THE

PUBLICATIONS

OF THE

Northamptonshire Record Society

FOUNDED IN DECEMBER, IN THE YEAR 1920

VOLUME XVI

FOR THE TWO YEARS ENDED 31 DECEMBER, 1953

THE BOOK OF
WILLIAM MORTON

ALMONER OF
PETERBOROUGH MONASTERY
1448-1467

TRANSCRIBED AND ANNOTATED BY

The Late W. T. MELLOWS

*(Formerly Chapter Clerk, Treasurer, and Archivist of
Peterborough Cathedral)*

EDITED BY

P. I. KING

WITH AN INTRODUCTION BY

C. N. L. BROOKE

PRINTED FOR THE
NORTHAMPTONSHIRE RECORD SOCIETY
BY CHARLES BATEY AT THE UNIVERSITY PRESS
OXFORD
1954

A "THOMAS ANTHONY MELLOWS MEMORIAL" VOLUME.

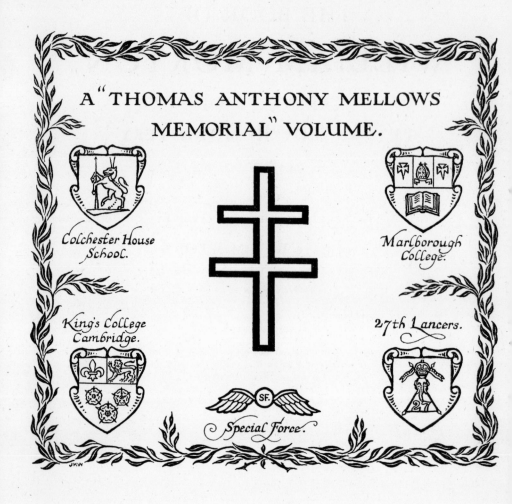

Colchester House School.

Marlborough College.

King's College Cambridge.

27th Lancers.

Special Force.

PRINTED IN GREAT BRITAIN

CONTENTS

LIST OF ILLUSTRATIONS   v

PREFACE   vii

ACKNOWLEDGEMENTS   ix

INTRODUCTION   xi
    I. THE MONASTIC COMMUNITY   xii
    II. WILLIAM MORTON AND HIS ADMINISTRATION   xvii
      A. The Obedientiary System   xix
      B. The Almoner   xxv
      C. Estate Management   xxxii
    III. THE BOOK   xxxix
      The Financial Status of Almoners   xlv
      The Watermarks in the MS.   xlvi

NOTE ON THE TEXT   xlvii

THE BOOK OF WILLIAM MORTON   1

SELECT GLOSSARY
    LATIN   170
    ENGLISH   172

INDEX OF PLACES AND PERSONS   177

INDEX OF SUBJECTS   193

ILLUSTRATIONS

Peterborough Cathedral from the south-east, from a water-colour drawing by Wilfrid R. Wood (1943)   *Frontispiece*

Facsimile of two pages of The Book of William Morton   *Facing page* xxxix

PREFACE

THIS book is the first to be issued of the ANTHONY MELLOWS MEMORIAL VOLUMES, an edition of a series of Peterborough texts designed by the late Mr. William Thomas Mellows of Peterborough in memory of his son, Thomas Anthony, who was killed in 1944 while on special service with the Maquis forces in the south of France.

The first two volumes of the series, of which *The Book of William Morton* is one, were already in the press at the time of Mr. W. T. Mellows's death in 1950, but the Introductions had not been written, and much remained to be done. The task of completing them he entrusted, in his own words, 'to my friends of the Northamptonshire Record Society'. Thus this volume now appears as a memorial to both father and son—to the devoted historian of Peterborough, the successor of Gunton and White Kennett, the friend and benefactor for thirty years of the Northamptonshire Record Society, on the one hand, and, on the other, to as promising, merry, and gallant a young Englishman as ever fell fighting for his King and country in the cause of freedom.

Professor M. Postan's guidance has been of the greatest help in carrying out Mr. Mellows's wishes with regard to this book. Our sincerest thanks are also due to Mr. P. I. King, who has collated the text with the original manuscript and upon whom has fallen the main burden of completing the edition. The Indexes are the joint work of Mr. J. Golson and Mr. Christopher Brooke. To Mr. Brooke we are further indebted for the Glossary, and, above all, for contributing the Introduction.

JOAN WAKE
Hon. Secretary,
Northamptonshire Record Society

LAMPORT HALL
NORTHAMPTON
July, 1954

ACKNOWLEDGEMENTS

INDIVIDUAL reference cannot be made to all those who helped Mr. Mellows in the early stages of this edition; but particular mention must be made of the late Professor A. Hamilton Thompson, who at one time lived at Gretton in Northamptonshire and who was an old friend of Mr. Mellows. In this, as in others of his books, some notes provided by Hamilton Thompson are distinguished by the initials A.H.T.

On my own account I would like to thank Mr. C. Dixon, Mr. J. Golson, Mr. P. Grierson, Dr. J. R. L. Highfield, Mr. P. I. King, Mr. R. E. Latham, and Mr. L. F. Salzman for advice and help on a variety of matters; Professor Bruce Dickins for assistance with problems in Middle English and with the glossary; Professor Dom David Knowles for advice and encouragement, and for most kindly reading the whole Introduction in typescript and offering invaluable comments and corrections; and my wife, who has given me constant encouragement and saved the reader from my worst infelicities.

It was originally arranged that the Introduction should be prepared by Professor Postan and myself, the economic aspect of the book to be treated by him, and the remainder by me; in the event, one section is his (Part II, C, pp. xxxii–xxxvii, except for the two final paragraphs on pp. xxxvii–xxxix). For this, for constant interest in the work, and for reading and revising my share of the Introduction, I am deeply grateful to him. To Miss Wake, for her generous help and advice, this volume and I owe a particular debt.

C. N. L. BROOKE

GONVILLE AND CAIUS COLLEGE,
CAMBRIDGE
April, 1954

INTRODUCTION

THE book of William Morton is the private account and memorandum book of an almoner of Peterborough Abbey in the mid-fifteenth century, of a man who, by virtue of his office, was concerned in all the multifarious duties, personal, legal, economic, and financial, of a medieval land-agent. The private notes of a great financier are rarely preserved for the eye of posterity. We normally have to view his activities, if at all, through the half-light of ledgers and published accounts; it is very seldom that we can meet him in the intimacy of office and counting-house, wrestling with addition and subtraction and petty cash in the regular humdrum of affairs. What is true of the great is equally true of the innumerable multitude of small-scale administrators, clerks, and private householders, so that the book before us is a very unusual document, one of the very few private account books to have survived from the Middle Ages. It is a friendly and revealing document, if it be not too much of a paradox so to describe an untidy packet of accounts. It gives us that kind of inside knowledge without which administrative work appears formless and unintelligible; it tells us, not only what it is suitable for the auditor to know, but what William Morton himself wished to record and to remember. It is thus in itself a chapter in the history of Peterborough in the fifteenth century and at the same time an important record of economic administration and finance.

The sources for the history of Peterborough monastery in the later Middle Ages are never fully balanced for any period, but they make a creditable showing among the documents for the other leading Benedictine houses.[1] A succession of chronicles and cartularies cover the twelfth, thirteenth, and fourteenth centuries, revealing a little of the interior polity of the convent, and a great deal of the political, economic, and litigious activities of the abbots. The *ordinale* (mid-fourteenth century, with some later additions)[2] gives elaborate details of rites and observances; but for the quality of the monastic life in the last two centuries before the Dissolution we have only the minute but one-sided witness of the visitation records in the years 1436–47[3] and again in the early sixteenth century. For the fifteenth and sixteenth centuries the main sources are the registers of Abbots John Deeping, Richard Ashton, and William Ramsey;[4] the few surviving obedientiary and manorial

---

[1] For a bibliography (valuable though not exhaustive) of the sources for the history of Peterborough Abbey see W. T. Mellows, *Henry of Pytchley's Book of Fees* (N.R.S. ii (1927)), pp. xxv ff. The best general account is that of A. Hamilton Thompson, *Associated Architectural Societies' Reports and Papers*, xxxiv (1917–18), pp. 259–75.

[2] Lambeth Palace Library MSS. 198, 198*a*.

[3] Edited with a translation and an admirable commentary by A. Hamilton Thompson, *Visitations of Religious Houses*, iii (L.R.S. xxi, 1929), pp. 269–302.

[4] British Museum Additional MS. 25288 (Deeping); Dean and Chapter of Peterborough Cathedral, Register Bird (Ashton and Ramsey). For the Peterborough registers cf. W. A. Pantin in *Historical Essays in honour of James Tait* (Manchester, 1933), p. 219.

account rolls;[1] the *Valor Ecclesiasticus*; and the account book of William Morton.

Morton's book contains the only surviving record of the finances of a Peterborough obedientiary over a period of years, and its detailed and workaday character gives many glimpses of the financial workings, the administration, the social structure of the monastery, and the relations of the monks with the convent's neighbours, tenants, and servants. It has also an intrinsic interest of its own as an account book of an almost unique kind; and it throws light on many dark places in the economic history of the period. In what follows each of these points will be briefly considered.

Of the personalities and normal routine of the monks such a book can tell us almost nothing: we therefore open with an interpretation of the contemporary visitation documents intended to provide a background to the rest of the story.

I. THE MONASTIC COMMUNITY

On 10 December 1437 William Alnwick, bishop of Lincoln, arrived at Peterborough to open his visitation of the abbey—the first of three visitations, whose *detecta*[2] form one of the most remarkable collections for any community of the later Middle Ages. Extensive *detecta* imply that all is not well in the house under scrutiny, and it has often been noticed that the state of Peterborough was unsatisfactory at this time.[3] It can be said at once that there is no trace of spiritual fervour in the house throughout the ten years 1437–47 covered by the documents. There is much evidence that the regular life was at a low ebb, that the liturgical round, the *Opus Dei*, was neglected, that there was little learning among the monks and inefficiency in the economic management of the monastic property. Above all, the spirit of faction, gossip, scandal, and backbiting peer out at us between the lines of these innumerable depositions—the forces most destructive of community life in any community in any age.

On the other hand, it is of the very nature of these visitation records that they should reveal abuses and be silent when all is well. The visitation system was founded as an investigation of how the Rule was kept; but in the later Middle Ages the normal good observance of a community and the sympathetic tact of the visitor could no longer be assumed. The visitation became a minute inquisition. It was a by-product, perhaps an inevitable by-product of the system that it called for the repetition of every kind of gossip as well as of serious complaints and well-founded accusations.[4] The monks were, so to speak, put on their conscience to reveal what they could, whether based on

---

[1] Cf. below, p. xxii, n. 2.
[2] i.e. the monks' depositions, the collection of which was the first stage in a visitation.
[3] e.g. by Hamilton Thompson, L.R.S. xiv, pp. li–lvi; G. G. Coulton, *Five Centuries of Religion*, iv (Cambridge, 1950), pp. 577 ff.
[4] The best discussion of the value and interpretation of visitation documents is to be found in M. D. Knowles, *The Religious Orders in England* (Cambridge, 1948), pp. 78 ff.

genuine information, personal spite, or idle rumour. On occasion vital information might be suppressed, but in general it is remarkable how exceedingly frank many depositions were. It is doubtless true, as Coulton so often stressed, that there were many abuses in medieval monastic life of which we have no record: it is also true that the abuses revealed in a visitation commonly appear in their most glaring colours. The visitation as practised in the later Middle Ages brought to the conscious level the stresses and strains and personal animosities which must be suppressed in the normal working of a healthy community. It had degenerated into a well-meaning effort to cure by an external administrative machinery the inherent weaknesses of a monasticism which had declined from its original fervour. A strong and active bishop like William Alnwick could do much good by patient and skilful application of the system. But it is scarcely surprising that it often bred disruption, and that the records make sorry reading.

I propose to scrutinize these visitation records, and by cross-questioning them to see what they reveal of the state of Peterborough Abbey—moral, social, and economic—in the two decades before the opening of Morton's book.[1] But I must start with the proviso that what we have here is a concentrated account of all that was abnormal—the common round, the daily routine, the normal relations of the monks are hidden from us.

The rule of two successive abbots—John Deeping (1409–38) and Richard Ashton (1438–71)—spanned more than half of the fifteenth century. The bulk of the charges contained in the *detecta* are against them, against both for their incompetence and mismanagement, and against Ashton for the strong rumour of his incontinence. But the figure who stands out most clearly is Richard Harlton, the prior, whose later years were devoted to the labour of Sisyphus: to restoring and preserving some regularity in religious observance and to the sound management of the abbey's economy. Four times in all—under Bishops Flemyng and Gray, Alnwick's predecessors, and again in 1437 and 1446[2]—he was given the charge or at least the first voice in a board of management to administer the abbey's affairs. Whereas brothers William Stamford and Thomas Gosberkirk prepared for a visitation by counting the tale of their personal animosities, Richard Harlton occupied himself with drawing up a reasoned schedule of abuses.[3] His own statements show an exact knowledge of the state of affairs, and almost all his complaints are confirmed by other monks.

[1] For a list of the monks in 1437 see L.R.S. xxi. 270 ff; and in 1471, below, p. 165, n. L.R.S., loc. cit., p. 270, n. 2, contains an analysis of the names of the monks. All but four have names of towns and villages in East Anglia or the east midlands—these names are mainly toponymics, i.e. not the monks' original surnames, but the name of their village of origin which they took on entering religion (N.R.S. xii. 51–2 has a list of the monks at the Dissolution, giving both surname and toponymic; cf. ibid., p. ix, n., and ibid. xiii, p. xxi). The practice apparently grew up in the thirteenth century or earlier, before surnames became at all stable, when it was necessary to distinguish members of the community with the same Christian name; being an established practice, it never lapsed (I owe this suggestion to Professor Knowles).

[2] L.R.S. vii. 101; xxi. 271–2, 275, 299–300.

[3] Ibid. xxi. 280–1 (identified by the references to the prior's schedule on pp. 275, 282).

The depositions of 1442 and 1446 suggest that preliminary discussion and lobbying had taken place: in 1437 the accusations are in the main exceedingly diffuse and haphazard.[1] The vague and petulant aspersions of Richard and William Stamford are suspiciously alike; two monks from the rest-house at Oxney, Richard Oxford and William Markham, had a notion that the prior was embezzling the reserve fund of the abbey. The subprior had achieved a wide measure of unpopularity, although the accusations are hard to reconcile. In general, however, it was the prior's schedule alone which represented anything like a consensus of opinion. The precentor and the abbot's steward (William Exton, of whom more anon) refer to it specifically and pronounce their agreement with it; all the important accusations are confirmed, some of them by a considerable number of witnesses.[2] Two monks looked back with regret to the days when the prior had had charge of the monastic economy; two more earnestly desired that he might have it again.[3]

The prior's charges may be summed up as follows: the *Opus Dei* was neglected and monks were too often absent from choir, partly because there was drinking late at night; discipline was lax and the monks received licence to roam too readily; and the abbot's administration was venal and inefficient. It came to this: the abbot, by his own confession, was elderly and incapable, and he could neither control his household expenses, nor his lay friends and counsellors, nor hold his own within the convent. He seems to have been easily imposed upon in financial matters.

The bishop's injunctions have not survived, but one or two points are clear: he forbade drinking in the town of Peterborough and other abuses likely to lead to scandal without and demoralization within.[4] He refused the abbot's request to be allowed to resign, but made the prior once again his coadjutor.

Two monks were absent from the monastery at this visitation, completing their studies at Canterbury College, Oxford—Richard Ashton and William Borough.[5] A little over eight months later they set out to return to Peterborough. They took a short holiday at Canterbury, and then spent a week-end in London on their way north. On the Monday (25 August 1438) they learnt that Abbot Deeping had resigned, that a new election was imminent, and that Richard Ashton was to preach before the election. At about the same time, as we learn from the fascinating letter which William Borough wrote to a friend at Oxford describing these events, they received their report from the warden of Canterbury College, addressed to the prior of Peterborough. They

---

[1] The visitation of 1437 is in L.R.S. xxi. 269–82 (depositions on pp. 272–82); of 1442, ibid., pp. 283–5; of 1446–7, pp. 285–302 (depositions on pp. 285–97). The depositions of individual monks are referred to in the index; for what follows I only give additional reference where it seems necessary or particularly desirable.

[2] Cf. pp. 280–1 and the editor's notes.

[3] William Exton (p. 275) and Thomas Deeping senior (p. 277); John Burnham (p. 278) and Thomas Gosberkirk (p. 282).

[4] Cf. pp. 283–5.

[5] For what follows see *Canterbury College Oxford*, ed. W. A. Pantin, iii (Oxford Historical Society, 1950), pp. 96–8; for the date of Ashton's election, below, p. xl, n. 3.

opened it and found it to be in the highest degree compromising: they were accused of haunting taverns and consorting with a woman, among other charges not specified. Needless to say, they destroyed it. William's letter is charming, intimate, and open-hearted; but it carries a postscript: 'Richard begs you to tell no one the story of the warden's letter addressed to our prior.'

Well he might: within a month—perhaps inspired by the eloquence of his sermon, or because the community was at loggerheads with itself, and turned in despair to a monk who had been for some time absent and was thus uncompromised—within a month Richard Ashton had been elected abbot of Peterborough.

At the time of his election Ashton seems to have been young and irresponsible: it cannot have been long before signs of that mismanagement which had become chronic by 1446 began to appear. But the visitation of 1442 passed quietly enough. The complaints are of negligible importance, and a large majority returned the verdict 'omnia bene—all is well'. To attribute this remarkable unanimity to collusion in the sense of a conspiracy to deceive would force us to assume far greater cohesion in the Peterborough community than the evidence suggests. The explanation seems to be that after the troubles of 1437–8 the leading spirits of the house were trying to keep the peace, and that it was in the interests of peace and to avoid frayed nerves and an atmosphere of suspicion that private grievances and any hints there may have been of mismanagement by the abbot were suppressed.

By 1446 this precarious equilibrium had vanished, and Ashton had lost control of the reins of discipline, of the monastic economy, and of his own reputation. The *detecta* are long and detailed, but the pattern which emerges is simpler to trace than that of 1437. We find faction, scandal, and a whispering campaign afoot: and a majority of the monks caring for neither the one side nor the other, but compelled to reveal the abuses of both.

Three monks, William Markham the treasurer, William Melton, and Thomas Gosberkirk, were accused of holding private meetings and carousals in the treasurer's office, and of fomenting discord. William Borough deposed that 'Thomas Gosberkirk, after that the abbot had received my lord's letter for this visitation, made conspiracies among the brethren, saying to them: "With whom will you be, on my side or the abbot's? If on the abbot's side, you will be accused first." '[1] Of the three, Gosberkirk was the spokesman and the fire-brand, but Markham was the elder statesman.

On the other side, it would seem that the abbot had a group of counsellors, partly lay, partly religious, led by his confessor, brother John More. More was accused of going to the abbot's chamber almost every evening after compline with some of the younger monks and retailing all the gossip of the convent; and old John Borough expanded this accusation into the time-honoured plaint—common to all communities and colleges—of the old against the idleness, refractory

[1] L.R.S. xxi. 294–5.

behaviour, and evil influence of the young. John More had already, in 1437, expounded to the bishop how bad an example was set by the older monks. It is of interest to observe that there was no love lost between More and William Morton: More accused Morton of drinking in the hamlets between Peterborough and Oxney of an evening; Morton accused More of stirring up strife between the abbot and the convent. In other matters, now as in 1437, Morton's deposition is mainly concerned with the monastic economy and administration.

The main burden of the charges was against the abbot, whose lack of discipline and gross maladministration stand clearly revealed, while we are presented at every turn with stories of his irregular life and incontinence. The last charge was the most serious, but it is impossible to say whether it was true. The abbot was defamed with three women of the neighbourhood, and the majority of the monks referred to this scandal, although not always in the same terms. The abbot and the three women and their husbands sedulously denied the charge, and the former was able to substantiate his innocence with one lady on the oath of a number of his fellow monks. Furthermore, the frequency with which the tale was repeated does not mean that it was supported by 'numerous and credible witnesses'.[1] Richard Harlton, for instance, had repeated the charge as a piece of public scandal, but was prepared to swear to the abbot's innocence with the third lady, Mrs. Est. It is clear that the story had been carefully disseminated, and we can trace from the depositions some of the plausible arguments by which it was fostered—that William Parker's wife is decked out beyond her husband's estate, that the three husbands had been too favourably treated, and the like. In any case, the strength of the rumour indicates that Richard Ashton was not a man of manifest good character.

The charges against the abbot's government were more specific, and possibly more substantial, although some of his offences are open to more than one interpretation. He had cut down and sold trees and even whole woods (as they tell us) to the loss of the abbey; manors and tenements were falling into ruin for want of proper maintenance; payments from the abbot's side of the financial system to the monks and conventual officials were in arrears; he had not presented any sort of accounts for two years. His fecklessness had led others astray, and some of the obedientiaries were alleged to be seven years behind with their accounts. He was also accused, as we have seen, of being over-friendly with the younger monks, of sitting up late of an evening with them, and of treating them with undue lenience. The unanimity with which the monks presented this outline of charges against the abbot shows how thoroughly Gosberkirk had carried out his campaign: it also shows why the abbot narrowly avoided deposition.

In the event, the bishop decided to remove Ashton to Oxney for a space and set up a board of management to direct the affairs of the monastery and set matters to rights. This was settled after a long day of consultation and debate; but next morning the abbot begged to be

---

[1] As stated by Coulton, loc. cit.

left in control, to avoid the scandal of even temporary degradation. His prayer was granted and the board was thus given a purely advisory function. It consisted of Richard Harlton, who had resigned his office a few days before, William Exton the new prior, William Markham, treasurer and insurgent, and William Borough (now steward).[1] Harlton was old and sick, and the other three were for the time being the leading figures in the reform and administration of the abbey. Exton and Markham appear from the visitation records to have been able and intelligent administrators. Borough we have already met as a student and a lively writer: he was now steward, later sacrist and cellarer; he sometimes acted as Ashton's proctor at the Benedictine general chapters.[2]

And so Richard Ashton was permitted to remain as abbot throughout the remainder of William Morton's life. Such slight evidence as survives[3] suggests a greater regularity in administration, and the absence of evidence to the contrary has been taken to indicate that his manner of life and rule improved. One thing is certain: Peterborough Abbey, on the brink of financial disaster in 1446, and always liable to overspend its income, weathered this storm like many others and was still solvent at the Dissolution. It has been argued that the failure of the monasteries in the fifteenth century was primarily financial, the product of chronic debt. But it is rare to find a house with more than a substantial overdraft—which is as common with an agricultural concern in the height of its prosperity as in the depth of mismanagement—and it is astonishing how quickly the greater houses could recover when threatened with serious disaster. Economic disorder had led to internal disorganization in the Peterborough community; but the true weakness and the true failure lay deeper, in the rarity of ardent religious vocation, failure to maintain the Rule, and the social and cultural changes which had already diverted the old influence and significance of the monastic order to other walks of life.

II. WILLIAM MORTON AND HIS ADMINISTRATION

The career of William Morton, as far as we can reconstruct it, shows no deviation from the normal routine of life of a Benedictine monk in fifteenth-century England. He was most probably born about the first decade of the century,[4] a member of a family which took its name from

[1] L.R.S. xxi. 299 ff.

[2] Cf. below, pp. 53 (steward); 69, 75, 81, 89, 111, 143 (sacrist); 168 (cellarer); *Chapters of the English Black Monks*, ed. W. A. Pantin, iii (Camden 3rd series, liv, 1937), p. 214, cf. also p. 250.

[3] e.g. in Ashton's register (cf. above, p. xi, n. 4) and in the present book. Between 1444 and 1465 Ashton was four times appointed by the general chapter of the English Benedictine Congregation to visit other houses (Pantin, *Chapters*, iii. 242).

A letter testimonial in his favour, in purely formal terms, was issued by the Chancellor and University of Oxford on 4 February 1447, while this visitation was in session (*Epistolae Academicae Oxon.*, ed. H. Anstey, i, Oxford Historical Society, 1898, p. 257; for the formula cf. pp. 80–1. The date is clearly 1447, not 1446 as stated). This letter shows that Ashton had proceeded D.D. since his election as abbot. His career ended with his resignation in 1471.

[4] Since he was already a monk and of age to be ordained acolyte in 1424 (see below).

one of the numerous villages called Morton in Lincolnshire and the east midlands. The account has a little to tell us of his family. Agnes Morton and her son Robert are frequently mentioned, and the presumption is that they were related to William.[1] Agnes we shall meet again, paying her debts by working for William; Robert was one of William's servants, and is often referred to as paying and receiving money and performing other tasks on the almoner's behalf. Both were clearly in a humble station. There is also passing mention of another Robert Morton, perhaps William's father; of another William Morton, a servant of the abbey, and of a younger Morton, Thomas, almost certainly related to the almoner, who paid the expenses of his entry into religion at Ramsey Abbey.[2]

William Morton must have made his profession c. 1420. In company with John York and Richard Ashton (later abbot), he was ordained acolyte in September 1424 by the archbishop's assistant, and deacon a year later by Henry Chichele himself, during the archbishop's administration of the see of Lincoln.[3] It is just possible that he studied at Oxford, since a monk of his name who was *decretorum doctor* was recommended by the University to the Benedictine general chapter in 1441.[4] His notebook shows that he was an educated man, but no great scholar. There is no evidence that he held any office within the community before he became almoner in 1448.

One of the most characteristic features of a late medieval monastery was the system of obediences: the system by which a wide variety of functions and revenues were assigned to a large and complicated hierarchy of officials.[5] It achieved its full development only in the more wealthy houses of the Benedictine congregations, and of these Peterborough was a characteristic specimen. Between a third and a half of the fully fledged monks were obedientiaries, with an office to themselves and a share in the revenues of the abbey, playing their part in the complex monastic economy and in the daily life of the convent. The

[1] That William was related to Thomas Morton (below, n. 2) seems clear, since William provided for his entry into religion at Ramsey Abbey—normally a relative's function; and it would be very curious under the circumstances if they were not related that they should both bear the name Morton. If this is accepted, it seems to follow that Morton was William's family name, and not merely his surname in religion (see above, p. xiii, n. 1).

It seems highly probable from the association of Agnes Morton with the elder Robert's anniversary on p. 40 that they were related; and it is hard to imagine why William Morton should spend so much on Robert Morton's anniversary (p. 25) if he were not closely connected with him. This creates a presumption in favour of the view that these four Mortons—Agnes, William, and the two Roberts—were related; and the presumption receives circumstantial confirmation from the close association of William with both Agnes and her son, the younger Robert (cf. p. 18). William was sufficiently interested in Agnes to include her private accounts in his book on one occasion (at the foot of f. 10r: this is the only entry of the kind), and sufficiently interested in Robert to take him into his service. But the relationship remains no more than a presumption.

[2] For the other William see pp. 74, 98, 113, 143 (possibly also pp. 66, 127); for Thomas, pp. 87 ff., 135. Richard Morton of West Deeping appears on p. 155; a Robert Morton, miller, on p. 130. It is of course far from certain that all these were William's relatives.

[3] *Register of Archbishop Chichele*, ed. E. F. Jacob, iv (Oxford, 1947), 363–4, 370, 372.

[4] *Chapters of the English Black Monks*, ed. Pantin, iii. 108.

[5] For the origins and nature of the system see Knowles, *Monastic Order in England* (Cambridge, 1940), pp. 427–39.

obedientiaries were appointed by the abbot, normally with the consent of the community: they were removable at will, and changes were frequent. At Westminster, where the lists of obedientiaries are almost complete for the fourteenth and fifteenth centuries, the average tenure for an almoner was less than five years;[1] similarly, at Peterborough, there were four treasurers in the period 1445–65.[2] Morton was almoner for fifteen years, an unusually long period. When he vacated the office (c. 1462) he became infirmarer and very shortly afterward (c. 1463–4), warden of Oxney, the rest-house, a small cell lying about three miles to the north-east of Peterborough.[3] His account book is comparatively full down to 1462, but after he had ceased to be almoner he only had occasion to enter a few disconnected memoranda. The latest date mentioned is Easter week 1467.[4] He must have died shortly after, perhaps in 1467, certainly by 1471.[5]

Although all the members of a monastic community were under the abbot's discipline, in the course of time, partly because of a deliberate papal policy, the method of government in a large Benedictine house had become oligarchical rather than despotic.[6] The abbot was dependent on the council of the senior monks in most of his administrative functions; and the finances of most houses were divided between abbot and convent, so that the administration of the abbot's household and of the rest of the monastery were to a large extent independent of one another. On the convent side the revenues were generally divided between the leading obedientiaries, so that each was more or less in independent control of the resources of his office. It is therefore necessary to discuss Morton's place in the system—his role as an obedientiary—before we can understand the details of his administration as almoner.

A. *The Obedientiary System*

With the origins and sources of the system we are not concerned: for our purpose it comes into view as part of the great change in the financial administration of the larger Benedictine houses which took place in the period 1150–1250. It was then (from c. 1150) that the formal division of monastic revenues between abbot and convent and of the convent's share between the leading obedientiaries first took place.[7] It

---

[1] E. H. Pearce, *The Monks of Westminster* (Cambridge, 1916), pp. 199–200. Cf. the elaborate charts of the Norwich obedientiaries in H. W. Saunders, *An Introduction to the Obedientiary and Manor Rolls of Norwich Cathedral Priory* (Norwich, 1930), pp. 193 ff.

[2] Thomas Maxey was treasurer in 1437 and 1442 (L.R.S. xxi. 282, 284 and n.); by 1446 William Markham held the office (ibid., pp. 294, 299). Markham was succeeded by Richard Harlton junior shortly before Michaelmas 1449 (below, pp. 27, 42), and he by William Leicester c. 1454 (pp. 62, 70, 75, 90–1). From c. 1455 Robert Nottingham was treasurer (pp. 75, 88, 93). Nottingham was subprior in 1471 (below, p. 165 n.).

[3] It is impossible to give exact dates to Morton's changes of office. He became almoner about the time the book opens, in 1448–9 (see especially p. 12); he seems to have relinquished the post c. Autumn 1462, to have been infirmarer c. 1462–3, and warden of Oxney c. 1463–7 (pp. 159, 162; 147, 163–4; 164 ff., especially pp. 167–8).   [4] p. 168.

[5] He does not appear in the list of monks drawn up at the election of the new abbot in 1471 (below, p. 165 n.), which seems to be exhaustive.

[6] Cf. Knowles, *Religious Orders*, pp. 271–2, 275–6.

[7] But some traces of informal earmarking of funds may be found, here and there, a century earlier.

was then, too (from *c.* 1200), that the abuse of monastic *proprietas* developed, the payment of sums of money to individual monks to buy clothes, food, spices, and the like, and the attendant growth of private property, which was as consistently condemned by monastic reformers as it had been by St. Benedict himself.[1]

The original reasons for these practices are complex and obscure. They may have a theoretical foundation, but at the practical level (in part at least) they were connected with the need to defend the community against the alienation of property (for feudal and other purposes) by the abbot; partly also with the natural tendency of such institutions to earmark funds for particular purposes. In the course of time—and it may well be that time is the major factor in this development—these allocations reached large proportions. Only a major reform would reverse this trend. Such a reform came in the thirteenth century; but the reversal was only temporary, and by Morton's time the detailed subdivision of revenue had reached its farthest point of development.

Financial decentralization had not been long established at Peterborough before it was discovered that it was possible for one department to be heavily in debt while the monastery as a whole was prosperous. The offices of sacrist, cellarer, and chamberlain were fully established by the middle of the twelfth century; the almoner received his main endowment from the great abbot Benedict (1177–93).[2] His successor, Andrew, allotted the rich manors of Alwalton and Fletton in Huntingdonshire to the cellarer for the maintenance of the monks' kitchen. But it was soon discovered that their revenues were inadequate, and under Robert of Lindsey (1210–22) they were supplemented.[3] This was the normal process: a temporary deficit might be made good by a single grant from another department, but whatever bade fair to be a permanent deficiency was covered by an increase in endowment, exactly measured for the estimated need. Decentralization normally took the form of assigning money to a stated task, which was then put in the charge of a particular official. The system was rigid, and often closely circumscribed the financial activities of the individual obedientiaries. It also meant that each obedientiary acquired a number of minor tasks unconnected with his original function.[4] In its later stages the system was not only complicated but incoherent.

The rigidity of the system could not survive without important changes, and there was naturally a limit to the extent to which impecunious offices could be shored up with additional endowments.

---

[1] Cf. especially Knowles, op. cit., pp. 287–9; Coulton, *Five Centuries of Religion*, iii (1936), chapters xxi ff.

[2] Swaffham's Chronicle, ed. J. Sparke, *Historiae Anglicanae Scriptores Varii*, i (London, 1723), pp. 101–2; his first recorded endowment was the church of Paston (*The Peterborough Chronicle of Hugh Candidus*, ed. W. T. Mellows (Oxford, 1949), pp. 129–30) in the time of Benedict's predecessor. For the other obedientiaries cf. Candidus and his commentators, ibid., pp. 122–3, 171–3.

[3] Swaffham's Chronicle, pp. 103, 111–12; Dean and Chapter of Peterborough MS. Swaffham's Register, f. cv *r–v* (where Abbot Robert makes the additional grants and gives an account of the reason for them).

[4] For an example see below, p. xxiv.

There were three possible solutions: the concentration of all finances in the hands of a central treasurer or treasurers, as happened at Christ Church, Canterbury, but was never, so far as we know, an established system at Peterborough; the formation of a central pool from which items of extraordinary expenditure, unaccounted for in the complete obedientiary system, could be supplied; or the transfer of funds from one official to another.[1] Such transfers were naturally common practice in all large houses in the later Middle Ages; and a central reserve fund in the charge of a treasurer or bursar, to whom new duties and unassigned income could be given, was established in many, if not most, in the middle or late thirteenth century. It was then that changing prices and the opportunities afforded by high farming led to an urgent demand for the centralization and redistribution of the funds. At Peterborough the office of conventual treasurer was set up shortly before 1248, became firmly established under the active and litigious abbot Richard of London (1274–95), and reached the zenith of its influence under the greatest of Peterborough's administrator abbots, Godfrey of Crowland (1321–38).[2] The shift in endowment can be clearly seen about this time in the story of the manor of Gunthorpe. It was purchased by Richard of London from an impecunious neighbour for 250 marks, and its profits were mainly given to the almoner; part of it was temporarily mortgaged to the cellarer to repay his contribution to the purchase price. Some years later the treasurer absorbed the almoner's share.[3]

[1] There is an excellent account of the first two in R. A. L. Smith, 'The *Regimen Scaccarii* in English Monasteries', *Collected Papers* (ed. Knowles, London, 1947), pp. 54–73.

[2] There is evidence of a convent treasury which seems to have been a kind of reserve fund under Abbot Walter of St. Edmund (Swaffham's Chronicle, pp. 103–4). His successor Abbot William (1246–8) ordained that there should be two monk wardens to administer the manors of the abbot, and two receivers (one for the abbot, the other for the convent) to handle all the revenues of the house (Whittlesey's Chronicle, ed. Sparke, p. 126). We seem to have here a system of centralized receipt and the offices of abbot's receiver and convent treasurer in embryo. But the system did not last, and the Peterborough treasurer was later in charge of a reserve fund only.

The treasurer was not among the endowed obedientiaries in 1254 (W. E. Lunt, *The Valuation of Norwich*, Oxford, 1926, p. 510), nor in 1268 (ibid., pp. 547–8); by 1291 his endowments were established (the best texts of the 1291 assessment for Peterborough are in the abbey registers: British Museum, MS. Cotton Vespasian E XXII, ff. 60–1, 121; Additional MS. 25288, ff. 91–2; and Ashton's register, for which see below, pp. 10–11, n.7). A garbled version also occurs in Morton's book (p. 1 below), very similar to that in Vespasian E XXII, ff. 60–1 (cf. Lunt, op. cit., pp. 23–4, n., where for 'Vesp. E xxiv' read 'xxii'). The endowment in 1291 only amounted to 30s. per annum, but was shortly after increased (see next note). The office was apparently established, then, between 1268 and 1291.

I imagine that Abbot William's ordinance (based perhaps on the example of Christ Church, Canterbury) was somewhat premature, and that the office was only finally established c. 1280–90 (cf. next note), when the movement for centralized finance and for setting up convent treasurers was beginning to get under way throughout the country (cf. Knowles, *Religious Orders*, pp. 39 n. 4, 58–60).

[3] There is some confusion about this transaction. According to the vendor's charter Gunthorpe was granted for the convent almoner (Swaffham Register, f. clxv); according to the contemporary author of the *Chronicon Petroburgense* (ed. T. Stapleton, Camden Society, 1849, p. 25) it was bought in 1277 for 550 marks, and the convent side received a rent of 10 marks per annum because they had contributed 155 marks to the cost. But the 1291 taxation shows the full annual revenue of 20 marks as the almoner's, and the surviving texts (cf. above) show that it later passed into the hands of the convent treasurer. In Whittlesey's Chronicle (which closes in 1321) the purchase price is given as 250 marks,

It is clear that under a strong and active abbot, and at times when economic enterprise demanded the maximum of financial flexibility, the incomes of the individual offices were far from stable, and their finances were closely integrated with the general administrative policies of the house. Some revenues could not be touched, particularly those which were allotted to almsgiving, and even in a community like Christ Church, Canterbury, where centralization was virtually complete, the almoner's income remained under his own control.[1] But the almost universal shift from the direct exploitation of land to a system of farms and fixed rents in the late fourteenth century destroyed the strongest motive for centralization; and natural centrifugal tendencies and the more limited administrative grasp of monastic superiors and their advisers combined, at Peterborough as elsewhere, to restore to the obedientiaries their fixed incomes and a measure of autonomy. The principle of the fixed income regained its sway : and although temporary loans or grants might be made down to the Dissolution to cope with local deficits, the normal method of restoring the finances of officers who could not pay their way was the settlement of a permanent grant from the purse of some more fortunate colleague. The surviving obedientiary rolls of the fifteenth century[2] show how far this process had gone. Almost every obedientiary received a number of payments from his colleagues, and made a number in return, sometimes to the same obedientiary from whom he had received an allowance. Such cases were, of course, no more than paper transactions, but the fact that they were solemnly recorded shows both the rigidity and the conservatism of the accounting organization.

Two factors helped to increase the complexity of this system. The growth in the number of lesser obediences in all monasteries in the late twelfth century has been often observed : it seems to have been partly due to the general tendency towards decentralization before the great reaction of the middle and late thirteenth century, but mainly to the growing complexity of the administration. It was sometimes encouraged

which is probably correct since the annual value was no more than 20 marks; of these the cellarer paid 88 : the convent register is cited as evidence. Under 1280 we are told that the cellarer is to receive £2. 15s. 4d. annually from the convent treasury until the 88 marks are repaid. A wood attached to the purchase went to the sacrist. Finally, Whittlesey says that in his time Gunthorpe was worth 20 marks per annum, of which 10 marks made up the abbot's anniversary (5 to the monks' refectory, 5 in distributions to the poor) and the remainder to the convent treasury *ad usum eiusdem* (Whittlesey, ed. Sparke, p. 147). It seems clear that the manor was originally in the almoner's hands, and that he still held it in 1291, but that it had been transferred to the treasurer well before Whittlesey wrote. The mention of the abbot's anniversary suggests that the transfer took place before Abbot Richard's death in 1295. The reference to the convent treasury under 1280 may be a confusion on Whittlesey's part, or it may be evidence of the existence of the office at that date.

[1] R. A. L. Smith, *Canterbury Cathedral Priory* (Cambridge, 1943), pp. 22–3; Knowles, *Religious Orders*, p. 62.

[2] About 25 obedientiary rolls (some of them fragmentary) survive in the archives of Peterborough Cathedral and elsewhere; there are transcripts of them among the Mellows transcripts in the Northamptonshire Record Office (vols. M (T) 23, 43, 44). Fragments of an account survive in Corpus Christi College, Cambridge, MS. 134; cf. also below, p. xxxviii. In no case is there a run of more than two consecutive years for the same official; none is contemporary with Morton's book (the nearest in date is that of William Markham as refectorer, for 1441–2).

by a strong abbot who feared the influence of a too well-endowed subordinate or the more serious danger of financial incompetence if too great a proportion of the subordinate funds were concentrated in a few hands. Some of the new officials, like the sub-almoner, were little more than juniors to a major obedientiary.; others, like the sub-sacrist and the master of the works at Peterborough, had independent incomes and separate functions, and were only to a small degree subject to the direction of the head of their side of the monastic economy.[1] In 1291 the cellarer, sacrist, sub-sacrist, almoner, chamberlain, pittancer, treasurer, and infirmarer all had separate incomes derived from land and other property.[2] Probably already, and certainly by the fifteenth century, a number of minor obedientiaries had sums allotted to them for the support of their office or for more specific purposes. A clear distinction emerges between the greater obedientiaries who maintained separate establishments, with two or three or more servants, and the lesser men who had only a few shillings to dispose of. Officials like the hostiller (or guestmaster) lay in between. In 1497–8 his income on paper was £2. 7s. 1d., of which about a third consisted in contributions from the sacrist and the almoner, and the rest in rents and oblations. His expenses came to £3. 2s. 7d., of which 17s. went as wages to his servants, 15s. 2d. in repairs to the buildings under his care, and the remainder, sundries apart, in small sums for the hostiller's summer party, the support of the prior, and other minor festivities. It would be absurd to measure the importance or judge the function of an obedience solely by its receipts and expenses; but for our present purpose this is the significant consideration. The numerous small expenses which have no conceivable connexion with hospitality, although they do not make up a large proportion of his income, illustrate the incoherence of function mentioned above.

The second factor was the growth of *proprietas*. The full significance of this is difficult to assess. In part it certainly reflected the growing deviation from the fully communal life of the Rule; but it was also an expression of the tendency to allot money for particular purposes previously catered for as need arose out of the common funds of the house. These private allowances were kept separate from the official funds of the obedientiaries, although an obedientiary who fell into debt was sometimes called upon to pay part of his debt out of his privy purse;[3] no rigid distinction of private and public accounts is to be looked for in medieval monastic records.

The monks' stipends were paid at Peterborough partly by the abbot's receiver, but mainly by the treasurer, a fact which indicates that they were instituted after the erection of that office in the second half of the thirteenth century. In 1522–3 the total paid was £115. 6s. 8d., of which £1. 6s. 8d. was for the support of the monks studying at Cambridge,

[1] The functions of the Peterborough obedientiaries are analysed by W. T. Mellows in *The Local Government of Peterborough* (Peterborough, 1919), pp. 215–41.
[2] For the best texts of the 1291 taxation return for Peterborough see above, p. xxi, n. 2.
[3] Cf. below, pp. 75–6; *Compotus Rolls of the Obedientiaries of St. Swithun's Priory, Winchester*, ed. G. W. Kitchin (Hants Record Society, 1892), pp. 77–8, 427; &c.

£22. 10s. for tunics on the feast of St. Luke, and £24 for spices on
O Sapientia. Almost a third of the total was paid out of funds supplied
by other obedientiaries: of the tunics allowance, for example, £10. 4s.
was supplied by the cellarer, the almoner, and the pittancer. In an age
before bank notes and mediums of exchange less cumbersome than
metal coin had been invented, it would obviously have simplified the
administration of the *stipendia* if the other obedientiaries had paid their
contributions to their fellow monks direct rather than through the
treasurer. In point of fact Morton's book proves that this was done.
Every year he records the payment to himself and to a certain number of
other monks of the *stipendia* for spices, tunics, and for the feast on
St. John the Baptist's day; the residue was paid to the treasurer, but
only on one occasion was it a sum of any size.[1] On the evidence of
Morton's book alone it would not be clear that it was the treasurer who
officially administered these funds;[2] on the evidence of the treasurer's
roll it would appear that the money actually passed through his hands.
The rigidity of the accounting organization was evidently not always
accompanied by an equal rigidity in administrative practice.

On the other hand, there can be no doubt that the treasurer retained
control over the distribution of the *stipendia*. The list of monks to
whom Morton paid his contributions always varies, at least to some
extent, from year to year; no doubt the treasurer issued instructions to
him how the money was to be laid out. This is but one of many
instances of the way in which the complexity of monastic finance must
have demanded a great deal of collaboration for the system to work
smoothly. The monks' diet offers a very clear illustration.[3] The regular
meals in the refectory were provided in the first instance by the cellarer,
who, with the aid of the garnerer, supplied the grain and other basic
necessaries; cooked in the convent kitchen, which was maintained
partly by the cellarer and partly by the abbot's receiver; and served
under the direction of the refectorer. Occasional additions to the normal
fare were made by the pittancer: and feasts or special dainties on
important festivals were provided by the abbot, the treasurer, the
almoner, the hostiller, the pittancer, and the chamberlain. Each of these
obedientiaries had other functions to perform, and each derived his
income from a wide variety of sources: from farms, rents, oblations,
and the like; and from the direct contributions of other departments in
the monastery. It is easy to see from this simplified picture that co-
operation among the obedientiaries themselves and control by the
abbot or council of senior monks was essential to the smooth working
of the monastic administration. It is easy to see, furthermore, why
Richard Harlton should complain in 1446 that the abbot's side was in
chaos because there was a multiplicity of officials without any clear
demarcation of function.[4]

---

[1] p. 93 (£4).
[2] But cf. p. 27, where there are hints that the treasurer organized the payments; furthermore a small residue of the payments is commonly paid to the treasurer.
[3] For what follows cf. the indications in Mellows loc. cit.
[4] L.R.S. xxi. 287.

In many other ways the independent action of the obedientiaries was limited and circumscribed. The close interrelation of functions in the daily life of the community; the annual audit of the accounts, which often involved adjustments and transfers of revenue; the ultimate controlling authority of the abbot, to whom in the last resort all owed obedience, and who had the power of appointing and removing the obedientiaries, in theory at least, as he wished; and perhaps most important of all, the ordinary give and take of community life, the dominant and imponderable factor in the history of monasticism, whether ruled by a kind of functional free trade or directed by the energy of a few leading personalities: all these combined to curb the autonomy of the obedientiaries and to provide a permanent check on the centrifugal tendencies of monastic administration.

Nevertheless the most striking fact about the obedientiaries remains their independence and autonomy. At times their financial activity may have been no more than accounting technique; but in the long run their independence was something far more significant. In England there was a temporary reaction against it shortly before the Dissolution, which took the form of centralization of a number of the major offices in the hands of a single Pooh-Bah, sometimes the abbot himself. But on the Continent devolution continued, until eventually the obedience became a benefice, and the holder legally irremovable. We are far enough from that. But the problem remains; and its solution, no doubt, lies deep in the sociology of late medieval monasticism.

B. *The Almoner*

Almsgiving has always been one of the principal duties of a monastic community, as of every religious institution: the support of the sick and poor is carefully enjoined in St. Benedict's Rule.[1] In early days the abbot himself was often directly responsible for it. But by the tenth century it was beginning to be the practice in some houses for the arrangements for almsgiving, as for many other duties, to be delegated to particular officials—first to the hostiarius and his subordinate the guestmaster (or hostiller), and later, and more commonly, to the almoner. The title is first met in the early customs of Cluny; and there is no doubt that it was from Cluny, through the medium of the Monastic Constitutions of Archbishop Lanfranc, that the almoner first came to England shortly after the Norman Conquest.[2] In the early twelfth century we find evidence of the almoner receiving an independent income in some English abbeys; by the end of the century he had taken his place in almost all, as one of the four or five leading obedientiaries with a separate office and an income of his own.[3]

The office of almoner, like the obedientiary system as a whole, awaits its historian: of its history on the Continent very little is known, while

---

[1] For what follows see P. Schmitz, *Histoire de l'Ordre de S.-Benoît*, especially ii (Maredsous, 1942), pp. 38 ff.
[2] Cf. *The Monastic Constitutions of Lanfranc*, ed. Knowles (Nelson's Medieval Classics, 1951), p. 89. For alms and almoners at Cluny see G. de Valous, *Le Monachisme clunisien*, i (Ligugé–Paris, 1935), pp. 161 ff. [3] Knowles, *Monastic Order*, pp. 482 ff.

the material already collected in this country, though considerable, is diffuse and hard to digest. I must therefore content myself with a few preliminary generalizations and conjectures, which may in the fullness of time be shown to be quite erroneous.

It would seem that in origin the almoner was not the official most directly concerned with alms as usually understood; nor was he ever their sole dispenser.[1] But he must always have been concerned in the distribution of money doles and of the food left over from the monks' meals; and no doubt he was from an early date the official subordinate of the abbot and cellarer in the disposal of their alms. In the Cluny customs and Lanfranc's Constitutions he appears as a sort of district visitor—visiting the sick and the aged in their homes or arranging for such ministrations—and the superintendent of a hospital (in the medieval sense of alms-houses or old peoples' home). Of the former function there is no trace after the eleventh century, and it presumably fell into abeyance. But the running of a hospital was the chief specific function of most English monastic almoners throughout the later Middle Ages.[2] The medieval conception of charity (in the narrow sense) was primarily concerned with the maintenance of the very old and the very young— that is, with hospitals and schools. Secular charitable foundations of the fourteenth and fifteenth centuries normally consisted of school and hospital combined, and Christ's Hospital is a living witness to the fact that no clear line was drawn between the two in the sixteenth century.

The monastic hospitals, on the other hand, were very rarely accompanied by schools. Postulants and novices apart, the only children supported by the monks were a few choir boys and the like, lodged in the almonry, but as commonly as not instructed in the local grammar-school.[3] By aid to the novices, by support of the almonry boys and occasionally of a choir school, as well as in other ways, the monastic almoner showed that his charitable functions were remotely connected with education. On Maundy Thursday, in every community, the monks washed the feet of an equivalent number of poor men chosen for the purpose, in commemoration of the Last Supper. The poor men were usually treated to a feast or at least a dole.[4] The organization of this ceremony was normally the work of the almoner (sometimes aided by the cellarer): it was commonly his one ritual function.[5] These specific

---

[1] Cf. below, pp. xxviii–xxix, xlv.

[2] Cf. the instances mentioned below, ibid. For medieval hospitals in general, R. M. Clay, *The Mediaeval Hospitals of England* (London, 1909).

[3] A. F. Leach, *The Schools of Medieval England* (London, 1915), pp. 213–34. Professor Knowles tells me that he believes Leach to have underestimated the amount of education undertaken in the almonries themselves.

[4] e.g. at Norwich and Winchester (below, p. xlvi).

[5] Cf. *Constitutions of Lanfranc*, pp. 29 ff.; Martène, *De antiquis mon. ritibus*, iii, c. xiii, nos. 51 ff.; *The Customary of Norwich*, ed. J. B. L. Tolhurst (Henry Bradshaw Society, 1948), pp. 80–1, cf. p. 238; *Ordinale of St. Mary's Abbey, York*, ed. the Abbess of Stanbrook and J. B. L. Tolhurst, ii (ibid. 1937), p. 278; *Registrum . . . prioratus beatae Mariae Wigorniensis*, ed. W. H. Hale (Camden Society, 1865), p. 107a (cf. *Paléographie Musicale*, xii (Tournay, 1922), pp. 65–6). For Peterborough cf. MS. Lambeth 198a (unfoliated): 'Surgat elemosinarius, ad claustrum pergat prospiciens si ea que ad mandatum pertinent bene ordinata fuerint.'

activities apart, he arranged for the distribution of food, clothing, and money to the poor according to the custom of each house.

The immense distributions of alms to the poor which took place at frequent intervals at St.-Denis and Cluny and other continental houses seem to have no parallel in England, nor is there any evidence of monasteries which allotted one-tenth of their income to alms, as is said to have been common abroad.[1] There is record in the eleventh and twelfth centuries of individual English abbots with an exceptional record for almsgiving. In the later Middle Ages it seems to have been reduced to a minimum: Professor Savine showed that the average compulsory alms—that is, the revenue from endowments specifically for alms—was well below 3 per cent. of the total monastic income in the *Valor Ecclesiasticus*, the tax returns of 1535.[2] The evidence he adduced is unexceptionable, since compulsory alms were exempt from tax, and would not be underestimated in the monks' claims. Furthermore, this evidence is confirmed by the surviving accounts of the later Middle Ages, which seem to show that in the main the total of voluntary alms added little to the compulsory. Occasionally even these small sums were diverted to another type of *pauperes*, the monks themselves.[3] An analysis of the functions of almoners and the expenses on alms in a few of the leading Benedictine houses makes this clear:[4] but one important proviso is necessary. A great deal of almsgiving can take place, in the shape of the distribution of food left over and used clothing, without making any impression on the accounts. Such distributions undoubtedly occurred and were perhaps of normal occurrence; in fact it is possible to imagine ways in which a spectacular distribution of alms could be made without leaving any trace in the official accounts. But there is no reason to suppose that the accounts are seriously misleading, and it is most unlikely that Savine's percentage was greatly exceeded in any house. The evidence suggests that by the fifteenth century voluntary alms were cut to a minimum. When money is scarce and it is difficult to balance the accounts, the reduction of alms is only too easy and obvious an economy. Sir Thomas More found so great a crowd of poor at the gate of Westminster Abbey that his road was blocked; but the actual expense to the monks of these distributions is known, and formed a small proportion of their total income.[5]

The income spent on alms was a small fraction of the monastic revenues as a whole; and although the almoner was not the only alms-giver—and sometimes not the most important—it is noticeable that the poor do not often bulk large in his accounts. In the budget of every almoner who had a separate establishment, the maintenance of his office, repairs to buildings and other property, the wages of his servants, and

---

[1] P. Schmitz, op. cit. v. 65–6.

[2] A. Savine, *English Monasteries on the Eve of the Dissolution* (Oxford Studies in Social and Legal History, ed. P. Vinogradoff, i, 1909), pp. 227–42, especially p. 238.

[3] Cf. Smith, *Canterbury Cathedral Priory*, pp. 47–8.

[4] See 'Note on the Financial Status of Almoners' on p. xlv.

[5] Savine, op. cit., pp. 240, 278: total of charity *c.* £265; gross income *c.* £3,912 (net *c.* £2,409). This is, in fact, the highest proportion known.

the like were always a large item. The proportion thus absorbed varied with the size and nature of the buildings to be maintained and the extent of the almoner's duties. It is not always fair to judge him by the fraction of his income actually spent on alms.[1] But frequently it seems to be small out of all comparison to his real function, and it is hard to see how his position can be justified. At Ely in the early fourteenth century, out of an income of about £100 a year, the almoner supported seven servants: but he also had a chaplain, and in 1328–9 two school-masters and twenty-three boys, apart from the regular distribution of old clothes, surplus food, and other doles to the poor. As the years passed, his staff and establishment remained as generous as ever, but the almonry boys sharply declined in numbers.[2] This kind of decay was probably quite common.

At Ely, as at Christ Church, Canterbury, the almoner was almost the only obedientiary whose finances were independent of the central treasurer.[3] No doubt the reason for this was originally a desire to give his office and its expenses greater stability. By the fifteenth century there was little difference in its workings in most houses from those of the other leading obedientiaries; but the almoner was always among the most independent.

The first calls on the purse of the Peterborough almoner were the maintenance of two hospitals and the distribution of certain small quantities of alms: the rest of his income went either to the support of other departments or to the upkeep of his own office, staff, and estates. There is no evidence of any almonry boys or of a song school.[4] The *Valor Ecclesiasticus* shows that the abbey claimed in the early sixteenth century to be paying about £60 a year in compulsory alms. It is im-possible to say exactly what proportion of this sum was actually paid by the almoner, although he presumably handled the greater part of it. Thus, for instance, 8*d.* a day (just over £12 a year) was issued by abbot and cellarer to certain poor men and women; 9 quarters of wheat were distributed to the poor—five by the almoner and four by the sacrist; 8 quarters of peas by the almoner; on Maundy Thursday the expenses in alms were assessed at £2. 18*s.* 4*d.*, of which the almoner paid 30*s.*, the chamberlain 15*s.*, and the cellarer 13*s.* 4*d.* The largest items were the payments to the eight poor men of St. Leonard's hospital (40*s.* each) and to the eight poor women of the hospital of St. Thomas of Canter-bury (33*s.* 4*d.* each).[5] By analogy, we should presume that these sums were paid by the almoner, but there is no evidence that such was the case, and it is very remarkable if so that there is no record of it in William Morton's book. In fact, such evidence as there is suggests that

---

[1] Because there is often no proper assessment of net income; he may have other functions to perform than purely eleemosynary; alms can be issued without appearing in his accounts; and he may organize ventures which are financed from other sources.

[2] *Ely Chapter Ordinances and Visitation Records*, ed. S. J. A. Evans (*Camden Miscellany*, xvii, 1940), pp. xi–xii.

[3] Ibid., p. 53; Smith, op. cit., pp. 23–4. At Ely the evidence comes from an ordinance of 1403; at Canterbury the anniversarian, and in part the prior, sacrist, and precentor were independent of the treasurers.   [4] But see below, p. xxx.

[5] *Valor Ecclesiasticus*, iv. 283–4; cf. Treasurer's Account 1522–3.

the ordinary maintenance of the poor in the hospitals was not paid for by the almoner but out of separate funds, partly supplied by the convent and partly by the parishioners of Peterborough, established perhaps before the endowment of the almonry.[1] It is possible but hardly probable that the sums mentioned in the *Valor* passed through the almoner's hands without being recorded in Morton's book, since he did not always note fixed annual payments there. Thus the distribution of bread on All Souls' Day is the only form of alms regularly referred to; otherwise there are only two passing mentions of alms; the Maundy Thursday expenses are never mentioned. The references to the sisters in St. Thomas's chapel (or hospital) seem to show Morton paying an annual sum of about 3s. 4d. or thereabouts to each of the sisters and some small sum to their servant, with occasional additions for robes and repairs to the fabric.[2] The numerous references to St. Leonard's hospital are all concerned with estate management, repairs, and the like. In any case it is certain that the almoner was the man primarily responsible for the administration of both the hospitals. This obscurity is a salutary warning of the danger of measuring an almoner's function solely by the details of his receipts and expenses.

The hospital of St. Leonard lay at the west end of the town: it had originally been a leper-house, and the first reference to it is in 1125, when it was already a flourishing institution. By the fifteenth century it had been converted into an ordinary hospital for about eight old bedesmen. The chapel and hospital of St. Thomas of Canterbury was founded by Abbot William of Waterville shortly before his deposition in 1175: the chancel still exists near the west gate of the precincts; the nave had been pulled down as early as 1402 to provide material for the new parish church in the market-place.[3]

Of his expenses within the convent, the most considerable were his payments to the treasurer already mentioned, amounting in 1522–3 to £8. 16s. 8d. or thereabouts, and £2. 3s. 8d. in rents.[4] He paid something towards the prior's sojourn at Oxney. To the infirmarer he owed a farm of £3. 6s., with the possibility of additional levies (as in 1379–80); to the hostiller a rent of 4s.; and to the precentor the usual small fee *pro ostensione librorum*.[5] Along with the sacrist and perhaps other obedientiaries, he paid an annual sum towards the support of the monks

[1] MS. Cotton Vespasian E XXII, f. 4; cf. Mellows, *Local Government*, p. 240.

[2] Cf. pp. 41 (28s. for 7 sisters and a servant for one year); 96 (3s. 4d. each to 3 sisters); 76 (2s. and 3s. 4d. to one new sister, possibly for successive years); and index, s.v. 'Peterborough, St. Thomas's Hospital'. For alms see index, and below, p. xlii.

[3] For the hospitals see W. T. Mellows, *Associated Architectural Societies' Reports and Papers*, xxxiv (1917–18), pp. 281–308 and *Local Government*, pp. 238–41; *Victoria County History of Northants.*, ii. 162; and for the foundation of St. Thomas's cf. *Peterborough Chronicle of Hugh Candidus*, ed. Mellows (Oxford, 1949), p. 130 (started by Abbot William de Waterville) and Swaffham, ed. Sparke, p. 101 (completed by his successor, Abbot Benedict). For the remains of St. Thomas's chapel see *Victoria County History*, ii. 456 and photograph facing; and for the destruction of its nave, below, p. 122, n. 1.

[4] A comparison of the items on the treasurer's roll of 1522–3 with those recorded in Morton's book shows that this sum would have been much the same in the mid-fifteenth century. What follows is not an exhaustive list of his payments to his colleagues.

[5] Infirmarer's roll, 1379–80; hostiller's roll, 1497–8; cf. below, pp. 34, 94, &c. (prior at Oxney); 27–8, 93–4, &c. (infirmarer); 75, &c. (hostiller); 17, 28, 49 (precentor).

studying at university.[1] In addition he gave a meal to some of his colleagues and their servants at Sexagesima and on the feast of St. Mary Magdalene, occasional small issues of wine to the convent, extra meals at the season of bloodletting, and tips to the abbey servants.[2] From time to time sums passed to the sub-almoner, whose functions are utterly obscure. He seems to have distributed a little alms and to have maintained an office; and a passing mention of *pueri in subelemosinaria* may possibly imply that he maintained almonry boys, but this is un-certain.[3] The almoner seems to have kept a wary eye on his subordinate official,[4] but there is surprisingly little reference to the sub-almonry in Morton's book. The remainder of his resources went to the upkeep and repair of his office and gardens, and to the payment of his vicar in choir, brother Thomas of St. Neot's,[5] and his servants and collectors.

At the heart of William Morton's administration lay his office, close by the east gate of the monastery, with its group of gardens and closes attached—the almoner's garden, 'the Trenches', and St. John's Close. It would seem that the old parish church of St. John lay immediately to the north of the almoner's property (by the road junction where St. John's Road now begins); near it lay the close or cemetery and the vicarage. The close was adjoining Morton's garden; in it he planted ash-trees and his servants caught rabbits for his table. Presumably it had fallen into his hands when the parish church was moved to its present site in the market-place in exchange for the nave of the Becket chapel, which had been granted to the parishioners for a quarry. St. John's Close is on the east side of what is now Vineyard Road; and Vineyard Road owes its name to the old vineyard of the monastery which lay to the west of it, whose southern part (now the garden of the Archdeaconry House) was evidently the almoner's garden. It may be that it was a formal garden for vegetables and flowers after the manner of those described in *The Goodman of Paris*: we only know that he planted herbs and leeks in it.[6]

---

[1] pp. 28, 52, 66, 93, 97, 107, 109, 144, 146, 158; cf. W. A. Pantin, *Canterbury College Oxford.* There are references to Peterborough monks in the surviving account rolls in 1454-5 (Pantin, op. cit. ii (1947), p. 179), 1459-60 (p. 180), 1462-3 (p. 182), 1466-7 (p. 185), &c., at intervals down to 1510-11 (p. 252). One of the rooms in the college was often called the Peterborough chamber, even when the Peterborough monks were not in it (e.g. pp. 200-1).

[2] e.g. pp. 23, 20, 34, 13-14, 94, and 137-8.

[3] p. 72 (and cf. *pueri in locutorio*, p. 134, and the frequent *clerici in subelemosinaria*, p. 39, &c.); cf. A. F. Leach in *Victoria County History of Northants.* ii. 202-3.

[4] See pp. 64-5, where Morton inquires into the status and morals of William Austhorp, *clericus mense in subelemosinaria.* [5] Cf. pp. 133, 139, 158.

[6] The above is a summary of Mr. Mellows's topographical notes to the text—see below, pp. 33, n. 2, 55, n. 7, 85, n. 6, 96, n. 6, 100, 101, n. 2, 122, n. 1 (there are further topographical notes on pp. 19, n. 4, 38, n. 1, 49, n. 2, 54, n. 6, 94, n. 3, 124, n. 1, 143, nn. 1 and 2). For the evidence of the site of the almonry see *The Foundation of Peterborough Cathedral,* ed. W. T. Mellows (N.R.S. xiii, 1941), pp. xlii, xliv and n., xlviii-xlix, lvi, lxxii; for the almoner's garden see also below, pp. 34, 113, 119-20, &c.; for medieval gardens cf. *The Goodman of Paris,* transl. Eileen Power (London, 1928), pp. 17-31, 195-204, 313, and Sir F. Crisp, *Medieval Gardens,* 2 vols. (London, 1924). On p. 146 below there is mention of a fruit garden or orchard in Howgate.

There are plans of the abbey precincts in *Victoria County History, ut sup.,* p. 448 and facing p. 440.

It was in his office that Morton must have spent most of his time, with his two or three servants, with his registers and records, his accounts, tallies, and money-bags. His chief book was his register, which was presumably similar in form to the almoner's registers which have survived at Durham and Worcester.[1] It would have been primarily a cartulary, a collection of title-deeds; but it seems also to have contained rentals and surveys, and, perhaps, notes of the almoner's duties and regular expenses. Of his legal records, court rolls, and the like, we know nothing apart from a few extracts in the present text and a reference to a book recording the process between Morton and the vicar of Maxey.[2] As almoner Morton was the tenant and the agent of a large estate; and the duties of a medieval land-agent were even more varied than those of his modern successor.

The names of about eight of Morton's servants occur in his book, but it seems doubtful if he employed more than three at any one time.[3] There are numerous references to John Coldwell from 1453 onwards and to Robert Morton from 1456: between them they clearly performed the bulk of his errands. John Coldwell in particular appears as his most trusted officer. His wages were 1s. 1½d. a week, paid in regular monthly instalments.[4] He was frequently employed in collecting money from Morton's debtors, and travelled on his behalf to Oxford and to London,[5] apart from frequent journeys nearer home. Morton had to keep very exact accounts with Coldwell, and these occur throughout the book; their transactions also show Coldwell holding a certain amount of property, and now and then selling a horse or the like on his own account.[6]

This staff may seem modest when compared with the seven servants of the Ely almoner, and in consideration of Savine's evidence that there were three laymen to every monk in many English monasteries on the eve of the Dissolution.[7] It is true that some departments in a monastery would need a far heavier staff than his; and it is true that Morton was not particularly prosperous among almoners. In any case it seems to have been adequate to his needs. Most of the ordinary tasks which needed doing were performed by local professionals—threshers, carpenters, thatchers, tilers, and the rest. But the men who played the largest part in Morton's affairs, apart from his servants, were his rent-collectors and the men who held his estates at farm. It is time to look somewhat more closely at the sources of his income and the range of his economic activities.

[1] The Worcester register has been edited by J. H. Bloom, *Liber Elemosinarii* (Worcs. Historical Society, 1911); cf. the register of the almonry of St. Paul's Cathedral, ed. M. Hackett (London, 1827).
[2] pp. 24–5, 117.
[3] Apart from Coldwell and Robert Morton there is reference to John Smythe, the almoner's clerk (p. 35), John Estaze, his *famulus* (p. 39), and John Baly, his *serviens* (p. 39, clearly his servant, not his serjeant); and see Subject Index; in 1456–7 we seem to be specifically told that there were three servants in the almonry—Coldwell, Morton, and John White (p. 94). One or two other men whose names occur may have been his servants.
[4] pp. 69, 84, 106.   [5] Cf. pp. 52, 58–9, 67, &c.
[6] e.g. pp. 108, 140.
[7] Savine, op. cit., pp. 218 ff., especially p. 222; for monastic servants cf. ibid., pp. 225–7, Knowles, *Monastic Order*, pp. 439–41.

C. *Estate Management*

The main sources of the almoner's income were profits of land, both rural and urban, and tithes. The urban rents were mostly in Peterborough itself, although dwellings to which no agricultural land was attached figured also among the almoner's possessions in such villages as Gunthorpe. However, by the middle of the fifteenth century the differences between these two sources of revenue—the form which their income took and the manner in which they were administered—were not as clearly marked as they may have been a century or two previously. Most of these properties, whether in the town of Peterborough or the purely rural parts of the Peterborough soke, yielded fixed money rents in various forms. Only pastures, woodlands, and some of the tithes produced fluctuating revenues in kind.

By the time of Morton's account the almoner's agricultural holdings had apparently ceased to be burdened by more than the vestiges of the regular obligations of personal service or to be associated with any customary payments denoting the unfree status of the tenants. The rents now represented the full money equivalent of all, or nearly all, the obligations which had once upon a time been borne by landholders. Customary holdings were presumably subject to limitations of sale and inheritance (the account tells us nothing about this). Here and there it is also possible to discover faint traces of surviving labour dues and personal obligations. When the almoner was engaged in building a mill at Sutton the *precarie* ('love boons') of the tenants provided much of the necessary carting.[1] The account also contains one or two fleeting references to suit of court due from some of the almoner's lands.

These lingering limitations and obligations, though few and no longer heavy, may account for the slight difference of yield between the almoner's customary rents and the rents he was able to charge for unrestricted leases. The rents for virgate holdings which were obviously customary, such as those of Sutton, listed on p. 48, varied according to the appurtenances and supplementary holdings attached to individual virgates, but never exceeded 10s. and were sometimes as low as 6s. 8d. A cottage with 4 acres in Sutton commanded the rent of 3s. 4d. and another cottage with 2 acres was let for 1s. 8d. These rents were substantially higher than the money payments due from similar holdings on the Peterborough estates at the time when they were still burdened with other customary dues, but apparently they were not higher than the thirteenth-century money rents from tenements held free of labour service. In at least one instance the account records a recent reduction in the customary rent of a virgate from 11s. to 8s.[2]

On the other hand, some of the almoner's land which had recently been let out and was not burdened by any customary obligations and not subject to any customary limitation, carried somewhat higher rent. Seven acres in the immediate neighbourhood of Peterborough were let for 4s., another 10 acres in the same area were let for 12s.[3] A similarly

[1] p. 105. [2] p. 48. [3] pp. 57, 86.

unrestricted lease of a holding of 26 acres with a large proportion of meadowland commanded a rent as high as 46s. 9d. or about 2s. per acre.[1] These may of course have been exceptionally dear lands, for meadowland was much more valuable than arable, and close proximity to Peterborough was also rated highly. Holdings and dwellings within the borough bore witness to the high level of urban rents: a mere cottage could be worth 6s. 8d. per annum.[2] On the other hand, the terminology of the account differentiates clearly between the 'assised rents' of customary holdings and the rents for the 'farms' or newly created leases, and the distinction was probably not merely one of nomenclature.

The bulk of William Morton's rents and revenues from land came from places within the soke of Peterborough—the borough itself, Gunthorpe, Sutton, Maxey, and Paston. The revenues in the borough came from lodgings and shops or else from meadows and woods on the outskirts. The account mentions the meadows at 'Mukhylle gap', at 'Fallam hyrne', at 'Stone Pyttys', and in miscellaneous crofts. The latter probably included the site of the hospital, that of at least one churchyard, and bits and pieces of land strewn all over Peterborough and its immediate vicinity. The almoner's woodlands in the Peterborough area are described as Eastwood and Westwood.[3]

The revenues in Gunthorpe consisted exclusively of tithes.[4] From Sutton the almoner derived both rents and profits of a church and a wood.[5] During the years covered by the account William Morton also constructed a water-mill by the Sutton bridge—the 'Brigmill'—which brought in about £2 per annum.[6] The main sources of income from Maxey and Paston came from their appropriated rectories.[7] The two rectories were apparently the two most valuable single properties in the possession of the almoner. William Morton did not exploit them in the same manner. The rectory of Maxey, which presumably had a considerable amount of glebe land attached to it, was as a rule let out to a lay 'farmer' for a fixed annual farm of £19. 10s. On the other hand, the

---

[1] pp. 49–50.   [2] p. 56; cf. also p. 78.

[3] For all these see Index, s.v. 'Peterborough, St. Leonard's Hospital', &c. Eastwood lay to the east of the city, in the parish of Eye; Westwood about a mile and a half to the west: they are represented today by Eastwood and Westwood Farms (cf. N.R.S. xiii. 13; J. E. B. Gover, A. Mawer, and F. M. Stenton, *The Place-Names of Northamptonshire*, pp. 228, 235).

The almonry had been endowed in the second half of the twelfth century with the manor of Sutton, the rectory of Maxey, the tithes of Paston and Gunthorpe (where Morton had a tithe barn; cf. below, pp. 10–11, 15, 36–7, 132, &c.), land in Warmington and Clapton, and some tenements in Peterborough itself, including land attached to St. Leonard's Hospital (which may at one time have constituted the almoner's home farm; cf. below, pp. 21–2, 32, 55, &c.). There had been some rearrangement and adjustment, but in the main this endowment seems to have been unchanged right through to the Dissolution. (For all this see above, pp. xx (twelfth century), xxi, n. 2 (1254, 1291), xxi, n. 3 (his brief tenure of the manor of Gunthorpe in the late thirteenth century) and *Valor Ecclesiasticus*, iv. 279 ff. (his holdings in 1535)). Gunthorpe apart, there is no evidence that his properties had altered between 1291 and 1535, although their relative values had no doubt shifted to some extent.

[4] Cf. pp. 10–11, &c.

[5] e.g. pp. 12–13, 48, 62–3.

[6] pp. 70, 103, 134; also pp. 62–3, 65, 72, 87, 91, 99, 102, 105, 107–9, 115–16, 130–1.

[7] pp. 29–31, and cf. next note.

profits of the rectory of Paston went in the first place to the rector, who accounted for them to the almoner or his receivers.[1]

The account suggests that the Maxey arrangement was not wholly satisfactory to Morton. From 1451 to 1454 we find him engaged in a protracted suit before the ecclesiastical authorities of the diocese of Lincoln and before the Papal Curia endeavouring to unseat the vicar of Maxey. It would be surprising if Morton's objections to the sitting vicar were provoked solely by the latter's spiritual failings or pastoral delinquencies. The document is, however, silent about any short-comings in the economic or administrative arrangements in the church of Maxey (some of the folios concerned with the case are missing), and the reader is left to his own speculation.

William Morton obviously was a careful and economically minded manager of his properties. On many manorial estates which were 'farmed' in the fifteenth century the 'farming' agreements made no pro-vision for the upkeep of land and buildings and equipment of their estates. But the almoner's properties were well looked after. Under his agreements with his tenants and 'farmers' he apparently bore the responsibility for repairs, and the account abounds with references to repairs and improvements carried out on his various properties, and above all to the upkeep of his farm buildings.[2] The references to the upkeep and reconstruction of the almoner's urban properties are also very frequent. On at least one of his Peterborough properties a 'shoppe wyndowe' was made at his expense.[3]

In addition William Morton also appears to have possessed and maintained buildings and 'capital equipment' which he himself used and occupied. For in spite of his being so pre-eminently a *rentier*, he was himself engaged in certain agricultural and quasi-agricultural activities. At one time we find him organizing the ploughing, sowing, and reaping of a small piece of land.[4] But arable occupations of this nature were not characteristic of his main interests. Much more characteristic and important were the operations which he had to carry out for the efficient management of his tithes and farms. Tithes, unless farmed for fixed sums of money, came in kind; and the account shows the almoner organizing their collection in sheaves and their transportation to his 'office' and his grange. We also find him repeatedly hiring men to thresh and winnow his tithe grain.[5] Whether his transactions with millers and bakers were, so to speak, a further stage in the management of his own produce we do not know. As almoner he would be expected to provide bread for the hospital and for occasional distribution. But there is little doubt that he made a great deal of malt, for we do find frequent references not only to malt-making but also to repeated sales of large quantities of malt to outsiders.[6]

---

[1] pp. 29–31, 66–7, 76–7, &c. In a later year the rector of Paston is shown 'buying' the almoner's share in the tithes of Paston (p. 134).
[2] pp. 12–13, 18, 51–3, 74, 79–81, 123, 135–6, 149–50, &c.
[3] p. 136.
[4] p. 135.
[5] pp. 10–11, 15, 36–7, &c.
[6] pp. 8, 11, 63, &c.

William Morton also exploited directly most of his woods and
pastures. We find him cutting and selling timber, firewood, and brushwood, and even bark for tanning. In these activities he reveals himself
as a careful and provident manager. He watches over the cutting of
trees and other dilapidations in his woods by tenants, and himself takes
care to maintain his plantations. The entries for 1456–7 describe the
planting—or perhaps the replanting—of a piece of woodland on land
adjacent to the old church of St. John the Baptist and in a place
described as 'le Trenchys'. We see him not only clearing and selling
the brushwood growing there but also planting a large quantity of
young trees: to be more precise, 700 ashes and two cartloads of willow
plants.[1]

Meadows could be and were exploited in several ways. Morton
obviously possessed and pastured on his meadows a herd of cattle of his
own, for he repeatedly records his sales of cows and calves for slaughter
and his frequent business dealings with Peterborough butchers—
especially with John Beylde and Robert Orwin, both described as
'bochers'.[2] We also find him 'lending' cows and calves to 'borrowers'
of cattle.

Another method of exploiting meadows was to grow hay for sale: an
activity well exemplified in the account. But in addition Morton also
let herbage for short periods or took in other people's cattle for agistment or grazing on his own land. The grazing agreements appear to
have been especially profitable, for pastures so close to the centre of the
borough as his commanded high prices.[3] It is therefore not surprising
that he should have tried to put to account every bit of grass he could
lay his hand on: in 'trenches', hedgerows, and cemeteries. The old
churchyard of St. John the Baptist which belonged to him was in
demand as a cow pasture.[4]

These and other transactions disprove the over-simple notions
current among historians about the universal slaughter of animals in the
winter. Winter keep was undeniably very costly, especially on the town
pastures of Peterborough. At 1s. 6d. to 3s. 6d. per beast it represented anything from a quarter to a half of the value of a full-grown
cow. There is, however, little doubt that Morton's meadows were
stocked in the winter. His table also bears witness to a steady supply of
meat throughout the year,[5] though it is impossible to know how much
of this was salted.

William Morton's involvement with pasture, herbage, cattle, and
butchers may also account for his frequent 'loans' of cows. It is, however, difficult to escape the suspicion that now and again Morton 'lent'
his cows and calves to cover up a little profitable money-lending.
According to the rough-and-ready principles which in the later Middle

---

[1] pp. 100–1.   [2] e.g. pp. 6–7, 60, 71–2.
[3] pp. 60–1, 71, 83, &c.; on p. 7 the charge for wintering 8 beasts appears to be 10s.
[4] In 1451–2 Robert Orwin leased the pasturage for four years at 6s. 8d. per annum (p. 7);
cf. also p. 55.
[5] The account reveals no discernible differences between his winter diet (pp. 13–14, 23–4,
55–6, 84–5, 96, 151) and his summer diet (pp. 20, 71, 89, 103, 122, 134, 154, 160).

Ages regulated the charging of interest, annual payment for the use of borrowed cows was not considered as usury, and loans of cows were therefore employed to legitimize petty borrowings on interest. When the account shows the almoner 'lending' a cow for a couple of years there is perhaps no reason for regarding the transaction as anything other than what it purports to be. But when we read that Morton lent cows for a period of five years, or a cow ten years old for three years at 3s. per annum with an understanding to repay a stipulated sum of money if the cow could not be 'returned', the impression that this is a disguised money loan is inescapable.[1]

Other loans to individuals of every station and profession will be found scattered all over the account. They are, as a rule, humble men and women owing small sums of money, sometimes for arrears of rent or for money owed for grain, malt, or firewood bought of the almoner, and sometimes representing petty loans of cash. At least one of the debtors, Agnes Morton, may have been a relative whom the almoner employed in all the occupations in which medieval women appear to have specialized—as an ale-wife, a maltster, a spinner of linen thread, and a maker of hair sieves.[2]

The only substantial men among Morton's debtors are the merchants with whom he has his business dealings, and among them his two butchers, who frequently buy from him agricultural produce—mostly cattle, grain, hay, and timber. In these sales credit, sometimes for periods as long as a year, is expected and given. The curious thing is that Morton, who is obviously a man of substance seldom short of cash, buys his own supplies (mainly spices, wine, building materials, such as sticks, bricks, lime, nails) on credit from suppliers who are often the same people who buy from him on credit. At regular intervals these mutual debts are set off against each other and net balances are either settled in cash or carried over for another term.[3]

These and other activities in which Morton engaged required a large amount of transport both by land and by water. It would hardly be an exaggeration to say that over the period covered by the account Morton was called upon to arrange for the transport of many hundred cartloads of goods. Considering the scattered character of his possessions, the scale and frequency of his dealings with carters and carriers is quite understandable, but his dealings also make it clear that Morton was able to manage his scattered possessions as he did on the assumption that the means of transport were sufficient for the purpose.

In other words, it looks as if medieval transport, inefficient as it was, made it possible to move bulky goods without prohibitive additions to costs. Water transport was of course cheaper than cartage; but the carting of goods within Peterborough can be assumed to have been cheap enough to justify a great deal of carting to Morton's 'office' from every part of the city. But Morton also transported large quantities of cheap and bulky produce—timber, firewood, clay, chalk, straw—to

[1] pp. 14–15, 54, 104, &c.   [2] p. 19; cf. above, p. xviii.
[3] pp. 6–7, 17, 25, &c.

and from his outlying possessions, most of them seven to eight miles away. The table below, which lists some of these cargoes, suggests that the average cost of cartage over these distances worked out at about 2*d.* per cart-mile.

Quantity (carts)	Commodity	Route	Distance (miles)	Cost per cart	Page
28	Timber	Eastwood to Peterborough	2½	7*d.*	1
6	,,	Castor to Peterborough	5	10*d.*	2
6	—	Gunthorpe to Peterborough	3	7*d.*	16
3	—	Peterborough to Sutton	5	10*d.*	32
3	Timber	Sutton Wood to the Hospital	6	1*s.*	62
2	—	Oundle to Warmington	3½	1*s.*	111
9	Timber	Sutton to Peterborough	5	10*d.*	121
5	Hay	'Mukhyll Gap' to Peter-borough	1½ (?)	3½*d.*	132
13	—	Between Peterborough and Gunthorpe (both directions)	3	8*d.*	141–2

As each payment probably included the charge for the return journey (and the costs of loading in the account make no other allowances for this item), the cost of Morton's transport does not work out much above, and must frequently have been well below, the 1*d.* per ton-mile, which, according to Thorold Rogers, was the average cost of transport by peasant carts. Expressed as a percentage of total costs Morton's charges do not greatly differ from corresponding costs in our own time. The carriage of 6,400 bricks by water from 'Wygnale' (? Wiggenhall, near Lynn, Norfolk) cost 6*s.* 5*d.* or about 28 per cent. of the cost of the bricks (23*s.* 4*d.*). The transport of 20 pieces of oak, worth 15*s.*, came to 1*s.* 2*d.* or about 8 per cent. of the total cost; 4 quarters of wheat, ground and baked into bread for distribution to the poor, cost 10*d.* to move from Maxey to Peterborough—about 3 per cent.[1]

In other words, the evidence of Morton's account bears out a conclusion reached elsewhere, that in the Middle Ages the proportion of transport costs to total costs may not have been higher than it is now, and that this may have been one of the reasons why men in the Middle Ages found it possible to trade as they did.[2]

To complete the picture of Morton's economy we need the aid of his annual account rolls: it is a misfortune that none of them have survived. They are frequently referred to in Morton's notebook—reference is made to earlier accounts to check rents and other dues, and entries are cancelled because they have been transferred to the official account roll.[3] In accordance with the almost universal practice among English landowners, religious and secular alike, these account rolls were drawn up

[1] pp. 87, 118, 52. The first of these leaves out of account 12½*d.* spent on moving 2,400 of the bricks from the wharf to the office and the hospital. This item shows the highest cost, except for the remarkable account for 10 cartloads of stone on p. 51—8 from Barnack and Walcot for 95 per cent. of cost (10*s.* 8*d.*: 11*s.* 4*d.*), and 2 from Wansford for 75 per cent. (2*s.* 6*d.*: 3*s.* 4*d.*).

[2] *The Cambridge Economic History of Europe*, ii (1952), p. 155.

[3] See below, pp. xlii, 95, 128 (cf. p. 123); for cancellations, pp. xlvii, 80 and n. 4, 99 and n. 1, &c.

in fair copy each year for the audit of the accounts of every limb of the monastic economy, from the bailiffs and collectors up to the abbot's receiver. The almoner's collectors' accounts were summarized on the almoner's roll: whether the almoner's roll was further summarized in a general statement of all the obedientiaries' accounts, such as was compiled at Christ Church, Canterbury, Norwich, and elsewhere,[1] is not known. It is clear from the evidence of Prior Richard Harlton, who could estimate fairly closely the normal total income of the convent side as well as of the abbot's, that when he had been in control of the audit it had been possible for him to assess the overall financial position of the abbey.[2]

In 1436, according to Harlton, the total income of the house was approximately £1,500 a year, of which the abbot's side had about £700,[3] the convent £800: a comparison with the abbot's receiver's account for 1415 seems to indicate that the gross income would have been somewhat higher.[4] In 1535 the total gross income is given as £1,979. 7s. 5⅞d., the net income as £1,721. 14s. 0⅞d.[5] This cannot be an over-estimate, and is probably not far wrong; we may say that the gross income was then about £2,000. The almoner's gross annual income in 1535 amounts to £82. 5s. 10¼d.: a comparison of certain items in detail seems to indicate that Morton's was somewhat higher.[6] But a statement of a

[1] Cf. R. A. L. Smith, *Canterbury Cathedral Priory*, pp. 19–20; H. W. Saunders, *Norwich Cathedral Priory*, pp. 17–18. [2] L.R.S. xxi. 273.

[3] This sum is confirmed by the abbot's receiver (ibid., p. 277).

[4] Additional MS. 25288, ff. 93–104: the gross income amounts to about £695, but only the period from Epiphany to Michaelmas 1415 is covered. Doubtless the income was higher under the high farming abbots of the late thirteenth and early fourteenth centuries; but the only figures which survive are the taxation assessments of the second half of the thirteenth century, which are quite useless for our purpose (cf. W. E. Lunt, *Financial Relations of the Papacy with England to 1327* (Cambridge, Mass., 1939), p. 353, and references there cited).

[5] *Valor Ecclesiasticus*, iv. 279–84; Savine, p. 279. For the relations of the 1535 assessment to actual income cf. ibid., pp. 31–75, especially pp. 73–5.

There is an error in the printed text of the *Valor* which upsets the entry relating to the almoner's spiritualities. The tithes of Peterborough are assigned both to the almoner and the sacrist: but it is clear that the phrase *Pertinen' officio elemos'* belongs to the preceding entry, and thus covers Maxey and Gunthorpe, as it should.

[6] The farm of the mill at Sutton was £2 in 1535, as in Morton's time, whereas the rectory of Maxey was assessed at £13. 16s. 8d. in 1535, while Morton drew from it £19. 10s. per annum (see above, p. xxxiii). On the other hand, it is possible that the latter figure included some of the temporal properties in Maxey (assessed at £5. 6s. 1d. in 1535), although they would normally be in the hands of the collector of Maxey (for whom cf. below, p. 29) not the farmer. The only other set of figures which can usefully be compared are those for the Gunthorpe tithes, and they only roughly. In 1535 they were assessed at £11; in 1448 they provided Morton with £12. 2s. 8d. gross (pp. 10–11), but this does not include the wheat render, which was consumed in the almoner's office. In 1449 he garnered 12 quarters of wheat and, in 1450, 8 quarters and 1 skep (pp. 15, 36–7), so that it looks as though this amounts to a substantial omission in the 1448 account; but unfortunately the cash yield from the tithe is never given in later years, and it is clear that it fluctuated considerably.

These figures, in so far as a conclusion can be drawn from them, suggest that Morton's income was higher than that of his successor in 1535; but allowance must be made for the fact (a) that we have only been able to compare the income from between a third and a quarter of his properties, and (b) that the assessment in the *Valor* may be too low (this seems particularly likely to apply to the Gunthorpe tithe, which fluctuated with the harvest, and would therefore be more open to under-assessment than a fixed rent or farm). No comparison is possible with the position of the almoner in earlier days.

Our only hint of the almoner's overall financial position is the note on p. 123 that

Facsimile of two pages of the Book of William Morton (Brit. Mus. Cotton. Vesp. A. xxiv. ff. 65v 66.)

gross annual income gives little real idea of an obedientiary's financial position. Without any of his account rolls, it is impossible to tell exactly how much of Morton's income went in customary payments and rents to his colleagues or how the resultant income was disposed. Morton's income was large, but there is no evidence from his book of real prosperity: at least, there is no indication of any unduly heavy expenditure on himself or his household. He seems to have lived quietly and on the whole economically—an able business man on a small scale—keeping his administrative machine in play: doing his accounts, organizing and maintaining his office and the hospital, keeping up his houses and barns, buying and selling, 'getting and spending'.[1]

III. THE BOOK

The manuscript to which we have given the title 'The Book of William Morton' is British Museum Cotton MS. Vespasian A XXIV. It is a small book of 99 folios, about $5\frac{1}{2} \times 8\frac{1}{2}$ in. (*c.* 145 × 220 mm.) written for the most part on paper, with two parchment slips inserted.[2] It is roughly and irregularly constructed and tightly bound, so that the following collation cannot be guaranteed in every detail; but it appears to be made up as follows: 1 parchment leaf + 1²⁴ (23–4, ff. 24–5, partly cancelled) + 2¹⁶ + 3²⁰ + 4?¹⁶ (ff. 62–76: a leaf seems to be missing between ff. 61 and 62³) + 5²⁰ (f. 94 is a parchment leaf inserted; ff. 95–7 are blank) + 2 sheets of modern paper. The last page of quire 5, f. 97*v*, is dirty, and obviously formed the back of the volume at one time.

The numerous cross-references and chronological data in the text show that the order of quires is correct and that in the main it is in the state in which it left Morton's hands. But they also show that between ff. 25 and 26 (i.e. between quires 1 and 2) a quire is missing. The lost entries covered the 14th and most of the 15th years of Abbot Richard. Two cross-references span the gap: ff. 7*r* (p. 13) to 34*v* (p. 62) are counted as 46 folios, and ff. 13*v* (pp. 25–6) to 45*r* (p. 81) as 50 folios; since Morton normally counts inclusively, this suggests that about 17 or 18 folios are missing, but his reckoning varied too much for an exact estimate.

On f. 58*v* (p. 106) we are referred to the penultimate folio of the book. The symbol and the cross-reference are unfortunately not to be found elsewhere; but since the tops of most of the folios towards the end have been defaced by damp, it seems probable that it once occurred there. The book now closes with the inserted slip (f. 94) and three blank leaves. The last folio on which there is writing is, properly speaking, f. 93; and the first entries which can be deciphered on f. 92*v* relate to metalwork, which would fit the cross-reference on f. 58*v*.

Morton's predecessor had received a *subsidium* of £6 in 1438–9; but this was probably a special allowance to deal with an exceptional expense.
[1] The subtitle of the third volume of Coulton's *Five Centuries of Religion* (after Wordsworth).
[2] ff. 1, 94.   [3] See 'Note on the Watermarks in the MS.' on p. xlvi.

This and the blank leaves at the end are sufficient to establish that the book is complete at its conclusion.

With the exception of four short passages the book is written in one hand of the mid-fifteenth century. The exceptions are as follows: the taxation assessment on f. *1r*; John Winwick's debtors and the account of the church on Stamford bridge for 1427–8, in different hands, on f. *3r–v*; the Sutton court roll on ff. *12v–13r*; and the curious historical jottings in the first paragraph of f. *23v*.[1] The Sutton court roll is relevant to and contemporary with its present context; the remainder seem to have been already written on the paper out of which the book was made—this must certainly be true of the Stamford account. The watermarks suggest that Morton collected old scraps of rough paper for his first quire, then added further quires as they were needed. The system of cross-references presupposes that the quires were roughly tacked together, at least, while Morton was using them.

Since the manuscript consists throughout of the rough accounts and memoranda of William Morton, it would seem natural to suppose that the single hand which wrote a large majority of the entries was his. Normally everybody is referred to in the third person, including Morton himself, but on the rare occasions when the first person singular occurs,[2] it always refers to Morton. If further proof were needed, I think a close scrutiny of the text leaves a strong impression that it was written by the almoner in person. It is, moreover, improbable that any one of his clerks or servants was in his employment from the time he became almoner right through to 1467.

The basic arrangement of the book is chronological. At the head of nearly every page is written the date, generally the year of Abbot Richard Ashton,[3] and approximately seven or eight folios are devoted to each year. But often entries relating to a number of different years are put down on the same page. A detailed inspection of the arrangement and of the handwriting reveals that many of the transactions were entered as they occurred, from day to day, but that at times a series of entries, covering weeks or even months, were made at once. The writer constantly turned back to the earlier pages of his book to make new entries, or to add marginal notes and cross-references. The number of these last is very large, and they enable us not only to check the original order of the quires but to see how Morton set to work. They provide us, as they provided him, with the signposts by which to follow out the purpose and uses of the book.

---

[1] These claim to be derived from the chronicle of William, prior of Peterborough, whom I have failed to identify (for the event it describes and its sources see W. E. Lunt, *Financial Relations of the Papacy with England to 1327* (Cambridge, Mass., 1939), pp. 230–8); from 'Chestr' ', which is a garbled extract from Ranulph Higden's *Polychronicon* (the passage occurs in the Rolls Series edition at viii. 270); and from another source unspecified. F. 94*v*. may also be in another hand.

[2] pp. 12, 29, 37 (*recepi*); 27 (*satisfeci*); 53 (*ego elemosinarius accomodavi*); 68 (*teste me ipso*).

[3] The *congé d'élire* for Ashton's election was issued on 27 August 1438; the royal assent was given on 24 September (L.R.S. xxi. 283, n. 2). The exact date of his election is not known, but it must have happened after 2 September (see above, p. xiv, n. 5 and reference there cited). For accounting purposes his year was clearly taken to begin at Michaelmas (see p. 168; for the *mutacio* of the regnal year there given, cf. also pp. 3, 63 and nn.).

As a record of Morton's administration the book is incomplete: his tallies and bills, his formal account rolls, his register, and the other stock-in-trade of a busy monastic official have disappeared without leaving a trace. Moreover, his revenues and expenses and all his activities were a closely integrated part of the complicated structure of the monastic economy. We have some other documents, very few of them strictly contemporary, with which to compare it; and by covering a period of twenty-odd years it provides a far more satisfactory picture than a stray account roll covering only one or two. But in the main it is isolated and without context, and that detracts from its value as evidence and the sureness of our interpretation of it. A person in Morton's position might be expected to keep accounts for four main reasons: as a record of the state of his dealings with creditors and debtors, as a check on the level of his expenditure, to observe his overall financial position—the balance of profit and loss—and to render an account of his stewardship at the annual audit. But the level of expenditure and the significant balance of profit or loss cannot be truly assessed by any routine method of book-keeping; and the medieval administrator had little idea of how to distinguish income and capital expenditure and rarely attempted a proper assessment of profit and loss. An obedientiary, as the head of a small department in a large non-profit-making concern, was apparently content to observe his general position as it emerged from the annual account roll compiled for the audit. The third and fourth needs were thus adequately covered by the account roll. This roll is the only sort of account which normally survives, and a specimen of it lies at the heart of all medieval English treatises on accounting and estate management.[1] The technique of accounting was based on the moral need to detect the unjust steward rather than on the dictates of economic suitability.

The medieval account roll represents the year's transactions in a conventional and simplified form. Behind them lay the complexity of everyday business, the give and take of cash and credit. How were individual debts and credits recorded? And how was this mass of detail translated into the annual account roll?

The answer to these questions is not at all clearly known. But there were two types of record which were fundamental: the tallies, notched and inscribed and then divided to form bill and receipt;[2] and the account rolls of previous years, which would clearly reveal those annual receipts and expenses which were unvarying. In an age when most of the monastic lands were let out at farm, and many payments fixed by custom, a great part of the obedientiary's roll would alter little from year to year.

William Morton's book may be said to bridge the gap between his

---

[1] For these treatises see the handlist by D. Oschinsky in *Economic History Review*, xvii (1947), 52–61, supplemented from Durham MSS. in Miss E. M. Halcrow's unpublished Oxford thesis on Durham administration; cf. also N. Denholm-Young, *Seignorial Administration in England* (Oxford, 1937), pp. 120 ff., 169–76.

[2] The fullest account of the tally is in H. Jenkinson, 'Medieval Tallies', *Archaeologia*, lxxiv (1923–4), 289–351.

tallies and his account rolls. Tallies are constantly referred to, and a very high proportion of the entries are presumably transcripts of them. A great number of transactions are cancelled or crossed out as having been transferred to the account roll—*scribitur*, *scribitur in compoto*, or the like. There are numerous marginal notes and headings, sometimes written at the same time as the entries beside them, sometimes added later; these help to analyse the transaction into groups. Sometimes the marginalia simply consist of the names of the debtor or creditor involved. Frequently they describe the type of transaction, and then in such terms—*custus in Burgo, forinseca expensa, Sutton recepta, Sutton compotus* or *Sutton* alone, and so forth—as would normally be the headings in a formal account roll, or something approximating to them. It is clear that these were put in not only for convenience of reference but also as a preliminary to the rearrangement of the material for the annual account. In addition, previous account rolls are sometimes referred to for comparison or to establish the size of some customary rent or the like.[1]

But a complete statement of his annual accounts cannot be recovered from his book. His annual payments of alms to the poor, apart from the distribution on All Souls' Day, are only twice mentioned.[2] They were small, but we know from other evidence that they existed.[3] His servants' wages are poorly represented: he records his first payments to Baly, Estaze, and Coldwell, but after three and a half years even Coldwell's disappear.[4] None of the annual payments to other monks or to his fellow obedientiaries is given for every year he held office. Examples could no doubt be multiplied: sufficient has been said to show that this book is not a complete record of his accounts. It is possible that with the aid of his tallies, his rolls, and his memory he could have constructed a complete account; and it is certain that the majority of his annual receipts and expenses is included here. It may be that he had other notebooks and documents in front of him.

What matters more is that this was not the only, nor perhaps the most important, purpose of Morton's book. It was also a record of the state of his account with all those with whom he had dealings, a cash book and a memorandum book.

In arrangement, as we have seen, it is fundamentally chronological, with numerous derangements of order and cross-references. Occasionally these are made to serve the second need of the accountant described above, to check the level of expenditure. Thus his expenses on the feast of St. Mary Magdalene 1449 were noted down immediately below those of 1450.[5] But the vast majority connect successive transactions

[1] p. 128 (cf. p. 123).
[2] p. 146 (10*s.* handed over to John Pytchley, apparently the hostiller, for distribution to the poor); p. 153 (3 cartloads of peas for distribution to the poor in Lent). But there is also reference to an alms-trough in the refectory (presumably for collecting scraps: p. 125; cf. p. 53).
[3] Cf. above, p. xxviii.
[4] See above, p. xxxi and n. 3. We cannot tell, however, what may have been lost with the missing folios.
[5] p. 20.

with the same person or successive entries relating to the same transaction. Apart from innumerable derangements, there are almost a
hundred cross-references of this kind. From these the individual
accounts could quickly be reconstructed: the completeness of this
cumbersome framework shows how essential a part of Morton's plan
this was. Gonville and Caius College, Cambridge, from the sixteenth
to the nineteenth century preserved two sets of account books in its
archives: the general annual statements, and the *Libri Rationales*. The
Liber Rationalis was a book containing the account of each fellow and
scholar with the college term by term and year by year. Fundamentally,
the book of William Morton is a rough draft of the same sort of
account.

This resemblance should not blind us to two fundamental differences
in character and purpose. First of all, this book clearly serves other
purposes, as we have seen: it was the basis of his account rolls and a
check on his expenditure; it also contains memoranda on other points
connected with his office, assessments of the number of loaves which
could be baked out of four quarters of corn, tables of weights and prices,
draft inventories,[1] and ephemeral memoranda of every kind.[2] Assessments and comparisons grow rarer as the years passed and Morton
grew more experienced, and in other ways the book develops and alters.
But its main layout changed little; and it is clear that for all its incoherence it suited its author well enough. It is essentially a private account
book, intended for his eye alone. It has all the lack of balance and
inconsequence which makes our private memoranda incomprehensible
to an outside reader but of intimate value and utility to ourselves.
Other medieval memoranda books which survive, like those of Henry
of Eastry, prior of Canterbury, and William de Ryckel, abbot of St.
Trond,[3] equally show a diffuse and seemingly inconsequential selection
of matter to be included. But behind them lay in fact the organizing
imagination, incisive intelligence, and breadth of grasp of two great
men of affairs; and any similarities with Morton's humble notebook are
at a superficial level—his vision was narrow, like the scope of his
activities. But his grasp was reasonably sure: if the multitude of disconnected entries of which it consists seems to us hopelessly confused,
it must be remembered that it covers a period of nearly twenty years,
and is so laid out that there is no reason to doubt the ability of the
author to find his way about. Under normal circumstances he would
only be using eight or nine folios at a time, with back references to ten
or a dozen more, and only very occasional intrusions farther back. The
more polished accounting techniques in use nowadays may be easier
to look at, and provide more exact insight into the workings of a modern business. But for William Morton's purposes a more primitive

[1] pp. 5–6, 9–10, 20, &c.
[2] e.g. on pp. 12 (a recipe for an eye-salve); 5, 44 (a pious jingle); 106, 115, 117 (notes
on books lent, &c.).
[3] MS. Cotton Galba E IV (cf. R. A. L. Smith, *Canterbury Cathedral Priory*, passim;
Knowles, *Religious Orders*, pp. 49–54, 322–5); *Le Livre de l'abbé Guillaume de Ryckel*, ed.
H. Pirenne, Gand, 1896.

instrument was not only adequate but probably more suitable.[1] There is no reason to doubt that he found it efficient.

Finally, Morton's book is a cash book: a register of actual cash transactions. The formal account roll, as a rationalized statement of accounts, is an essential guide to the economic position and the broad nature of the transactions of a medieval accountant. But for the technique of these transactions, the way by which money actually passed, we have to turn to a cash account like the present book. The difference is illustrated in two ways. First, by the use of credit, and the manipulation of the complicated cross-fire of accounts between the obedientiaries; of this we have already given a description. Secondly, it is shown by actual descriptions of the payment of cash. It is true that the majority of payments are given in pounds, shillings, and pence, which tells us nothing of the coin involved; and that the book throws little light on the vexed question of how small change was manipulated in the fifteenth century. But there are numerous references to coins larger than a penny, to groats and gold nobles, and even on occasion to gold halfpennies and gold farthings.[2] On f. 42v there is a list of the rector of Paston's payments over the years 1456–9: at some date in 1458 Morton notes that one lot included a forged groat; on 27 January following he noted three forged groats received; and on 28 April *memorandum de multis falsis denariis*.[3] Apart from this, references to forged coin are rare. But perhaps the clearest statement of the nature of a transaction is in the account with the sacrist, William Borough, in 1455–6.[4] On 21 December 1455 Morton paid Borough 'in part payment of 5 marks, 20s. in groats, and one gold noble; one "sort" of figs and raisins worth 15s.; and 2,000 red tiles (bricks) worth 12s.: total 53s. 8d., and he owes 13s.' Payments of this kind in food and materials are commonly referred to; and many of Morton's more humble tenants and neighbours paid their rent in work. Agnes Morton was employed from time to time at the rate of 3d. a day: on one occasion she worked off 2s. of a debt by handing over 9 chickens and 2 geese (12d.) and working for 4 days at the hospital (12d.).[5] On ff. 14–15 we have a series of accounts of the almoner's farmers and collectors, which clearly reveal the nature of the book as an index of tallies; the phrases *per talliam* and *ut patet per talliam suam* frequently occur. In general it may be said that the large, regular debts were paid off in somewhat irregular instalments, while the smaller sums were allowed to accumulate, sometimes over a period of years, to avoid the constant passage of small change. This is no more than what we should expect at a time when coin was a cumbersome commodity.

Our final impression, on closing Morton's book, is that it was the work of a meticulous man in a meticulous age. Payments are identified not only, for obvious reasons, by the name of the man who actually

---

[1] For a discussion of the rise of double-entry book-keeping and the suitability of different sorts of accounts for small concerns see B. S. Yamey, *Economic History Review*, 2nd series, i (1948–9), 99 ff., especially p. 105.

[2] pp. 54, 81, etc.   [3] pp. 76–7.   [4] p. 81.   [5] p. 18.

received the money, often one of the almoner's servants, but by place and often by witness. Every part of the monastery appears sooner or later as the home of the money-changers, from the almoner's office to the abbey choir during mass;[1] and a high proportion of the other obedientiaries are involved as witnesses to payments or contracts. The last were further validated by the oath of the contracting party (who swore with his right hand raised, as Morton frequently observes).[2] These references seem to reflect the formalism of the fifteenth century in legal and financial matters alike; and also perhaps the personality of William Morton, painstaking, conscientious, and precise, a man genuinely interested in his business concerns, a faithful and efficient steward, even if wanting in the finer points of office technique.[3] Once, and only once, the account shows us William Morton face to face. On f. 17v (p. 35) we have a pretty little dispute with two debtors who owed 8d. each, which they claimed to have paid. It seems that when they expostulated with him, Morton gave the customary creditor's grunt of scepticism, and entered in his book: 'paid—so he says' by each. The two waxed indignant, and pressed the point home. The final result is that Morton has written over the first entry: 'Paid, so he says. And it's true, it's true, it's true!' Over the second we read: 'Paid, so he says: it's true—he's paid, paid, paid, paid, paid!' But even this, vivid as it is, tells us all too little of Morton as a man, and nothing at all of Morton as monk and priest.

Note on the Financial Status of Almoners

THE following is a brief analysis of the almoner's position at Bury, Canterbury, Norwich, and Winchester; for Durham cf. Durham Account Rolls, ed. J. T. Fowler, iii (Surtees Society, 1901), pp. xxxviii–xlv; for Ely see above, p. xxviii; for other cases, the Valor Ecclesiasticus, passim. But there is a wealth of material, of which only a limited proportion is dealt with here: Westminster in particular would repay study.

At Bury St. Edmunds the almoner's income in 1535 consisted of £43. 10s. 4½d. out of a total income of over £2,000, and of this £15. 8s. 9d. was for compulsory alms. But the cellarer and hostiller disposed of far larger charitable funds (£191. 19s. 1d. and £86. 14s. 5d. respectively); and the alms of abbot, treasurer, and sacrist also exceeded the almoner's (Valor Ecclesiasticus, iii. 459–65; Savine, p. 235). This is an extreme case; but it is common for the almoner's share in the alms distributed to be less than half the total. It may well be that he had a hand in the distribution of some of the other alms.

Of the size of the almoner's income and the proportion spent on alms, Bury is not an exceptional case. The almoner of Christ Church, Canterbury, had a similar income, of which some proportion was spent on the support of a chapel and a school, but only about ½ per cent. on alms to the poor in the early fourteenth century (apart from considerable issues of corn and cloth);

[1] The choir during mass occurs on p. 68.
[2] pp. 25 (2), 55, 60 (2), 65, 92, 113, 114, 118, 162, 163.
[3] Morton's book may be more than a chance survival—the very fact that it was written may well indicate, as Professor Postan has pointed out to me, that Morton was more of a business man than the majority of medieval obedientiaries.

the remainder of his income went to maintain his household and servants and in allowances to fellow monks (Smith, *Canterbury Cathedral Priory*, pp. 47–8).

At Norwich the main expense on alms was the support of a grammar school for thirteen poor boys (£21 a year in 1535) and of a hospital (more than £28 a year); the almoner also spent £2. 2s. and 26 quarters of grain for distribution to the poor; 6½d. a week for the support of twelve poor men in the cathedral; and £10 for the Maundy Thursday feast. (*Valor Ecclesiasticus*, iii. 287, 289; Savine, p. 234; cf. H. W. Saunders, *Norwich Cathedral Priory*, pp. 121–7. It is not clear what part the almoner played in maintaining the grammar school and hospital.)

At Winchester Cathedral priory the almoner was chiefly supported from the proceeds of Hinton Manor, which gave him between three-quarters and four-fifths of his income (in the early fourteenth century *c.* £30 or a little more, out of a total of *c.* £39) and a favourite holiday resort. His main expense was the maintenance of the sisters in the Sustern Spital, who with their chaplain took up just over a half of his income. The remainder went on his office, on numerous sundry expenses, in small sums to the sub-almoner and the boy bishop, in the expenses of the Maundy Thursday feast, in distributions on obit days to monks and to the poor, and, in alms, about 17s. or a little more. In the fifteenth century his income fell slightly; but his loss was more than compensated by a reduction in the number of sisters at the hospital, which stood at 22 in 1311–12, fell sharply after the Black Death, and became fixed at 16 from *c.* 1405 (*Compotus Rolls*, ed. Kitchin, pp. 74–8, 138–41, 389–467). Charity, like many other commodities, became formalized in fifteenth-century England.

Note on the Watermarks in the MS.

The evidence of the watermarks in the MS. divides the quires into three sets, as follows.

1. Quire 1. In this quire the watermarks occur irregularly—a fragment, probably the handle of a pair of keys (similar to C. M. Briquet, *Les Filigranes*, Paris, 1907, i, no. 3835,&c.) in f. 3, and an indecipherable design three times elsewhere, spanning six of the leaves. Clearly the quire is composed of heterogeneous material; and the notes on ff. 1, 3, and 23 (see p. xl) suggest that it was made up out of earlier notes or note-books.

2. Quires 2–4. In quires 2–3 one watermark, possibly representing an eagle, occurs regularly, four times in quire 2, five times in quire 3, spanning half the leaves in each quire. It is not certain on other grounds that quire 4 consists of more than ff. 62–75; but in these fourteen leaves the same watermark occurs four times, spanning eight leaves. I therefore conclude that quire 4 (like quire 2) originally consisted of sixteen leaves—i.e. that f. 76 is a part of it, and that a leaf is missing between ff. 61 and 62. It is probable but not certain that this leaf was cancelled by Morton himself.

3. Quire 5. In this quire a different mark, an ox's head (very similar to Briquet, op. cit., iv, no. 15068, recorded in 1462), occurs five times, spanning ten out of the twenty leaves.

Presumably, then, Morton started his note-book by using a part or the whole of quire 1; when this part was complete he added to it quires 2–4; and finally, towards the end of his career, quire 5 also. But this suggestion cannot, of course, be wholly proved: it is possible that all the quires were collected at one time.

NOTE ON THE TEXT

WE have attempted to reproduce what Morton wrote as exactly as is consistent with a reasonably lucid and presentable text: to establish this a certain amount of compromise is essential, and four particular difficulties have had to be overcome.

1. *Cancellations.* A great number of words and entries in the book are cancelled; sometimes these are mere corrections; sometimes entries were cancelled when an account was closed or transferred to another part of the book (*quia melius alibi*, &c.), or to his account roll (*scribitur in compoto*, &c.), or because the account was wound up (*neuter debet alteri nisi caritatem* or something of the kind). He cancelled either by crossing out or erasing or by dots—and sometimes a long entry is cancelled by a single dot in the margin. To show every one of these cancellations would disfigure the text excessively; nor is it really possible, since some of his dots are stray blots of ink, and since, in addition, he was not himself consistent about it—ideally, no doubt, the whole book should ultimately have been cancelled. Odd letters or words which were clearly a slip of the pen and were instantly corrected have generally not been recorded in this edition; passages crossed out or erased and passages inserted into the text have been shown by the symbols given below; except for a few cases where it seemed essential to show it, cancellation by dots has not been noticed.

2. *Latin Grammar.* Morton's grammar was far from impeccable, and his book was a private record, certainly not intended for the eye of an expert latinist. His favourite error was to confuse the dative and ablative of the third declension, which he renders by *-i* and *-e* almost indiscriminately (this is an extreme case of a common medieval practice); but eccentric spellings and minor errors (like *in uno libra* on p. 59) abound. These have been faithfully reproduced, but they are so frequent that it seemed undesirable to disfigure the text with [*sic*] on every occasion: most of Morton's errors have therefore been silently incorporated.

3. *Extensions.* The manuscript is heavily abbreviated, and abbreviations have been extended throughout unless there is serious doubt what Morton intended. Doubtful extensions are shown in italics: Latin words have been given their correct terminations (where possible)— and only in the rare cases where Morton is consistent in his solecisms has an ungrammatical form been devised. A ruthless consistency would have given a false impression of Morton's book and of Morton's mind; and in minor matters we have not attempted it.[1] Personal names are also frequently abbreviated—Morton's, for instance, sometimes appears as 'W.M.'. Where there is no reasonable doubt of the full name, it has

---

[1] Where a common abbreviation can be extended in two different ways, we have sometimes had to make an arbitrary decision—e.g. *eq*; has normally been extended *equet* and *ponder'* *ponderans*, although there is warrant for *eque* and *ponderis*. Cf. below, p. 8, n. 8.

been extended; otherwise we print the initial alone or extend in italics. The various forms for the personal names are gathered together in the index, where place-name forms are also collected and identified.

4. *Marginalia*. These are of two kinds: summary headings to groups of entries (e.g. *Sutton recepta, forinseca expensa*), and occasional notes or additions to the text. The former have been printed as headings to the entries to which they refer, so that they clarify the text in the way in which Morton intended (see also above, p. xlii); the latter have been noted as marginal insertions. Morton frequently wrote the word *N' ,No',* or *Nota* in the margin, so frequently that its insertion in the text would only add to the confusion: it has generally been omitted.

The following symbols have been used throughout:

(   ) enclose an addition or interlineation in the text (made by Morton himself);

(d   ) an entry deleted or cancelled by Morton (see above);

[   ] an omission in the text, a passage which is either indecipherable or nearly so, or an editorial addition.

The following abbreviations have been used:

Cal. Rot. Pat.   Calendar of Patent Rolls
Gunton   S. Gunton, *The History of the Church of Peterborough* (London, 1686)
L.R.S.   Lincolnshire Record Society
N.R.S.   Northamptonshire Record Society.

The dates of most of the transactions are given in the notes. Dates between 1 January and 25 March are usually given in both styles; but where a single year occurs, it is that of the New Style.

THE BOOK OF WILLIAM MORTON

ALMONER OF PETERBOROUGH MONASTERY [1448–1467]

[*From the original manuscript in the British Museum, Cotton Vesp. A XXIV*]

[*f. 1r.*][1] Summa totalis taxacionis bonorum abbatis et conventus de Burgo Sancti Petri, tam temporalium quam spiritualium, existencium sub colectione abbatis Oseneie

		Inde decima[2]		
Totalis porcio abbatis taxatur a . . .	ij^clxxiiij*li*. xiiij*s*.	vj*d. ob.q.* xxvij*li*.	—*s*.[3]	v*d. ob.*
Item manerium de Belasyse taxatur a . .	— c*s*.	viij*d*.	x*s*.	i*d*.
Item ecclesia de Wermyngton cum pencione taxatur a	xxxviij*li*. —	—	lxxvj*s*.	—
Item maneria de Alwalton et Fletton' taxantur .	xxvj*li*. xiij*s*.	—	liij*s*.	iiij*d*.
Item totalis porcio sacristie taxatur a . .	lxiiij*li*. iij*s*.	—	vj*li*. viij*s*.	iiij*d*.
Item totalis porcio elemosinarie taxatur [4 . .	]	[		]
Item totalis porcio camerarie taxatur a . .	vj*li*. xiij*s*. iiij*d*.	—	xiij*s*.	iiij*d*.
Item totalis porcio thesaurarie conventus taxatur a	— xxx*s*.	—	— iii*s*.	—
Item totalis porcio pitanciarie taxatur a . .	— xxvj*s*. viij*d*.	—	ij*s*.	vij*d*.
Item totalis porcio infirmarie taxatur a . .	— vj*s*.	—	—	vij*d. q.*
Manerium de Gosberkyrk' taxatur [a] . . .	xlij*li*. xij*s*. iij*d*.	iiij*li*.	vj*s*.	ij*d. ob.q.*
Summa[5] totalis taxacionis :	iiij^c lxxviij*li*. viij*s*.	viij*d. ob.q.*		
Inde decima . .			xlvij*li*. xvij*s*.	xj*d. q.*

[*f. 1v.*] ESTWOODE. In (solutis pro)[6] una roda meremii (empta) ibidem, xxxiij*s*. iiij*d*. In eadem succidenda, xx*d*. Et in solutis ij hominibus ibidem laborantibus circa meremium dressyng' et cariandum, iij*s*. iiij*d*. Et in xxviij carectatis ejusdem meremii cariandis ad Burgum, carectata ad vij*d*., xvj*s*. iiij*d*.; et in datis carectariis et aliis ad potum per vices, xij*d*. Summa, 55*s*. 8*d*., tamen summa predicta est minor per xvj*s*. receptos

---

[1] Folio 1, which is of parchment, is only about half the size of the majority of folios and has been bound in sideways, so that on both recto and verso the last line of writing is nearest the edge by which the folio is found in. For this assessment, see above, p. xxi, n. 2.

[2] In the manuscript the words 'inde decima' occur before each entry in this column and the text runs straight on. The columnar arrangement is adopted here for the sake of clarity.

[3] The figure ix has been omitted by accident in the MS.

[4] There is an erasure; the words erased seem to be 'a lx*li*. xiiij*d*.' and 'vj*li*. j*d. ob.*'. See pages 10–11, note 7, for details.

[5] This total excludes the £42. 12*s*. 3*d*. of the immediately preceding entry but includes the £60. 1*s*. 2*d*. of the almonry. The actual totals on the same basis are £478. 8*s*. 4¾*d*. and £47. 16*s*. 11¼*d*. compared with the manuscript figures £478. 8*s*. 8¾*d*. and £47. 17*s*. 11¼*d*.

[6] The numbers and words in round brackets ( ) are interlineations written above the lines of the text.

pro xij carectatis de thect' vel fowel venditis. (Vera summa est xxxix*s*. viij*d*.)

CASTUR WODE. In solutis pro lx peciis quercinis, (x*s*.), longitudo earum, xxiiij (pedes), xx (pedes), xvj pedes; grossitudo sive sirculus earum in medio, Anglice ye cowmepasse of theyme in ye myddys (decorticatis), xxviij polices sive inchys, 24 (polices), 20 (polices), 18 (polices), 16 (polices), 15 (polices) inchys. Item in vj carectatis, vel in cariagio ad Burgum, v*s*. In scapulacione earum, iij*s*., et memorandum quod scapulaciones venduntur pro iij*s*. Item memorandum quod Johannes N. carpentarius scapulavit eas in v diebus ferialibus ante et post festum Sancti Gregorii Pape.[1]

[*f. 2r*.] Meremium expensum et appreciatum per Walterum Dowcheman et ij filios Johannem et Walterum ad messuagium quondam Petri Stonley in Westgaate. Memorandum quod isti supradicti erant tres carpentarii, qui fecerunt molendinum ventriticum extra villam versus Thorppe.[2] 28 sper*ts*[3] [   ] a pec'; 7 sper*ts* in coquina, 4*d*. a pec'; 2 gutt*ur*pec*s*, 10*d*. ambo; 4 post*s* pro hostiis, 4*d*.; 2 wyf*ur*pec*s*, 10*d*.; 14 wynbem*s*, 12*d*.; 3 walplat*s*, 18*d*.; 3 beem*s*, 2*s*. 6*d*.; j mapylpec', 4*d*.; 3 wyf*ur*bem*s*, 6*d*.; j beeme und*ur* splynt' sum'. 12*d*.; j p*ur*lyn in coquina de wyche 10*d*.; j slep*er* super le Porche; 6 slep*er*sse, 62 taylfeete etiam f*ur*yng' tymb*ur*, 3*s*.; gutt*ur* bord*s* simul cum evysse borde, 5 tabule, 15*d*. Item meremium in aula apreciatum fuit per carpentarios ad 6*s*. 8*d*.; item mille sclatte, 10*s*.; item 12 c lathe et 7 c lathepynn*s*, 12*s*. 4*d*.; item 4 fod*ur* calcis cum cariagio, 8*s*. 8*d*.; item 4 carectate [4   ] 10*d*.; item pro carpentria aule et camere, iij*s*., preter le coquin et gu[ttir].

Item pro 5 rodis sclattyng, 25*s*.; et bat*ur*yng' et [5   ] de xx*c* sclatte, 4*s*.; item pro 8 stoon' plumbi (precium fact*ur*'), 4*s*. 8*d*.; item 5 carectatis [5   ], 15*d*.; item 8 carectatis terre rubie, 2*s*.; item 5 (mille) lathenayle, 5*s*. 10*d*.; cc grosse spyk', 10*d*.; cc mydylspyk', 6*d*.; ccc spl[   ], 9*d*.; item pro bemfyllyng duobus lathamis et 2 servitoribus et [5   ] unius muri in aula, unius gabuli in camera per 5 dies, 7*s*. 6*d*.; item in 24 crest*s* emptis, 4*s*.; item pro le dawbyng' (unius [   ]) et stramine ad illud ibidem, x*d*.

Memorandum quod media decima solvenda domino regi pro ecclesia Burgi est xxiiij*li*. ix*s*. ij*d*.[6]

[CERA.] (*d7* . . .; item 32 *lb*. de Croyland; de herciis et de re[ddicione] xiij *lb*. *dim*. Summa totalis 13*xx* 8 *lb*. *dim*. Expenduntur hoc anno x*xxvj lb*. et remanent lxij *lb*., unde in torche3 32 *lb*. et in pura cera 30 *lb*. et *dim*.)

---

[1] *10–14 Mar.*
[2] Woodhithemilne. These last two sentences are written in 17 short lines from the middle of the top of the page towards the centre, in a blank space marked off from the rest of the text by a line.
[3] Where the compiler of this valuation did not know the Latin word describing an article, he wrote it down in English.
[4] Indecipherable; the first letters may be 3at.
[5] Indecipherable.
[6] At the foot of this page in a modern hand: 'Compotus ecclesiæ Sancti Petri de Burgo.'
[7] Written sideways in top right corner.

(ᵈ OLEUM. Remanent lagena dimidia; de empcione iiij lagene dimidia, ut infra, 4 lagene dimidia. Summa 6 lagene. De quibus expenduntur hoc anno v lagene, et remanet j lagena.)

CERA.¹ Remanent de anno preterito lxxj [*lb.*], unde in torchysse, xxxix *lb.*, et in pura cera, 32 *lb.* De empcione cxliiij *lb.*; item 32 *lb.*, de Croyland; item xiij *lb.* dimidia, de herciis et de reddicione. Summa ccxlviij (*dim.*) *lb.* Expenduntur hoc anno in pura cera et in torche₃, xˣˣ *lb.* sive ccxx [?] *lb.* Et remanent lviij *dim. lb.* [²].

[*f. 2v.*] (ᵈ iiij³ sowlebac*s*, iij*s*. iiij*d*.; xiiij stothys, xiiij*d*.; j beeme cum j teybalk, x*d*.; ij ayhepec*s*, iij*d*.; ij welowpec*s*, ij*d*.; splent*s* emptis de Roberto Morton, xiij*d*.; in rewardis datis, xx*d*. Summa:—viij*s*. vj*d*.)

(ᵈ In solutis carpentario pro sullevacione et carpentria unius q*u*ernehowse ejusdem ad messuagium quondam *Johannis* Wart*re* [⁴]; item pro reparacione facta per W*illelmum* Mason in loco [⁴].)

*Anno domini 1449, anno regni regis Henrici sexti xxvij et anno domini Ricardi Ayheston abbatis xj.*⁵

Willelmus Payne debet (ᵈ iiij*li*.; (xxxvj*s*. viij*d*.); pro brasio xiij*s*. iiij*d*.), xviij*d*. Ricardus Lucasse debet (ᵈ xv*s*. viij*d*. ad Circumcisionem domini) xxx*s*. Willelmus Sand*ur* debet (ᵈ viij*s*. vj*d*.). Johannes Eyyr', collector de Sutton (ᵈ xxxix*s*.). T*homas* Balle de Newerk (ᵈ xv*s*.) iiij*s*. x*d*. cum aliis debitis. Willelmus Ravon debet, omnibus computatis, (ᵈ ij*s*. viij*d*.). Willelmus Neffe debet (ᵈ xij*s*.); item pro breve domini regis.

Memorandum quod ij f*r*ayl' de fygg*s* ponderantes viij*ˣˣ* libras et j f*r*ayle *r*esyngg*s* lij *lb.* et deliberantur refectorie anno Ricardi [abbatis] xij,⁶ precium xiij*s*.

It is to haffe in mynde that a pece of tymb*ur* in cowmepasse xxi(ᵈiij) inchysse wyl beer' v inchysse squar' ev*er*y wey; item vj in cowmepasse inchys wil be squar' v inchis; item vij inchi[s] a bowte vj inchis squar'; item viij inchis in compas vij inchis squar'; item ix inchis in compas wil be viij inchys squar'.

[*f. 3r.*] HEC SUNT DEBITA QUE DEBENTUR FRATRI JOHANNI WYNWYK'

(Debitores)			[*li.*]	[*s.*]	[*d.*]
Ricardus Grymbold de Weston	.	.		xij*s*.	iiij*d*.
Johanna Port*ere*, relicta Ricardi Port*ere*	.			iij*s*.	—
Ricardus Confort de Wycle	.	.	xiiij*li*.		
Willelmus Mason de Dosthorp	.	.		viij*s*.	vj*d*.
Johannes Brigman de Eye	.	.	.		xvj*s*.	
Ricardus Gyldale pro officio receptoris	.	iiij*li*.		ij*s*.	viij*d*.
Officium pitanciarie, (ᵈ iiij*li*. xix*s*.)	.	.	iiij*li*.	vj*s*.	vij*d*. ob.
Johannes Est de Wynwyk' senior,	.	.		xxxij*s*.	iiij*d*.

---

¹ Written sideways on left margin of leaf.   ² Indecipherable.
³ First line worn and illegible.
⁴ These words cannot be read owing to the binding.
⁵ As to the precise period occupied by a year of Abbot Richard of Ashton see below, f. 35*r*, p. 63, and f. 93*v*, p. 168; and above, p. xl, n. 3.
⁶ *1449-50.*

	[*li.*]	[*s.*]	[*d.*]
Walterus Est de eadem, ...		x*s*.	—
Johannes Burbroke, ...		xiiij*s*.	viij*d*.
Willelmus Wygtoft de Ou*er*ton, . . .		xviij*s*.	—
unde rec*epit* iij*s*. iiij*d*.			
Alicia Thurleby, Edmundus Rypse et ceteri quorum nomina scripta sunt in quodam papiro debitorum predicti fratris Johannis Wynwyk',	x*li*.	v*s*.	j*d*.
Officium receptoris			
Officium receptoris, pro viij quarteriis brasii Johannis Dyllynge non allocatis . . .		xl*s*.	—
Et pro x quarteriis brasii Johannis Waryn, .		liij*s*.	iiij*d*.
Et pro pipa vini rubei, ...		liij*s*.	iiij*d*.
Et pro xxj coleriis equinis, ...		xvij*s*.	vj*d*.
Et solvit Johanni Hood pro cathenis et aliis necessariis pro gaola et alibi, . . .		vj*s*.	viij*d*.
Et ob periur*ium* Hen*rici* ball*ivi* de Ondell', .	iiij*li*.	—	—
Et de oneratis in compoto receptorum de anno xviij Johannis[1] Abbatis pro wych', . .	iiij*li*.	—	—
Et de brasio empto de Johanne Incle, . .		xij*s*.	—
Et pro xj quarteriis ordei emptis de Johanne Deynes de Thorp, ...		xxiij*s*.	x*d*.
Et pro brasio inde faciendo, . . .		v*s*.	vj*d*.
Et pro brasio empto de Johanne Flo*ur*, .		xxxiij*s*.	ix*d*.
Thomas[2] Bayly de Sutton, ...		vj*s*.	viij*d*.
Willelmus Port*er*e de Burgo, . . .		vj*s*.	v[iij*d*.]
Johannes Est de Burgo, ...		c*s*.	viij*d*.
Willelmus Vyncent, ...		vj*s*.	viij*d*.
Johannes Smyth de Sutton, . . .		v*s*.	[3]
(recepit ij*s*.)			
Walterus Plomere de Stang[round], . .			xij*d*.
Johannes Leche de Stanford' pro obligacione,	vj*li*.	—	—
Nicholaus Conway miles, ...		lx*s*.	—
Item idem Nicholaus miles, . . .		xlvj*s*.	

[*f. 3v.*] Compotus Johannis Leche goldsmyth de Stan*ford* prepositi ecclesie be[ati Thome] ad pontem Stan*ford* anno sextò Regis Henrici sextı post conquestum.[4]

Recepta. De Thoma Basset, Johanne Whytside, Johanne Leche, Roberto Smyth et aliis parochianis dicte ecclesie (^d ad fabricam ejusdem ecclesie) ut patet in quodam rotulo (scripto) de denariis concessis per dictos parochianos ad fabricam ecclesie predicte in denariis receptis, xlvij*s*. v*d*. Et remanent denarii levandi, ut patet per dictum rotulum, ix*s*. x*d*. *ob*. Summa, xlvij*s*. v*d*.

---

[1] Abbot John Deeping, 1409–38.
[2] This is the first of a second column of entries.
[3] Torn.   [4] *1427–8.*

Pravo per chorum qui versum legit istum⎞ versum Deo istum reci-
pravo per Christum qui versum legerit istum⎠ tanti choro capistrum

EXPENSE. In emendandis campanis, vj*s.*; et solutis pro meremio et
ferro, xiiij*d.*; et cera empta pro ij torchis faciendis, xv*s.* iiij*d.*; et pro
cathenis, vij*d.*; et solutis Thome Harpmaker' pro emendacione de le
schafte, (xl*d.*); et solutis pro ij torchis faciendis, xxij*d.*; et solutis pro
glutino, xj*d.*; et solutis pro plumbo rubeo, (ij*d.*); et in expensis pro
port[eragio] de le schafte, viij*d.*; et solutis pro j belropp, viij*d.*; et
solutis pro nerfis ad le schafte, j*d.*; et pro cordula empta, ij*d.*; et solutis
pro le plo*m*bh*u*r, iij*s.* iiij*d.*; et in panno empto pro le schafte, xj*d.*; et
pro rebus scribendis, ij*d.*; et in datis histrionibus, vj*d.*; et solutis pro
locione manutergiorum, iiij*d.*; et pro emendacione librorum x*d.*; et in
filo empto pro canapeo, j*d.*; et pro locione naparie et manutergiorum,
v*d.*; et in corio empto ad funes campanarum, ij*d.*; et in victualibus
emptis pro Ricardo Keruer' et fratre Rowsby, v*d.*; et in (datis) cuidam
carpentario Keruere pro le rodelofte videndo, vj*d.*; et solutis bigario
Johannis Whytside, ix*d.*; et solutis Thome Glasyer' pro emendandis
fenestris ecclesie, v*s.*; et solutis Johanni Ropere pro j corda campane,
xj*d.*; et eidem pro alia corda, x*d.*; et in filo empto pro vestimentis, j*d.*;
et solutis Agneti 3onge et aliis, x*d.*; et solutis Thome Basse pro j
baudryk', vj*d.*; et solutis Ricardo Keruere, xxx*s.*; et solutis pro uno
arculo ad campanam, iiij*d.*; et in cera empta ad commune lumen, iiij*s.*
Summa

[*f. 4r.*] *Anno domini 1448, anno Henrici regis xxvij et anno domini Ricardi*
[*abbatis*] *xj incipiente.*

CERA.

			[*li.*]	[*s.*]	[*d.*]
iiij*d.*	j *lb.* cere	Centena		xxxvij*s.*	iiij*d.*
iiij*d. obolum*	j *lb.* cere	Centena		xlij*s.*	—
v*d.*	j *lb.* cere	Centena		xlvj*s.*	viij*d.*
v*d. obolum*	j *lb.* cere	Centena		lj*s.*	iiij*d.*
vj*d.*	j *lb.* cere	Centena		lvj*s.*	—
vj*d. obolum*	j *lb.* cere	Centena		lx*s.*	viij*d.*
vij*d.*	j *lb.* cere	Centena		lxv*s.*	iiij*d.*
vij*d. obolum*	j *lb.* cere	Centena		lxx*s.*	—
viij*d.*	j *lb.* cere	Centena		lxxiiij*s.*	viij*d.*
viij*d. obolum*	j *lb.* cere	Centena		lxxix*s.*	iiij*d.*
ix*d.*	j *lb.* cere	Centena	iiij*li.*	iiij*s.*	—

Cera rubea, j *lb.*, vj*d.*; cera viridis, vj*d.*

SPECIES.		[*li.*]	[*s.*]	[*d.*]
Piper,	j *lb.*			x*d.*
Zinsiber,	j *lb.*			xv*d.*
Crocus,	j *lb.*		viij*s.*	—
Clowes,	j *lb.*		iij*s.*	—

	[*li.*]	[*s.*]	[*d.*]
Macs,	j *lb.*	iijs.	—
Notmug',	j *lb.*		xxd.
Ryce,	j *lb.*		iijd.
Reysyngs of			
Corinth	j *lb.*		iijd.
Annes,	j *lb.*		ijd. ob.
Lycorice,	j *lb.*		ijd.
Almawnds,	j *lb.*		ijd.
Greyns,	j *lb.*	iijs.	—
Sugur,	j *lb.*		xviijd.
Sawndurs,	j *lb.*		xviijd.
Galyngale,¹	j *lb.*		xvd.
Grenezynsiber,	j *lb.*		xxd.
Cinamonium,	j *lb.*		xxd.
Quaterna papiri,			iijd.
Coton,	j *lb.*		vijd.
Barelle sope,		xixs.	—
Orgeyse, dim. cent.	iiij*li.*		—
Orgeyse, xxiiij, }			
Lyng', iiij salsati, }		xxs.	—
Lyng' (salsati), xxvj,		xs.	—
et ij in avawntagio.			
In solutis pro ij matts,			vja.
In uno cornu pro venatore,			xxd.
In una sorte, scilicet:—			
ij frayl' fygg' et			
una frayle reysynggs,		xiiijs.	

[At the foot of this folio upside down]

. . .] W. Comesse *dim. lb.* et j unciam de kandila et iiij *lb.* et iij quarteria cere.

[*f. 4v.*] *Anno Ricardi abbatis xij incipiente ad festum Michaelis.*²

ROBERTUS ORWYN. Dominus Willelmus Morton elemosinarius et Robertus Orwyn computaverunt, et, omnibus computatis cum uno haukyd ster' et una vacca venditis Henrico Wycle bocher', predictus Willelmus elemosinarius debet supradicto Roberto ix*li.* xiijs. jd.

Item postea predictus elemosinarius vendidit Johanni Beylde bocher' unam vaccam rubei coloris et Roberti Orwyn pro vjs. viijd. Item (elemosinarius) vendidit j vaccam nigri coloris (Roberti Orwyn) Willelmo Gattele et Willelmo Ryder' bochersse pro vjs. viijd. (ᵈ Roberti Orwyn). Item predictus elemosinarius debet dicto Roberto Orwyn pro ij cadys de rubeis sperlyng' iijs. iiijd. et debet pro una sorte de ficubus et racemis, xiijs. pro anno xij Ricardi abbatis. Item Robertus emit j quarterium ciliginis, ijs. vd. Omnibus computatis modo (elemosinarius)

---

¹ A second column begins here in the MS.　　　² *1449–50.*

debet xj*li*. iiij*d*.; tamen Robertus supradictus debet pro le wynt*ring*'
de vij bestiis pro ij annis et unum bovem debilem (vide postea)
wint*u*ryng', (x*s*.). Item frater Willelmus Morton debet (Roberto
Orwyn) pro x petris albe lane.

Anno Ricardi (*abbatis*) *xiij*.[1]

Idem Robertus Orwyn recepit ij quarteria ciliginis, precii vj*s*. Tamen
notandum quod precium j quarterii ciliginis in foro, illo tempore, erat
iij*s*. vj*d*. Idem Robertus recepit iiij eskeppas pisarum, xij*d*. (in foro,
bussellus iij*d*. obolum). Idem Robertus recepit j quarterium ciliginis,
precium de eodem et eodem tempore in foro, iiij*s*. viij*d*. (*d* Idem
elemosinarius debet Roberto predicto pro ficubus et reysyng*s*, xij*s*. vj*d*.;
solvit Geordio mercatori xiij*s*.) Item pro ij cadys de sp*er*lyng', iij*s*.
Idem Robertus debet pro ij carectatis straminis ordei et pro feno,
iij*s*. iiij*d*. Idem Robertus debet pro crofto, vj*s*. viij*d*. Idem Robertus
debet pro wynt*ring*' de bestiis, ut supra, x*s*.

Anno Ricardi abbatis xiij in crastino Sancti Dunstani.[2]

Frater Willelmus Morton debet Roberto Orwyn x*li*. ix*s*. iiij*d*. et
Georgio mercatori de Stan*ford* pro ficubus et racemis, xij*s*.

Anno xiiij,[3]

Idem Robertus Orwyn debet fratri Willelmo Morton pro le wynt*u*ryng'
de x bestiis, scilicet:—vaccis et vitulis triennalibus per xiiij ebdomadas,
et pro factura unius rakke, (x*d*.), pro eis et meremio, xx*d*. (*d* Idem
debet pro lx salicibus, videlicet settyngs, 12*d*.) (ex dono). Idem Robertus
debet dicto elemosinario pro herbagio cimiterii Sancti Johannis Baptiste
per iiij annos, xxvj*s*. viij*d*.

Anno xvij,[4]

Item dictus Robertus accomodavit dicto elemosinario vj*li*. iij*d*. Lon-
doniis pro materia Johannis Hopkyn; et notandum quod dominus
Johannes Ham*er*ton, rector de Paston,[5] solvit dictas vj*li*. iij*d*. Roberto
Orwyn iterum. Item debet dictus Robertus pro ij salsatis pissibus, 18*d*.
Robertus Orwyn debet pro carectata feni, ij*s*. vj*d*.

[*f. jr*.] *Anno domini 1448, Henrici Sexti xxvij et anno Ricardi abbatis
xj incipiente*.

T*homas* Balle debet fratri Willelmo Morton, xv*s*.; item [pro] le
wynt*u*ryng unius vacce; item [pro] reparacione unius celle, (scilicet
xxxij*d*.). Inde solvit per manus prioris in aula minucionis, ij*s*. v*d*.;
item per Henricum Holond, alia vice, in die Sancti Theodori,[6] xviij*d*.;
item per priorem et uxorem predicti Tome, xij*d*.; item eodem die per
ipsam, vj*s*. viij*d*.; item de eadem uxore ij virgas de blanket, (precii)
xiiij*d*.; item per

---

[1] *1450–1*. [2] *20 May 1451*. [3] *1451–2*. [4] *1454–5*.
[5] Rector *c*. 1448–60. [6] *9 Nov. 1448*.

Anno 1449.

Ricardus Lombe de Wysbeche emit lvij quarteria (iiij eskeppas) brasii de domino Willelmo Morton elemosinario, precium j quarterii, iij*s*., viij*li*. xij*s*. vj*d*. Inde solvit xx*s*. [et habet] dies de residuo Pascha et Pentecosten; idem per T*homam* Hawme post festum Sancti Martini anno Ricardi abbatis xiij[1] solvit elemosinario xl*s*.; item in die Sancte Lucie virginis[2] per T*homam* Havme, xx*s*.; item per Ricardum Paalle, ut in x*c* bryc vel rubeis tyl', vij*s*.; item v*s*.; item ad Wysbeche, xiiij*s*. viij*d*.; item unam equam cum pullo suggente, precium xx*s*.; item x*s*. propter sewtte in partem solucionis, xx*s*.

Require plus in folio 29 sequente ad tale ⊕. ([d] Ricardus Derneforde debet ix*s*. iiij*d*., propria computo. Inde solvit per laborem in fossatis et aliis laboribus per xviij dies dimidium ut in avena[3].)

Nota. Memorandum quod frater Willelmus Morton elemosinarius computavit cum Ricardo Derneford in die Sancti Felicis[4]; omnibus computatis Ricardus Derne*forde* debet viij*s*. (8*d*.) supradicto elemosinario, et inde solvit ut in precio, scilicet unius cade vel meyse rubie alle*cie* (scilicet ccccc), iiij*s*. viij*d*. Item memorandum quod convenit inter predictum elemosinarium et Ricardum supradictum quod Ricardus solvet v*s*. ad festum Sancti Johannis Baptiste proximum futurum,[5] testante Willelmo Goldesmythe.

Nota. T*homas* Havme. Elemosinarius, frater Willelmus Morton, computavit cum T*oma* Havme ad festum Michaelis anno Ricardi abbatis xiij incipiente,[6] omnibus computatis inter illos, T*omas* Havme debet v*s*.; item pro j quarterio pisarum, xx*d*.

Memorandum[7] quod Frater Willelmus Morton elemosinarius debet Johanni Styv*ur*, v*s*. Inde solvit iij*s*. et ij*s*.

Idem frater debet domino Willelmo Kysby xxiij libras plumbi. Solvit et eque.

[*f. 5v.*] *Anno domini 1448.*

Debitum. Ricardus Lucas debet fratri Willelmo Morton viij*d*. de veteri debito (solvit);[8] item xv*s*., per limitacionem domini Tome Maxey,[9] (solvit,) scilicet pro ultimo quarterio anni precedentis.

Anno domini 1449.

Item xv*s*. pro primo quarterio anni; item xv*s*. pro secundo quarterio. Item debet pro ij quarteriis pisarum, iiij*s*. [in] festo Sancti Johannis

---

[1] *11 Nov. 1450.*   [2] *13 Dec. 1450.*
[3] These three words are written in the margin.
[4] *8 Mar.*   [5] *24 June.*   [6] *29 Sept. 1450.*
[7] At the foot of this folio, written upside down.
[8] The word 'solt', which has been inserted above the line in numerous paragraphs of this MS., has been extended and printed 'solvit'. It might be 'solvitur'.
[9] See L.R.S. xxi. 283–4, 290, 293, as to his former office of bursar. It was alleged in 1447 that contrary to religious discipline he walked up and down among the monks at study in cloister, chattering with them and hindering their study, etc.

Baptiste;¹ item pro ij quarteriis ordei, vjs. festo Johannis Baptiste, vel tantum ordeum in autumpno. Item debet pro tercio et quarto quarterio xxxs.

SCAPULACIO MEREMII. Elemosinarius, frater Willelmus Morton, convenit cum ij carpentariis quod ipsi scapularent meremium, scilicet viijˣˣ v pecias quercinas et fraccinas, iij pecias semper pro vd., xxijs. xjd.; item in rewardis et potu, xxd. Item nota quod meremium supradictum scapulatum erat in xxviij diebus ferialibus post Purificacionem Beate Marie virginis.²

(ᵈ SOLUCIO RICARDI LUCAS.
Supradictus³ Ricardus et cariagium ejus. In primis (ᵈ xj) xix carectate terre rubee, v carectate arundinis de Bole ȝaate⁴ usque Sowter row, viij carectate de fimo; item ix columbelle, precium iijd.; item unum casium, precium ijd., ponderans iiijli. et quarterium; item una carectata potyngthac de Burowbryg' ad Westegat; item ij carectate pisarum; item j carectata straminis frumenti de Gonthorppe usque Burgum; item xiij carectate terre rubie ad ustrinam; item iij carectate petre velute ibidem; item iiij carectate terre rubie ad aliam domum ibidem.)⁵

(ᵈAnno domini 1449.)
Solucio Ricardi Lucas pro primo quarterio anni. In primis (cariagium) iiij carectarum spinarum; item ij carectate straminis de Gonthorp ad Burgum etc. alibi.

*Xij anno domini Ricardi abbatis.*⁶
In solutis Johanni Ravon et Willelmo Phylyppe carpentariis de Melton Mowbr' pro scapulacione de iiijˣˣ quercinis peciis meremii (vs.);⁷ longitudo earum xxiiij (pedes), xx (pedes), xvj (pedes); grossitudo sive sirculus earum in medio decorticatarum xxiiij inchys, xx inchys, xvj inchys. Memorandum quod meremium supradictum erat scapulatum in quinque diebus ferialibus ante et post festum Gregorii pape.⁸

[f. 6r.] Memorandum quod [de] j eskeppa sive bussello frumenti ponderis liij librarum de molendino, furfur vel panes possunt fieri inde xxx, quelibet panis ante furnicionem ponderans ij libras dimidiam et postquam furnitur ij libras [et] j quarterium. Item j bussellus sive eskeppa frumenti ad molendinum liij libre et de molendino liij libre, furfur inde ij libre, panes possunt fieri xxix ponderantes ante et post furnicionem modo quo supra.

Item probatur alia vice ad et de molendino ij eskeppe frumenti et ciliginis dimidia eskeppa ponderis vjˣˣ et x librarum, furfur inde iiij libre, panes iijˣˣ xij, quelibet panis (ponderans) ij libras dimidiam ante furnicionem. Item probatur, ad molendinum et de molendino, j eskeppa

¹ *24 June.* ² *2 Feb.–(?) 6 Mar.*
³ The following paragraph was struck out and the word *vacat* was written in the margin.
⁴ Probably Bolithegate. ⁵ The end of the deleted paragraph.
⁶ *1449–50.* ⁷ Note in left margin: In compoto anni xj.
⁸ *10–14 Mar. 1450.*

frumenti et ciliginis dimidia eskeppa ponderans iij^{xx} xij libras, furfur inde j libra, panes xxxviij [possunt fieri] quelibet panis ponderans ij libras dimidiam ante furnicionem.

Alia vice, ad molendinum et de molendino, j eskeppa dimidia frumenti et ciliginis dimidia eskeppa ponderans simul v^{xx}ij libras, furfur inde iij libre, panes xliiij, quelibet panis ponderans iij libras ante furnicionem.

Item alia vice, ad molendinum et de molendino, j eskeppa frumenti et ciliginis dimidia eskeppa ponderans iij^{xx}xviij libras, scilicet knockyd et ample mensura. Furfur inde vel panes xxxiij, quelibet panis ponderans iij libras ante furnicionem et post furnicionem. Omnes panes scilicet xxxiij ponderantes simul iiij^{xx} xviij libras sive vel vij petras. Alia vice, ad molendinum et de molendino, j eskeppa et dimidia frumenti et ciliginis de mensura str*i*kyd. Furfur inde [possunt fieri] v libre dimidia panes xxxvij quelibet panis ponderans ij libras dimidiam ante furnicionem.

Memorandum quod furnitur[1] pro die Animarum anno Ricardi abbatis xij[2] iiij quarteria frumenti, prima furnicio viij^{xx} vj panes; secunda furnicio viij^{xx} viij; tercia viij^{xx} xij panes; quarta furnicio ix^{xx} panes; quinta furnicio viij^{xx}xij. Summa xlij^{xx}xviij panes.

Anno Ricardi abbatis xiij prima furnicio viij^{xx} xij panes; secunda viij^{xx} vij; tercia furnicio vij^{xx} x; quarta viij^{xx} xvj; quinta vij^{xx} ix; sexta vj^{xx} iiij. Summa xlvj^{xx} et xviij panes.

Item nota quod quilibet panis ponderat ante furnicionem ij libras j quarterium.

Alia vice, ad molendinum et de molendino, ij eskeppe frumenti furfur inde iiij libre, panes xlij, quelibet panis ante furnicionem ponderans iij libras.

Anno Ricardi abbatis xiiij.[3]

Pro die Animarum[4] prima furnicio vij^{xx}iiij panes; secunda ix^{xx}vij; tercia ix^{xx}ij; quarta viij^{xx}xij; quinta vj^{xx}xij; sexta vj^{xx}; et quilibet panis ante furnicionem ponderat ij libras et j quarterium. Summa xlvj^{xx}xvij panes.

[*f. 6v.*] (^d COLLECTOR DE SUTTON. Johannes Eyr de Sutton debet fratri Willelmo Morton elemosinario Burgi xxxix*s*., per limitationem domini T*ome* Maxey[5] sacriste.)

Anno domini Ricardi abbatis x et (xj incipiente[6].)

Elemosinarius Frater Willelmus Morton.[7] In solutis Johanni Pye de Gonthorp pro collectione garbarum decimalium de iiij campis ibidem,

---

[1] This is one of very few indications in the whole book of a distribution of food to the poor, which one might consider the normal dury of a monastic almoner (see above, pp. xxvi ff).　　[2] *2 Nov. 1449.*
[3] *1451-2.*　　[4] *2 Nov. 1451.*
[5] See above, p. 8, footnote.　　[6] *1447-8; 1448-9.*
[7] Upon the levying of the tenth granted by the clergy of the province of Canterbury to Henry VI in 1444 (Cathedral Library, The Book of Roger Bird, ff. 15 et seqq.), a list of

xiiij*s.*; item in solutis Johanni et Tome Beylde pro cariagio ejusdem ad grangiam[1] ibidem, xxxvj*s.* x*d.*; item in datis eis ad potum per vices, vj*d.*; item in solutis Johanni Pye et T*ome* Hawme pro trituracione et ventilacione, anglice threysyng' et wenowyng', de ix quarteriis, iiij bussellis frumenti, vj quarteriis ciliginis, iij^{xx}iiij quarteriis iij eskeppis ordei, xxxix quarteriis v eskeppis pisarum, vj quarteriis v eskeppis avenarum. Summa cvj vel vj^{xx} et vj quarteria j bussellus, quarterium trituratum et ventilatum pro ij*d. ob. qu.* Summa xxviij*s.* x*d. ob.*; item in datis ad potum per vices, vj*d.*

Memorandum[2] de vj carectatis straminis ordei expensis cum bestiis; item [de] vj carectatis ad facturam brasii; item [de] ij carectatis propter unam domum cooperiendam.

VENDICIO PALEI ET STRAMINIS SIVE STRAMENTI IBIDEM.[3]

De paleo (pisarum) (^{d}vendito) de le mow inter ostia grangii vel stramen venditur pro xx*d.* (solvit) Roberto Beylde (Wryte); item paleum, scilicet owre chaffe straminis pisarum et avenarum de secundo arconio (mow), venduntur Ricardo Eston pro iij*s.* Item paleum tercii arconii (scilicet govyl mow) cum stramine pisarum venduntur Stephano Lyst*er*, T*ome* Beylde et J*ohanni* Hopkyn pro iij*s.* iiij*d.*; item paleum (totum) de le foor' mow (arconio) frumenti et ordei venditur pro ix*d.*; item paleum totum (ordei) de le govyl mow (arconio) venditur T*ome* Hardy pro xx*d.*

VENDICIO BRASII. Ricardus Lombe de Wysbeche emit lv quarteria dimidium brasii, quarterium iij*s.*, (x bussellos pro quarterio), viij*li.* vj*s.* vj*d.*

NOTA FRUMENTUM. Frumentum expenditur in officio.

VENDICIO PISARUM. Item pise albe (ij busselli) et nigre (xxxvj quarteria) venditur pro lx*s.*; item iij quarteria dimidium pisarum venditur [pro] vj*s.* viij*d.*

the assessable estates of the abbot and obedientiaries of the monastery of Peterborough according to the valuation of 1291 was written in that register. The following paragraph relates to the assessment of the estates of the almoner (see above, pp. xxi, n. 2, xxxiii).

	£	s.	d.
The Almoner has of rent in Water Newton in the deanery of Yaxley from the abbot of Thorney, per annum		2	6
The same officer has in Gunthorpe in lands and rents	13	6	8
[Over the word Gunthorpe, there is written the word 'thesaurarius', indicating that this estate subsequently passed to the bursar of the monastery.]			
In Sutton in lands rents and other possessions	6	2	—
In the hospital of St. Leonard [in Peterborough]	6	—	—
In Clapton in lands and rents	2	16	8
In Warmington and Cotterstock	3	13	4
A portion [of the tithes] in the parish of Paston [including Gunthorpe]	13	6	8
The rectory of Maxey which is assessed at	14	13	4
Total	60	1	2
A tenth thereof	6	—	1½

---

[1] Carriage of tithes to the tithe barn.   [2] In left-hand margin.
[3] i.e. at the Gunthorpe tithe barn.

NOTA PROPTER VISUM. Take ye galle of a clene blac el (anguille) *and* hony, ye quantite of a smal notte (nucis), *and* ye thyrde p*a*rte of a sponefulle of fayr' wat*u*r, ande myng' theys togedyr, tylle they be liquitte, notte to thyk, nor to thyn, *and* putte yis in a lytil glasse, *and* wythe a dovisse fed*u*r, putte su*m* of ye lyk*u*r in ye eye (oculo) lyyng' or restyng' up on a bedde.

[*f. 7r.*] *Anno domini 1449.*

SUTTON. Thomas Pr*i*ur, firmarius de Sutton solvit iij*s*. iiij*d*. de precio dimidii apri; item vj*s*. viij*d*. per uxorem suam in Sabbato Sexagesime;[1] item ij nobilia auri per manus proprias in Sabbato secundo Quadragesime;[2] item per Johannem Eyr', collectorem de Sutton, vj*s*. viij*d*. in presencia fratris Ricardi Stanforthe[3] (scilicet in camera sua); item x*s*. ad Sutton per manus T*o*me Pr*i*uur in aula (ibidem); item alia vice Sabbato ante festum Michaelis[4] per uxorem suam, xxvj*s*. viij*d*.; item predictus firmarius solvit Johanni Rothewel iij*s*. iiij*d*. pro debito elemosinarii; item xxx*s*., Sabbato ante Nativitatem domini.[5]

Summa soluta c*s*. et sic quietus est pro anno xj Ricardi abbatis.

Annus secundus.[6]

Sutton. Tomas firmarius supradictus solvit anno xij Ricardi abbatis in feria iiij ebdomade Pasche[7] elemosinario in presencia Roberti Conqueste et Johannis Ivysse, xx*s*.; item vj*s*. viij*d*. Sabbato ante dies Rogacionum;[8] item vj*s*. viij*d*. in infirmaria et in presencia Roberti Conquest et Johannis Eyyr et in die Sanctorum Marcelli et Petri;[9] item xx*s*. in ebdomada Exaltacionis Sancte Crucis,[10] per Robertum Conquest. Item per T*homam* Havme in die Quatuor Coronatorum,[11] xx*s*. (vacat quia in solucione Roberti Conquest); item in crastino,[12] per T*homam* Havme, xx*s*.; item per Robertum Conquest in Sabbato ante Purificacionem,[13] xiij*s*. iiij*d*.; item in solutis pro vij quarteriis calcis, iiij*s*. viij*d*. et debet modo viij*s*. viij*d*., unde recepi [*sic*] vij*s*. iiij*d*. et xvj*d*.

Annus 3.[14]

Memorandum quod Robertus Conquest firmarius de Sutton solvit in primis xx*s*. per T*o*mam Havme; item recepi de predicto Roberto ut in precio de lxiij sper*r*s sive tignis, v*s*.; item ut in iiij gallinis et iiij pulcinis, xiij*d*. Item Robertus solvit (latamo) pro emendacione ostii stabuli ibidem, iiij*d*. Item Robertus Conquest solvit Johanni Rothewel, xx*d*. pro carpentria unius schep koote;[15] item ij*d*. pro traccione tignorum de aqua; item xviij*s*. iij*d*. in vigilia Pasche;[16] item in ([d] vigilia) die Sancti Laurencii,[17] vj*s*. viij*d*.; in vigilia Assumpcionis Beate Marie,[18] xiij*s*. iiij*d*.

---

[1] *16 Feb. 1449.*   [2] *8 Mar. 1449.*
[3] See L.R.S. xxi. 271, 276, 280–1, 289. In 1437 he was the chamberlain; see his criticisms of the abbot in 1437 and 1447.

[4] *27 Sept. 1449.*	[5] *20 Dec. 1449.*	[6] *1449–50.*
[7] *8 Apr. 1450.*	[8] *9 May 1450.*	[9] *2 June 1450.*
[10] *14–19 Sept. 1450.*	[11] *8 Nov. 1450.*	[12] *9 Nov. 1450.*
[13] *30 Jan. 1451.*	[14] *1450–1.*	[15] Sheep cot.
[16] *24 Apr. 1451.*	[17] *9 Aug.*	[18] *14 Aug.*

per Johannem Cooke alias bacst*er*;[1] et debet 26*s*. x*d*. Postea idem Robertus solvit in die Sancti Edmundi regis et martiris,[2] vj*s*. et x*d*.; item xx*s*. in die Sancti Vincencii martiris,[3] et sic quietus est pro anno terciodecimo.[4]

Annus 4 elemosinarii Morton.[5]

Item in die Sancti Vincencij, iij*s*. iiij*d*. Item xx*s*. per diversas parcellas reparacionis nove boverie ad Sutton in manerio. Item solvit xlvj*s*. viij*d*. in die Sancti Stephani (anno Ricardi abbatis 16[6]) pro anno xiiij[7] 3*li*. 10*s*. et debet 23*s*. 4*d*., unde solvit xx*s*.; item iiij tyld*s* et j schold*ur* de brawne, precium xx*d*.; item xx*d*. pro fratre Ricardo Stanfor ad unam fenestram capelle de Sutton dat', et equet pro hoc anno (14). Quere plus in xlvj folio sequente ad tale signum ⊕[8]

[*f. 7v.*] *Anno domini 1448 finiente; anno regni regis Henrici Sexti post conquestum xxvij et anno Ricardi abbatis xj incipiente.*

CUSTUS ELEMOSINARII IN MINUCIONIBUS TERCII PRIORIS

	[*s*.]	[*d*.]
Minucio prima tercii prioris pridie Nonas Octobris,[9] .		40*d*.
Secunda minucio Idus Novembris,[10] . . .		40*d*.
Tercia minucio xviij Kal. Januarii,[11] . . .		40*d*.
Minucio quarta vij Kal. Februarii[12] die Dominica in iiij caponibus, ij aucis etiam volatilibus (wilde fowle),	ij*s*.	—
[*In margin*] Minucio inter Nativitatem domini et Purificacionem Beate Marie.[13]		
Feria secunda, in iiij pastellis et aliis curialibus, .	ij*s*.	viij*d*.
Feria tercia, in uno porcello, ...		vj*d*.
Dominica Sexagesime,[14] Die dominica ad prandium, [in] j tyylde et dimidio apri, in uno ferculo cocto et alio assato et j*d*. ad cenam, ...		vj*d*.
Feria secunda,[15] in uno et dimidio tyyld apri; item in uno pleno ferculo ad prandium et cenam, . .		vj*d*.
Item in tribus capitibus vitulinis, . . .		iiij*d*. ob.
Ad cenam in ij gallinis et ij pulcinis, . . .		vj*d*.
Feria tercia, j et dimidio tyylde apri; item in uno pleno ferculo cocto et assato pro prandio et cena, . .		vj*d*.
Item in carne porcina salcata pro colloppys, iiij*d*. et lx ovis, iij*d*. ad fricsandum, ...		[vij*d*.]
Ad cenam in ij gallinis et ij pulcinis . . .		vj*d*.
Feria iiij, nichil.		

---

[1] The payments made add up to £3. 6*s*. 6*d*., which is expressed at this point by a series of dots, six for sixpence, etc.
[2] *20 Nov.* [3] *22 Jan. 1451/2.* [4] *1450–1.*
[5] *1451–2.* [6] *26 Dec. 1453.* [7] *1451–2.*
[8] See below, p. 62. [9] *6 Oct. 1448.* [10] *13 Nov. 1448.*
[11] *15 Dec. 1448.* [12] *26 Jan. 1448/9.*
[13] *i.e. between 25 Dec. 1448 and 2 Feb. 1448/9.*
[14] *16 Feb. 1448/9.* [15] *17 Feb. 1448/9.*

[*s.*] [*d.*]

Feria quinta, in j pestel porci, j*d. ob.*, propter priorem;
in ij caponibus et ij gallinis (ᵈ vij*d.*), . . . x*d.*
et ad cenam in carne ovina pro una sew et speciebus, iiij*d.*
item in tribus gallinis, ... vj*d.*
[*In margin*] Item quere ebdomada Sexagesime, v folio
postea.
Dominica Quinquagesime,¹ in uno pestel porci et
capite vitulino, iij*d.*; unum ferculum apri et in uno
capone, ij*d. ob.* in una assacione, Anglice a rooste,
j*d. ob.* . . . . [vij*d.*]
Ad cenam in una gallina . . . . . ij*d.*

Summa:— . . . . vj*s.* —

Minucio quinta in ebdomada prima Quadragesime,²
in solutis coco . . . . . . 40*d.*

[*In margin*] Anno domini 1449.

SEXTA MINUCIO IN EBDOMADA PASCHE.³
Feria secunda, in uno agno, viij*d.*; item in speciebus
pro salciamentis, j*d.* . . . . . [ix*d.*]
Feria tercia, in quatuor caponibus, xj*d.*; item in ovis
propter iusselle, ij*d.* et in speciebus, ij*d.* . . [xv*d.*]
Feria quarta, in greene fyhesce vel in viridibus pissi-
bus, vij*d.*; in butiro, j*d.* . . . . [viij*d.*]
Feria quinta, in uno porcello, ... vj*d.*
Minucio septima in ebdomada proxima post Roga-
ciones,⁴ . . . . iij*s.* iiij*d.*
Minucio octava ad festum apostolorum Petri et Pauli,⁵ iij*s.* iiij*d.*
Minucio ix in Dominica ante festum Sancti Oswaldi,⁶ iij*s.* —
Decima minucio ad Nativitatem Beate Marie Virginis
per quatuor dies continuando, Dominica, in iiij pul-
cinis et j porco, ... x*d.*
Die Nativitatis Marie,⁷ in iiij caponibus, . . xij*d.*
Feria tercia, in iij aucis, ... xij*d.*
Feria quarta, in uno dentrice, . . . vij*d.*

[*f. 8r.*] *Anno domini 1449. Anno regni regis Henrici xxvij et anno domini
Ricardi abbatis xj.*⁸

Memorandum quod frater Willelmus Morton elemosinarius, in festo
Invencionis Sancte Crucis,⁹ ad firmam tradidit pro tribus annis sequentibus Johanni, coco ducis Som*u*rsette, unam vaccam, piyde sive fleckyd,
etatis 4 annorum, cum uno vitulo, annuatim (sive omni anno), pro

---

¹ *23 Feb. 1448/9.* ² *2–8 Mar. 1448/9.*
³ Easter Day was on 13 Apr.: *13–19 Apr. 1449.*
⁵ *29 June 1449.* ⁶ *3 Aug. 1449.* ⁴ *25–31 May 1449.*
⁸ *1448–9.* ⁹ *3 May.* ⁷ *8 Sept. 1449.*

ij*s*. vj*d*., per equales porciones ad duo festa Sanctorum Johannis Baptiste et Michaelis archangeli proxime sequencia; et notandum quod liberabit eandem vaccam cum vitulo suo sive precium, scilicet ij*s*.; item precium vacce, si aliquid contingat ei per malam gubernacionem, vj*s*. viij*d*.

Item predictus dominus Willelmus Morton elemosinarius (eodem die quo supra) dimisit Johanni Yonghe de Burgo unam nigram vaccam (x annorum) cum vitulo pro tribus annis, annuatim pro iij*s*., reddendo sive solvendo per equales porciones ad duo festa ut supra, et liberabit vaccam et vitulum sive precium ut supra; item precium vacce viij*s*. si quid contingat ut supra.

RECEPTUM[1] GRANGIE DE GONTHORP[2] ANNO XI FINIENTE ET ANNO XII INCIPIENTE.[3]

VENDICIO STRAMINIS ET PALEI AD GONTHORP.

Memorandum quod Frater Willelmus Morton elemosinarius vendidit in die Sancti Eustachii sociorumque ejus[4] Tome Beylde et Johanni Crosse de Wytheryngton totum stramentum ordei cum paleo primi arconii[5] scilicet de le govyl mow in grangia decime ad Gonthorp pro v*s*. Item elemosinarius vendidit (*d* eodem die supradictis Thome et) Johanni Pye totum (stramentum pisarum) paleum secundi arconii, Anglice ye seconde mow, pro xij*d*.; et stramen reservatur ad officium. Item elemosinarius vendidit paleum cum stramine primi arconii pisarum, scilicet gouil mow, Johanni Bernerde pro v*s*.; item stramen pisarum secundi mow venditur pro ij*s*. et cum paleo, exceptis duobus walheschysse; item stramentum totum in medio domus scilicet inter ostia venditur cum paleo pro xxij*d*., (solvit).

Nota:—Frumentum receptum videlicet, xij quarteria de mensura strikyn. Ciligo, xij quarteria v eskeppe per mensuram strikyn. Ordeum, iij^xxvj quarteria iij eskeppe per mensuram supradictam. Avene, iiij quarteria ij eskeppe per mensuram strikyd. Pise albe, ij eskeppe. Pise nigre, xlij quarteria per mensuram supradictam. Summa vij^xxij quarteria iiij eskeppe per mensuram strikyd.

Nota:—In solutis Johanni Pye et socio suo pro trituracione ventilacione et ryyng de vj^xxv quarteriis et iiij eskeppis, videlicet xxij quarteria pro viginti, xxviij*s*. viij*d*.

[*f. 8v.*] *Anno xij Ricardi abbatis.*[6]

Johannes Pypwel debet fratri Willelmo Morton in primis (pro messuagio in quo manebat) pro ultimo quarterio tempore fratris T*o*me Maxey[7] elemosinarii, ij*s*. iij*d*.; item pro proximo anno sequente, scilicet anno Ricardi abbatis xj,[8] pro messuagio supradicto, vij*s*. Item predictus Johannes mituatus est de fratre Willelmo Morton ij*s*. propter emere frumentum. Item Johannes emit unam carectam ferream, precii xviij*s*.

---

[1] Margin.　　　　[2] Gunthorpe tithe barn.　　　　[3] *1449.*
[4] *2 Nov.*　　　　[5] Stack.　　　　[6] *1449–50.*
[7] Note the name of the preceding almoner. For his other offices see pp. 8 (n. 9), 10, and 19. William Morton also occupied several offices successively. See pp. xix and 163 ff.
[8] *1448–9.*

Item predictus Johannes debet pro veteri meremio grangii [*sic*] ibidem, vj*s*. Idem Johannes debet ij*s*. et cariagium pro redditu anni xij Ricardi abbatis.[1]

Memorandum quod idem Johannes solvit ut in cariagio de ij carectatis thac de Thorney fen, xiiij*d*.; item vj carectatis de Gonthorp ad Burgum, iij*s*. vj*d*. Idem Johannes Pipwel solvit ut in thackyng', iij*s*. vj*d*. Idem solvit, ut in dawbyng' per ij dies et dimidium, ix*d*. Item solvit vij*s*. per vices; item ut in ij porcellis, (*d* viij), ix*d*.; in ij pulcinis, ij*d*.; item in thakyng' ad hospitale, (*d*ij*s*.); item ryggyng' ibidem per (*d* j diem et dimidium) xij dies, v*s*.

Anno Ricardi abbatis xiij incipiente in die Lucie Virginis.[2]

Omnibus computatis Johannes Pypwel debet domino Willelmo Morton, viij*s*.; item pro veteri meremio. Idem solvit [pro] mille cooperture, precium vij*s*.

Memorandum quod anno Ricardi abbatis xij[3] Willelmus Castelle[4] debet domino Willelmo Morton elemosinario xij carectatas petre velute. Item recepit de fratre Johanne Wynwyc,[5] anno Ricardi abbatis ix,[6] iij*s*. iiij*d*. Idem recepit de fratre Willelmo Morton iij*s*. iiij*d*. Item uxor Willelmi Castelle debet pro uno superlectulo de nigro sago et uno pelow, ij*s*. vj*d*. Idem debet pro pastura unius vituli, xv*d*.

(*d* Memorandum quod anno Ricardi abbatis xij[7] Johannes Bernarde debet pro uno cartebody (solvit); j plowbem (solvit); et una pecia fraccina (solvit); pro *tri*bulis faciendis, (*d* ij*s*. ij*d*.,) xx*d*., (solvit.). Idem debet pro stramine pisarum et owr' chaffe, v*s*., (solvit domino abbati);[8] item pro j quarterio pisarum, xxij*d*. (solvit iiij*d*.; solvit sacriste, xx*d*.). Idem Johannes solvit ij capones, (juvenes), precium v*d*. Item idem solvit in precio de barow lymmys et ij rotis, iiij*d*. Neuter debet alteri ad festum Purificacionis anno Ricardi abbatis xiiij.[9]

Memorandum[10] quod Johannes Incle succidit salices elemosinarii. Item Johannes Browny succidit arborem quercinam. Item Johannes Hopkyn de B*ur*go succidit arborem fraccinam elemosinarii sine licencia.

[*f. 9r.*] *Anno domini Ricardi abbatis xij.*[11]

Memorandum quod T*omas* Beylde et Johannes Beylde, (omnibus materiis computatis clare), debent fratri Willelmo Morton pro frumento et ciligine, iiij*d*.; item anno sequente, Pascha,[12] pro ciligine j quarterium.

---

[1] *1449–50.*   [2] *13 Dec. 1450.*   [3] *1449–50.*

[4] L.R.S. xxi. 274, 280. As to the family of Castell see *Cal. Rot. Pat. 1467–77*, 8 (8 Feb. 1468). Isabel Castell late of Peterburgh in Northampton 'wedowe', and John Castell late of Peterburgh 'gentilman' executors of the will of William Castell late of Peterburgh 'gentilman'.

[5] L.R.S. xxi. 282, 284. At one time fraterer.   [6] *1446–7.*   [7] *1449–50.*

[8] When a payment was made afterwards, either in cash, or by a set-off for goods supplied, the relevant entry in the draft cash book was deleted, with such an explanation as has been printed within brackets above.   [9] *2 Feb. 1451/2.*

[10] The following note at the foot of this folio is written upside down.

[11] *1449–50.*

[12] *25 Apr. 1451.* This word has been inserted and may refer to the next entry.

Memorandum quod Johannes Belamy junior debet ix*s*. pro ij fratribus Ricardo et Johanne Mason de dos[?].

Memorandum quod Willelmus Plowman recepit pro labore ad Sutton per vices, vij*s*. viij*d*. Idem recepit de uno de Wetlyssey,[1] nomine elemosinarii, vj*s*. viij*d*.

Memorandum quod frater Johannes York debet fratri Willelmo Morton, iiij*s*. pro materia Willelmi Mekness de Stanford'. Tamen notandum quod idem frater Willelmus Morton stipavit predicto fratri Johanni York[2] ij*s*. iiij*d*. pro servisia; item iij*s*. pro ostencione librorum pro iij annis. Idem frater Johannes recepit pro puero suo Johanne Bolton', iij*s*. iiij*d*. vide in v folio sequente; item xij*d*. pro ostencione librorum pro officio elemosinarii.

Memorandum quod Johannes carpentarius cum barba tustata debet de redditu ad Nativitatem domini anno Ricardi abbatis xij,[3] xij*s*.; item iij*s* iiij*d*. (pro subpriore.)
  Idem solvit inde uno coopertori, ij*s*. ij*d*. Idem solvit ut in opere carpentrie per vj dies, (in Heygate), ij*s*. vj*d*. Idem solvit per fact*ur*am [*sic*] j fumerel, xx*d*. Idem solvit in opere carpentrie, ubi Willelmus Reeste maneret, per (d iiij) v dies, ij*s*. j*d*. Idem solvit per opus [*sic*] carpentrie per ij dies (d et dimidium) in schoppa copbularii, (x*d*.) Idem solvit per opus carpentrie ad hospitale per j diem, v*d*. Idem solvit in scapulacione magni meremii, iiij*d*. Idem solvit fratri Willelmo M*e*rkam[4] v*s*. iiij*d*. de debito fratris Willelmi Morton et equet.

Ad Epiphaniam domini anno suprascripto.[5]
Idem Johannes carpentarius debet iiij*s*. pro ij terminis, videlicet Annunciacionis Beate Marie et Johannis Baptiste. Predictus Johannes carpentarius solvit ut in opere carpentrie per iij dies, ca*piens* in die v*d*.

Anno Ricardi abbatis xiij incipiente.
Idem Johannes carpentarius debet elemosinario pro tribus terminis vj*s*. de redditu; inde solvit ut in opere carpentrie per vj dies dimidium ij*s*. ix*d*. Quere in secunda parte xiiij folii sequentis.

Johannes Drap*er* debet fratri Willelmo Morton, omnibus computatis, ad Natale Domini anno suprascripto,[6] iij*s*. viij*d*. Idem debet pro viij bussellis ciliginis. Item debet pro ij eskeppis pisarum, v*d*.; item uxor ejus pro ij eskeppis ordei, viij*d*.

(dMemorandum quod dominus Willelmus Morton debet T*ome* Hawme ad Natale Domini anno suprascripto, omnibus computatis, xvij*s*. vj*d*. preter robam suam, scilicet xx*d*. Inde predictus Tomas recepit vij*s*. vj*d*.; item vj*s*. in presencia J. Eyyr; item ij*s*.; item vj*d*.)

---

[1] Whittlesey, Cambs.   [2] L.R.S. xxi. 296 n.   [3] *Thursday, 25 Dec. 1449.*
[4] See L.R.S. xxi. 278, &c. (cf. p. 22, n. 11).
[5] *6 Jan. 1449/50.*   [6] *25 Dec. 1449.*

(ᵈMemorandum¹ quod anno domini Ricardi abbatis xij incipiente²
frater Willelmus Morton et Agnes Morton computaverunt. Omnibus
computatis predicta Agnes debet xx*s.* et ij juvencas. Idem [*sic*] Agnes
recepit ex mutuo xij*d.* per filium Robertum; item ij*s.* (ᵈ frumento);
item ij*s.* Idem Agnes fecit ad elemosinarium predictum lx quarteria
brasii pro xx*s.* Idem Agnes vendidit elemosinario (ix) pullos et (ij)
aucas, xij*d.* Idem Agnes laboravit per iiij dies ad hospitale, xij*d.* Agnes
debet v*s.*)

[*f. 9v.*] *Anno xj domini Ricardi abbatis.*³

Memorandum quod Johannes Warde tegulator fecit in opere suo,
(scilicet poynetyng') pro elemosinario ad grangiam (et granariam) in
rectoria de Maxey. In primis xxij rodas et iij quarteria rode, precium
unius rode, xvj*d.*, xxx*s.* iiij*d.* Item ad hospitale fecit iij rodas et terciam
partem rode de novo tegulat*o*, precium unius rode iiij*s.* vj*d.*, xv*s.* Item
fecit ij rodas et unum quarterium rode poynetyng', roda xvj*d.*, iij*s.*
Idem vendidit elemosinario viij mille de lathepynnys, ij*s.* Idem fecit
in officio elemosinarii ij rodas et iij quarteria, scilicet poynetyng', iij*s.*
viij*d.* Idem fecit, ubi Johannes Waldyng' manet, j rodam et dimidiam
poynetyng', ij*s.* Idem fecit, ubi Henricus Palm*er* manet, de novo
tegulato fere j rodam, iiij*s.*

Idem Johannes Warde recepit de domino Willelmo Morton elemosinario
xvj petras nigre lane, precium unius petre ij*s.* viij*d.*, xlij*s.* viij*d.* Idem
recepit iij virgas panni c*u*rialiter texti, precium virge xx*d.*, v*s.* Idem
recepit per vices xiij*s.* Idem recepit vj virgas pro una roba, precium
v*s.*, et ij dies in labore tegulatoris.

(ᵈ Memorandum⁴ quod Johannes Balle senior debet pro iij quarteriis
pisarum, v*s.* vj*d.* Idem solvit per cariagium feni, vij*d.* Item idem solvit
per cariagium de Gonthorppe ad B*u*rgum, videlicet ij carectatarum
ordei. Idem solvit per cariagium de bryc ij carectatarum iiij*d.* Idem
solvit per manus Agnetis Morton, iiij*d.*, iiij*d.*)

(ᵈ Memorandum quod Johannes Gonowr' de Cast*u*r debet pro pisis
j quarterium et dimidium, iij*s.*, (non solvit). Idem debet pro ij
quarteriis avenarum, iij*s.* iiij*d.*, (non solvit). Idem (ᵈ solvit) debet pro
v quarteriis pisarum receptis ad grangiam (de Gonthorp), x*s.*, quos
solvit in argento et per cariagium.)

(ᵈ IN OFFICIO. *Anno xij Ricardi abbatis.*)⁵

(ᵈ In solutis Johanni Warde pro diversis parcellis super bachows et
coquina in officio, et in anno xij Ricardi abbatis, ij*s.*; item in solutis
eidem Johanni, pro j roda de novo coperienda, iiij*s.* vj*d.*; item eidem
pro dimidia roda poyntyng' super 'Vetus Scaccarium',⁶ viij*d.*)

---

¹ This paragraph is written at the foot of the folio upside down.
² *1449–50.*   ³ *1448–9.*
⁴ The following paragraphs were deleted as shown by the letter 'd'.   ⁵ *1449–50.*
⁶ The old exchequer (of the treasurer or another official), on the site of which houses had
been built.

(d SUTTON.)

(d Item pro ij mille de lathepynns, vij*d*., Sutton. In vij quarteriis calcis cum cariagio, iiij*s*. viij*d*.; in solutis pro dimidia roda de novo coperienda, ij*s*. iij*d*.; item pro iij rodis (et) iij quarteriis rde [*sic*] poynetyng', v*s*. Memorandum quod, omnibus computatis in Sabbato ante Nativitatem Beate Marie, Johannes Warde debet elemosinario iij*s*. et laborem j dierum [*sic*].)

(d Memorandum[1] quod Hugo Barkar, fidejussor Willelmi Neffe, pro xxiiij solidis solvendis domino Willelmo Morton elemosinario, preter expensa pro breve domini regis in primis solvit in die Sancti Albani[2] iiij*d*. per talliam, continuando omni dominica etc.)

[*f. 10r.*] *Anno domini Ricardi abbatis xj.*[3]

Memorandum quod elemosinarius deliberavit domino T*ome* sacriste, ex mutuo, xij tracinas; item Johanni Waldyng' v pecias ad unum pentes faciendum; item pro hostiis in Cowgate, scilicet dernysse lyntell' et aliis ibidem faciendis, in fenestris, etiam in tecto, ubi Willelmus Depyng' manet. Item diverse pecie deliberate sunt ad Sowt*er* Row; item ad Sutton lx sp*err*s vel tingna; item xvj alie pecie; item pro uno cotagio in Paston in ten*ura* T*ome* Noblette viij pecie deliberat*e*; item pro uno cotagio in Heygate ij sowlebac*s* cum diversis peciis, ubi Johannes carpentarius cum barba tustata manet; item totum meremium pro uno p*ari* de travysse super Chapel row,[4] deliberat*ur* de officio; item Henrico Palm*er* ij pecie longe ad unum pentesse faciendum. Memorandum quod frater Willelmus Morton deliberavit de proprio meremio ad Sutton (ij pecias, 15*d*.) et Cowgaate (iiij pecias, 16*d*.) et pro uno mantylpese (8*d*.). Item deliberavit ad diversa loca in Sutton unam carectatam meremii per Henricum W*er*mele. Item deliberavit ad Clopto*n* j carectatam meremii, videlicet xxj pecias pro collectore. Item deliberavit ad ij mansiones super Vetus Scaccarium xvj pecias fraccinas et quercinas; item manerio [*sic*] de Sutton' carectatam, videlicet xiiij pecias ad hustrinam ibidem; item ad messuagium ubi T*omas* Hab*ur*gyl manet in Cowgate iiij stothys 4 sp*err*s cum multis splent*s* groncell' et aliis; item ad manerium de Sutton, scilicet, ad coquinam ibidem, j carectatam grossi meremii cum certis sp*er*ris; item alia vice per Robertum Conqueste et Johannem Ivysse iiij carectatas ad dictam coquinam et hustrinam. Item deliberavit ad Depyng' ij carectatas grossi meremii Johanni Trott*er*.

(d Ricardus Sewale[5] debet Agneti Morton in primis pro fact*ura* de vj quarteriis dimidio brasii et pro howsyng' de xvj brasii quarteriis, iiij*s*. vij*d*.; item pro spynnyng' de flax j libram, ij*d*. *ob*.; item pro lagena lactis, j*d*.; et debet pro j har syffe, ij*d*. Summa, v*s*. *ob*.

---

[1] Written at the foot of the folio upside down.
[2] *22 June*.   [3] *1448–9*.
[4] A row of shops, on the site of the former nave of the Becket Chapel, which was demolished to provide materials for building the new parish church on the Market Hill.
[5] At the foot of the folio upside down, afterwards deleted.

Agnes Morton debet Ricardo Sewale in primis pro salicibus, iiij*d*.; item pro cariagio, iiij*d*.; item pro fod*ur* ad animalia, iiij*s*. iiij*d. ob*.)

[*f. 10v*.] *Anno domini Ricardi abbatis xij*.[1]

INVENIUNTUR IN ELEMOSINARIA :—ij chargyrsse, vij platersse, vij poty-gersse, ix sawc*er*sse; item vj olle enee, prima ponderat [[2]]; secunda, [ ]; tercia, [ ]; quarta, [ ]; v, [ ]; sexta, [ ]; item j vern ponderans [ ]; ij cob*er*d*s*, [ ]; j furca ferrea ponderans [ ]; unum mensale operis Parisie [ ]; item j breede tubbe, precii x*d*.; item j dooc*er* vel hallyng' cum quatuor imaginibus cum scripturis Sancti Jacobi apostoli.[3]

iij sawcersse, ij holle potygersse, item j alia potiger, ij platersse cum ⊞[4] [*a line left blank*]

Providencia fratris Willelmi Morton elemosinarii (erga festum Sancte Marie Magdalene) anno Ricardi abbatis xij.[5] In pane, ij*d*.; in servisia (villana), xij*d*.

Ad cenam in vigilia :—pro clericis, in uno humero ovino, j*d. ob*.; pota-gium in die de pisis; item servicium [*sic*] de coquina; in ii pik*s* sive dentricibus, longitudinis xx policum, xx*d*.; in j anguilla assabile, ij*d*.; item in xij anguillis propter unum sorr', iij*d*.; in grene pissibus, butiro, xxx ovis, melle et speciebus propter unum froyse, iiij*d*.; in ij tenchis, v*d*.

Ad secundam cenam :—ova sorbilia de coquina conventus; residuum de prandio servatum (et pescoddis); in datis T*ome* Rowcebi coco pro suo labore, ij*d*.

Providencia erga festum Sancta Marie Magdalene anno Ricardi abbatis xj.[6]

In servisia empta, x*d*.; in pane, ij*d*.

In vigilia ad cenam: in carne vitulina iiij*d*.; potagium in die de pisis; in ij ferculis grossarum carnium, vj*d*.; in j gallina, ij*d*.; in j auca, iiij*d*.; in j porcello, v*d. ob*.; item eadem die potagium de pisis pro capellano (capelle) Sancti T*home* Martiris et uno hospite jejunantibus; in grene pissibus et salcatis anguillis, iiij*d*.

Ad secundam cenam: in una garbage et carne vitulina propter unam sew, ij*d*.; in j humero vitulino, j*d. ob*.

[*f. 11r*.] *Anno domini Ricardi abbatis xij*.[7]

Computacio facta inter dominum Walterum W*er*mingtone[8] et fratrem Willelmum Morton elemosinarium in festo Sancti Wolstani episcopi[9] neuter debet alteri.

---

[1] *1449–50*.   [2] The weights were never inserted.
[3] Several lines were left blank, followed by the following list upside down, the first line of which is missing.
[4] A sign whose significance is unknown.   [5] *22 July 1450*.
[6] *22 July 1449*. Note that this entry concerning the 11th year follows that of the 12th.
[7] *1449–50*.   [8] See L.R.S. xxi. 280, 282, 295.   [9] *19 Jan. 1449/50*.

Computatis omnibus inter dominum Ricardum Oxforthe[1] seniorem et dominum Willelmum Morton elemosinarium tercio Kal. Februarii,[2] nullus eorum debet alteri.

IN HOSPITALE. In solutis Johanni Poope laboranti ad hospitale per viij dies (in domo prostrato, et quia portavit splent*s* illuc), et in gardino infra officium per j diem, capienti in die iiij*d*. iij*s*.; item eidem pro j camino juxta Henrici Palm*er* deponendo sive prosternendo, (aretro[3]).

Memorandum quod frater Willelmus Morton vendidit (T*ome* Hawme) j equum coloris grey et etatis iiij annorum pro iiij*s*. vj*d*.; festo Sancti Michaelis solucio.

ARETRO. Memorandum quod frater Willelmus Morton elemosinarius solvit ij carpentariis pro scapulacione de iiij^xx vj peciis quercinis et fraccinis, v*s*. iiij*d*. *ob*.

HOSPITALE. In solutis eisdem pro opere carpentrie in una grangia ad hospitale simul cum emendacione j stabuli ibidem et—

CUSTUS IN BURGO—emendacione ij cotagiorum (per unum diem) in Bongate per v dies, capientes [*sic*] in die x*d*., iiij*s*. viij*d*.; item ad potum, ij*d*.; in solutis supradictis carpentariis pro imposicione unius som*ur*pese, ij threyschold*s* cum aliis defectibus emendatis super Sowter row in grosso ij*s*.; in cariagio illius som*ur*pese cum magnis lapidibus de hospitale illuc et ad unum ibidem prope, iiij*d*.

IN OFFICIO. In solutis supradictis carpentariis pro emendacione de le bac hows (in officio) per iij dies, ij*s*. vj*d*.; item in rewardo illis dato, vj*d*.

(^d Memorandum quod lathamus [*sic*] recepit, ij*d*.; item xij*d*. in parte solucionis de xx*s*. pro factura unius camini super Chapel row.)

IN CONVENTU. In solutis pro j jaale servisie in presencia prioris, et pro rastura noviciorum, iiij*d*.

IN OFFICIO. In j tribulo et j mokeforc ferri emptis, iiij*d*.

NECESSARIA. In solutis pro uno roope de canabo ponderante xxij libras et dimidiam (iiij capistris, ij kolers, ponderantibus iij libras dimidiam), precii xxiij*d*.

IN OFFICIO. In solutis pro una situla nova cum iij circulis ferreis bene ligata.

NECESSARIA. In solutis pro reparacione et emendacione de tribus frenis, xviij*d*.; in solutis pro ij ventilabris emptis, v*d*.

IN HOSPITALE. In solutis T*ome* Style et Johanni Medow pro dawbyng' unius stabuli et j gabule in una grangia ad hospitale, in grosso, ij*s*. ij*d*.

NECESSARIA. In j singulo equino empto, ij*d*.

IN OFFICIO. In uno senevecterio novo empto, xiiij*d*.

---

[1] See L.R.S. xxi. 277–8, 284.   [2] *30 Jan. 1449/50.*
[3] In margin.

Anno Ricardi[1] *abbatis xij.*[2]

RECEPTA DE HOSPITALE. In primis 40*d.*
Columbelle[3] deliberate selerario domini abbatis, domino Johanni
B*u*rneham,[4] xxvj. T*ome* Rowseby, xxiiij columbelle; item iiij; item
Johanni Dey, ix.

[*f. 11v.*] *Anno domini Ricardi abbatis xij.*[5]
Debita fratris Willelmi Morton elemosinarii que debet certis confratri-
bus et secularibus scripta in dominica prima Quadragesime:—[6]
Domino Johanni T*u*rvey,[7] v*s.* pro speciebus, quos solvi in ebdomada
Pasche scilicet feria vj,[8] (solvit); domino Johanni Northoppe, v*s.* pro
simili; inde solvi, ij*s.* vj*d.*; item ij*s.* vj*d.*; et equet (solvit); domino
Ricardo Bysle,[9] vj*s.* pro consimili, (solvit); domino Willelmo Melton,[10]
iij*li.* vj*s.* pro redditu assise et pro sacrista, (solvit); domino Willelmo
M*e*rkam,[11] xij*s.*, (solvit. Nota stipand' est hic iij*s.* iiij*d.* pro parte); item
(pro co*nt*[   ] de Oxney) vj*s.* vj*d.*, (solvit); domino T*ome* Maxey, c*s.*;[12]
domino Johanni York,[13] [   ]; domino Willelmo Stanforde,[14] xvj*d.*
pro fratre Willelmo Alwyncle, quos solvit; domino Willelmo Gretteforde,[15] ij*s.* vj*d.* pro tunica sua, (solvit); domino Johanni Pychele[16] et
fratri Willelmo Spaldyng', x*s.* pro speciebus, inde solvit v*s.*; xx*d.*; iij*s.*
iiij*d.*; (solvit); domino Willelmo Ufforthe, x*s.* pro speciebus, (solvit);
inde solvit v*s.*; item xiij*d.*; item vj*s.*; j*d.*; et equet inter illos; domino
Johanni Ryalle, v*s.*, pro consimili, quos solvi [*sic*] ad ostium minucionis; domino Willelmo Hontyngdon, iij*s.* iiij*d.* pro consimili, (solvit);
inde recepit ij*s.*; iiij*d.*; xij*d.*; et equet; domino Johanni Baston, v*s.* pro
speciebus, sol*u*cio ad Pascha[17] facta est, (solvit); domino regi pro decima
sua concessa per clerum vij marcas, (solvit); Roberto Orwyn, ut in
8 folio ante et ut alibi postea; sororibus capelle, (solucio facta est), et
clerico ejusdem [*sic*] (solvit); clericis in subelemosinaria: satisfactum
est eis; pauperibus ad hospitale, ij*s.*, (solvit); Willelmo M*e*rkawnte,
xx*d.*, (solvit); Johanni Styv*u*r, ij*s.* (solvit); T*ome* Hawme, vj*s.*; item
[[18]   ]; (xij*s.* ad diem Sancti Elpegi);[19] Willelmo Maydelette, [[18]   ];
Johanni Pye, [[18]   ]; Johanni Beylde, (Wryhete) vel draffe; Petro
Barbur et Johanni Exton, vj*s.* viij*d.* (solvit); Johanni Rothewel de
Sutton, nichil. (d Frater Willelmus Walmysford debet fratri Willelmo
Morton pro Johanne Browny vij*d.* (xij*d.*) de redditu; solvit ut dicit.)

(d Memorandum[20] quod anno Ricardi abbatis xij, vij Idus May,[21] omnibus
computatis Johannes Smyth vel Clark de Wodcrofte debet elemosinario,

---

ij*s*. viij*d*. quos solvit et sic quietus est pro anno xj Ricardi abbatis. Idem solvit x*s*. alia vice pro anno xij et debet x*s*.)

[*f. 12r.*] *Anno domini Ricardi abbatis xij.*[1]

NOTA. Quere expensas ebdomade Sexagesime anni precedentis folio v ante.

Dominica Sexagesime[2] ad prandium: in primis, brawne; in j ferculo de grossa carne cocto et alio assato, v*d*.; (ᵈ item ad cenam, j*d*.) (ᵈ Feria secunda, brawne;) in tribus carnibus vitulinis, iiij*d*. *ob*.; item ad cenam, in iiij pulcinis emptis, iiij*d*.

Feria secunda: brawne; in grossis carnibus pro prandio et cena, v*d*. Item in carne porcina salcata pro colloppys, iiij*d*.; in sagine j*d*.; in ovis, iij*d*. Ad cenam in pedibus vitulinis et cepe, iij*d*. Feria tercia: brawne; in uno ferculo cocto, alio assato, v*d*.; in una gallina, ij*d*. Ad cenam in iiij gallinis, viij*d*. Feria iiij: nichil. Feria v: brawne; in j ferculo cocto et alio assato, v*d*. In iiij gallinis pro camino, viij*d*.; in uno mallard pro fratre Johanne B*urr*ow, senescallo,[3] ij*d*. Ad cenam in carne pro uno sew et garbage gallinarum, iij*d*.

Dominica quinquagesime[4]: iiij lechis apri pro uno ferculo tantum hac die; item in j capite vitulino et j pestel porci, iij*d*.; in una assacione, j*d*. *ob*.; ad cenam, in una gallina, ij*d*.

Ebdomada Sexagesime anno Ricardi abbatis xiij.[5]

In solutis pro victualibus emptis (per elemosinarium) pro ebdomada Sexagesime,[6] ij*s*. v*d*.; item in solutis T*ome* Rowseby, coco, pro victualibus per illum emptis eadem ebdomada cum Dominica Quinquagesime,[7] iiij*s*. ij*d*. *ob*.

Quere expensas minucionis tercii prioris in Nativitate domini anno xiiij Ricardi abbatis,[8] vicesimo folio sequente.
Ebdomada Sexagesime[9] et minucio tercii prioris anno Ricardi abbatis xiiij.

Dominica. In aprina ut supra, in anno xij Ricardi abbatis,[10] et in carnibus grossis per quatuor dies eadem dominica; in quatuor capitibus vitulinis, vj*d*.; in ij aucis, viij*d*.; in carne vitulina, 8*d*.; ad cenam in hoggysse chek*s* cum pedibus sowsydde, iiij*d*. Feria *ij*. In aprina et grossa carne ut supra; in carne porcina salcata sagine et ovis, vij*d*.; in iiij gallinis, 8*d*.; in j porcello, v*d*.; ad cenam, in wyldefowle, vj*d*.

Feria tercia. In aprina et grossa carne, ut supra; in carne vitulina, 8*d*.; ad cenam in pedibus vitulinis, iiij*d*. Feria v. In aprina et grossa carne, ut supra; in ij capitibus vitulinis, 4*d*.; in uno pestel porci, ij*d*.; in una auca, 4*d*.; in ij gallinis, 4*d*.; ad cenam in ij gallinis, iiij*d*.

---

[1] *1449-50.*
[3] See note concerning Richard Oxford senior, p. 21.
[5] *28 Feb. 1450/1.*   [6] *28 Feb.–6 Mar. 1450/1.*
[8] *25 Dec. 1451.*   [9] *13 Feb. 1451/2.*

[2] *8 Feb. 1449/50.*
[4] *15 Feb. 1449/50.*
[7] *7 Mar. 1450/1.*
[10] *1449-50.*

Dominica quinquagesime.[1] In aprina, nichil; in uno pestel porci cum
j capite vitulino, iiij*d.*; in uno ferculo assato, ij*d.* Ad cenam in j ferculo
porci, j*d. ob.*

[*f. 12v.*] SUTTON. Magna Curia ibidem in die Lune iiij [*sic*] die mensis
Aprilis anno regni regis Henrici Sexti xxviij,[2] et anno domini Ricardi
abbatis xij, fratre Willelmo Morton tunc elemosinario Burgi.

ESSONIATI. Willelmus Blogwyn', Willelmus Geffron', Thomas Tayl-
lour', sunt essoniati. Thomas Pryour' junior, *Thomas* Fadyrman', ipse
est inoccup*atus* tenent' ibidem.

INQUISICIO HOMAGII videlicet Thomas Pryour', Johannes Rowell',
Ricardus Uppyngham, Johannes Dureham, Johannes Panke, Willelmus
Laye, Henricus Wormeley, Johannes Ivys, Thomas Tallour de Caster,
presentant quod in crofto vocato Lundys yard' defecit clausura in
defectu Ricardi Uppyngham ([d] tenentis ibidem). Et quod ([d] Thomas
Pryour' senior) dominus elemosinarius debet clausur' j croft*i* vocat*i*
Malyn yard'.

Et quod Hugo Schelford', (ij*d.*), Nicholaus Walker', (ij*d.*), Thomas
Rothewell' (ij*d.*) sunt venatores in j crofto vocato Malynyard' et ceperunt
cuniculos. Et quod domus mer*emii* Ricardi Uppyngham est in defectu dicti Ricardi [in] meremio et aliis necessariis ibidem ([d] in defectu)
est in defectu domini elemosinarii Burgi.

LIBERI TENENTES videlicet:—Thomas Pryour' senior, Robertus Wymyche, Johannes Eyre ju*rati* presentant quod homagium predictum
bene et fideliter presentant et nichil concelaverunt etc.

AFFURATORES   Johannes Ives
Johannes Rowthwelle.

v carectate terre rubie per Belamy juniorem. Johannes Pypwel laboravit ad Hospitale per v dies.

Anno[3] *Ricardi abbatis xij* et ad festum Nativitatis Sancti Johannis
Baptiste,[4] omnibus computatis Walterus Laveroc debet elemosinario
iiij*s.* viij*d.* de redditu. Idem debet elemosinario pro proximo termino,
v*s.* x*d.*, videlicet pro ultimo termino anni supradicti Ricardi abbatis.[5]

Anno Ricardi abbatis xiij. Idem Walterus debet v*s.* x*d.* elemosinario ad
Nativitatem domini.[6]

[*f. 13r.*] Memorandum quod j acra terre jacet in campis de Upton et
abbuttat super Sowthwel brok' Est et West. Henricus Redyll[7] clamat
quod elemosinarius (Burgi) debet sectam curie suam pro dicta acra
terre ibidem. Nunc est in manu domini.

ITEM dimidia acra terre nuper in tenura Willelmi Clerk' jacet in Long
dalle ibidem. Henricus Ridell clamat quod elemosinarius Burgi debet
sectam curie pro simili ibidem.

[1] *20 Feb. 1451/2.*   [2] *1450.* If this is right, Monday should be 6 Apr.
[3] Written at foot of this folio upside down.
[4] *24 June 1450.*   [5] *29 Sept. 1450.*   [6] *25 Dec. 1450.*
[7] For Ridel family see Henry of Pytchley, *Lib. Feod.*, N.R.S. ii. 26 *et passim.*

Item dimidia acra terre in campo de Sybberton ibidem, quod [*sic*] Thomas Seymerk'[1] clamat, quod dominus elemosinarius Burgi debet sectam curie suam ibidem pro dicta dimidia acra terre ibidem.

Memorandum quod Henricus Wyncle debet xiij*d.* fratri Willelmo Morton, (solvit).

Elemosinarius computavit cum Ricardo Lucasse in vigilia Sancti Bartholomei Apostoli anno Ricardi abbatis xij.[2] Omnibus computatis Ricardus debet xxxij*s.* x*d.* pro firma ad Hospitale. Item Ricardus debet pro pisis, iij*s.* viij*d.* Item Ricardus debet elemosinario ij quarteria ordei.

(d Memorandum quod predictus Ricardus Lucas solvit per cariagium iiij carectatarum zabuli de le Beyche usque Merket stede; item j carectat'[3] rubei tyle sive bryk illuc; item j carectat' straminis ordei ad officium pro litera. [*In margin*] Nota ij caretat' feni in dubio.)

Anno Ricardi abbatis xiiij incipiente[4] *in crastino Sancti Luce Ewangeliste.* Omnibus computatis Ricardus predictus debet (elemosinario) clare xxxij*s.* vj*d.* Idem Ricardus postea solvit ut de precio unius porcelli, vj*d.* [*In margin*] Memorandum de xix*d.* receptis pro casio et lacte.

Memorandum quod idem Ricardus Lucasse et Willelmus Lucasse venerunt ante festum Omnium Sanctorum ad elemosinarium, anno Ricardi abbatis xiiij,[5] et fidem fecerunt levando dexteram manum in presencia Johannis Halle et Johannis Hynton' et aliorum, quod ipsi solverent viij*s.*, (solverunt), ad festum Annunciacionis Beate Marie proxime (sequens);[6] item viij*s.* ad festum Sancti Johannis Baptiste (proximum);[7] item viij*s.* ad festum Michaelis (proximi);[8] item viij*s.* et vj denarios (per breve regis) ad (proximam) Nativitatem domini,[9] sub pena duplicacionis vel xx marcarum.

Anno 16[10] Willelmus Lucas promisit solvere ad festum Michaelis anno Ricardi abbatis xvj incipiente,[11] 7*s.* domino Willelmo elemosinario; item ad festum Martini proximum,[12] vij*s.*; et ad Epiphaniam,[13] vij*s.* iij*d.*, levando manum coram fratre Johanne Borow, [et] Willelmo Port*er*.

Dies[14] *tercius anniversarius Roberti Morton*[15] *sive annus tercius.* In pane, x*d.*; in servisia, videlicet quatuor tankard*s* vel xx lagenis cervisie, xx*d.*; item vicario, (6*d.*); v sacerdotibus, (15*d.*); et clerico, (2*d.*); item Johanni campanerio, ij*d.*; in caseo, viij*d.*

[*f. 13v.*] Memorandum quod rector de Norb*u*rrow accepit decimam

---

[1] Ibid., p. 26 *et passim.*   [2] *23 Aug. 1450.*
[3] An alternative reading would be 'item [per cariagium] unius carectate . . . item unius carectate'. The cost is not stated.
[4] The royal assent to the election was given on 24 Sept. 1438 and the temporalities were restored to him on 14 Oct. *Incipiente* does not mark the actual start of the year. All that it means is that 19 Oct. came in the early days of the 14th year. A. H. T. Cf. above, p. xl, n. 3.
[5] *c. 31 Oct. 1451.*   [6] i.e. on *25 Mar. 1452.*   [7] i.e. on *24 June 1452.*
[8] *sic,* i.e. on *29 Sept. 1452.*   [9] *25 Dec. 1452.*   [10] *1453-4.*
[11] *29 Sept. 1453.* See, however, note 4 above; the actual date for payment is doubtful.
[12] *11 Nov. 1453.*   [13] *6 Jan. 1453/4.*   [14] Written at foot of folio upside down.
[15] Who was Robert, and when was his anniversary commemorated? John the sexton apparently rang the bells on this day.

unius acre prati jacentis in Marram mette buttantis super Mer' dik'. Idem rector accepit decimam de j acra terre arabilis jacente in Sowthe felde (fere in medio), buttyng' super Heygaate. Et memorandum quod dicta terra est de parochia de Maxey et infra bundas de Maxey.¹ Idem rector retinet decimam in aliis ibidem.

Item memorandum quod rector de Peykyrc retinet decimam unius acre prati jacentis in Marram mette.

Memorandum quod domina Colepep*ur* petit sectam curie de elemosinario ad Wodecroft pro tenemento ibidem.

Item memorandum quod Johanna Jaxson retinet (decimam) de vj acris dimidia (prati) jacentibus in Maxey prato; tamen loquendum est cum Margareta Reynolde, quondam uxor Willelmi Reynolde de ista materia, et de solucione decime in campo de Norb*ur*row. (Notandum quod non dant decimam, ut dicitur.)

(ᵈ BEYLDE. *Anno xij Ricardi abbatis.*²

Johannes Beylde boch*er* mutuatus est iiij*s.* de elemosinario. Idem Johannes Beylde debet elemosinario pro una vacca, vij*s.* vj*d.* Inde solvit elemosinario per carnes deliberatas coco infirmar*ie* sive [aule] minucionis ad diem Assumpcionis Beate Marie,³ x*s.* x*d.* Modo debet viij*d.* Postea supradictus Johannes deliberavit coco infirmarie per talliam.)

Omnibus computatis ad festum Michaelis Archangeli⁴ anno xiij Ricardi abbatis incipiente, elemosinarius debet Johanni Beylde bocher' (ᵈⁱ)j*s.*, (quos soluit).

Radulphus Bakyl de Wermyngton' fecit fossatum et plantavit salices super unam foreram domini elemosinarii de Burgo sine licencia et ideo etc.

Memorandum quod, anno Ricardi abbatis xij,⁵ elemosinarius satisfecit domino Ricardo Oxford⁶ pro clerico suo *Roberto* Bawnce. Idem elemosinarius, anno Ricardi abbatis xiij in Concepcione Beate Marie,⁷ solvit domino Johanni Yorc⁸ pro anno xj Ricardi abbatis propter clericum suum Johannem Bolton, iij*s.* iiij*d.*

Anno xj Ricardi⁹ abbatis frater *Tomas* Depyng debet fratri Willelmo Morton (elemosinario) iij*s.* iiij*d.* pro alneto celerarii; item ij*d.* propter ciminum. Idem debet Willelmo elemosinario xij*d.* pro pondis in Werkery ʒard' pro anno xij.¹⁰

Memorandum quod Johanna Jaxson et Willelmus filius ejus tenuerunt

¹ As to Maxey and adjoining parishes, Woodcroft and Northborough, see 'The Articles of the cleymer, demaunder, compleyntes and greuances of Richard abbot of Peterburgh, shewed to the right noble and worthy prince the Erle of Somerset, nowe duke', etc., Roger Bird, f. 25.
² *1449–50.*   ³ *15 Aug. 1450.*   ⁴ *29 Sept. 1450.*   ⁵ *1449–50.*
⁶ Either Richard Oxford senior (see above, p. 21, n. 1) or junior (see L.R.S. xxi. 284 n).
⁷ *8 Dec. 1450.*
⁸ See L.R.S. xxi. 280, 282–3, 296. In 1471 Yorke was a very old man in the farmery.
⁹ *1448–9.*   ¹⁰ *1449–50.*

ad firmam de Willelmo Reynold et solverunt ei xviij*s.* pro prato in Est medow (cum decima[1] ibidem) et Nunton holme pertinente ad rectoriam ecclesie de Maxey.

Memorandum quod [[2]   ] Murkote de Peykyrc habet iiij acras terre prope Nabbe Wode in campo de Werryngton, et rector de Peykyrc clamat decimam illarum, ideo inquirendum est.

Fidejussores Willelmus Reynolde, Willelmus Moyses, Johannes Kyllam, Robertus Cast*ur*, Willelmus [*fo. 14r, foot*] Garrad. Memorandum quod clericus de Marram sit informa*rius* elemosinarii de jure suo de decimis in Est medow.

[*f. 14r.*] *Anno domini 144[9]; item anno regni Henrici Sexti xxviij et anno domini Ricardi abbatis xij incipiente.*

Expensa fratris Willelmi Morton in officio elemosinarie anno Ricardi abbatis xij incipiente.[3]

Memorandum quod satisfeci [*sic*] fratri Willelmo M*e*rkam pro tunicis de anno xj Ricardi abbatis.[4]

Soluciones. In primis fratri Ricardo Oxford seniori, x*s.*; item fratri Willelmo Alwynkyl,[5] x*s.*; item fratri Roberto Lydyngton,[6] x*s.*; item fratri Willelmo Morton, x*s.*; item vj*s.* viij*d.* de xiij*s.* iiij*d.* ad festum Sancti Michaelis, quando frater Willelmus M*e*rkam recessit de officio thesaurarii. Memorandum quod frater Willelmus M*e*rkam retinuit et non solvit istos vj*s.* viij*d.* fratri Willelmo Morton propter plenam solucionem de xlvj*s.* viij*d.*

Soluciones ad dominum Willelmum M*e*rkam xxx*s.* hic

Item memorandum quod frater Willelmus Morton elemosinarius solvit domino Willelmo M*e*rkam, gardiano de Oxney,[7] vj*s.* vj*d.* (pro comunibus) de anno xij Ricardi abbatis ad hostium vestiarii, in presencia Henrici Freyr collectoris de Clopton; item x*s.* (ad Oxney); item iij*s.* iiij*d.* (ad Oxney); item iij*s.* iiij*d.*; 6*s.* x*d.* Quere plus ex altera parte istius folii.

Soluciones. Item predictus elemosinarius solvit in vigilia Natalis Domini[8] fratri Willelmo Gretf*ord*, subelemosinario, vj*s.* viij*d.* in parte solucionis de x*s.* solvendis subelemosinario; item x*d.*; iij*s.* iiij*d.*

Soluciones. Memorandum quod frater Willelmus Morton elemosinarius solvit fratri Willelmo Melton infirmario per manus Tome Rowceby in die Sancti Johannis Ewangeliste[9] xx*s.* per tallium in parte solucionis de lxvj*s.*; item in vigilia Pasche[10] in presencia Walteri Qhwyte, xxs.; item in vigilia Trinitatis,[11] xiij*s.* iiij*d.*, in presencia supradicti Walteri et

---

[1] It was the tithe apparently and not the meadow which belonged to the rectory, but owing to abbreviations the meaning of the text is not clear.
[2] Christian name omitted.   [3] *1449–50*.   [4] *1448–9*.
[5] L.R.S. xxi. 290, as to his keeping a jack and other arms of offence in the dorter.
[6] Ibid. 293, his complaint against Thomas Maxey.
[7] After his retirement from the office of bursar; see above.
[8] *24 Dec. 1449.*   [9] *27 Dec. 1449.*
[10] *4 Apr. 1450.*   [11] *30 May 1450.*

in camera infirmarii.[1] Et de aliis solucionibus require postea in xv folio (sequenti) ad tale signum ⊙.

De anno Ricardi abbatis xij incipiente.[2]

SOLUCIONES. Memorandum quod frater Willelmus elemosinarius debebat domino Willelmo Exton priori,[3] ixs. xd. Idem frater Willelmus Morton elemosinarius solvit priori in minucione supprioris in Adventu[4] in presencia sociorum ibidem, vijs. viijd. (Idem) elemosinarius stipavit penes priorem (pro oblacione in capella Beate Marie), xjd. de debito fratris Johannis Spaldyng'; vjd. pro ostencione librorum de debito fratris Ricardi Depyng';[5] item ijd. ob. de debito fratris Willelmi Talyngton.[6] (Idem) prior habuit in manibus vijd. fratris Willelmi Morton ob memoriam rotulorum (caucionem), et sic equet, preter vjd. ob. ([d] Idem elemosinarius solvit priori pro scolaribus (pro) anno xj Ricardi abbatis.) Idem elemosinarius solvit priori in parte solucionis de jalez pro anno Ricardi abbatis xj obolum auri, (iijs. iiijd.), in minucione Johannis Rycheman presentis ad prandium. Idem solvit domino priori anno domini 144[7] ad festum Pasche pro cursu suo xls. de grossis.

[f. 14v.] Anno Ricardi abbatis xij.[8]

Memorandum quod frater Willelmus Morton elemosinarius solvit pro tunicis fratri Willelmo Merkam, ut patet in prima parte istius folii.[9] Item idem elemosinarius solvit supradicto domino Willelmo Merkam, in parte solucionis de xxiiijs., vjs. viijd. Idem elemosinarius solvit per manus Johannis Carpentarii cum barba tustata, vs. iiijd. Idem gardianus recepit per Henricum Bawnce 3 Idus Decembris[10] iijs. iiijd.; item iijs. iiijd. ad ostium Willelmi Ravon, in previgilia Natalis Domini.

Anno xiiij Ricardi abbatis.[11]

Item xxd. pro redditu assise in Westgate. Idem gardianus recepit per manus Johannis Waldyng', viijs.; item per Henricum Bawns, ijs. 4 Kal. Februarii.[12] Idem gardianus recepit in die Sancti Mathie Apostoli sequente[13] iijs. iiijd. in camera. Quere in folio 7 sequente. [In margin] Summa solucionum, xxxiijs. viijd.; 4li. 6s. iiijd.

Memorandum quod collector de Clopton solvit de collectione suo de anno xj Ricardi abbatis, xxs. per tallium. Item memorandum quod Ricardus Dodley occupat dimidiam acram prati injuste modo per quatuor annos et notandum quod jacet in Olde Forthe buttant' [sic] usque austrum super Tychemer broc. Ideo consulendum est cum etc.

Idem collector solvit per tallium et per manus Tome Hawme, xjs. Item idem solvit per Tomam Hawme primo Sabbato Quadragesime,[14] xiiijs. ixd. ob.; item xxxjs. jd. ob. Item allocantur Henrico collectori pro reparacione in cotagiis Johannis Egyston, Johannis Hartte et aliis

---

[1] The chamber of the infirmarian, now a canonry house.
[2] *1449–50.*   [3] L.R.S. xxi. 299.   [4] *On or after 30 Nov. 1449.*
[5] L.R.S. xxi. 275, 282, 285, 290; as to his carrying arms, ibid. 290.
[6] Ibid. 295.   [7] Left blank.   [8] *1449–50.*   [9] See f. 14r.
[10] *11 Dec. 1449* (?).   [11] *1451–2.*   [12] *29 Jan. 1452.*   [13] *25 Feb. 1452.*
[14] *1 Mar. 1448/9.* Ash Wednesday was on 26 Feb.

materiis, ixs. ijd. ob.; et quietus abiit pro anno xj Ricardi abbatis; item xxs.; item xxxijs.; item pro roba anni precedentis, 6s. 8d.; item xvjd. Modo recepi [sic] 3li. 5s.; 2s. 8d.; xijs.; 4d.; item iiijs.; et equet pro anno xij, quia elemosinarius perdonavit collectori jd. ob.

Collector de Wermyngton solvit elemosinario, ut patet per tallium suum in Sabbato ante Conversionem Sancti Pauli[1] cum vijd. receptis ad curiam, xxs.; item in Sabbato dominice Passionis,[2] viijs. iiijd.; item in festo Apostolorum Petri et Pauli,[3] xjs.; item ijs. iiijd.; item vjd.; item pro anno 2, xiijs. iiijd.; item iijs. vjd.; item iijs. ijd. in dubio; item in Vigilia Omnium Sanctorum[4] anno Ricardi abbatis xiiij vjs., pro 2 anno elemosinarii; item xvjd. [In margin] 3li. 9s. 6d.

Collector de Sutton solvit elemosinario, ut patet per tallium inter eos, xiijs. iiijd.; item per manus Willelmi Lay, vijs.; item per manus Johannis Yvis, xiijs. Item idem collector solvit in die Sancti Mathie[5] in capite Quadragesime iijs. iiijd.; item vijs. in capella noviciorum; item in Vigilia Trinitatis[6] ad hostium vestiarii, ixs. in presencia Roberti Conqueste; item per Johannem Eyr' et Ricardum Uppyngham in Vigilia Sancti Nicholai,[7] xxs.; item iiijs. per manus Johannis Yvis etc. Quere plus in vj folio sequente. [In margin] 3li. 16s. 8d.

Collector de Maxey solvit elemosinario, ut patet per tallium inter eos, xs.; item iijs. iiijd. Item unus tenens solvit in orto abbathie inter metas ibidem, iijs. viijd. (Notandum hic); item viijs. in Vigilia Sancti Martini per Tomam Havme;[8] item in Sabbato ante Nativitatem domini,[9] xiijs. iiijd.; item eodem die xxd. Summa, 40s.

   Item per Johannem Irnerde, xiijs. iiijd. in presencia Tome Honte; item xiijs. iiijd. primo Sabbato Quadragesime;[10] item vjs. viijd. de Willelmo Brewster et Johanne Castur Sabbato ante Dominicam Palmarum;[11] item vjs. viijd. in Sabbato in ebdomada Pasche[12] de Willelmo Brewster; item in presencia Roberti Gardiner, vjs. viijd.; item xxs. Sabbato ante festum Nicholai;[13] item per Willelmum Jacson, 26s. 8d.; et per Johannem Clerk de Wodcroft, xxs.; et de Willelmo Reede, 4s.; et de Roberto Paums, 7s. SUMMA RECEPTE, 6li. 26d. [sic]

Memorandum de xxd. receptis ad curiam de Sutton de j tenemento ibidem pro anno xij Ricardi abbatis.

[f. 15r.] Anno Ricardi abbatis xij.[14]

Memorandum quod Johannes Irnarde firmarius rectorie de Maxey solvit pro firma sua ut patet per tallium suum. In primis solvit Tome Hawme, xiijs. et iiijd. in presencia Johannis Caastur; item xxs. per tallium in die Sancti Antonii;[15] item Kal. Marcii[16] per Thomam Hawme,

vj*s*. viij*d*.; item xx*s*. in Sabbato ante Dominicam in ramis palmarum;[1]
item x*s*. per Thomam Hawme in Invencione Sancte Crucis;[2] item in
die Sanctorum Primi et Feliciani,[3]iiij*li*.; item de rectore de Norborow,
x*s*., (solvit); item ut in caseo, xvj*d*.; item in reparacione portarum
ibidem, xij*d*.; item in die Sanctorum Septem Dormiencium[4] per Johannem Smythe, xxvj*s*. viij*d*., (per tallium); item per Johannem Irn*er*de in
die Sancti Oswaldi[5] (per tallium), xxvj*s*. viij*d*.; item in Assumpcione
Beate Marie[6] (per tallium), xl*s*.; item per T*omam* Havme in crastino
Sancti Luce Ewangeliste[7] anno Ricardi abbatis xiij, xxvj*s*. viij*d*., (per
tallium); item per eodem [*sic*] T*omam* Havme in die Quatuor Coronatorum,[8] vj*s*. viij*d*., (per tallium); item in crastino Coronatorum,[9] (per
tallium,) xx*s*., per T*omam* Havme; item xx*s*. per Johannem Yrn*er*de in
crastino Sancti Vincentii martiris.[10] Summa, 16*li*. 9*s*.; item in Sabbato
Sexagesime[11] per idem [*sic*] firmarium, iij*li*. vj*s*. viij*d*.; et debet modo
iiij*s*. iiij*d*.[12]

Memorandum quod anno Ricardi abbatis xiij feria v in Cena Domini,[13]
et in presensia Roberti Smythe vel Hok', Johannes Yrn*er*de solvit pro
firma rectorie de Maxey pro anno xij Ricardi abbatis iiij nobilia auri.
Item idem Johannes, firmarius, solvit v die mensis Junii[14] in presencia
Roberti Hok' et Johannis Cast*ur* iiij marcas; item in Sabbato ante
Exaltacionem Sancte Crucis[15] in presencia Roberti Palm*s*, iij*li*.; item
feria v post festum Sancti Andree,[16] in presencia Johannis Carpentarii
alias vocati Bradbyry, xl*s*. Summa recepte, 9*li*. pro xij anno Ricardi
abbatis; item xx*s*. anno xiiij Ricardi abbatis in Vigilia Natalis domini;[17]
([d] item iij*li*. in Sabbato). Summa recepte x*li*. Item idem firmarius solvit
in previgilia Nativitatis domini anno xv Ricardi abbatis[18] xl*s*.; item in
Vigilia,[19] xxxiij*s*. iiij*d*. per Johannem Coldewelle; item iij*li*.; Summa
soluta xvj*li*. xiij*s*. iiij*d*. et debet lxvj*s*. viij*d*.

Memorandum quod anno Ricardi abbatis xiiij xj Kal. Marcii[20] Robertus
firmarius rectorie de Maxey solvit primo in presencia Roberti Paulm*s*
et Johannis Irn*er*de iiij*li*. Idem solvit Sabbato in ebdomada Pasche in
presencia Johannis Irn*er*de iiij*li*. Idem solvit per manus Nicholai
Smythe, vj*li*. Idem solvit per Johannem Irn*er*de, iij*li*. Idem solvit l*s*.
in presencia Stephani Gardyn*er*; item per rectorem de Norb*ur*row, x*s*.
et equet.

Anno Ricardi abbatis xv.[21] Robertus Hok' firmarius ibidem solvit per
Johannem Coldewel, vj*s*. viij*d*. in Vigilia Nativitatis domini[22] et per
dictum Johannem in Vigilia Purificacionis,[23] 13*s*. 4*d*.; item 3*li*. 13*s*. 4*d*.;
item xx*s*. Item solvit xxviij die Aprilis,[24] iij*li*. vj*s*. viij*d*. Item solvit

---

[1] *28 Mar. 1450.*
[5] *5 Aug. 1450.*
[8] *8 Nov. 1450.*
[11] *6 Mar. 1450/1.*
[14] *1451.*
[17] *24 Dec. 1451.*
[20] *20 Feb. 1451/2.*
[23] *1 Feb. 1452/3.*

[2] *3 May 1450.*
[6] *15 Aug. 1450.*
[9] *9 Nov. 1450.*
[12] Written later.
[15] *11 Sept. 1451.*
[18] *23 Dec. 1452.*
[21] *1452-3.*
[24] *1453.*

[3] *9 June 1450.*

[4] *27 July 1450.*
[7] *19 Oct. 1450.*
[10] *23 Jan. 1450/1.*
[13] *22 Apr. 1451.*
[16] *2 Dec. 1451.*
[19] *24 Dec. 1452.*
[22] *24 Dec. 1452.*

in Vigilia Corporis Christi[1] per Johannem Coldewel, vj*s*. viij*d*.; item in vigilia Sancte Margarete Virginis,[2] v nobilia; item iiij*li*.

[*f. 15v*.] *Anno domini 14* [3] *regni regis* [*Henrici Sexti*] *xxviij Ricardi abbatis xij*.[4]

In solutis Johanni Rothewel de Sutton pro diversis laboribus ibidem, v*s*. et memorandum quod elemosinarius debet, omnibus computatis, x*s*.; tamen supervidendum est de mensura murorum, et idem Johannes Rothewel debet redditum pro anno instante. Memorandum de solucione ei antea, videlicet xxj*s*.; xv*s*.; vj*s*. viij*d*.; iij*s*. iiij*d*.; et ad j capicium, xviij*d*.

SUTTON. In solutis Henrico W*u*rmele pro uno muro prosternendo sive deiciendo, separacione petre velute, et preparacione fundamenti unius domus, (scilicet stabuli), ibidem, vj*d*.; item eidem pro cariagio de xx carectatis petre velute, xx*d*.; in solutis eidem pro xiij carectatis terre rubie, xiij*d*.; item in solutis Johanni Rothewelle pro factura unius muri ibidem, videlicet (longitudinis) ij rodarum altitudinis 9 pedum, viij*s*., meremium de preempcione; in solutis Johanni Rothewel pro factura unius tecti ibidem xxv coplys, iiij*s*.; item pro bemfyllyng' Henrico W*u*rmele, iiij*d*.; in solutis pro copertura, (scilicet iiij carectatis), et cariagio illius, vj*s*.; item in solutis Henrico W*u*rmele pro ij carectatis straminis ordei, xx*d*.; in solutis pro arundine, scilicet watlyng', etiam baston roope, ij*s*. vj*d*.; in uno coopertore conducto pro dicta domo coperiendo in grosso, iiij*s*. vj*d*.; in uno serviente ei pro stramine et copertura trahendis ad supradictum opus, in grosso, iiij*s*. vj*d*.; item in datis eis ad potum, iiij*d*.

NOTA DE FACTURA GRANGIE HENRICI W*u*rMELEY, que vacatur quia melius postea. (d In solutis Johanni Rothewel pro emendacione murorum et tecti grangie ibidem in grosso per xv dies, v*s*.; in vj carectatis cooperture emptis simul cum cariagio, vj*s*. vj*d*.; in (d v) ix carectatis terre rubie propter muros et ad ryggandam dictam grangiam, ix*d*.; in uno coopertore conducto per v dies, ij*s*. j*d*.; et in uno serviente conducto per vj dies, ij*s*.)

Memorandum quod Henricus W*u*rmele de Sutton petit allocacionem (et habet) de elemosinario pro grangia sua. In primis pro ix carectatis terre rubie, ix*d*.; item pro iij carectatis straminis, ij*s*. vj*d*.; et pro cariagio (coperture) de M*o*rcoote usque Sutton factu' [*sic*] per Henricum W*u*rmele et Willelmum Lay, xx*d*.; et pro uno coopertore cum suo serviente conductis per v dies, iiij*s*. j*d*., (vacat).

[*f. 16r*.] *Anno xij domini Ricardi abbatis*.[5]

In solutis pro v carectatis cooperture emptis de Johanne Yvysse de Sutton, iiij*s*. ij*d*.; item in uno coopertore cum suo servitore conductis per vij dies pro domibus Johannis Yvisse coperiendis, iiij*s*. viij*d*.; et

---

[1] *30 May 1453.*   [2] *19 July 1453.*   [3] Left blank.   [4] *1449–50.*
[5] *1449–50.*

in iij carectatis terre rubie, ij*d*.; in solutis pro stramine et ryggyng'
grangie Willelmi Reynolde, viij*d*.; in solutis uno copertori conducto
per ij dies, ubi Johannes D*u*rham, et aliquando Willelmus Haale
manent, vj*d*.; in solutis pro meremio tractato (contra annum futurum)
de aqua ad j domum Roberti Conquest, ij*d*.

Anno xj Ricardi abbatis.[1] In solutis Johanni Ivys pro cariagio trium
carectarum meremii et watlyng' et roope, ij*s*. vj*d*.; item eidem pro
cariagio trium carectarum thac de Botylbrige,[2] ij*s*.; in solutis pro ij
carectatis stipule, xvj*d*.; in solutis eidem pro cariagio petre velute et
terre rubie, vij*s*.; in solutis Willelmo Lay et Henrico W*o*rmele pro
tribus carectatis de B*u*rgo ad Sutton, ij*s*. vj*d*.; item eisdem pro tribus
carectatis de Botilbrige, ij*s*.; item Willelmo Lay pro iiij carectatis petre
velute ad messuagium Henrici W*u*rmele, iiij*d*.

HOSPITALE. In solutis pro ij mille [de] thac cum cariagio illius et alie
cooperture empte xv*s*.; in solutis pro wattlyng' videlicet garbe lv,
ix*d*.; in roope xij bonche, xij*d*. (et remanent 4 bunches); in solutis
(Johanni Pipwel) coopertori per (d v) xij dies pro grangia ibidem cum
stramine cooperienda (et rygg*an*da), v*s*.; item solutis servitoribus pro
coopertura, tractanda et adaquanda Margarete Offecyal per xj dies
et dimidium, ij*s*. x*d*. *ob*.; inde predicta Margareta recepit x*d*. *ob*.; et
elemosinarius stipavit ij*s*. pro redditu aretro; et dicta Margareta debet
in previgilia Pentecostes,[3] de redditu, Johanne Drap*er* teste, iij*s*.; item
in solutis Alicie Stawnton alias Melton per vj dies, xviij*d*.; item Agneti
Morton per iiij dies, xij*d*.; in rewardo dato Johanni Pampe pro labore
suo ibidem, vj*d*.

Anno Ricardi abbatis xij[4] *et xiij Ricardi abbatis.*[5] In v mille [de] thac
de uno de Wytlissey emptis, simul cum cariagio ad hospitale, xxxij*s*.
vj*d*. (Nota precium de uno mille, v*s*. vj*d*.)[6]

ANNO XIIJ.[5] Item in quatuor carectatis de stramine ciliginis emptis
cum cariagio, vj*s*. viij*d*.

ANNO XIIIJ.[7] Item in tribus carectatis straminis ciliginis emptis cum
cariagio. Memorandum quod vastatum est per Johannem Hopkyn (et
per Johannem Pipewel). In solutis pro uno wyndyng' de ferro ponderante ij libras, 4*d*., empto de Willelmo M*er*sche; (d item pro tribus
carectatis straminis ciliginis, anno xiiij Ricardi abbatis;) (vacat hic quia
parens superius, videlicet secunda linia.)

ANNO 15. (dIn vj*c* longhe thac emptis pro veteri aula ibidem, v*s*. vj*d*.;
et in cariagio ad hospitale [8]; item, ad eandem vj*c* thak, v*s*. iiij*d*.;
et in cariagio). [*In margin* postea]

[*f. 16v.*] *Anno domini Ricardi abbatis xij.*[4]

In solutis Roberto Columbyne et T*ome* Tayl*ur* pro quatuor peciis

---

[1] *1448–9*.　　[2] A parish adjoining Orton Longueville, Hunts.　　[3] *22 May 1450*.
[4] *1449–50*.　　　　　　　　　　　　　　　　　　　　　　[5] *1450–1*.
[6] If the price was 5*s*. 6*d*. per 1,000, the thatch cost 27*s*. 6*d*. and the carriage 5*s*.
[7] *1451–2*.　　　　　　　　[8] No space left for figures.

quercinis emptis, vij*s.*; et in solutis pro cariagio de Westewode usque
ad officium, xvj*d.*; item in solutis pro lathys factis videlicet viij*c* dimidio, xiiij*d. ob.*

Solucio pro contribucione de lez O, ad festum Sancti Johannis Baptiste.
In primis fratri Johanni Northorpe (*d* iij*s.* iiij*d.*) vj*s.* viij*d.*; fratri Johanni
Turvey, vj*s.* viij*d.*; fratri Willelmo Morton;[1] (*d* fratri Johanni Baston,
iij*s.* iiij*d.*; item eidem alia vice); fratri T*o*m*e* Gosm*er*kirc [*sic*] (vj*s.* viij*d.*
in capella Sancte Anne); item thesaurario in claustro, iij*s.* iiij*d.*

[IN OFFICIO] (*d* In solutis T*o*m*e* Rowseby pro ij peciis quercinis, una
longitudinis 20 pedum, alia x pedum; et in cariagio de Estwode ad
officium elemosinarii, vij*d.*; et in potu, j*d.*)

BONGAT ET HOSPITALE. In solutis pro v*c* thac emptis ad Stang*ro*nde,
simul cum cariagio, iij*s.*, ad Bolle yaate; item pro cariagio in villa,
iiij*d.*; item eis in potu, j*d.*

CUSTUS IN OFFICIO. In solutis pro iiij fod*ur*s calcis emptis, food*ur* [pro]
xviij*d.*, vj*s.*; et in cariagio, viij*d.*

ROBERTUS STEYNTON. In solutis Roberto Steynton, laboranti in gardino
per xviij dies, capienti in die, ij*d.*, iij*s.*; item eidem Roberto pro labore
in fodiendo et coligendo petras ad muros Sancti Johannis juxta vicariam
Burgi[2] per ij dies, capienti in die, iij*d.*, vj*d.*

JOHANNES RYCHEMAN. In solutis Johanni Rycheman pro iiij lagenis
dimidia vini in festo Petri et Pauli, iij*s.*

NOTA CARECTATAM. In solutis T*o*m*e* Rowsby (ij*s.* vj*d.*) pro ij peciis
quercinis, una longitudinis 22 (xxij) pedum et in circuitu in medio
(pecii) decorticati, sive circulus vel grossitudo ejus in medio iiij pedes
dim'; secunda pecia longitudinis x pedum et grossitudo [*sic*] in medio
et decorticata iiij pedes dim', et in cariagio (scilicet bona carectata) earum
de Estwode, vij*d.*; in potu, j*d.*

NECESSARIA. In solutis Johanni Davy de Stang*ro*nde et socio suo pro
sarracione de iij rood*s* dimidia de tabulis quercinis, roda ad iiij*s.* vj*d.*,
xiiij*s.* vj*d.*; item in solutis supradictis pro sarracione de tabulis fraccinis
cum subscriptis, videlicet (*d* item in solutis predictis pro) legg*s* pro
ostiis faciendis et monyell' pro fenestris, (*d* iij*s.*); item in solutis sepe-
dictis pro una pecia quercina empta de fratre Willelmo Walmysf*ord*[3]
sarranda, de qua pecia post sarracionem vij*xx* pedes habentur in tabulis,
xviij*d.*

[*f. 17r.*] *Anno xij Ricardi abbatis.*[4]

IN OFFICIO. In solutis Willelmo Fyscherr' de Eston pro dimidio mille
[de] sclatt*s* emptis, iij*s.*; item xx*d.* pro viginti grossis sclatt*s.*

[1] No space left for figures.
[2] The earliest vicarage, here referred to, was situated on the east side of Boongate Hook,
now known as the junction of St. John's Street, St. Mary's Street, Granby Street, and Vineyard Road. The adjoining parish chapel of St. John the Baptist evidently served as a quarry
for the almoner, who had allowed the parishioners to pull down the nave of Becket's
chapel, which was under his control, to build the present parish church in the middle of
the Market Place.
[3] L.R.S. xxi. 279–80, 296.   [4] *1449–50.*

Robertus Steynton, secunda vice. In solutis Roberto Steynton laboranti in gardino per xviij dies, iijs.; in solutis pro porrettis et plantacione earum, xd.; in solutis Johanni Rothewel in parte solucionis majoris summe, ijs., Henrico Wurmele portante.

Nota. Frater Willelmus Morton vendidit Willelmo Hauxby de Lynne x petras lane, precium petre xxd., xvjs. viijd.

In Burgo ad caminum. Nota solucionem MM bryc.

In conventu. In solutis Nicholao Smythe pro vino in die Assumpcionis Marie,[1] videlicet:—v lagenis (^{d} et j quarte) et j potell, iijs. viijd.

[Oxney.] In solutis priori ad Nativitatem Beate Marie[2] pro mora sua ad Oxney, xvjs. vjd.

In elemosinaria. In solutis Nicholao fabro pro cura j equi de vivysse,[3] vjd.

Sutton. In solutis, pro iij paribus de heyngl', stoks, ryngys, plats, (ij katt'), et pynnys ferreis, ponderantibus l libras, precium libre, ijd. (ad grangiam de Sutton, ubi Johannes Yvis manet).

Custus in Burgo. In una tabula quercina empta de Willelmo Cowper, viijd. pro ij loversse inde faciendis super Vetus Scaccarium; item in solutis Johanni carpentario cum barba tustata pro factura de loversse supradictis et aliis defectibus ibidem emendandis (scilicet ij trheyscholds), viijd.; in solutis Johanni Elyotte pro ccccc (^{d} mille) de thac, iijs.; (^{d} item in cariagio ejusdem (2 fol' ante) ad Sutton, videlicet vj c et (ad alia loca) iiij c).

Providencia fratris Willelmi Morton elemosinarii ad nundinas Sancti Mathey Apostoli et Ewangeliste.[4]

Anno Ricardi abbatis xij.[5]

In solutis pro ij libris amigdalarum (iardyns), vd.; in dimidia libra piperis empta, vd.; in dimidia libra zinziberi, viijd.; in iiij unciis croci, ijs. iiijd.; in ij unciis clows, iiijd.; in ij unciis macs, iiijd.; in dimidia libra reysyngs, ijd.

In elemosinaria. In garthewebbe pro singulis equinis, videlicet:— xij virgis, vjd.; in ij boltys de sec clothe, viijs. viijd.; in ij[6] skeynys de pacthreede, ijd.; in vj libris candele Parisie, vjd.; in ij mille de walnotts, iijs. iiijd.; in solutis pro ij scaphis emptis, viijd.

In necessariis. (In solutis pro uno siffe, iijd.;) in solutis pro uno cribro, iiijd.; in wody roope (baste sive lyng' roope) emptis pro scafolds ligandis, iiijd.

In Burgo. In (^{d} v) iij mantyll' de meremio faciendis pro (tribus) caminis, unde de empcione altera ij de officio, xiiijd.

[*f. 17v.*] *Anno Ricardi abbatis xiij.*[7]

(Ista materia Johannis Bernerde vacat hic, quia ante in folio x.)[8]

---

[1] *15 Aug.* [2] *8 Sept.*
[3] Glanders. [4] Peterborough Bridge Fair. [5] *1449-50.*
[6] MS. 'vj^{ij}' of which 'vj' has been crossed through. [7] *1450-1.*
[8] This note is written above the first line of the first paragraph: see p. 15.

(^d Johannes Bernerde senior debet pro j quarterio pisarum.) Willelmus
frater ejus debet pro ij quarteriis, (solvit). Willelmus Bernerde filius
vel junior debet pro (^d ix bussellis) (j quarterio) pisarum, (ij*s.*, solvit).
Johannes frater ejus debet pro v bussellis (xiij*d. ob.*). Robertus Samon
debet (v*d. ob.*,) pro ij bussellis. Johannes Pye debet pro vj bussellis,
(solvit). T*omas* Hardy debet pro ij quarteriis, (solvit). Johannes Beylde
de Walton debet (xj*d.*) pro iiij bussellis. Johannes Penel debet (xxij*d.*)
pro j quarterio, (solvit). Johannes Pye debet pro iiij bussellis brasii,
xx*d.*, solvit, ut dicit.

Johannes Drap*er* debet pro viij bussellis siliginis, xvj*d.*, (solvit) (et
debet pro ij bussellis pisarum albarum). Johannes Bernerde junior
[debet pro] ij quarteriis, v*s.* iiij*d.* Robertus Rolston de Paston debet
pro siligine, viij*d.* (solvit).

Willelmus Bernerde (junior) debet pro iiij bussellis siliginis, xvj*d.*
Johannes Bernerde junior debet pro iiij bussellis siliginis, xvj*d.*
Robertus Samon debet pro quatuor bussellis (siliginis), xvj*d.* T*omas*
Derby debet pro j quarterio siliginis, ij*s.* viij*d.*, (solvit). Willelmus
Bernerde debet pro ij quarteriis ij bussellis avene [¹]. T*omas* Smythe
de Ey debet pro ij bussellis siliginis, viij*d.*, (solvit ut dicitur et verum
est²). Ricardus Bryghe de eadem debet pro ij bussellis siliginis, viij*d.*,
(solvit ut dicitur: verum est, 'solvit'³).

T*omas* Boys. In solutis T*ome* Boysse in primis xx*d.* in domo sua; item
ibidem alia vice, iiij*d.* pro jantaculo suo in scriptura compoti; item ij*s.*
in camera sua in abbathia per Johannem Smythe clericum elemosinarie.
Item T*omas* Boysse stipavit (^d ix*d.* de xix) (xviij)*d.* de redditu in Bondegate pro ij annis; item ix*d.* pro eodem redditu de tercio anno.

IN BURGO. In solutis pro ij^c de copertura, cum cariagio, ad cotagium
in Bondegate, ubi Agnes Garlonde et Margareta Offycial manent, xiij*d.*

CUSTUS DOMUUM IN BURGO. In solutis copertori pro labore suo per
iiij dies ibidem, xx*d.*; item eidem copertori, alia vice, per v dies, ubi
supra, (^d iiij) ij*s.*; in solutis servienti (Margarete Ofcyel [per] vij dies
dimidium), ij*s.* iij*d.*

CUSTUS IN BURGO. Item in solutis pro copertura ibidem, cum cariagio
videlicet:—ij^c, xvj*d.*; (^d item in j bonche de bastonrop, j*d.*).

IN NECESSARIIS. Item pro le ryggyng', videlicet iij carectatis terre rubie,
vj*d.*; in solutis pro ij duodenis baston rop, ij*s.*; (^d in calce empto
dimidio fod*ur*, viij*d.*, anno Ricardi abbatis xiiij incipiente; vacat).

In⁴ solutis Willelmo Plowman ad messuagium in Westegate per vj dies,
ij*s.* vj*d.*

[*f. 18r.*] *Anno Ricardi abbatis xiij.*⁵

CUSTUS CAMINI. Item in solutis pro viij carectatis terre rubie ad
caminum, xx*d.*; item in aliis locis (vj carectatis terre rubie, xv*d.*); item

---

¹ Left blank.   ² Repeated thrice.   ³ Repeated four times.
⁴ At foot of folio upside down.   ⁵ *1450-1.*

pro cariagio zabuli, videlicet iiij carectatis calcis, ij carectatis meremii propter scafolds, hyrdl', tabulas et aliis necessariis illuc, xv*d.*; in solutis Johanni Browny pro zabulo fodiendo et cribrando per ij dies, viij*d.*; in solutis fratri Johanni Bronham pro uno webbe plumbi ponderante viij petras et dimidiam, precium petre ix*d. ob.*, vjs. vj*d.*; item in iij libris reedyng' pro colore ad caminum, iij*d.*

Willelmus Bernerde senior debet pro ij quarteriis pisarum, iij*s.* viij*d.*, (solvit per Johannem Pye); j quarterio ciliginis, 32*d.* (negat); Willelmus Bernerde junior debet pro j quarterio pisarum, ij*s.*, (solvit); iiij bussellis siliginis, xvj*d.*, (solvit).

Item Willelmus Bernerde senior vel junior debet pro ij quarteriis ij bussellis avenarum.

Johannes Bernerde junior debet pro v bussellis pisarum, xiij*d. ob.*; item pro iiij (viij) bussellis siliginis, xvj*d.* (xxxij*d.*)[1]

Nota. Johannes Beylde de Walton debet pro iiij bussellis pisarum, xj*d.* Item debet pro ciligine, videlicet iiij bussellis, 16*d.* T*omas* Beylde de eadem et Johannes Crosse debent pro stramine et paleo, vij*s.* (sol' sacrist'). Robertus Samon debet pro ij bussellis pisarum, v*d. ob.* (solvit T*ome* Maxe, sacriste). Item pro iiij bussellis siliginis, xvj*d.*; Johannes Pye debet pro vj bussellis pisarum [   ]; item pro iiij bussellis brasii, xx*d.*; solvit ut dicit. T*omas* Hardy debet pro ij quarteriis pisarum; solvit ut dicit. Johannes Penel debet pro j quarterio pisarum, xxij*d.* (solvit sacriste Maxey); idem debet pro j carectata straminis ordei, vj*d.*; (solvit). Robertus Rolston debet pro ij bussellis siliginis, viij*d.*; (solvit).

Paston. T*omas* Derby debet pro j quarterio siliginis, ij*s.* viij*d.*; item xviij*d.* pro tribus acris terre; Johannes Bernerde de Paston debet pro (di)j quarteriis (ciliginis) (d v*s.* iiij*d.*) xxxij*d.*, (di)j quarteriis avenarum, 40*d.* (xx*d.*).

Focale venditum. Elemosinarius vendidit Ricardo Hatle j carectatam focalis pro (d ij*s.*) xx*d.*; item Johanni M*er*che scissori iij carectatas focalis pro vj*s.*; dies solucionis Natale et Pascha.

In Burgo. In emendacione j hostii et darn*s*, ubi Johannes Gryssle manet, 4*d.* Memorandum cla' [*sic*]. Elemosinarius vendidit Johanni B*ur*gesse iiij (dimidia) eskeppas brasii pro xx*d.*

Necessaria. In solutis pro viij^c grossis spyk*s* emptis de Johanne fabro de Denby [*sic*], iij*s.* iiij*d.*; mydylspyk*s* vj^c, ij*s.*; stowryng vel splentyng' nayle vj^c, xv*d.*; clowtenal' vj^c, xij*d.*; lathenal' iiij mille, iij*s.*

Chyppis vendite. In receptis pro l lepfulle de chyppys sive de ij carectatis quisquiliarum venditis Johanni Smythe de Yaxle, iiij*s.* ij*d.*

[*f. 18v.*] *Anno Ricardi abbatis xiij incipiente.*[2]

Recepta frumenti apud Gonthorp. Prima vice propter diem Animarum iiij quarteria; item j quarterium vj eskeppe; item ij quarteria

---

[1] Above the line.   [2] *1450–1.*

iij eskeppe—Totalis summa frumenti recepti viij quarteria j eskeppa, (inde Johanni trituratori 4 eskeppe, et Johanni B*ur*gesse j eskeppa).

RECEPTA CILIGINIS. In primis recepi v quarteria de quibus vj eskeppe; item iiij quarteria, v eskeppe. Summa totalis ciliginis recepte x quarteria iij eskeppe.

RECEPTA ORDEI. In primis xij quarteria (*d* deliberatum Roberto Orwyn j quarterium) (vacat); item viij quarteria iiij eskeppe (vacat); item xx quarteria (vacat); item vj quarteria (vacat), iiij eskeppe (vacat). Summa recepta ad Annunciacionem Beate Marie[1] lviij quarteria, j bussellus caret.

Summa totalis ordei recepti, octoginta iij quarteria iiij eskeppe.

RECEPTA AVENARUM. Prima vice vij eskeppe; item iij quarteria j eskeppa. Summa totalis recepta, iiij quarteria.

RECEPTA PISARUM. In primis per T*omam* Havme, j quarterium; per Robertum Wryhete, iij[2] quarteria; per Johannem Pye, iij eskeppe; item xj quarteria vj eskeppe. Summa totalis recepta, xxvij quarteria, videlicet viij eskeppe strykyd pro quarterio.

Memorandum quod Johannes Beylde triturator trituravit in toto iij[xx] xv quarteria 4 eskeppas, videlicet de simplice mensura, scilicet 8 eskeppas strikyd pro quarterio; tamen nota quod verum pactum sive convencio est xxij quarteria pro xx quarteriis, precium ad quarterium trituratum, ij*d. ob. q.* Summa de plena mensura scilicet xxij quarteria pro viginti quarteriis ad tascam, lxviij quarteria iiij eskeppe; in solutis pro lxviij quarteriis 4 eskeppis, xv*s.* viij*d.*

Item memorandum quod Johannes Burgesse trituravit lvij quarteria iiij eskeppas de simplice mensura; et in solutis pro lij quarteriis iiij eskeppis per mensuram xxij quarteria pro viginti, xij*s. ob.*

In[3] solutis Johanni Beylde et Johanni Burgesse trituratoribus decime ad Gonthorp; in primis Johanni Beyl, vj*s.* et j supra; ut in iiij bussellis et dimidio (brasii) precii xx*d.*; item iij*s.* iiij*d.*; item vj*d.*; item Johanni Beyl iiij eskeppe ciliginis, precii xxij*d.*; Johanni Burges iiij*s.* vj*d.*; item Johanni Beyl, xiiij*d.*; item ij*s.* j*d.*; item eidem Johanni Beylde iij eskeppe pisarum, precii xj*d.*; nota quod Johannes Beylde recepit modo, xij*s.*; item Johannes Beyl, xx*d.*; item Johannes Beylde, ij*s.*

[*f. 19r.*] *Anno Ricardi abbatis xiij.*[4]

CUSTUS CAMINI. In solutis Roberto Doutte (alias Grey) de Tyryngton,[5] et Waltero collectori pro factura de ij caminis novis super Chapel Row, xxv*s.*; et in datis eis (et famulo suo) pro rewardo in se, xij*d.*; item in solutis pro factura unius fenestre (ibidem) Johanni carpentario cum barba tustata, vj*d.*; et in j pari henglis et stok*s* cum j snac et latche, iiij*d.*

SOORELLE. In solutis pro cura unius equi de vyvisse, vj*d.* Et nota

---

[1] *25 Mar. 1451.*   [2] One i marked for deletion.
[3] This paragraph at the foot of the folio is written upside down.
[4] *1450–1.*   [5] Terrington in Norfolk.

[quod] Nicholaus faber ad Barnax crosse warantizavit¹ quod equus nunquam haberet illam infirmitatem postea sub pena unius nobilis.

DE ALIIS CAMINIS. In solutis supradictis latamis pro ij caminis emendatis, ubi Johannes Waldyng' [manet], et aliis defectibus ibidem per [ ] dies, iiij*s*.

IN FORINCESIS. In decimis² solutis domino regi, iiij*li*. xiij*s*. iiij*d*.; in solutis pro generali capitulo,³ videlicet j*d*. ad merke, xvij*s*. vj*d*.

FRUMENTUM DELIBERATUM. In primis Johanni Draper (pro Johanne heremita⁴) j eskeppa; Johanni Roper, dimidia eskeppa; Agneti Morton, j eskeppa, (ix*d*.); item Johanni Burgesse, j eskeppa; item Johanni Beylde juniori iiij eskeppe ex mituo, (solvit).

CILIGO DELIBERATA. In primis Roberto Orwyn ij quarteria, vj*s*.; Johanni Draper iiij eskeppe, xx*d*.; Johanni Roper dimidia eskeppa; Agneti Morton dimidia eskeppa, (ij*d*. *ob*.); iiij eskeppe Johanni Penel (pro sacrista); Johanni Pye (pro sacrista) ij eskeppe; Willelmo Trett' (patri) iiij eskeppe, (xxij*d*.); et Willelmo (filio) iiij eskeppe, (xxij*d*.), solucio midlenton.

Johanni Beyld vel Wryte iiij eskeppe, xxij*d*., (solvit); Ricardo Sylk iiij eskeppe, xxij*d*.; Agneti Morton dimidia eskeppa, iij*d*.; T*ome* Hardy j quarterium, iiij*s*.

AVENE deliberate propter farinam faciendam v eskeppe; item in prebenda equorum, ij busselli; j bussellus; item Emme Tylar j quarterium, xx*d*.; (solvit) duodecima die post Natale.

PISE deliberate Roberto Orwyn, iiij eskeppe, xiiij*d*.; T*ome* Hawme, j quarterium; Roberto Wryhte, ij quarteria, [ ]; Johanni Pye, iiij eskeppe, (non solvit); domino Abbati, iiij quarteria iiij busselli, precium quarterii, ij*s*. ij*d*.; T*ome* Edows, ij quarteria, precium 4*s*. 8*d*.; Nicholao Smythe iiij eskeppe, xiiij*d*. (solvit); Willelmo Bernerde juniori, v eskeppe, xviij*d*., (solvit); item domino T*ome* Maxey, iiij quarteria iiij busselli, precium de j quarterio, ij*s*. iiij*d*.; Johanni Crosse, 4 busselli (solvit); item G. Rog', j quarterium, ij*s*. iiij*d*., (solvit); item Johanni Burges, j bussellus; Ricardo Eston j bussellus; Johanni Wryhte, 3 busselli; item uxori Roberti Rycheman, [⁵]. Summa xxvij quarteria j eskeppa pisarum.

ORDEI. Agneti Draper, ij eskeppe, precium vij*d*.

¹ Nicholas the blacksmith of Barnard Cross, which was situated at the junction of Long Causeway and Westgate, acting as a horse-doctor, not only cured one of the almoner's horses of the glanders, but warranted a complete cure, with a penalty of one noble.
² Tenths payable to the King from the almoner's fee.
³ A levy of one penny per mark of income, paid by the almoner towards expenses, at a general chapter of the Benedictine Monks.
⁴ Probably the hermit who had a cell adjoining the chapel of St. Mary Magdalene or the Park Kirk at Newark. (See Book of Roger Bird, f. 20—a charter by which the abbot Richard Ashton granted to John Scenefield a site for the building of a hermitage there, dated 12 Jan. 1446/7.)
⁵ Left blank.

[*f. 19v.*] *Anno Ricardi abbatis xiij.*[1]

Johannes Baly, serviens elemosinarii recepit de elemosinario pro stipendio suo in vigilia Omnium Sanctorum,[2] iij*s.*; (item ij carectatas de chyppys, iiij*s.* ij*d.*); (*d* item alia vice). Memorandum quod totum sive plenum stipendium istius Johannis supradicti fuisset (per annum integrum), xiij*s.* iiij*d.*; item una toga precii vj*s.* viij*d.* Item quoad victualia habuisset panem sicut clerici in subelemosinaria, potum sicut familia in aula abbatis; item j quarterium frumenti, j quarterium ciliginis, j quarterium ordei, j quarterium pisarum, et ij eskeppas avenarum. Notandum quod Johannes supradictus incipiebat servire ad festum Sancte Marie Magdalene[3] et (causa minucionis) recessit in die Animarum,[4] tamen postea reveniebat in crastino Sancti Edmundi regis et martiris[5] ad satisfaciendum quod deliquid [*sic*]. Idem serviens recepit, vj*d.*; item in vigilia Sancti Andree,[6] viij*d.*; item iiij*d.*

Johannes Estaze famulus elemosinarii recepit de magistro suo ut in uno pari ocrearum (in vigilia Omnium Sanctorum),[7] xvj*d.*; item viij*d.*; item viij. (ad caligas emendas); item iiij*d.* calcaria (sp*o*rris, Anglice). Memorandum quod elemosinarius dedit predicto Johanni Estasse unum pullum equinum; item j sistam, precii xviij*d.*; item vj*d.*, Sabbato post festum Martini;[8] item in vigilia Sancti Andree, ij*d.*;[9] item viij*d.* eodem die; item vj*d.* in die Sancti Damasi;[10] item in crastino Sancti Thome apostoli,[11] ij*d.*; item ij*d.* ad casium emendum; item in die Nativitatis domini[12] iiij*d.*; item xij*d.*, in vigilia Circumcisionis,[13] ad emendum pannum nigrum; item ij*d.*; item iiij*d.*; item iiij*d.*; iiij*d.*; item xij*d.* propter ij camisias emendas; item xij*d.* propter femoralia et alia emenda; item xij*d.*; item iiij*d.*; item viij*d.* (transeundo) ad Wermyngton; item iiij*d.*; vj*d.*; item xvj*d.*, propter caligas et sotulares emendas; et Johanni Roper patri ejus ij*d.*, ex dono; item ij*s.* iiij*d.* transeundo ad Stanford; item in j ulna linie tele empta ad Stanford, iij*d.*; item iiij*d.*; item j*d.*; item xij*d.*, transeundo ad patrem et matrem; item ad Stanford xij*d.* ad emendum j dagarrum; et in datis eidem, iiij*d.*; item in liberatis ei vj*d.*; item xij*d.*, propter sotulares. Assencio; item xij*d.* in festo Pentecostes[14], ad j dowbelet; in vigilia Trinitatis,[15] vj*d.*; item ij*d.*; ij*d.*; ij*d.*; (*d* xij*d.*); propter caligas emendas, xvj*d.*; item iiij*d.* in vigilia Advincule Sancti Petri;[16] item in vigilia Assumpcionis,[17] iiij*d.*; item vj*d.*, pro ocriis pedulandis; item iiij*d.*; item ij*d.*; item vj*d.*, propter caligas; item ad unam vaginam emendam cum aliis, iiij*d.*;[18] item vj*d.* propter sotulares; item j*d.*; j*d.*; item in recessu suo, xij*d.*; item unum pullum ex dono, precii iij*s.*

Anno[19] *Ricardi abbatis xiij et in die Sancti Leonardi*[20] omnibus computatis Agnes Morton debet domino Willelmo Morton elemosinario, vij*s.*; item ij vitulos vocatos brennyng*s*; item pro redditu; item pro una

[1] *1450–1.* [2] *31 Oct. 1450.* [3] *22 July.* [4] *2 Nov.*
[5] *21 Nov.* [6] *29 Nov.* [7] *31 Oct.* [8] *14 Nov. 1450.*
[9] *29 Nov.* [10] *11 Dec.* [11] *22 Dec.*
[12] *25 Dec.* [13] *31 Dec.* [14] *13 June.*
[15] *19 June.* [16] *31 July.* [17] *14 August.*
[18] The total sum is expressed here in dot-notation as £1. 6*s.* 2*d.*
[19] At foot of folio upside down and afterwards deleted. [20] *6 Nov. 1450.*

carectata focalis cum cariagio de capella Sancte Marie Magdalene,[1]
xvj*d*.; item iiij*d*., ex mituo; item xij*d*.; item in Vigilia Trinitatis,[2]
xij*d*.; xij*d*.; xij*d*.; item ad vel propter anniversarium Roberti Morton,[3]
iiij*s*. x*d*.

[*f. 20r*.] [SUTTON]. Memorandum quod Johannes Eyr' solvit (elemosinario) xiij*s*. iiij*d*., in Sabbato ante Purificacionem,[4] de redditu de
Sutton, de anno xij Ricardi abbatis; item ([d] xj*s*. x*d*.) ix*s*., de tenemento
in Merham; item vj*s*. viij*d*.; item xvj*s*., in presencia Johannis Yvis;
item xx*s*., per Johannem filium Johannis Eyre.

SUTTON. Memorandum quod Johannes Yvis solvit per reparacionem
factam in anno Ricardi abbatis xij ix*s*., ut patet in principio quarti
folii ante.

([d] Memorandum de cariagio T*ome* Prio*ur*.) Quere plus in folio quintodecimo sequenti ad tale signum ☉.··

In vij quarteriis calcis emptis, j quarterio cum cariagio, viij*d*., iiij*s*. vj*d*.
pro aula ([d] grangie) manerii de Sutton; in solutis Johanni Warde pro
dimidia roda de novo coperienda, ij*s*. iij*d*.; item in solutis eidem
Johanni pro tribus rodis et iij quarteriis rode pictandis, v*s*.; in lathepynn*s* emptis, vij*d*.

INFIRMARIA. Anno Ricardi abbatis xiij, in vigilia Natalis Domini,[5]
frater Willelmus Morton elemosinarius solvit fratri Johanni Burneham
xx*s*. in aula minucionis, et in presencia prioris.

SUBELEMOSINARIA. Elemosinarius solvit subelemosinario in eadem
vigilia[5] iij*s*. iiij*d*. pro anno precedente.[6]

RECEPTA. Memorandum quod Emma, uxor Willelmi Brasyar' de
Wysbeche, solvit domino Willelmo Morton elemosinario, in Sabbato
ante Purificacionem Beate Marie,[7] anno Ricardi abbatis xiij, xx*s*. pro
brasio; et modo debent [*sic*] elemosinario xxvij*s*., (solvit).

SOLUCIO. In solutis fratri Willelmo Leycet*ur* pro officio crucis,[8] x*d*.;
item xvj*d*.

INFIRMARIA. In solutis T*ome* Rowceby, in dominica Sexagesime,[9] pro
fratre Johanne Burnham, infirmario, ix*s*., in aula minucionis, et in
presencia domini R*icardi* Oxford[10] et Petri servientis ibidem.

INFIRMARIA. Item in solutis fratri Johanni Burnham, infirmario[11] pro
secundo quarterio, xxix*s*. ad Oxney.

SUBELEMOSINARIA. In solutis fratri Willelmo Gretford,[12] ad ostium
coquine conventus, in medio Quadragesime anno xiij,[13] v*s*. de anno

[1] In Newark.   [2] *19 June*.   [3] See note, p. 25 above.
[4] *31 Jan. 1449/50*.   [5] *24 Dec. 1450*.
[6] On account of his stipend for the year 1449–50.   [7] *30 Jan. 1450/1*.
[8] Probably warden of the altar of Holy Cross. He was also sub-sacrist. See f. 20*v*.
[9] *28 Feb. 1450/1*.
[10] Cf. above, p. 26, n. 6.
[11] Ibid., p. 278; formerly cellarer on the part of the abbot, in 1437.
[12] Ibid., p. 279. In 1437 a monk in deacon's orders.
[13] *4 Apr. 1451*.

Ricardi abbatis xij;[1] item ebdomada Pasche, vjs. viijd. (Nota cum favore de ijs. vjd.)

In solutis Willelmo Plowman pro emendacione unius lover super Raton row, iiijd.; in solutis Regi pro medio decime sibi concesse per clerum Cantuariensem, xlvjs. vijd. q.; in solutis Johanni Wryhette pro factura j haache pro gardino in officio, simul cum emendacione unius speyrr'[2] juxta [domum] Johannis Waldyng', vjd.; in solutis Willelmo Plowman [3]; in solutis pro x[c] rubie tyle vel bryc emptis de Johanne Palle, vijs.; item in cariagio ejusdem de Boyl yaate [sic] ad officium, [3].

SOLUCIO SORORIBUS IN CAPELLA SANCTI TOME. Memorandum quod anno Ricardi abbatis xiij elemosinarius solvit vij sororibus capelle, et servienti earundem, (ad Pascha),[4] xiijs. iiijd., pro anno xij° precedente. Memorandum quod elemosinarius debet modo residuum; item, alia vice, xiiijs. viijd., et quietus est elemosinarius pro anno xij° Ricardi abbatis. Idem elemosinarius solvit alia vice predictis sororibus et ancille earundem, pro anno xiij° Ricardi abbatis, xijs.; inde plenius in xij° folio sequente.

Anno[5] Ricardi abbatis xiij ad Natale domini, omnibus computatis, Henricus Palmer (debet) elemosinario, vs.; item iijs. iiijd., pro uno hostio.

[f. 20v.] ([d] EXPENSA. Tome Haame et Johanni Palle prima vice versus Wysbeche, xxd.; secunda vice Tome Haame, transeundo et redeundo, xiijd.; tercia vice Johanni Smythe, transeundo et redeundo illuc, xiiijd.; quarta vice Tome Haame, transeundo et redeundo, ijs. viijd.; quinta vice idem [sic] Tome Haame, xixd.; sexta vice domino Willelmo Morton, transeundo feria sexta (et Sabbato) ante Rogaciones,[6] simul cum rewardo ductoris ad Wysbeche, ijs.; et in expensis factis super Willelmum Brasiar et uxorem ejus (prima vice 8d.) propter etc.; item predictis supervenientibus in Nativitate Beate Marie,[7] ad vinum, iiijd.; septima vice predicto elemosinario domino Willelmo Morton transeundo et equitando feria sexta ante festum Michaelis[8] ad Wysbeche, ijs.; et ad Welle,[9] xijd.

Memorandum quod Johannes ([d] Korner) Corner et Johannes Hacbyche de Wysbeche, fidejussores Ricardi Lombe, solverunt et satisfecerunt, ut patet in folio xiiij° sequente, videlicet, per xlviij quarteria avenarum, recepta per fratrem Willelmum Morton.

BURNEHAM. Memorandum quod frater Willelmus Morton elemosinarius solvit in die Pasche, anno Ricardi abbatis xiiij°,[10] pro ultimo quarterio elapso, xiiijs. vjd., in parte solucionis de xxixs., fratri Johanni Burneham, infirmario; item in presencia.)

In[11] vino empto de fratre Willelmo Leycetur, subsacrista pro conventu, in die Pasche, anno xiiij° Ricardi abbatis,[10] videlicet iij lagenis, j potelle, j quarte, et j pynte, iijs. iijd.; (solvit).

WILLELMUS MERKAM. Memorandum quod frater Willelmus Morton, anno xiiij Ricardi abbatis, in die Sancti Geordii,[1] solvit gardiano de Oxney, iijs.; item, anno Ricardi abbatis xiiij⁰ in Octabis Sancti Laurencii,[2] iijs. iiijd.; item in vigilia Nativitatis Beate Marie,[3] iijs. iiijd. Anno Ricardi abbatis xv⁰, sexto Kal. Decembris,[4] idem frater Willelmus Merkam recepit de elemosinario, per manus fratris Ricardi Stanford, iijs., ijs., xs., per vices. Idem elemosinarius solvit xiijs. iiijd. dicto domino Willelmo Merkam ([d] per stupacionem pro Willelmo) in Nativitate domini.[5] Summa soluta dicto gardiano cjs. viijd. Idem recepit de elemosinario, anno xv, ut in precio de xxxvij quarteriis et dimidio quarterii et uno pekke brasii, vjli. vs. jd.; item xxs. anno xvj⁰ [6] pro officio infirmarie, de anno xv⁰. ([d] Summa soluta, xxxvijs.)

([d] Anno[7] Ricardi abbatis xiij⁰ in ([d] previgilia) Annunciacione Sancte Marie,[8] omnibus computatis, frater Willelmus Morton, elemosinarius, debet fratri Willelmo Merkam, gardiano de Oxney, pro communibus ibidem, 13s. [?], item 6s., pro officio thesaurarii.)

[*f. 21r.*] (Furnitur[9] ij eskeppe in die Sancti Albani[10] in panes, xlij, quelibet ponderans iij libras.)

Solucio pro tunicis per elemosinarium de anno Ricardi Abbatis xij⁰.[11]

In primis fratri Johanni Turuey, xs., (solvit); fratri Johanni Northop, vs., (solvit); fratri Johanni Moour, vs., (solvit); fratri Willelmo Morton, elemosinario, xs.; fratri Johanni Pychele,[12] xs., (solvit); et memorandum quod frater Ricardus Harlleton, thesaurarius, habet vjs. viijd., de cameraria fratris Willelmi Morton, et sic satisfactus est pro hac solucione.

SOLUCIO PRO SPECIEBUS POST NATALE DOMINI, ANNO RICARDI ABBATIS XIIJ⁰.[13]

In primis fratri Johanni Turvey, vs.; item ijs.; item [[14]]; item xvjd.; et equet; fratri Johanni Bernak,[15] vs.; item vs., in presencia Alicie Lowthe et Willelmi Austorp; fratri Ricardo Stanford, vjs. viijd. et fratri Ricardo Harleston[16] (seniori), iijs. iiijd., (solvit, famulo suo teste); fratri Johanni Northop, vs.; item ijs.; item iijs., ad ostium claustri; fratri Willelmo Morton, xs.; fratri Willelmo Walmisford,[17] vjs. viijd.; item xijd. (pro Johanne Browny nativo domini abbatis); item ijs. iiijd.; fratri Tome Gosberkyrc,[18] vs., in presencia prioris; item vs., in camera Gosberkirke ad noctem, et equet; fratri Willelmo Ufforde, xs., in vigilia Pentecostes,[19] (solvit,) et equet; fratri Willelmo Gretteford,[20] xs.; fratri Willelmo Depyng', vs.; item ijs.; item xvjd.; item xxd., et equet.

[1] *23 Apr. 1452.* [2] *17 Aug. 1452.* [3] *7 Sept. 1452.*
[4] *26 Nov. 1452.* [5] *25 Dec. 1452.* [6] *1453-4.*
[7] At foot of f. 20v. upside down. [8] *25 Mar. 1450/1.*
[9] This note was inserted at the head of the folio, above the first line.
[10] *22 June.* [11] *1449-50.* [12] L.R.S. xxi. 293 n.
[13] *1450.* [14] Left blank.
[15] L.R.S. xxi. 280 n., 282, 284, 286, 296.
[16] Formerly prior. [17] L.R.S. xxi. 279-80, 296.
[18] Ibid. 291-6. Gosberton, Lincs.
[19] *12 June 1451.* [20] L.R.S. xxi. 279-80, 284, 295.

Anno Ricardi abbatis xiij⁰.[1]

Memorandum quod frater Willelmus Morton elemosinarius stupavit penes Johannem Martyn, balivum Burgi, vijs. iiijd., propter debitum domini abbatis, penes dictum fratrem Willelmum Morton elemosinarium, statim post Purificacionem.[2]

In solutis pro iij virgis (dimidia) nigri panni, pro una tunica fibulata, iijs.; item in lineo panno ad eandem, jd.; et in solutis Johanni Granger, pro factura ejusdem, viijd., quia cum dowbyllynyng vel iij folds.

SUTTON. In solutis pro heynglys et stoks, ubi Johannes Royewel [sic] et Johannes Yvysse manent, ponderantibus vj libras dimidiam, xiijd.

NECESSARIE. In una heryng barelle empta propter sowsyng' de brawne, viijd.; in vasis circulandis, videlicet j cowle et j bolle; in uno brenlet sive tripode (d ponderante) iiijd.

FORINCECE EXPENSE. In expensis elemosinarii ad privandum vicarium de Maxey de beneficio suo prima vice ad Depyng' et Stanfordiam, ijs., videlicet feria v post festum Sancti Gregorii Pape, scilicet xv Kal. Aprilis[3] anno domini mcccclj; item in victualibus (et vino) pro magistro Ricardo Dyklyng', magistro W. Rave et feno et prebenda pro equis suis in villa, xxd.; item in expensis vini feni et prebende equorum supradicti magistri Ricardi redeundo [sic] de Londoniis, xvjd. Verte folium ad tale signum ◎[4]

[*f. 21v.*] *Anno domini Ricardi Abbatis xiij.*[1]

In solutis pro mille de potyng' thac emptis de Willelmo Plowman, vjs., et in cariagio ad hospitale et ad alia loca, xvd.

Memorandum quod omnibus computatis inter Johannem Smythe de Wodcroft et elemosinarium in ij⁰ Sabbato Quadragesime[5] predictus Johannes debet xijd.

Item in solutis Willelmo Plowman pro mille garbis cooperture, vs. viijd.; in cariagio [6   ].

In solutis Tome coco pro ebdomada Sexagessime pro victualibus emptis, iiijs. ijd. ob.; item in victualibus emptis per elemosinarium pro ebdomada supradicta cum (d ebdomada) dominica Quinquagesime, ijs. vd.; item in solutis Tome coco pro victualibus in minucione prime ebdomade Quadragesime, (solvit.)

[THE DEPRIVATION OF THE VICAR OF MAXEY (CONT.)]◎

In solutis pro vino dulci misso domino Ricardo Dyklun usque Depyng', vjd.; item in solutis predicto domino Ricardo pro adquisicione instrumenti iiij notariorum, simul cum rewardo Johanni Dyklon, ijs. viijd., ad consistarium Stanfordie; item in solutis [6   ] magistro (Ricardo) Myl' (d doctori) in decretis et uno alio cum eo, equitantibus ad Lyncolniam pro j sitacione optinenda ad sitandum vicarium de Maxey comparere

---

[1] *1450–1.*   [2] *2 Feb. 1450/1.*   [3] *18 Mar. 1451.*
[4] See below as to the further expenses incurred in the proceedings for the deprivation of the vicar of Maxey, where the special sign ◎ appears; see also p. 58. At the bottom right-hand corner the figure 5 in dot-notation appears followed by s', i.e. 5s.
[5] *20 Mar. 1450/1.*   [6] Blank.

coram vicario generali Lincoln*ie* respondere ibidem coram eo super diversis defectibus, iij*s.* vij*d.*; item in datis vicario Burgi uno notorio- rum ibidem pro suo consilio,[1] iiij*d.*, et iij eskeppe (prebende); item in datis magistro Willelmo Raffe, pro suo consilio, xij*d.*; in expensis elemosinarii, cum ij servientibus, equitantis ad Stanfordiam, pro materiis contra dominum T*homam* Bakon, vicarium de Maxey, in con- sistario Stanford', feriis iiij[a] et v ante dominicam Palmarum, anno Ricardi Abbatis xiij°,[2] ij*s.* vj*d.*, quia per ij dies ibidem exspectantes; item in datis magistro Johanni Bunghe et magistro [   ] Tyssington, ij*s.* iiij*d.*; in vino dato magistro Ricardo Dyklon in presencia domini abbatis, v*d.*; et in solutis pro feno et prebenda equorum, j*d. ob.*; item in solutis vicario de Depyng pro summonicione vicarii de Maxey ad compariendum coram vicario generali ecclesie Lincolniensis, et pro uno certificato illuc de summonicione predicta, iiij*d.*

Expense elemosinarii ([d] equitantis) cum domino Ricardo Dyklun et vicario de E*st* Depyng, equitantis versus Lincolniam et redeundo, propter materiam vicarii de Maxey, per iij dies, xxiiij*s.* vj*d. ob.*; (memorandum de commissione et sitacione optentis); in datis vicario Burgi ([d] pro sitacione) ad sitandum vicarium de Maxey et certificato, iiij*d.*; in datis vicario de E*st* Depyng et Ricardo Undyrwode capellano subito supervenientes [*sic*], vij*d.* ad vinum et victualia.

[*Footnote*][3] Pravo per chorum qui post versum legit istum. Pravo per Cristum, qui post versum legerit istum. Versum [*sic*] deo istum reci- tanti Criste capistrum. [*in dot notation*: £1. 6*s.* 3*d.*]

[*f. 22r.*] *Anno Ricardi abbatis xiij°.*

[DEPRIVATION OF THE VICAR OF MAXEY (CONT.)]

Item in datis fratri Rogero Sothworth, ordinis minorum, propter laborar', ad declarandum in curia Pape, videlicet verba in confirmacione sive dotacione vicarii de Maxey. Et vicarius sustinebit omnia onera illius ecclesie debita et consueta, viij*d.*; in solutis vicario Burgi propter procuracionem script' ad mittendum curie Romane, vj*d.*

Con[si]starium apud Stanf*ordiam*, iiij° et tercio Idus May.[4] In solutis Rogero Jorden scriptori, anglice scribe, propter multa facienda, xx*d.*; in vino dato domino Ricardo Dyklun, iiij*d.*; in datis magistro Willelmo Rathe, xij*d.*; item in victualibus primo et secundo die, simul cum vino pro elemosinario et aliis supervenientibus, et prebenda pro equis, iij*s.* ij*d.* Alia vice in vino, servisia, magistro Ricardo Dyklun superveniente,

---

[1] His name was John Hare. For the names of other notaries engaged in these and other proceedings see Roger Bird, f. 61, 20 Sept. 1463—the appointment by the abbot Richard of Ashton as proxies jointly and severally of William Rathe, bachelor of laws, John Hare, John Prutwell, and Thomas Upex, notaries public, John Hamerton, chaplain, Thomas Newthorpe and John Rawlyn, laymen of the diocese of Lincoln, to appear before the arch- deacon of Northampton at his visitation, or before any commissary or official principal in the absence of the abbot, bearing his excuses and in his stead.

[2] *14 and 15 Apr. 1451.*

[3] This is a note at the foot of the folio of the MS. See above, pp. xliii, 5.

[4] *12 and 13 May 1451.*

x*d*.; et in pane pro equis suis, j*d*.; in vino misso supradicto magistro Ricardo cum magistro Willelmo Rathe, v*d*.; iterum in solutis Rogero Jorden adveniente usque Depyng' et pro una sitacione ad instanciam domini abbatis et conventus Burgi scripta, xx*d*.; in datis diversis latamis magistri Ricardi Dyklun, iiij*d*. et in expensis equorum, viij*d*.; item in carnibus ovinis ad cenam, ij*d*.; item in solutis pro procurasia [*sic*] script' per dominum Ricardum Und*ur*wode, et missa London*ias* per eundem dominum Ricardum, iij*s*. viij*d*.; (nota quod non deliberavit, ut magister J. Lorde dicit); item in servisia eidem revenienti de London*iis*, j*d*. *ob*. et in j quarte vini, iij*d*., missa magistro Ricardo Dyklun.

CONCISTORIUM APUD STANFOR*DIAM* VJ IDUS JUNII.[1]

In expensis elemosinarii ibidem per ij dies, in victualibus pro homini-bus et prebenda equorum, xxj*d*.; in rewardo magistro Willelmo Rathe, xvj*d*.; in consimili dato magistro Johanni Paynyll' pro renovacione instrumenti notarii, ij*s*.; in datis domino Ricardo Und*ur*wode, vj*d*.; item domino Ricardo Dyclon sedenti cum vicario[2] Burgi et aliis ad cenam, iiij*d*.; item magistro Rogero Jorden, xij*d*.; item in servisia ij*d*.; item, feria ij Pentecostes,[3] in datis vicario Burgi propter quandam citacionem, cum certificacione, de novo factam, iiij*d*.; item in solutis pro prebenda equorum magistri Ricardi Dyklun, equitantis, secunda vice, London*ias* in vigilia Trinitatis,[4] ij*d*. *ob*.; item in uno potelle vini dato eidem magistro Ricardo revenienti de London*iis* per manus vicarii Burgi, v*d*.; item in solutis vicario Burgi pro una litera missa magistro Ricardo Reynyll, xj*d*. [   ]; item in expensis elemosinarii equitantis ad Stan*ford* et Uffyngton, ij*d*.

CONCISTORIUM IBIDEM IN CRASTINO[5] SANCTI TOME MARTIRIS.[6]

In expensis elemosinarii per duos dies ibidem, ij*s*. iiij*d*.; in vino (propter hospi), xiij*d*.; in pane pro equis, ij*d*.; in feno, iiij*d*.; in rewardis [datis] magistris Willelmo Rathe, xx*d*.; Johanni Paynyll, ij*s*.; Rogero Jorden, xij*d*.; in vino dato magistro Johanni Tyssyngton supervenienti, per manus vicarii Burgi, iiij*d*.; in solutis Willelmo Norton [*sic*], pro una procuracia scripta, ij*d*. Quere plus de ista materia in vj*to* folio sequente ad tale signum ⊕.[7] [*In dot notation*: £2. 6*s*. 3*d*.]

[*f. 22v.*] *Anno Ricardi abbatis xiij°.*[8]

JOHANNES CARPENTARIUS. Idem Johannes carpentarius solvit ut in factura unius hache et emendacione unius sp*err*' vel schrene juxta Henricum Palm*er* per unum diem, v*d*. (Idem solvit per emendacionem unius grangie in Westgate, xx*d*.)

MARGARETA OFCYEL. Memorandum quod Margareta Offcyel anno xiij Ricardi abbatis, ad festum Pasche,[9] debet elemosinario iiij*s*. j*d*. *ob*. (Item quere amplius vel magis ex altera parte sequente.)

---

[1] *8 June 1451.*
[2] Note the part taken by the vicar of Peterborough in the proceedings for the deprivation of the vicar of Maxey.   [3] *14 June 1451.*   [4] *19 June 1451.*
[5] *Probably* translationis.   [6] *8 July 1451* (?).
[7] Lost, see above, p. xxxix.   [8] *1450–1.*   [9] *25 Apr. 1451.*

Memorandum quod Willelmus Brewster de Maxey debet elemosinario, post Pascha, iiij*d*.

Anno Ricardi abbatis xiij°.[1]

In solutis Nicholao Smythe, pro cura et medicam*ine* unius pulli, Sorelle nomine, xx*d*.

SOLUCIONES PRIORI. In solutis priori, pro mora sua post Pascha, xx*s*. (et ad cariagium prioris, iiij*d*.); item alia vice [2   ]. In solutis pro emendacione unius selle monachalis, x*d*.; et in ij coriis vitulinis, xij*d*.

HOSPITALE. In xviij*c* potyngthac emptis, viij*s*.; et in cariagio per Johannem Hopkyn ad hospitale, scilicet x carectatarum [2   ].

CLOPTON. Memorandum quod frater Willelmus Morton, elemosinarius, deliberavit Johanni Egiston iij*s*. iiij*d*., ad plenam reparacionem grangii sui; item xx*d*., de redditu suo; item iij*c* thac cum cariagio; item meremium, scilicet tingna, j coplys [*sic*] stothys cum splent*s*. Item allocatur eidem iiij*d*. pro scapulacione unius mayst*ur* copil ac etiam scapulati.

CLOPTON. Idem elemosinarius dedit tenentibus de Clopton viij*c* coperture, precii iiij*s*., videlicet Johanni Egyston iij*c* ad grangiam ut supra, Henrico collectori ad grangiam suam ij*c*, et aliis tenentibus ibidem residuum inter se.

SUTTON. Memorandum quod Johannes Rothewel de Sutton recepit iij*s*. iiij*d*., in vigilia Pentecostes,[3] in presencia Roberti Conquest in parte solucionis de xiiij*s*. pro factura murorum et carpentria unius bovarie ibidem. (Vacat hic.)

SOLUCIO ELEMOSINARII AD FESTUM SANCTI JOHANNIS BAPTISTE[4] PRO LE O ANNO RICARDI [ABBATIS] XIIJ°.

In primis fratri Johanni Northop, vj*s*. viij*d*., (solvit); item fratri Willelmo Morton, vj*s*. viij*d*.; item fratri Johanni Pychele, vj*s*. viij*d*. receptos per Petrum Barb*ur*, (solvit); item fratri Willelmo Ufford, vj*s*. viij*d*., (solvit); fratri Johanni Turvey, iij*s*. iiij*d*., (solvit in auro).

JOHANNES CARPENTARIUS. Johannes carpentarius cum barba tustata debet (elemosinario) de redditu, ad festum Reliquiarum, anno Ricardi abbatis xiiij°,[5] omnibus computatis, viij*s*. x*d*.; item viij*s*. pro quatuor quarteriis anni. Inde solvit xij*d*.

Allocatur[6] de redditu Henrici Palmer:—in primis pro Johanne Pye, xiij*d*., propter sotulares; item pro ij pueris, xx*d*.; item pro una sera, et una tabula quercina, viij*d*.

[*f. 23r.*] *Anno Ricardi abbatis xiij°.*[7]

In solutis Johanni o ye Halle, (alias dicto Cosyn), servienti elemosinarii:—in primis in ebdomada Pasche,[8] xx*d*.; item in vigilia Sancti

---

[1] *1450–1.*
[3] *12 June 1451.*
[5] *21 Oct. 1451.*
[7] *1450–1.*

[2] Left blank.
[4] *24 June 1451.*
[6] Note at foot of folio upside down.
[8] *25 Apr.–1 May 1451.*

Augustini,[1] versus Depyng', xx*d*.; in vigilia Trinitatis,[2] xx*d*.; item xx*d*. ad emendum unum hatte; item xx*d*. in vigilia Sancti Petri Advincula;[3] item propter unam camisiam emendam in festo Sancti Agapiti,[4] xx*d*.; in die Sancti Bartholomei,[5] xij*d*.; in campo de Paston, xvj*d*.; item xvj*d*.; item per manus uxoris Roberti Wryhete, xiiij*d*.; item xiiij*d*.; item in Sabbato post Exaltacionem Crucis,[6] xvj*d*.; item ij*s*., in die Sancti Mathye;[7] item in die Sancti Michaelis,[8] xij*d*.; item xij*d*., per T*omam* Hardy, pro pisis. Summa recepte, xx*s*., xvj*d*., et elemosinarius debet predicto Johanni ij*s*., omnibus computatis. Idem Johannes recepit postea iiij*d*.; item vij*d*.; item xiij*d*.; item x*d*. ad caligas emendas; item unum par ocriarum, precii xx*d*.; item xx*d*., pro rewardo; et neuter debet alteri modo. Idem habuit unum signum de cera; item vj*d*., pro labore in gardino.

Memorandum quod elemosinarius solvit Willelmo Bernard juniori et T*ome* Hardy, in die Sancti Laurencii,[9] pro cariagio decime faciendo ad Gonthorpe, xvj*s*. in parte majoris summe, videlicet:—xxxiij*s*. iiij*d*. Item iiij eskeppe brasii deliberantur eis ex convencione, (pro rewardo); item Willelmo predicto j eskeppa brasii, precii iiij*d*.; item iiij*d*.; item T*ome* Hardi viij*s*. viij*d*.; item Willelmo Bernard viij*s*. et equet pro hoc anno.

MARGARETA OFFECYEL. Memorandum quod Margareta Offecyel computavit cum elemosinario in Dominica ante Exaltacionem Sancte Crucis anno Ricardi abbatis xiij° omnibus computatis ipsa debet iiij*s*.; item xij*d*., pro termino sequente; et nota quod juravit per fidem suam levando dexteram manum, in presencia Tome Style de Burgo et T*ome* Hontte firmarii de Cast*ur*, quod solveret vel satisfaceret per laborem infra annum.

Memorandum[10] quod Matilda Ʒong' solvit iiij*s*. elemosinario, ad Natale Domini,[11] anno Ricardi abbatis xiiij°, et liberavit nigram vaccam cum vitulo, et equet. (d Item illa solvet xij*d*. elemosinario ad Purificacionem proxime sequentem[12] et xij*d*. ad Carniprivium[13] proxime sequentem et equet.)

[*f. 23v.*] *Anno domini Ricardi abbatis xiij°.*

(d clero[14] per ij annos per litteram domini Pape supplicatoriam et per inducionem et consensum Archiepiscoporum ad opus domini Edwardi, pro expensis suis apud Acon. Cronica domini Willelmi prioris de Burgo Sancti Petri. Anno domini millesimo ducentesimo septuagesimo tercio. Circa hunc annum jubente domino Papa Nicholao taxate sunt in Anglia ecclesie, secundum verum valorem, et vocatur ex tunc

[1] *25 May 1451.*	[2] *19 June 1451.*
[3] *31 July 1451.*	[4] *18 Aug. 1451.*
[5] *24 Aug. 1451.*	[6] *18 Sept. 1451.*
[7] *21 Sept. 1451.*	[8] *29 Sept. 1451.*
[9] *10 Aug. 1451.*	[10] Upside down at the bottom of the page.
[11] *25 Dec. 1451.*	[12] *2 Feb. 1451/2.*
[13] (?) *c. 23 Feb. 1451/2.*	[14] The first part of this paragraph is missing.

'Taxacio Norwycensis'. Chestr' fol' [¹   ]. Anno domini MCC nona-
gesimo primo. Rex Edwardus dominium regni Scocie est adeptus et
destructio civitatis.)²

SUTTON. De Johanne Rothewel, ix*s*., pro j virgata terre et prati, videlicet, j acra dimidia; de Johanne Yve, x*s*., pro j messuagio et iij cotagiis
(et croftis) cum j virgata terre; de Johanne Yve, vj*s*., pro j tofto et
j virgata terre, quondam Daw Annys. Memorandum de hedpense (scilicet
ij*s*.) in certo vel non; de Willelmo Blogwyn, vj*s*. viij*d*., pro j tofto et
j virgata terre quondam in tenura Dycon (Ricardi) Prio*ur*; de Ricardo
Uppyngham xij*s*. pro j messuagio, j virgata terre, et quatuor parcellis
terre dominice in quatuor campis; de T*o*m*a* Priour, (modo Conqueste),
vj*s*. viij*d*., pro j grangia et j domo, xij acris terre et prati; de Johanne
Eyr' viij*s*., pro j tofto et j virgata terre quondam Lunsthynk; de
Johanne Yve vij*s*., pro j messuagio, j virgata terre, j cotagio incluso
infra etc., quondam Willelmi Holande.

De³ T*o*m*a* Prio*ur* seniore ix*s*., pro j messuagio et j virgata terre, quondam (*d* Malersse) Malynsthynk.

(A).⁴ De Johanne Rothewel, vj*s*., pro j tofto et j virgata terre, quondam
Benetholde.

(B). De Henrico W*u*rmele, vj*s*., pro j messuagio, j virgata terre, quondam [in] tenura Teysse.

(C). De Willelmo Gefron, viij*s*., pro j messuagio (grangia) et j virgata
terre, et solebat reddere xj*s*., et vocatur Newbonde ty*n*k.

De iij cotagiis supra dimissis Johanni Yve; de quarto cotagio tamen
collector denegat; de T*o*m*a* Fad*ur*man, xij*d*., pro j cotagio, j crofto,
continente iij rodas; de Willelmo Stacy, iij*s*. iiij*d*., pro j cotagio cum
crofto iiij acris terre et iij rodis prati; (de⁵ J. D*u*rram, (xx*d*.), pro cotagio
ij acris dimidia terre, et prati j roda et quatuor pedibus); de [¹   ]
Haale pro j cotagio, crofto et ij acris terre adjacentibus, nuper in tenura
T*o*me Fad*ur*man, igno*ur* [?]; de Willelmo Gefron, xij*d*., pro ij toftis,
croftis et dimidia j acre terre, quondam Parker; de Willelmo Lay, xij*d*.,
pro j cotagio cum crofto continente iij rodas in ij sellionibus, quondam
Potton; de Johanne Yvis, ij*s*. pro ij aliis cotagiis cum crofto continente
j acram dimidiam, quondam Sydrak*s*; de Roberto Conquest, vj*d*. pro
j tofto cum iij sellionibus, vel quondam Wolffe yerde; de Willelmo Lay,
vj*s*. pro j messuagio, cum crofto et viij acris terre et prati modo in
tenura Roberti Mownecelle; de Henrico W*u*rmele vj*s*. pro j messuagio
crofto, x acris terre et prati et j acra ad Snypewel hyl juxta; de eodem,
vj*s*. pro j messuagio, crofto et j virgata terre et iij dimidiis acris prati,
quondam Laver*o*k*s*; de Willelmo Reynold, iij*s*. iiij*d*. pro j messuagio,
crofto cum certis parcellis terre; de Roberto Wymysse, j*d*. pro vj sellionibus jacentibus juxta Woodmyl dyk*s*.

¹ Left blank.
² A line is drawn on the left side of this incomplete paragraph, with the word 'Vacat'.
They are also in a different hand: cf. above, p. xl and n. 1.   ³ In margin: Conqueste.
⁴ The letters a, b, and c are written in the left margin of this folio, the order in the MS.
being b, a, c.   ⁵ Above the line.

Nota de Cast*ur*, (x*s*.) et Me*r*ram, (a marc') [*sic*].

4*li*. 6*s*. iij*d*. summa ut collector asserit. Redditus assisus xxij*s*. ix*d*.

[*f. 24r*.]¹

Dominus Abbas debet fratri Willelmo Morton in primis pro Halbotfen, ij*s*. viij*d*.; item pro tenemento in Comersgate pro v annis, x*s*.; item ad finem ville² versus hospitale (pro v annis), v*s*. x*d*.; item pro tenemento in Newerk pro uno anno et ij quarteriis, iij*s*.; item pro dimidia acra terre apud Hawyaate, ij*d*. *ob*. pro v annis; item v*d*. pro Stoxmans acr*e*; de eodem [abbate] pro ostencione librorum, viij*s*. iiij*d*.; de eodem, xx*s*. pro rectore de Pychele; nativo de Cambrige; alio nativo de Wer-myngton.

Anno xvᵒ ³

Item pro officio elemosinarie, iiij*d*., pro j acra (ᵈ terre) prati in Egersle pro ij annis; item xij*d*. pro j tofto in Gonthorp, pro ij annis, vocato Foleschank; item ij*s*. pro v acris in Holmys de Paston; item xij*d*. pro terris in campo de Wethryngton dimissis domino abbati per novum rentale; item xxx*s*. pro croftis apud Newerc; item pro iiij quart*e*riis (dimidio) pisarum, precium quarterii in foro ij*s*. viij*d*., x*s*. v*d*.; [*in margin*:—iiij quarteriis pisarum, precium quarterii, ij*s*. viij*d*.]; item pro iiij clav*ibus*, xij*d*.; item iiij*d*. ex mituo propter fraternitatem Sancti Tome; item pro emendacione unius parve serure, iij*d*. Verte folium.

[*f. 24v. upside down.*]

Item pro ij acris et dimidia in Hamons medow, pro ij annis aretro, precium acre, iij*s*. iiij*d*., viij*s*. iiij*d*.; (ᵈ de domino abbate, pro terra vocata Childryns londe, pro [⁴   ] annis [   ]; de eodem pro gardino et crofto T*o*me Balle; de eodem pro alio crofto ibidem nuper in tenura T*o*me Boysse, x*s*.; de eodem pro una acra prati in Egerley per [⁴   ] annos [⁴   ]; de eodem pro uno tofto in Gonthorp de feodo Folschanc, [⁴   ]; de eodem pro v acris in lez Holmz de Paston); de eodem pro iij quarteriis, (vij*s*.), iiij eskeppis, (xiiij*d*.), pisarum precium j quarterii in foro, ij*s*. iiij*d*. Idem abbas recepit per stupacionem solucionis Johannis Be*r*narde, v*s*.; Johannis Benette, cop*er*, xx*s*. Idem abbas debet fratri Willelmo Morton, (ᵈ iij*s*., et nota) [quod] frater Willelmus Lecet*ur* habuit residuum pro vino; item ij quarteriis pisarum, v*s*. vj*d*. Item debet pro Johanne Grynston et trowhe, 9*s*.

[*f. 25r*.]⁵

F*IRMA MESUAGII* xxvj *ACRARUM TERRE* j *ACRE DIMIDIE* j *RODE PRATI.*

De Ricardo Sapcot,⁶ ix*s*.; de H. Haw, vj*d*.; de J. Woode, ij*d*.; de Waltero Myller, j*d*.; de W. Cak*er*, (ᵈ vj) ij*d*.; de J. Alwarde, *ob*.; de

---

¹ A small leaf stitched in the book.
² i.e. at the west end of Westgate.
³ Written in the margin at this point. There is nothing to show whether this refers to all the entries on the scrap of paper or only to those which succeed this note.
⁴ Left blank.   ⁵ Another small piece sewn in.
⁶ The names and amounts are written in two parallel columns.

Radulfo Bacyl, *ob.*; de J. Stok, iiij*s.* x*d.*; de Willelmo Alwarde, j*d.*; de J. Ayleton, v*d.*; de J. Greene, iiij*d.*; de Ricardo Baate, xij*s.* pro j virgata terre; de H. Browme et J. Cresby, xij*s.* iiij*d.*; de Ricardo Gaale, vj*d.* pro j tofto; de Willelmo Ferm*ur*, vj*s.*; de J. Roper, ij*d.* Summa (vera) totalis xlvj*s.* ix*d.*

Memorandum quod balivus domini regis de hondreda de Willybroc clamat sectam curie ibidem apud Wodnewton de elemosinario.

De Johanne Cresby j*d.* pro dimidia acra buttante super Bolwelgate, et est redditus assisus.

Memorandum de una roda dimidia terre arabilis nuper in tenura Walteri Lesse, postea in tenura Johannis filii ejus, et modo in tenura Ricardi Bate, et jacet ad finem ville de Egyllethorp, inter terram Jacobi ex parte boriali, et terram [   ] ex parte australi.

[*f. 26r.*][1] *Anno xv Ricardi abbatis.*[2]

In solutis Willelmo Plowman, tectori, pro veteri copertura deicienda, anglice:—baryng et paryng, fere medietatem veteris aule pauperum ad hospitale,[3] per iiij dies, xvj*d.*; in solutis pro vj carectatis petre velute, cum cariagio, (18*d.*); item pro vij carectatis terre rubie pro muris emendandis (et) bemfillyng, x*d.* (*ob.*), (ᵈ et ryggyng tocius domus.)

(b) In scapulacione de xv coplys tingnorum cum alio meremio scilicet walplat*s*, beemys, wyfyrs, nichil, quia Johannes Skarlet unus pauperum ibidem operatus est, meremium de officio.

(a)[4] In solutis uno latamo pro emendacione murorum aule supradicte, xxij*d.*; in cervisia operariis et pauperibus ibidem, (per vices), viij*d.*; in cariagio iiij carectarum meremii scapulati illuc, xij*d.*

(b) Item pro cariagio ix carectatarum arundinis et thak de Coksholme.

(a) In xijᶜ (long) thak emptis, x*s.* x*d.*; in uno copertore conducto pro novo opere in grosso, 9*s.*, (ᵈ ix); item eidem et suo servienti per vj dies laborantibus super eandem domum, capientibus in die viij*d.*, iiij*s.*; item in datis Willelmo Schepey, Willelmo Plowman, Roberto Fuller et aliis adjuvantibus in le reysyng' novi tecti ibidem, per unum diem, xviij*d.*; item pro beemfyllyng, vj*d.*; item pro le ryggyng' viij carectate terre rubie, xvj*d.*; item in solutis copertori pro le ryggyng tocius domus per [5   ] dies [5   ] wattlyng et roope de stauro.
    Summa:—xxxvij*s.* viij*d.* *ob.*

(ᵈ Memorandum de recepto de Ricardo Clokmythe pro redditu per Johannem Coldwel. Item Johannes Smythe de Wodcrofte, omnibus computatis, debet iiij*s.* ij*d.*, quos solvit.)

---

[1] Folio 25*v* is covered with letters of the alphabet and other scribbles.
[2] *1452–3.*
[3] Repairs to the hall of St. Leonard's hospital or the Spittle.
[4] The letters a and b which are in the original above the line or in the margin indicate that these sentences are to be transposed.
[5] Left blank.

[*f. 26v.*] *Anno domini Ricardi abbatis xv finiente et xvj incipiente.*[1]

FACTURA NOVE AULE AD HOSPITALE CUM LE GARRETTE.[2]

In primis in convencione facta cum Johanne Hopkyn pro muris ibidem deponendis separandis et [pro] preparacione fundamenti nove aule ibidem, vj*s.* viij*d.*; item eidem pro preparacione alterius muri cum camino et latrina, x*d.*; item Johanni Roome fodiendo et valyng in le yaatehows ibidem, per vj dies (dimidium), capienti in die, iiij*d.*, ij*s.* iij*d.*; et in fodicione et cariagio de vij^{xx} j carectatis terre rubie, (^d capienti pro carectata), xviij*s.* j*d.*; item pro [³] carectatis terre rubie ad unum murum ex transverso domus ibidem [³]; item pro fodicione de cxxx^{ta} carectatis petre velute, xiiij*s.*; item in cariagio ejusdem ad hospitale, dando pro (cariagio) carectate, ij*d. ob.*, xxv*s.*; item pro xl carectatis petre velute, vj*s.* viij*d.*; item in x carectatis petre libere emptis, unde ij carectate de Walmysforde, iij*s.* iiij*d.* et in cariagio ad hospitale, ij*s.* vj*d.* et octo carectatis de Bernak et Walcotte, xj*s.* iiij*d.*, et in cariagio ad hospitale, carectata [pro] xvj*d.*, x*s.* viij*d.*; in solutis pro ij wyndyngg*s* de ferro, pro fine unius walleplaate ligando, ponderantibus in libris [³].

Item una carectata rubie thegule de stauro; item (pro camino) ij carectate calcis et zabuli (de stauro); et in solutis Willelmo Schepey pro x scaffold herdlys (novis) cum cariagio de Upton, ij*s.* vj*d.*; item in solutis dicto Willelmo Schepey, latamo, pro parietibus petrosis ibidem faciendis, (^d unde), quorum vj rode altitudinis xiiij pedum, item ij rode et dimidia altitudinis xxj pedum cum camino et latrina omnia de novo, iiij*li.* xiij*s.* iiij*d.*; item in solutis pro dictis parietibus cooperiendis in tempore yemali, ij*s.* iiij*d.*

Memorandum de walleplat*s*, wyfrysse, bemysse, somyrsse, de pre-emcione; et in solutis pro vj (grossis) coplys tignorum cum cariagio, vj*s.* viij*d.*, et residuum meremium de Sutton woode, (exceptis walplatis, beemys et wyf*ur*s); (in sarracione de wyf*ur*s et xxxiiij lat*s*, ij*s.* v*d.*); in convencione facta cum uno carpentario pro xl coplysse faciendis, xl*s.*; (in jantaculo dato operariis post meremium exaltatum super muros nove aule, ij*s.*); item in solutis pro sclatt*s* videlicet viij mille, precium de mille viij*s.* iiij*d.* cum cariagio, lxvj*s.* viij*d.*; item [pro] mille ccc latt*s* longitudinis trium pedum, precium vij*s.* ij*d.*; item in solutis pro magnis portis de le garrette factis ibidem, viiij*s.*

Memorandum[4] de lx creest*s* emptis (cum cariagio), pro tectis de le sclatte howsysse ad hospitale, 7*s.*

[*f. 27r.*] *Anno domini Ricardi abbatis xvij° incipiente.*[5]

Item dccc latt*s* de preemcione; item xiiij mille lathepynnysse, iiij*s.* viij*d.*; item vij mille lathenayl' de preemcione; item iij fymerell' de dono

---

[1] *1453.*
[2] The following paragraphs on fos. 26*v.* and 27*r.* were struck out, without explanation, no totals of payments being stated. It is not clear, therefore, whether they were transferred to the almoner's official *compotus* or to any other record.
[3] Left blank.
[4] Note below text subsequently deleted.   [5] *1454–5.*

domini abbatis; item iij fod*ur*s calcis de preemcione; item ij carectatis
zabuli cum cariagio, xiiij*d*.; et in xxx creests de preemcione; item in
solutis Johanni Aspschaw, tegulatori, pro vj rodis et dimidia cooperiendis, roda ad v*s*., xxxij*s*. vj*d*.; item in rewardo, (scilicet caligis), ei
datis et servisia sociis suis, xx*d*.[1]

[*f. 27v*.] *Anno domini Ricardi Ayheston abbatis xvj*.[2]

In solutis Davy Belle pro dimidia roda tabularum quercinarum sarrata,
xxij*d*.; in solutis Thome Sawar pro una roda sarrata, 3*s*. 8*d*.; item eidem
pro dimidia roda, xxij*d*.; item Davy Belle pro una roda, iiij*s*.; item in
solutis dicto Davy pro una roda et dimidia tabularum quercinarum cum
alio meremio videlicet iij pecysse de walnut treysse, vj*s*.; item eidem pro
una longa pecia et ix tracynsse sarratis, viij*d*.

In solutis pro quatuor quarteriis frumenti, pro distribucione in die
Animarum,[3] emptis, unde tria quarteria de Johanne Clark de Wodcrofte, precium quarterii, v*s*. viij*d*., xvij*s*., et unum quarterium de
Johanne Cast*ur* de Maxsey, precium (^d vj*s*. vj*d*.), vj*s*.; et in solutis
Willelmo Payn pro pistura et factura de viij ^c et xx panibus vel (^d lx)xlix^xx
panibus, quilibet ponderans post furnicionem ij libras, iij*s*.; item in
solutis molendinario de Maxey, (per Johannem Castur), pro multura
ejusdem, xij*d*.; et in cariagio ejusdem, x*d*.; (vacat:—in solutis pro
tribus brasyn whelys ponderantibus xxj libras, v*s*. vj*d*.; item in uno
ferreo pyn ad unum polen vel ferne ponderante ij libras, iiij*d*.)

EXPENSE FORINSECE. In expensis Johannis Coldewel, famuli elemosinarii, redeuntis de Oxon*ia* cum duobus equis in die sanctorum Crispini
et Crispiniani[4] postquam adduxit dominum Johannem Malden ad
Universitatem, primo ad scolas ibidem [   ], ij*s*.

(In solutis capellano Henrici Greene pro uno waranto scripto ad
capiendum Johannem Hopkyn et filium suum Willelmum, pro pace
contra Ricardum Ay, viij*d*.; item in datis Willelmo Castelle,[5] (ij*s*.), et
Ricardo janitori, (iiij*d*.), pro certis causis in ista materia, ij*s*. iiij*d*.; item
in servisia et vino, (x*d*.); item in rewardo dato famulo Henrici Greene
venienti super negotio magistri sui et elemosinarii ad Robertum Orwyn
et Willelmum Sand*ur*, xx*d*.)[6]

[*f. 28r*.] *Anno Ricardi abbatis xvj*.[7]

In solutis Roberto Bryghe carpentario pro opere carpentrie, per xvj
dies dimidium, capienti in die v*d*., vj*s*. x*d*. *ob*., videlicet scapulando
xl tingnos et alia ligna sarranda cum diversis walplat*s*; item eidem
carpentario pro scapulacione (meremii) per ij dies, x*d*.; in solutis eidem
Roberto alia vice pro sē et servo suo per vij dies in opere carpentrie
faciendo iij ostia (pro hospitale) et scapulando ad P*ar*kekyrc, cum aliis

---

[1] Two thirds of this folio were left blank.
[2] *1453-4*.   [3] *2 Nov. 1453*.
[4] *25 Oct. 1453*.   [5] See p. 16.
[6] This paragraph is marked 'vacat' in the margin.   [7] *1453-4*.

in officio faciendis, infra octabas Epiphanie,[1] iijs. vjd.; item in solutis dicto Roberto carpentario pro framyng novi tecti aule ad hospitale per vices, iijs. iiijd.; xxd.; xijd.; ijs.; xijd.; item iijs.; item xvjd.; item viijd.; item xxd. SUMMA SOLUTA, xvjs. iiijd. Nota quod dictus carpentarius est aretro de ([d] x)xijd. Item memorandum quod ego elemosinarius accomodavi iijs. iiijd. dicto carpentario, ultra soluciones perantea scriptas, teste Johanne Coldwe[lle]. Item dictus carpentarius habuit iij carectatas focalis per convencionem pro regardo.[2]

In solutis Johanni Bolton clerico mense in Parascheue xxd. in parte majoris summe, scilicet xlijd.; in solutis pro ij scafis pro elemosina servanda, iiijd.

Johannes Balle recepit pro heggyng ad Parke kyrc, ijd.; xijd., (iiijd.; vjd.) Robertus Awsthorp recepit pro Johanne Browne, vs.; Ricardus Brygghe de Eye, ijs. jd.; Ricardus Blome, xxd.; xxd. In solutis episcopo Lincolniensi pro una dimissione tempore visitacionis sue, xs.

([d] Robertus Sawndur recepit pro fodicione petrarum, xijd.; xijd.; viijd.; (vs.); item iijs. iiijd.; item ij bussellos sive eskeppas frumenti et ciliginis; item lx poma.

[f. 28v.] *Anno domini Ricardi Ayston abbatis xvj°.*[3]

([d] Memorandum quod frater Willelmus Borowhe senescallus Burgi stupavit xiijs. iiijd. ad festum Michaelis Archangeli[4] de communibus fratris Willelmi Morton pro domino abbate. Idem senescallus recepit ixs., de Roberto Fullebroke peuturer', de redditu elemosinarii pro debito dicti elemosinarii penes dominum abbatem.)

Anno Ricardi abbatis xvij°.[5]

VINUM. In vino empto de Johanne Tylly pro conventu in festo Pentecostes,[6] videlicet, iiij lagenis et j quarte, ijs. xd.; item in vino empto de Johanne Tylly pro conventu eodem anno, videlicet, iij lagenis et dimidia in festo apostolorum Petri et Pauli,[7] ijs. iiijd., (solvit). ·2·[8]

SOLUCIO ELEMOSINARII PRO TUNICIS AD FESTUM SANCTI LUCE EWANGELISTE PRO ANNO 15.

In primis domino Johanni Turvey, vs.; item vs. in camera sua tempore Natalis domini; domino Ricardo Stanford, xs.; domino Willelmo Morton, elemosinario, xs.; domino Johanni Pychele, xijd.; item viijd.; vjs. viijd.; xxd.; solvit et equet; domino Ricardo Harleton, thesaurario, vjs. viijd. et equet pro hac solucione.

Anno Ricardi abbatis xvj°.

SOLUCIO FRATRIS WILLELMI MORTON ELEMOSINARII PRO SPECIEBUS.

In primis domino Willelmo Morton elemosinario, xs.; domino Ricardo Stanford, vjs. viijd., item obolum auri per Willelmum Sylk in cathedra

---

[1] *13 Jan. 1453/4.* [2] A blank space of 2 inches. [3] *1453–4.*
[4] *29 Sept. 1453.* [5] *1454–5.* [6] *25 May 1455.*
[7] *29 June 1455.* [8] In margin. See p. 65.

Sancti Petri;[1] ([d] domino Johanni Pychele [   ]); domino Willelmo Markam, vj*s*. viij*d*.; item ij quadrantes auri ad ostium minucionis; domino T*ome* Gosberkyrc, vj*s*. viij*d*.; item iij*s*. iiij*d*. in cathedra Sancti Petri prope altare Sancte Crucis; ([d] domino Johanni Moo*ur*,[2] vj*s*. viij*d*.); domino priori, xiij*s*. iiij*d*.; domino Johanni Northoppe, v*s*., item v*s*. in officio camerarii; domino Johanni Turvey, v*s*.; item v*s*. in cathedra Sancti Petri super formam juxta pulpitum; domino Willelmo Rampsey, x*s*., receptos per priorem; domino Willelmo Huntyngdon, v*s*.; idem recepit in capella noviciorum super mensam, v*s*.

Memorandum de solucione pro le Ooz ad festum Sancti Johannis Baptiste, ut in iij folio sequenti.

[*f. 29r.*] *Anno domini Ricardi Ayheston abbatis xvj°.*

FIRMARIA BURGI. In solutis fratri Willelmo Markam, infirmario Burgi, pro anno xvj° Ricardi abbatis; in primis xx*s*.; item xx*s*.; item T*ome* Rowsby, x*s*., ex precepto dicti infirmarii; item eidem coco obolum auri; item in solutis dicto M*er*kam, per fratrem Johannem Pychele, xij*d*., et viij*d*., per vices; item pro brevibus portandis ad Rampsey, Croyland, Thorney, Spaldyng et Stawnforde, Hontyngdon', xvj*d*.; item iiij*d*.; item fratri Johanni Pychele, pro jantaculo famulorum infirmarie et sartrine, xx*d*. Idem frater Willelmus Morton elemosinarius solvit per carnes emptas et deliberatas T*ome* Rowceby, coco, pro officio infirmarie per iiij ebdomadas, ([d] i) x*s*. ([d] xj*d*.) iiij*d*.; item pro ij intermissis feriis quintis, vj*d*.

Anno Ricardi abbatis xv.

[Johannes] Clericus de Oxney et Matilda uxor ejus convenerunt cum fratre Willelmo Morton, elemosinario, et conduxerunt iij vaccas habentes iij vitulos suggentes ad terminum quinque annorum reddendo annuatim ix*s*. ad ij terminos; et nota quod dictus (Johannes) clericus et Matilda uxor ejus ad finem quinque annorum, quasi in medio mensis May, deliberabunt istas tres vaccas cum tribus suggentibus vitulis vel valorem, sicut possunt concordare. Memorandum quod solverunt iij*s*. viij*d*.; item ij*s*. iiij*d*.; item anno xix Ricardi abbatis in Vigilia Natalis domini[3] per Johannem Coldwel, vij*s*. Memorandum quod in deliberacione, videlicet in fine quarti anni scilicet ([d] cum) supradictis iij vaccis cum uno vitulo duobus carentibus et cetera. Item supradictus clericus solvebat fratri T*ome* Kydde, Gardiano de Oxney, pro fratre Willelmo Morton, xiiij*s*. ([d] In solutis[4] pro iij scaphis emptis, unde ij pro subelemosinaria, et una pro officio, vij*d*. In solutis pro vino dato Magistro Henrico Greene,[5] senescallo Burgi, 8*d*.; Sororibus Capelle[6] cum ancilla

---

[1] *22 Feb. 1453/4.*

[2] L.R.S. xxi. 280, 284, 292, 297, 299; the abbot's confessor.

[3] *24 Dec. 1456.*   [4] Notes at foot of page afterwards cancelled.

[5] Note the distinction between Master Henry Greene, High Steward of the honour or liberty, a layman, and the monastic steward Brother William Borough, a monk mentioned on f. 28*v*.

[6] A reference to the sister house near the Becket Chapel. See above, p. xxix.

earundem, in Vigilia Natalis domini (et Pasce per vices), xvs.; item xvs. In solutis Sare Esex¹ pro sacrista per elemosinarium vjs. viijd.; item xld. et robam.)

[f. 29v.] *Anno domini Ricardi abbatis xvj°, tercio die Januarii.*²

[SUTTON]. MEMORANDUM quod dominus Willelmus Morton, elemosinarius, convenit cum filio Johannis Yvisse et cum uno alio ad Sutton, quod ipsi foderent et facerent unam foveam ibidem prope orientalem fenestram capelle, longitudinis [³   ] perticarum, ita quod dicta fovea esset latitudinis in fundo trium pedum et in summitate quinque pedum, et in profunditate quatuor pedes et omnis pertica longitudinis xxj pedum, et habebunt pro omni pertica (vd.,) videlicet, cum viva sepe trino ordine posita, Anglice:—with quyk hegghe be thre rowys sette. Item tercio die Januarii dictus elemosinarius convenit cum Johanne Rothewelle quod ipse emendaret unam gabulam ibidem ad Sutton, ubi Johannes Ivysse manet, cum imposicione unius magni balk, factura unius beenke, cum novo speyr; item splentyng ex utraque parte atrii ibidem, cum ij novis ostiis et uno hatche, cum emendacione unius walleplate et (unius) threysholde, (pro) iiijs. vjd. et chyppysse et offalle pro rewardo.

[HOSPITAL]. Vicesimo die Junii Ricardus Pyndar et Willelmus Sewalle de Burgo emerunt (de elemosinario) totum proficuum graminis magni crofti ad hospitale usque festum Purificacionis Beate Marie⁴ proxime sequens et fecerunt fidem levando dexteras manus solvere elemosinario xs. ad festum Advincula Sancti Petri,⁵ et xs. ad Natale domini anno ut supra, (solverunt).

[ALMONER'S ESTATE IN THE VILL.]

(ᵈ MEMORANDUM quod Johannes Drewus junior venit ad elemosinarium xxiij° (die) Januarii,⁶ et cepit unum messuagium super Ratonrow pro T*homa* Palle, reddendo per annum viijs., hoc notato quod elemosinarius reparabit muros et tectum, et Johannes Drewus et [Thomas] Palle adinfra)

[f. 30r.] *Anno domini Ricardi abbatis xvj°.*⁶

MINUCIO TERCII PRIORIS IN NATALI.

Die dominica, in ij capitibus vitulinis, iijd.; in j porcello, vd.; feria secunda, in ij aucis, ixd.; in j porcello, iiijd.; feria iij, in ij capitibus vitulinis, iijd.; in iiij caponibus, xijd.; item in ij aucis, ixd.; item in ovis pro frytu*r*s, ijd.; et in sagina scilicet j quarte, iiijd.; item in pomis, ijd.; item in quatuor volatilibus, viijd.; item quatuor cuniculi de cimiterio⁷ Sancti Johannis Baptiste; ad cenam: j copylle konys; item ij volatilia, iijd.; feria quarta: videlicet, ad unum fricsum in salcatis pissibus, ijd.;

---

¹ The senior sister of the sister-house.   ² *1454.*   ³ Left blank.
⁴ *2 Feb. 1453/4.*   ⁵ *1 Aug. 1454.*   ⁶ *1453-4.*
⁷ Note that there was a rabbit warren in the graveyard of St. John the Baptist. This must refer to St. John's close near the original parish church on the eastern side of the present Vineyard Road, where there is now a playing-field [1947].

in bituro [*sic*], ij*d*.; in ovis, iij*d*.; in reysyngg*s* korawns,[1] j*d*.; in speciebus per istos ij dies, scilicet, pipere et croco,[2] ij*d*.

EBDOMADA SEXAGESIME ET MINUCIO TERCII PRIORIS.

Dominica: in aprina ut in annis precedentibus; in grossis carnibus nihil hoc die; in ij capitibus vitulinis, iij*d*. *ob*.; in ij aucis, ix*d*.; in uno agno, v*d*.; ad cenam: in v wyldefowl, vj*d*.; feria secunda: in uno ferculo grossarum carnium cum una assacione ad prandium, et cum alia assacione in cena, v*d*.; item in carne porcina salcata propter collops, iiij*d*.; in ovis, iij*d*. *ob*.; in sagina, ij*d*.; in ij loyn*s* vitulinis (cum aliis carnibus), viij*d*. (*ob*.); item in v volatilibus, vij*d*. *ob*.; ad cenam: in vj volatilibus, vj*d*.; feria tercia: in uno ferculo grossarum carnium cum una assacione ad prandium et alia ad cenam, v*d*.; in v caponibus et gallinis, xij*d*.; in ij loyn*s* et j schold*ur* vitulinis, ix*d*.; ad cenam: in uno garbage vel ferculo cum carne ovina et vitulina ad unum sew, iiij*d*.; feria quarta: in uno tenche, (iij*d*.), et xvj pycrell' o x et xij inchys, (vij*d*.); feria v: in uno pestelle porcino, (ij*d*.); item quatuor cuniculi de cimiterio Sancti Johannis; ad cenam: in vj volatilibus, vj*d*.

Dominica Quinquagesima. In uno pestelle porcino, (ij*d*.); capite vitulino, (ij*d*.), cum una assacione ad prandium, (ij*d*.), et alia ad cenam, (ij*d*.) Summa.

[*f. 30v.*] *Anno domini Ricardi abbatis xvj*.[3]

Memorandum quod omnibus computatis inter fratrem Willelmum Morton elemosinarium Burgi et Thomam Smyth de eadem in festo Annunciacionis Beate Marie Virginis anno regni regis Henrici Sexti xxxij^do ita quod dictus Thomas debet prefato elemosinario ad predictum festum viij*d*. preter iij quarteria redditus unius cotagii ibidem juxta, v*s*. (Require de ista materia plus in 28 folio sequente ad tale signum 28.)[4] Quere plus de T*o*ma Fabro in xxviij folio sequente, videlicet, aliam computacionem, ut ibidem ad tale signum 28.

Omnibus computatis inter dominum priorem et elemosinarium, elemosinarius debet priori ad festum Annunciacionis Beate Marie anno ut supra[5] cum x*s*. pro fratre Willelmo Spaldyng, xvj*s*. viij*d*.; item 6*s*. 8*d*. In solutis Johanni Lek pro j quarterio iiij eskeppis pisarum, iiij*s*. vj*d*.; item eidem pro vj eskeppis pisarum, ij*s*. iij*d*.; item uno alio per T*o*mam Hawme, pro uno quarterio pisarum, iij*s*; item in solutis pro j quarterio empto per Johannem Coldewelle, ij*s*. viij*d*.; item per eundem Johannem, iiij eskeppis, xvij*d*.; in solutis T*o*me Beylde pro iiij eskeppis pisarum, xviij*d*.; in solutis Ricardo Cok*er* pro iiij eskeppis avenarum, xv*d*.; in solutis T*o*me Beylde pro iiij eskeppis avenarum, viij*d*.; item in solutis pro ij quarteriis avenarum emptis ad Clopton, v*s*.

In solutis T*o*me Beylde pro iiij eskeppis frumenti, ij*s*. viij*d*.; item eidem pro ij bussellis frumenti, xvj*d*.; in solutis Johanni Bernewelle pro uno quarterio frumenti, v*s*. iiij*d*.; item dicto Johanni Bernewelle pro ij eskeppis frumenti, xvj*d*.; item in solutis Johanni Smythe de Wodcrofte

[1] Raisins of Corinth or currants.   [2] Saffron.   [3] *1453–4.*
[4] See below, p. 106.   [5] *25 Mar. 1454.*

pro iij quarteriis frumenti, xvij*s*.; item Johanni Cast*ur* de Maxsey pro uno quarterio frumenti, vj*s*.[1]

Prima ebdomada, j quarterium; secunda ebdomada, vj eskeppe; tercia ebdomada, ij eskeppe dimidia, j eskeppa, iij eskeppe; ebdomada quarta, ij eskeppe, ij eskeppe et [   ] eskeppe; ebdomada quinta, iiij eskeppe dimidia, ij eskeppe dimidia; ebdomada sexta, iiij eskeppe.

[*f. 31r.*] *Anno domini Ricardi abbatis xvj*°.[2]

IN OFFICIO. In solutis Ricardo Surdo pro factura unius coote[3] cum petra veluta in orto officii juxta gardinum herbarum per quatuor dies, (xij*d*.); item eidem pro aliis laboribus in gardino per v dies, xv*d*.

HOSPITALE. Item eidem ad hospitale per j diem, iij*d*.

SUTTON. In solutis pro una cerura empta pro domo Johannis Yvysse ad Sutton, iiij*d*.

IN CONVENTU. In solutis pro mille walnutt*s*[4] emptis emptis [*sic*] pro conventu in Quadragesima, xij*d*.

NECESSARIA. In solutis Reginaldo Humb*ur*ston pro emendacione unius celle monachalis.

CUSTUS IN BURGO. In solutis Johanni Fylyngham juniori pro cariagio de vij carectatis terre rubie ad Kowgate, xiiij*d*. (14*d*.); item eidem pro cariagio de iij (4*d. ob.*) carectatis petre velute illuc, et in fodicione ejusdem Willelmo Belamy, iij*d*.; et in solutis Willelmo Schepey laboranti ibidem super unum gabulum per vij dies, ij*s*. xj*d*.; item in servisia, ij*d*.

[SUTTON WOOD.] ([d] In solutis pro hegyng' ad Suttonwode, xx*d*.) Memorandum quod Johannes Eyr junior solvit elemosinario in Cena Domini[5] xx*s*. per talliam; et idem dictus Johannes mituatus est xx*d*. ad solvendum pro hegyng ([d] ut supra). ([d] Johannes Waldyng' solvit vj*s*. viij*d*. elemosinario pro calceto sibi vendito).

NOTA DE SEPTEM ACRIS DIMIDIA TERRE DIMISSIS.
Memorandum quod Willelmus Belamy venit ad fratrem Willelmum Morton, elemosinarium, feria tercia in ebdomada Pentecostes[6] et conduxit vij acras terre arabilis et dimidiam acram reddendo per annum iiij*s*., unde una acra et dimidia buttant super Westwode prope Botol sok, nuper in tenura Henrici Hopkyn bedelli; item ij acre terre ad Gatelond style (nuper in tenura Johannis Hopkyn cum sequentibus); item ij acre terre ad M*er*ram gate; item dimidia acra terre ibidem; item dimidia acra subtus Westwod; item dimidia acra iacet juxta Hodis medow; item dimidia acra ultra viam versus Burgum.

SOLUCIO ELEMOSINARII PRO LE O AD FESTUM SANCTI JOHANNIS BAPTISTE.
In primis elemosinario, 6*s*. 8*d*.; item fratri Johanni Turvey, iij*s*. iiij*d*.; item eidem iij*s*. iiij*d*.; ([d] item eidem); item fratri Johanni Pychele, xx*d*.; item eidem xij*d*.; xij*d*.; item residuum (fratri Willelmo Hontyndon);

---

[1] A blank space of 1 inch with the words following at the foot of the folio.
[2] *1453–4.*   [3] Dovecote.
[4] Walnuts in Lent.   [5] *18 Apr. 1454.*   [6] *11 June 1454.*

item tesaurario in manibus, iijs. iiijd.; item fratri Willelmo Huntyngdon pro fratre Johanne Pycheley et pro se ipso, ixs. viijd.; et equet.

Memorandum quod Robertus Bryg' carpentarius mituatus est iijs. iiijd. de elemosinario per mensem, (solvit.)

[f. 31v.] Anno Ricardi abbatis xvj°.[1]

MAGISTER WYTTHAM, THOMAS HALDENBY, WILLELMUS EST CUM SEX ALIIS.[2]

·ꝗ· Item[3] ad Londonias xvij Kal. ([d] May) Junii[4] in solutis pro uno pari sotularum pro vicario Burgi, vijd.; item ad jantaculum pro victualibus, vd.; ad cenam in duobus quarteriis agni, vjd.; in ij rabitts, iijd.; in ij pulcinis, iijd.; in uno scholdur motun, iijd.; in pane, iijd.; in servisia, viijd.; item xjd.; in pane equino, videlicet xj panes, iiijd.; in avena cum pane equino, iijs.; feria sexta: ad prandium, xijd.; item in solutis pro navigio de Westmonasterio, jd. ob.; sabbato: ad jantaculum pro vicario Burgi, iijd.; ad prandium cum sorore fratris Willelmi Burrow, viijd.; item ad vinum in presencia Tome Dyvys, Ricardi Pytts, Symoni [sic] Burton, Ricardi Armeston cum aliis, vijd. ob.; item in servisia eisdem, ijd.; item barbitonsori, iijd. Dominica, (vicario Burgi presente), pro jantaculo, vjd.; in rewardo dato doctori Sugur ex precepto Magistri Willelmi Wyttham,[5] vjs. viijd.; ad cenam, iiijd.; in pane equino, ijd.; feria secunda: ad iantaculum, ijd.; ad cenam, iijd.; in itinere Johannis Coldewelle famuli elemosinarii equitantis de Londoniis ad Sandewyche continuando per iij dies dimidium propter consilium Magistri Ricardi Reynylle[6] in materia placiti contra vicarium de Maxey, ijs. xjd.; item pro ferrura equorum, iiijd.; in emendacione unius celle monachalis cum freno, viijd.; in navigio ad Westmonasterium, jd.; item barbitonsori et pro servisia ibidem magistro Roberto Barkbe, ijd. ob.

Nota quod Johannes solvit hic et computavit ijs. xd., solutos de tercio nobile, et remanent in manibus dicti Johannis Coldewelle iijs. xd.; unde dictus Johannes solvit in minutis expensis, xxjd. Idem Johannes Coldewelle solvit Johanni Broke pro victualibus per unam septimanam, iijs. iiijd.; in feno et litera pro ij equis et aliquando pro quatuor equis per xxij dies, vijs.; in dimidia libra piperis empta pro dono vicarii Burgi, vjd.

Die Augustini[7] in computacione pro equis, xix dies, vjs. ixd. ob.[8]

---

[1] 1453-4.
[2] See Cal. Rot. Pat. 1459, 553—grant for life to the King's servant, William Est, yeoman of the chamber, by the mainprise of Thomas Haldenby of Milton, co. Northampton, 'gentilman', and Richard Skirmote of Peterburgh, 'gentilman', of the keeping of the manor of Upton, co. Northampton, and all other lands, rents, and services in Upton and Eylesworth, co. Northampton, pertaining to the manor, in the King's hands by the forfeiture of Richard Duke of York, at the rent of 100s. yearly.
[3] The following paragraph is evidently a continuation of the expenditure concerning the proceedings for the deprivation of the vicar of Maxey. See above, pp. 43-45.
[4] 16 May 1454.
[5] See p. 59.   [6] See p. 45.   [7] 26 May 1454.
[8] Or ijs. ixd. ob. An almost illegible note at the foot of this folio.

[*f. 32r.*] *Anno Ricardi abbatis xvj°.*[1]

Item in uno [*sic*] libra reysyngg*s* of Corawnse dicto vicario ex dono, iij*d.*; item in solutis pro quatuor zonis et v duodenis de rubiis poynt*s* pro liberatis, Anglice livereysse, (xiij*d.*); item in datis Johanni Coldewelle et Tome Ay ad duas piliones emendas, viij*d.*

In expensis dicti vicarii Burgi redeuntis in febribus[2] de London*iis* ad Burgum cum ij equis, v*s.*; in tribus carectatis feni, in feno et pane equino pro ij equis per ij dies, ix*d.*; in uno jantaculo et cena pro Johanne Coldwelle, ij*d.*; in solutis pro ij lectis per quatuor noctes, vij*d.*; in uno pari culltellarum pro elemosinario, viij*d.*; in ferrura equorum, ij*d. ob.*; in servisia, (ij*d.*); et barbitonsori, (j*d.*). Ad Waar';[3] in pane et servisia, ij*d.*; in uno pulcino cum carnibus ovinis coctis, ij*d. ob.*; in vino (albo), ij*d.*; in prebenda et feno, v*d.* Royston; ad jantaculum ij*d. ob.*, in prebenda et feno, ij*d.* Hontyngdon; in victualibus, j*d.*; in pane et feno, ij*d.* Stilton cum sena [*sic*] in Burgo et prebenda equorum, vj*d.*; item Magistro Willelmo Wy*t*tham in vigilia Sancti Oswaldi[4] in uno potello vini, iiij*d.*; item in viij columbellis sibi datis, ij*d. ob.*

Item in expensis Johannis Coldewelle equitantis usque Stanford, xiij Kal. Octobris,[5] propter concilium Magistri Willelmi Wy*t*tham et propter evidenciam in custodia Magistri T*ome* Rawscotte nuper defuncti, iij*d.*; item in expensis dicti Johannis Coldewelle secunda vice equitantis ad Stanford ix et viij Kal. Octobris,[6] pro materia ut supra, viij*d.*

Item memorandum de columbellis datis vicario Burgi de columbari ad hospitale; et nota quod habuit clavem illius domus per v ebdomadas (*d* usque ad) ante festum Michaelis[7] anno quo supra; item in datis dicto vicario equitanti ad vicarium de Maxey in ij negociis, primum negocium pro consuetis ecclesie de Maxey ad episcopum Lincolniensem, et aliud negocium pro elemosinario, iiij*d.*; item in vino dato Magistro Willelmo Wyttheham in Octabis Sancti Johannis Ewangeliste[8] in domo (*d* vicarii) Johanne Heydon', iiij*d.*

[*f. 32v.: this folio is blank.*]

[*f. 33r.*] *Anno Ricardi abbatis xvj°.*[9]

[VINUM.] In vino empto de Johanne Tylly ad festum Apostolorum Petri et Pauli[10] pro conventu, videlicet iiij lagenas [*sic*] (solvit), j potel (solvit), et j quarte (solvit); item in vino empto pro conventu in festo Sancti Oswaldi[11] de (*d* Johanne Tylly) subsacrista videlicet iiij lagenas et (*d* v) ij pynt*s* precium lagene, viij*d.* Nota quod solvit iiij*s.* iiij*d.*

[1] *1453–4.*
[2] Apparently the vicar had an attack of influenza (or something worse), which caused him to return home immediately.
[3] Ware in Herts. Note the route taken by the sick vicar of Peterborough by way of the old North Road from London to Peterborough with the almoner's servant John Coldwell in attendance.
[4] *4 Aug. 1454.*   [5] *19 Sept. 1454.*   [6] *23 and 24 Sept. 1454.*
[7] *29 Sept. 1454.*   [8] *3 Jan. 1454.*   [9] *1453–4.*
[10] *29 June 1454.*   [11] *5 Aug. 1454.*

In officio, plantacio de porrettis. In solutis Ricardo Grawnte et uxori sue pro plantacione de porrettis in gardino elemosinario per ij dies, vj*d*., et ad potum, j*d*.

Fodicio zabuli. In solutis Johanni Been pro fodicione et cribracione de quatuor carectatis zabuli, unde ij carectate pro officio et in villa, et ij carectate pro hospitali, xiiij*d*.

Cariagium zabuli ad hospitale. Item in solutis Johanni Fylyngham juniori pro cariagio de ij carectatis zabuli supradicti ad hospitale, vj*d*.

Cariagium zabuli in officium. Item eidem pro cariagio duarum carectatarum in officium, iiij*d*.

Terra rubia pro muris Sancti Johannis et gardini.[1] Item eidem [Johanni Fylyngham] pro v carectatis terre rubie ad muros Sancti Johannis Baptiste vij*d*. *ob*.; in uno latamo (conducto) ad emendandum (dictos muros scilicet) tria loca ibidem, 16*d*.

Cariagium terre rubie ad hospitale. (d Item eidem pro iij carectatis terre rubie ad hospitale pro ryggyng veteris aule ibidem, iiij*d*. *ob*.), [cancelled with an explanation] quia antea in vij folio cum aliis.

Memorandum quod Johannes Beylde, bocher, emit de elemosinario v acras prati et terre frisce, (per perticam xvj pedum), ad Swynys medow solvendo pro acra iij*s*. [   ] et nota quod primus dies solucionis est ad festum Martini[2] et residuum videlicet x*s*. vel, (ad libitum elemosinarii), unum present [*sic*] pro domino abbate ad festum Pasche proxime sequens et fecit fidem levando dexteram manum observare convenciones ut in proxima parte istius folii.

Memorandum quod iste Johannes Beylde mituatus est xiij*s*. iiij*d*. Nonas Octobris[3] de elemosinario et juravit levando dexteram manum in presencia [   ] Michelle, Johannis Coldewel et aliorum quod solveret et deliberando carnes propter coquinam minucionis quousque solverit debitum. Idem recepit xiij*s*. iiij*d*. et habet diem Hyllarii[4] x*s*. et Purificacionem[5] iij*s*. iiij*d*. (d Memorandum de vj*s*. viij*d*. receptis pro camerario ex parte domini abbatis de festo Pasche solvenda [*sic*] et aliis.)

[*f. 33v.*] *Anno domini Ricardi abbatis* xvj°.[6]

Idem Johannes Beylde bocher emit pratum vocatum Koksholme, continent*em* x acras cum fossatis, de elemosinario pro xxiij*s*. iiij*d*. et fecit fidem (levando dexteram manum) sigillare unam obligacionem et servare certos dies solucionis, ut postea, in presencia Ricardi Grawnte et Johannis Coldewelle famuli elemosinarii videlicet vj*s*. viij*d*. ad festum Michaelis proxime sequens;[7] item vj*s*. viij*d*. ad festum Omnium Sanctorum proxime sequens;[8] item x*s*. vel unum present [*sic*] pro domino abbate ad festum Nativitatis Domini proxime sequens[9] ad libitum elemosinarii.

[1] See below, p. 85 n. 6.   [2] *11 Nov. 1453.*
[3] *7 Oct. 1453.*   [4] *13 Jan. 1453/4.*   [5] *2 Feb.*
[6] *1453-4.*   [7] *29 Sept. 1454.*   [8] *1 Nov. 1454.*
[9] *25 Dec. 1454.*

In forincecis. A.[1] Prima solucio domino regi,[2] xl*s*.; secunda, xxx*s*. (^d viij*d*.); tercia, xxxiij*s*. iiij*d*.
B. In expensis factis pro equis studencium hoc anno statim post Translacionem Sancti T*ome* Martiris,[3] iij*s*. iiij*d*.; in una decima cum una parte (alterius) decime ultra, domino regi per clerum Cantuariensem sibi concessa hoc anno, ciij*s*. iiij*d*.

Necessaria. In iij fodursse (et dimidio) calcis emptis, iiij*s*. viij*d*. et in cariagio ad officium, (vj*d*.)

Johannes Kyrcby. Memorandum quod Johannes Kyrcby recepit xxxiij*s*. pro sclatt*s* in parte solucionis majoris summe, videlicet liij*s*. ij*d*. (^d Nota 26*s*. per J. Wakerley. Item ij*s*. viij*d*. et v*s*. pro elemosinario, solvit; item iiij*s*.; item xx*s*.; item pro expensis unius equitantis ad Dodyngton, 12*d*.; item vj*s*. viij*d*. Summa soluta, iij*li*. xj*s*. ij*d*.)

Memorandum quod modo Johannes Kircby debet elemosinario clare xvij*s*. viij*d*.

Ricardus Frytthe. Memorandum quod dictus Ricardus Fritthe anno quo supra statim post festum Petri et Pauli[4] venit ad dominum Willelmum Morton elemosinarium et cepit et conduxit x(^d iij)j acras terre et prati ad Fallam herne ad terminum trium annorum reddendo per annum vj*s*. (viij*d*.) videlicet iij*s*. (^d vj*d*.) iiij*d*. ad Pascha et iij*s*. (^d vj*d*.) iiij*d*. ad festum Michaelis. Item nota quod non scindet neque intromittet se de spinis, nisi tantum ad clausuram ibidem, et memorandum quod ipse habuit pratum ibidem in suo ingressu, scilicet anno Ricardi Abbatis xvj°, et ideo non habebit in suo egressu.
Nota quod satisfecit pro anno primo et sic dimisit.

(^d Memorandum quod frater Robertus Notyngham accomodavit elemosinario ij sportas calcis et vj eskeppas); item frater Ricardus Harlton accomodavit elemosinario 12 eskeppas.

[*Note at foot of folio*] usque in crastinum Sancti Oswaldi[5] elemosinarius solvit Johanni Coldwel [*the remainder is illegible*]

[*f. 34r.*] *Anno domini Ricardi abbatis xvj°.*[6]
Sutton. In sclatt*s* bastard cum cariagio, emptis ad Walcotte, viij*d*.; item in solutis T*ome* Hadd*ur*le conducto ad emendandum unum par graduum ad ostium camere in manerio de Sutton, cum emendacione unius ston3ate (juxta) ibidem per quatuor dies, xx*d*.; item in uno serviente ei per idem tempus, xij*d*.; in solutis pro tribus quarteriis calcis, ij*s*. emptis ad Clyffe.[7]

Hospitale. In solutis Willelmo Ploman conducto cum uno serviente per vj dies laborantibus super orientalem gabulum aule pauperum et eisdem laborantibus super borialem gabulum unius sclatte hows ibidem obturando propter ventum (^d per diem), ij*s*.; item ij*s*. v*d*.

---

[1] This sentence is written near the foot of the page.
[2] Tenths, see above, p. 38.   [3] *7 July 1454.*   [4] *29 June 1454.*
[5] *6 Aug.*   [6] *1453–4.*   [7] A blank space of 1½ inches.

Pro anno sextodecimo Ricardi abbatis.[1]

SOLUCIO ELEMOSINARII PRO TUNICIS AD FESTUM SANCTI LUCE EWANGE-
LISTE

In primis elemosinario, x*s.*; item domino Ricardo Oxford sen[iori],[2]
ut in focali empto de elemosinario, viij*s.*; item in argento, x*d.*; item
in solutis Willelmo Lucasse (Man) et Johanni Elyotte pro cariagio dicti
focalis ad domum Ricardi Oxford, xv*d.*; item fratri Johanni Northoppe,
iij*s.* iiij*d.*; item eidem, iij*s.* iiij*d.*; item eidem tercia vice; item fratri
Willelmo Aldewynkille, viij*s.* iiij*d.*, et residuum condonavit; item fratri
Ricardo Harlton thesaurario in manibus, vj*s.* viij*d.*; et equet.

Memorandum[3] quod dominus Willelmus Morton solvit Roberto Style
clerico mense in subelemosinaria in suo recessu de Burgo ij*s.*; Johanni
Bocher, ij nobilia; Kyrby, v*s.*; Bryg', xl*d.*, xx*d.*, xij*d.*

[*f. 34v.*] ⊕ SOLUCIO ROBERTI CONQUESTE FIRMARII DE SUTTON. Quere
in xlvj folio ante plus.

Anno Ricardi abbatis xvj°.[4]

Memorandum quod Robertus Conqueste firmarius de Sutton in die
Sancte Margarete virginis[5] solvit elemosinario pro manerio de Sutton,
xx*s.* Item idem Robertus solvit ut in reparacione facta in gradibus
petrinis et in uno ostio petrino (vel muro ibidem juxta) emendando,
ut in parte antea, iij*s.* iiij*d.*
Idem[6] solvit in Octabis Dedicacionis anno xvij incipiente, xx*s.*; item
in cariagio de iij carectatis (tignorum) de Suttonwode ad et propter
Hospitale, iij*s.* (*d* viij*d.*) Idem solvit pro calce empto ut in parte antea
videlicet iij quarteriis ij*s.*, et debet elemosinario xlv*s.* pro anno xv°
Ricardi abbatis unde solvit ut in ij tingnis, viij*d.* Idem solvit in
Sabbato Quinquagesime,[7] xxj*s.* Idem solvit in vigilia Pentecostes[8] xxiij*s.*
iiij*d.*, et sic quietus est pro anno xv°.
Item idem solvit pro anno xvj° in crastino Beati Mathei Ewangeliste[9]
anno Ricardi abbatis xvij° xx*s.* Item dictus Robertus solvit elemosinario
Sabbato proximo post festum Martini,[10] xij*s.* ix*d.*, et residuum scilicet
iij*s.* et j*d.* per meremium venditum pro boveria ibidem noviter tractum;
item vij*s.* vj*d.* pro uno termino stupato propter Brygmylle. Item idem
solvit in die Pauli primi heremite[11] xiiij*s.* x*d.*; item vij*s.* vj*d.* pro alio
termino stupato propter Brygmille; item in vigilia Pentecostes,[8] xv*s.*
x*d.*; et vij*s.* vj*d.* obstupavit propter Brigmylle; item in vigilia Sancti
Jacobi[12] xv*s.* x*d.*; et vij*s.* vj*d.* in obstupacione propter Brigmylle; item
in Vigilia Sancti Leonardi[13] anno nonodecimo xv*s.* x*d.* per Johannem
Coldwelle pro anno xvj (nota hic) domini Ricardi abbatis; (item) cum
obstupacione pro Brigmylle scilicet vij*s.* vj*d.*; item in die Sancti Vincencii,[14] xv*s.* x*d.* cum obstupacione propter Brigmylle, vij*s.* vj*d.* Item

---

[1] *18 Oct. 1453.*
[2] Or senescallo; cf. pp. 21, 26.
[3] A footnote to the text.
[4] *1453–4.* See p. 13.
[5] *20 July 1454.*
[6] This paragraph is inserted in a smaller handwriting.
[7] *9 Mar. 1453/4.*
[8] *8 June 1454.*
[9] *22 Sept. 1455.*
[10] *15 Nov. 1455.*
[11] *10 Jan. 1456.*
[12] *15 May and 24 July 1456.*
[13] *5 Nov. 1456.*
[14] *22 Jan. 1456/7.*

idem Robertus Conquest solvit lxiij*s.* iiij*d.* xix Kal. Februarii[1] videlicet pro iij quarteriis de anno xix et primo quarterio de anno xx, ut in cariagio et alio labore ad Brigmylle. Item dictus firmarius solvit, ut in precio de xiiij tabulis quercinis, iiij*s.*; item ut de precio ordii, avenarum [et] pisarum, v*d.*; item ut in cariagio propter Brigmylle, xij*d.*; item x*s.* vj*d.*; et in stoppyng pro Brigmylle, vij*s.* vj*d.*; item xiiij*s.*, Sabbato proximo post festum Sancti Jacobi;[2] item per cariagium de sclatt*s* propter cameram in infirmaria; item vij*s.* vj*d.* in stoppyng propter Brigmylle; item xv*s.* x*d.* et in obstupacione ut supra.

Quere plus de ista materia in folio 38 sequente ad signum 38.[3]

[*f. 35r.*] *Anno*[4] *Ricardi abbatis xvj° finiente.*

WILLELMUS PAYN. Memorandum quod anno sextodecimo finiente [*sic*] in festo Decollacionis Sancti Johannis Baptiste,[5] Willelmus Payn de Burgo emit (de elemosinario) l quarteria brasii mensura rasa, hoc est de mensura aquatica xl quarteria, precium quarterii, iiij*s.*, viij*li.* et dictus Willelmus Payn habet ij dies solucionis, primum in Dominica Ramis Palmarum iiij*li.* (proxime sequente[6]); secunda ad festum Michaelis proximum sequens,[7] per obligacionem (anno 17) unde solvit xl*s.* iij Idus Julii;[8] item per Johannem Coldwelle viij° Kal. Octobris,[9] xx*s.*; item per dictum (Johannem), x*s.*; item anno xviij° Sabbato secundo Quadragesime,[10] x*s.*; ∅˙ item in Octabis Sancti Johannis Baptiste,[11] xiij*s.* iiij*d.* per Johannem Coldewelle; item x*s.* xxiiij^mo die Octobris;[12] item in meremio empto de dicto Willelmo Payn propter Brigmylle, xx*s.*

Memorandum[13] quod, omnibus computatis inter dominum Willelmum Morton et Willelmum Payne de Burgo in festo Translacionis Sancti Martini episcopi anno domini Ricardi abbatis xxij,[14] *dominus Willelmus Morton* elemosinarius debet Willelmo Payne, x*s.*

HOSPITALE. Anno xvj°[15] finiente dominus Willelmus Morton elemosinarius emit carectatam (octo) tignorum quercinorum de Johanne Tylly, precium tigni, vj*d.*, iiij*s.*; et nota quod post scapulacionem le squar' erat in majore fine septem polices vel inchysse; et in cariagio ad officium, iiij*d.*

Memorandum quod dominus Willelmus Morton vendidit (et deliberavit) Johanni Hunnyng et Agneti uxori ejus ad vel circa festum Nativitatis Beate Marie ix quarteria et dimidium brasii de mensura fori, precium quarterii iiij*s.*, xxxvij*s.*; item frater Willelmus Morton solvit vij*s.* Johanni Avenam.

IN HOSPITALE. In solutis Johanni Smythefelde pro sarracione de (iiij wyfurs et) xxxiiij lac*s* vel bond*s* ad aulam cameram et le garret ad

---

[1] *14 Jan. 1457/8.*   [2] *29 July 1458.*   [3] See below, p. 130.   [4] *1453–4.*
[5] *29 Aug. 1454.* From this entry it would appear that a year of abbot Richard of Ashton was deemed to end on 29 Aug., but *finiente* does not mark an exact date. (A.H.T.) See p. xl.
[6] *30 Mar. 1455.*   [7] *29 Sept. 1455.*   [8] *13 July 1455.*   [9] *24 Sept. 1455.*
[10] *21 Feb. 1455/6.*   [11] *1 July 1456.*   [12] *1456.*
[13] The following paragraph is repeated in the text, except for the three words in italics.
[14] *4 July 1460.*   [15] *1453–4.*

hospitale, ij*s*. v*d*.; item in uno jantaculo (cum cena et rewardis, ij*s*.) datis carpentario et vj aliis hominibus adjuvantibus in meremio sive tecto nove aule exaltando supra muros ibidem. Johannes Coke, pybak*er* anno xvij° Ricardi abbatis infra octabis Apostolorum Petri et Pauli emit de elemosinario totum proficuum graminis quinque acrarum in Swynys medow pro x*s*. et habet diem solucionis festum Michaelis proxime sequens.

Memorandum de v tankard*s* bone cervisie receptis de Willelmo Payne; (item) dimidio tankard; item dimidio; item j, j, j, j; item de mediocre cervisia xij tankard*s*; item j tankard; item j tankard; item j, j, j, j, j; item de bona [cervisia] dimidio tankard.

[*f. 35v.*] *Anno Ricardi abbatis xvij°.*[1]

(d NAYL'[2] In solutis pro mille [de] lathenayll' ponderante vj libras, xij*d*.; item in solutis pro iiij mille lathenayl', mille ponderans x libras, v*s*. vj*d*.; item in solutis pro ij mille, mille ponderans ix libras, ij*s*. iij*d*.; item pro ij^c clowtenayl', iiij*d*.; item pro vij^c b*ur*denayl', xix*d*.; item pro ij^c midilspyk*s*, vj*d*.; item in solutis pro iiij^c grossis spik*s*, xix*d*.; in solutis pro uno parvo sacco pro supradictis nayl' cariandis, iiij*d*.; item in expensis unius equitantis ad Stanfordiam pro supradictis nayl' emendis, xvj*d*.)

(d NECESSARIA. In solutis fratri Johanni Pychele pro ij scalis emptis ab eo, una quercina xiij steel' vel rongg*s*, altera fraccina longitudinis xviij stel', unum ferreum poleyn ponderans xj libras et dimidiam, unum poleyn meremium, unum magnum cabylle cum uno ferreo gunfo, una forma, item xij peciis quercinis propter barrys pro hostiis et fenestris de novo faciendis, iiij*s*.)

RICARDUS AY. Memorandum quod septimo die Octobris dominus Willelmus Morton elemosinarius conduxit Ricardum filium Johannis Ay de Fodrynghay servire dicto elemosinario per annum, Johanne Coldewelle teste, pro xiij*s*. iiij*d*., una nova toga, et xij*d*. ad unum par ocriarum, vel ad unum par caligarum, et nota quod dictus Ricardus Ay habuit pro arra in prima convencione, iiij*d*., unde dictus Ricardus Ay recepit per talliam de stipendio ut patet ibidem etc.

NOTA DE WILLELMO AUSTORP. Memorandum quod Willelmus Austhorppe erat clericus mense in subelemosinaria in monasterio Burgi anno domini Ricardi abbatis ix° et x° et domino T*o*ma Maxey elemosinario.[3] Idem Willelmus Austhorppe (erat) clericus mense (per xxiiij ebdomadas) anno xj° domini Ricardi Ayston abbatis et tempore domini Willelmi Morton elemosinarii, et nota quod dominus Willelmus Exton posuit istum Willelmum Austorppe propter supler' ibidem annos Henrici Lynne, postquam dictus Henricus attonsus erat, et sussepit habitum monachale. Item iste Willelmus Austorp erat magnus venator nec transivit ad scolas nec adjuvabat in servicio ad capellam Sancti

---

[1] *1454-5.*
[2] *The following paragraph was cancelled with a marginal note:* Item quere in folio sequente plures nayl'.
[3] *1446-8.*

T*home* martiris, nec fecit jantaculum pueris in subelemosinaria, tamen habuit xij*d*. de domino [*f.36r, foot*] Willelmo Morton elemosinario, et non erat dignus.

[*f. 36r.*] *Anno Ricardi abbatis xvij°.*[1]

Memorandum quod Robertus Wymyheste de Sutton clamat certam terram, videlicet infra Schort wod, et ibi sucsidit spinas et abducit, ideo inquiratur quomodo. Item Henricus Rydelle habet terram ibidem, ut dicitur, ex parte orientali, ideo inquiratur (tamen falsatur). Longitudo de Brigmylle xij virge, latitudo (in occidentali fine) infra muros fere xij pedes. Altitudo murorum ix pedes. Memorandum quod sunt ibidem in aqua lxxij pecie quercine.

Memorandum quod Robertus Bryg carpentarius abstulit focale de Sutton wod.

Memorandum quod Robertus Conqueste solvit in (d festo) crastino Sancti Dionisii[2] pro Malynsse thynk etiam Bakons thynk xiij*s*. iiij*d*. in parte solucionis majoris summe, videlicet xv*s*. viij*d*.

(d Memorandum de sarracione unius querci ibidem ad Sutton.)

(d CUSTUS IN BURGO. In solutis Johanni carpentario pro factura unius pentysse et unius hatche super Sowter Row, xiij*d*.)

Memorandum quod in vigilia Sancti Edwardi regis et confessoris[3] Petrus Lorre et Willelmus Gedney (de Wiryngton) fecerunt fidem levando dexteras manus domino Willelmo Morton in presencia Roberti Brigghe carpentarii et Johannis Coldwel, quod ipsi solverent iiij*s*. ad Natale domini proximum (solverunt), et iiij*s*. ad proximum Pascha (unde solverunt 4*s*.; item 4*s*. ut in pisis.)

(d RICARDUS CLOCSMYTH.) Memorandum quod Ricardus Cloksmyth anno Ricardi abbatis xvij ad festum Nativitatis domini[4] debet viij*s*. iiij*d*. Memorandum quod idem Ricardus solvit ad festum Purificacionis Beate Marie anno xviij Ricardi abbatis[5] xxvj*s*. viij*d*.

(d VINUM PRO CONVENTU. Quere in viij folio ante ad tale signum:—•&•)[6]

(d NOTA PROPTER HOSPITALE. Memorandum quod Frater Robertus Notyngham accomodavit fratri Willelmo Morton iij cofnos, Anglice leepysse, plenos calce; item vj eskeppas calcis. Item frater Ricardus Harlton accomodavit elemosinario viij eskeppas et iij carectatas [de] sclatt*s* scilicet xv*c*.)

SORORIBUS CAPELLE SANCTI THOME MARTIRIS cum ancilla (earundem) in vigilia Nativitatis domini et Pentecostes per vices, xxx*s*.; item Johanne Gattle, ij*s*. in festo Sancti Petri quod dicitur ad vincula, videlicet anno xviij°.[7] Item nota quod Johanna Gattele recepta erat inter sorores ad festum Annunciacionis anno xvij°.[8]

[1] *1454–5.*   [2] *10 Oct.*   [3] *12 Oct. 1454.*
[4] *25 Dec. 1454.*   [5] *2 Feb. 1455/6.*   [6] See above, p. 53.
[7] *1 Aug. 1456.*   [8] *25 Mar. 1455.*

[*f. 36v.*] *Anno domini Ricardi abbatis xvij°.*[1]

(d FRUMENTUM. In solutis pro xij eskeppis frumenti, v*s.*; item in solutis pro ij quarteriis emptis per Johannem Coldewelle, vj*s.* viij*d.*; et memorandum de quatuor eskeppis frumenti ultimi anni; item pro ij eskeppis frumenti emptis (in foro), x*d.*)

[THE PARK KIRK.][2] Memorandum de reparacione facta per Johannem Asppeschaw sclatt*er* (cum filio suo) ad capellam Beate Marie Magdalene per unum diem ex devocione.

CHAPEL ROW. Item in reparacione facta per dictum Johannem super domum ubi Ricardus Cloksmyth manet super Chapel Row per unum diem, vj*d.*; item Willelmo Ploman coopertori cum suo serviente per unum diem et dimidium cooperiendo ibidem, xij*d.*

(d AVENE. In uno quarterio avenarum per Johannem Coldewelle, xiij*d.*; item iij eskeppis de Willelmo Craane, v*d.*; item xij eskeppis ex dono (domini) episcopi; item iiij essceppis emptis de Johanne Barnewelle, [3   ]; item xij eskeppis emptis de uno de Holondia [*sic*], xviij*d.*; item de Ricardo Pyndar iiij eskeppis, (vj*d.*). Summa vj quarteria iij eskeppe; item de Ricardo Pyndar j quarterium avenarum, xv*d.*)

NECESSARIA. In solutis pro una cella seculari omnia [*sic*] de novo facta, iij*s.* viij*d.*

(d PISE. In solutis pro vij bussellis, item iiij bussellis pisarum emptis per Johannem Coldewelle, ij*s.* iij*d. ob.*; item (de) Willelmo Morton pro iiij bussellis, (x*d.*); item de eodem [pro] iij bussellis, [3   ]; item de Johanne Pye [pro] viij eskeppis, xx*d.*; item pro ij eskeppis, v*d.*)

(d NAYL'. In solutis pro cccccc de midil spyk*s*, ij*s.*; item iij mille latnayl' et v^c, iij*s.* xj*d.*)

PYKAX. Memorandum quod Johannes Yvysse de Sutton habet unum pykax domini Willelmi Morton.

POLEYN. Item Robertus Mownselle molendinarius habet unum poleyn de meremio.

(d IN FORINCECIS. (In anno xvj°.[4]) In expensis factis pro equis studencium Oxon*iam* eundo et redeundo, vj*s.*; et nota quod unus infirmabatur et expectabat ad Towcet*ur* a festo Sancti Oswaldi[5] usque ad festum Omnium Sanctorum.)

Rector de Paston solvit elemosinario per vices, in primis quatuor nobilia; item iiij nobilia; item xx*s.*; item v nobilia; item xx*s.*; item x*s.*; (d item xvj playtes linee tele); item xx*s.*; item viij marcas, videlicet per stupacionem factam per Robertum Orwyn; item iiij nobilia per rectorem; item xiij*s.* vij*d.* per stupacionem, ut supra; item lix*s.* vij*d.* per dictum rectorem; item, alia vice, per dictum rectorem v nobilia. [SUMMA] 19*li.* 16*s.* 6*d.*

---

[1] *1454-5.*   [2] At Newark.   [3] Left blank.
[4] *1453-4.*   [5] *From 5 Aug. till 1 Nov. 1454.*

[*f. 37r.*] *Anno domini Ricardi abbatis xvij°.*[1]

FIRMARIUS DE MAXEY. Memorandum quod Robertus Hook*s* firmarius rectorie de Maxey computavit cum fratre Willelmo Morton, elemosinario in die Animarum anno quo supra, videlicet xvij°,[2] et omnibus computatis, dictus Robertus solvit xix*li*. x*s*. pro anno xv[3] domini Ricardi abbatis; tamen memorandum quod rector de Norb*ur*row debet x*s*. pro eodem anno cum ceteris (*d* solidis) debitis per antea. Item memorandum quod Robertus firmarius, ut supra, recongnovit quod ipse debet pro anno xiiij° Ricardi abbatis[4] xxx*s*. et rector de Norb*ur*row, x*s*. Item dictus Robertus solvit vj*s*. viij*d*.; item Sabbato post Purificacionem,[5] xxxiij*s*. iiij*d*.; item in cena Domini, scilicet feria v ante Pascha,[6] iiij marcas; item in Translacione Sancti Martini,[7] xiij*s*. iiij*d*. per Johannem Coldewelle; item in Vigilia Sancte Margarete Virginis,[8] vj*li*.; item Sabbato ante festum Symonis et Jude, xl*s*.;[9] item Sabbato in die Sancte Lucie[10] quatuor marcas; item iij*li*. vj*s*. viij*d*. in Sabbato Quinquagesime;[11] item in festo Apostolorum Phylyppi et Jacobi,[12] iiij*li*.; item in festo Sancti Oswaldi Martiris,[13] iiij*li*.; item in festo Bricii (anno xix),[14] xl*s*. pro anno; (*d* item); item in festo Sancti Mauri abbatis eodem anno, scilicet xix[15] pro anno [[16]   ] in presencia Roberti Webster (carpentarii), iiij*li*.; item eodem anno in Cena Domini,[17] iiij*li*. in presencia Johannis Grawnte; modo solvit pro anno [*sic*] xvj et xvij in parte majoris summe scilicet xl*li*. nisi xxxvij*li*. vj*s*. viij*d*.; et debet pro anno xvij*mo* hic xl*s*.; xiij*s*. iv*d*.; unde solvit (4*li*.); item in previgilia Sancti Petri et dicitur advincula,[18] xx*s*.; item ad nundinas Mathei Ewangeliste anno xix[19] pro anno xviij°, iij*li*.; modo debet pro anno 18, 14*li*. xiij*s*. iiij*d*.; unde solvit xl*s*.; item, alia vice in festo Sancti Stephani[20] per manus Johannis Coldwel, iiij*li*.; item eodem die, cum vij*s*. vij*d*. obstupatis pro reparacione in grangia ibidem, xl*s*.; modo idem firmarius recognoscit et fatetur se debere pro sexto anno[21] scilicet xviij Ricardi abbatis, 6*li*. 13*s*. 4*d*.; unde solvit xl*s*. secundo sabbato Quadragesime;[22] modo debet 4*li*. et x*s*.; unde solvit per Johannem Coldwelle iiij*li*. sabbato in ebdomada Pasche.[23] Unde xxxj*s*. x*d*. predictus Johannes Coldwel obstupavit propter debitum suum, et solvebat in manibus dicto elemosinario, xlviij*s*. ij*d*. Item dictus firmarius solvit ut in diversis parcellis ostensis in una cedula de reparacione in rectoria per dictum firmarium facta, viij*s*. iij*d*. Item solvit xxj*d*. et equet pro sex annis.

Quere plus de ista materia in 26 folio sequente 26.

[1] *1454–5.* [2] *2 Nov. 1454.* [3] *1452–3.*
[4] *1451–2.* [5] *8 Feb. 1454/5.* [6] *3 Apr. 1455.*
[7] *4 July 1455.* [8] *19 July 1455.* [9] *25 Oct. 1455.*
[10] *13 Dec. 1455.* [11] *14 Feb. 1455/6.* [12] *1 May 1456.*
[13] *5 Aug. 1456.* [14] *13 Nov. 1456.* [15] *15 Jan. 1456/7.*
[16] Left blank. [17] *14 Apr. 1457.* [18] *30 July 1457.*
[19] At Peterborough Bridge Fair on 21 Sept. 1457. For the charter granting this fair, 14 July 1439, see Roger Bird, f. 10; Gunton, 158. There are some interesting copyhold leases of booths in the fairground to merchants and a non-molestandum in Bird, f. 35 (*r.* and *v.*).
[20] *26 Dec. 1457.*
[21] i.e. Robert Hook's sixth year as farmer of the rectory of Maxey: cf. *pro sex annis* below
[22] *25 Feb. 1457/8.* [23] *8 Apr. 1458.*

Rector de Paston debet elemosinario ad festum Sancti Georgii, anno Ricardi abbatis octavodecimo[1] pro duobus annis preteritis, xxix*s*. ix*d*.; et pro tercio anno octo marcas; unde solvit xxvj*s*. v(^{d}iii)*d*.

[*f. 37v.*] *Anno Ricardi abbatis xvij°.*[2]

Nomina confratrum solutorum pecunias suas recipiendas ad festum Purificacionis Beate Marie[3] per fratrem Willelmum Morton, elemosinarium:—

In primis fratri Willelmo Morton, x*s*.; fratri Johanni Turvey in Dominica Sexagesima,[4] v*s*., (solvit); item v*s*., (solvit); fratri T*ome* Gosmerkyrc in Dominica Sexagesima, vj*s*. viij*d*., (solvit); item iij*s*. iiij*d*.; fratri Johanni Northorpe, v*s*., (solvit); item v*s*. (solvit); fratri Willelmo Walmysford, viij*s*., (solvit) teste me ipso; item ij*s*. per stupacionem de uno roope; fratri Willelmo Stanford, vj*s*. viij*d*., (solvit); item fratri Johanni Glynton, iij*s*. iiij*d*., (solvit); fratri Roberto Lydyngtone, v*s*., (solvit); item in parcellis, v*s*., (solvit); fratri Roberto Notyngham, vij*s*. (solvit); item per stupacionem pro stagnis in le werkr' ʒarde, iij*s*.; fratri Ricardo Oxforde juniori, x*s*., (solvit); frater Willelmus Melton recepit x*s*. in choro Dominica Sexagesima[4] ad missam, (solvit).

(^{d} IN CONVENTU. In solutis pro iiij mille de avellanis[5] emptis ad Lynne, 32*d*.)

(^{d} SUTTON: JOHANNES WAARDE. In solutis Johanni Warde, tegulatori, conducto per v dies et dimidium ad emendandos diversos defectus in manerio ad Sutton, ij*s*. iij*d*.; et nota quod modo neuter debet alteri, nisi caritatem.)

RECEPTA. In receptis pro salicibus crescentibus per foveam juxta cimiterium Sancti Johannis et venditis Willelmo Payn et Roberto Orwyn, vj*s*. viij*d*.; in receptis pro calceto elemosinarii inter pratum infra officium elemosinarii et Snorshylle vendito Roberto Orwyn et Willelmo Payn in ebdomada Quinquagesime anno quo supra,[6] xl*s*.; item de Johanne Waldyng' pro calceto ad australem partem prati elemosinarii ibidem, vj*s*. viij*d*.; item de Roberto Orwyn pro calceto inter alnetum celerarii et pratum elemosinarii suprascriptum, xx*s*.

Memorandum quod collector de Weryngton recepit iiij*d*. de Johanne Syyr; item iiij*d*. de Willelmo Pye.

[*f. 38r.*] *Anno Ricardi abbatis xvij°.*

CAPELLA BEATE MARIE MAGDALENE.[7] In solutis (vitriario) pro reparacione magne fenestre ad capellam Beate Marie Magdalene cum plumbo sowd*ur* et victualibus emptis, iij*s*. iiij*d*.

---

[1] *23 Apr. 1456.* [2] *1454–5.* [3] *2 Feb. 1454/5.*
[4] *9 Feb. 1454/5.* [5] Walnuts or hazel-nuts. [6] *16–22 Feb. 1454/5.*
[7] Probably, but not certainly, the Park Kirk in Newark; see p. 38.

Minucio tercii prioris tempore Natalis domini anno ut supra.[1]

Elemosinario existente London*iis* propter materiam Johannis Hopkyn, videlicet propter falsum indictamentum dicti elemosinarii et Roberti Orwyn cum aliis duobus per falsam imaginacionem Jacoby Stamford.[2]

EBDOMADA SEXAGESIME. In diversis expensis pro conventu preter vel citra aprinam, vj*s*. iiij*d*. (*d ob*.)

IN FORINCECIS. In solutis pro ij virgis et dimidia de kanvasse[3] ad involvendum Robertum Karynton, qui obiit in carcere feria tercia prime ebdomade Quadragesime,[4] viij*d*.

[SISTER HOUSE]. In solutis Isabelle uxori Nicholai Halle pro xj virgis et dimidia de blankette pro roba[5] Sar*e* Essex, et aliis, vj*s*.; item in solutis Johanne Lytst*er* pro tinccione ejusdem, iij*s*.; item pro scheryng ejusdem, ij*d. ob*.

NECESSARIA. In solutis pro uno tribulo[6] empto de N[undinis], iiij*d*.; in solutis pro una nova vanga [7   ].

[CALX.] In solutis fratri Willelmo Burrowhe sacriste pro ix fodursse calcis ab eo emptis, precium unius fodur xv*d*., xj*s*. iij*d*.; item in cariagio ad officium de quinque fodursse, x*d*.; item de iiij fodurs, unde iij fodurs ad hospitale, ix*d*.; item in cariagio unius fodur ad officium Magistri Operis quia pro mituato calce, ij*d*.

[GARDINUM]. In solutis pro plantacione de wort*s* in gardino Ricardo Grawnte et uxori sue xviij Kal. Julii[8] cum victualibus, vj*d*.

(*d* Memorandum[9] quod computatis omnibus inter elemosinarium et Johannem Coldwelle famulum dicti elemosinarii, in Dominica iiij, scilicet media Quadragesime,[10] neuter debet alteri nisi caritatem.
Anno xvij domini Ricardi abbatis, ut infra.
Item pridie Idus Aprilis[11] Johannes Coldwel recepit iiij*s*. vj*d*.; item quinto Idus May,[12] iiij*s*. vj*d*.; item vj Idus Junii,[13] iiij*s*. vj*d*.; item pridie Non. Julii,[14] iiij*s*. vj*d*.; item tercio Non. Augusti,[15] iiij*s*. vj*d*.; item pridie Kal. Septembris,[16] iiij*s*. vj*d*.; item in Vigilia Michaelis,[17] iiij*s*. vj*d*.; item 7 Kal. Novembris,[18] iiij*s*. vj*d*.; item 9 Kal. Decembris,[19] iiij*s*. vj*d*.; item in die Sancti Tome Apostoli,[20] iiij*s*. vj*d*.)

[*f. 38v.*] *Anno domini Ricardi abbatis xvij°.*[21]

(*d* CUSTUS AD HOSPITALE. In solutis Willelmo Qwhyte, conducto pro

---

[1] Further particulars of this bloodletting are not given. There is a dividing line in the text after the word 'supra' followed by a capital letter 'Elemosinario'. It is not clear whether the sum given in n. 2 related to the bloodletting or to the almoner's journey to London, where he would probably stay in the abbot's lodgings in Fleet Street.

[2] *In left margin:* 39*d*. scilicet iij*s*. iij*d*.

[3] A shroud for the burial of a prisoner, who died in the abbot's jail.

[4] *25 Feb. 1454/5.*   [5] A robe for the sisters in St. Thomas's hospital.

[6] Probably a shovel.   [7] Blank.   [8] *14 June 1455.*

[9] Note at the foot of the folio upside down, afterwards cancelled.

[10] *16 Mar. 1454/5.*   [11] *12 Apr. 1455.*   [12] *11 May.*   [13] *8 June.*

[14] *6 July.*   [15] *3 Aug.*   [16] *31 Aug.*   [17] *28 Sept.*

[18] *26 Oct.*   [19] *23 Nov.*   [20] *21 Dec.*   [21] *1454-5.*

diversis defectibus in fossatis clausure ad hospitale emendatis, fodiendo ibidem per iij dies preter mensam, ix*d.*)

Custus in officio. Item in solutis dicto Willelmo pro suo labore in heggynge in le trenchys, plantacione de salicibus ibidem cum aliis laboribus in gardino simul cum victualibus per xiij dies, iij*s.* iij*d.*

Convencio de muris faciendis ad Brigmylle. Notandum xxiiij^to die Aprilis (^d dominus Willelmus Morton elemosinarius) in presencia Johannis Eyr' (baliui et) collectoris de Sutton, Roberti Conquest firmarii ibidem, Johannis Coldewelle famuli dicti elemosinarii et aliorum, frater Willelmus Morton elemosinarius convenit cum Willelmo Schepey latamo quod dictus latamus faceret murum petrinum de Brygmylle longitudinis xxxviij pedum, altitudo muri, preter fundamentum, x pedum; dencitas sive spissitudo de ij gabulis ibidem ij pedum per virgam regiam; item dencitas aliorum murorum ibidem ij pedum et dimidii per virgam regiam, cum tribus bot*u*rasse, videlicet ij bot*u*rasse ad le Watyr ʒate in australi parte et unum bot*u*rasse ex altera parte dencitatis in fronte trium pedum per virgam regiam.
[*In margin*] 23*s.* 4*d.*[1]

(^d Custus in Burgo. In solutis Johanni Fylyngham pro tribus carectatis terre rubie (vj*d.*), pro domo Ricardi Cloksmythe; item in solutis Willelmo Ploman cum uno serviente ei per unum diem ad (cooperiendum et) ryggandum ibidem, viij*d.*; item pro uno muro (terreo) plastrando et emendando, iiij*d.* ibidem; item in uno tegulatore conducto cum serviente suo per j diem ibidem, viij*d.*)

(^d Terra rubia. In solutis Willelmo Maydelette et T*home* Multon pro (cariagio de) iij carectatis terre rubie usque Raton row, ubi Willelmus Rogg*er* manet, vij*d. ob.*)

Memorandum ad petendam allocacionem.

[*f. 39r.*] *Anno domini Ricardi abbatis xvij°.*[2]
Nomina confratrum solutorum pecunias suas recipiendas pro lez O ad festum Sancti Johannis Baptiste[3] per fratrem Willelmum Morton, Elemosinarium.
In primis fratri Willelmo Morton, elemosinario, vj*s.* viij*d.*; fratri Johanni Northoppe, xx*d.*; item iij*s.* iiij*d.*; item xx*d.*; fratri T*ome* Gosmerkirc, vj*s.* viij*d.*; item fratri Willelmo Leycet*ur*, thesaurario, x*s.* in manibus.

Jaxson. Memorandum quod ad festum Sancti Johannis Baptiste Willelmus Jaxson debet elemosinario pro Paynys holme,[4] vj*s.* viij*d.* anno quo supra xvij°, (solvit.)

Custus in Burgo. In solutis pro mundacione sewere ad capellam Sancti T*home* Martiris, iij*d.*

T*homas* Pep*ur*, circa primum diem Junii, in presencia Johannis Hynton

---

[1] A blank space of 1 inch.   [2] *1454–5.*   [3] *24 June 1455.*
[4] A meadow in Peakirk.

et uxorum suarum¹ convenit cum Johanne Coldewelle habere totum
proficuum graminis magni crofti ad hospitale continentis xviij acras
usque ad festum Beate Marie in Quadragesima² cum wedysse et gramine
in orto juxta grangiam ibidem, et item occupare medietatem grangie
ibidem cum bladis usque festum Pasche³ proxime sequens reddendo
pro supradictis proficuis xvs. ad Nativitatem Domini; item xvs. ad
Pascham proxime sequentem; et nota quod fecit fidem servare predictos
dies solucionis, unde solvit xiijs. iiijd. in Dominica Quinquagesime;⁴
item xijs. ut in uno presentte facto sive misso domino abbati ad festum
Pasche, exceptis caponibus missis per elemosinarium, et sic predictus
Tomas Pepur debet elemosinario, iiijs. viijd.; unde solvit ut in reparacione ostii borialis grangie ibidem, viijd. Item idem Tomas Pepur debet
ijs. pro una carectata focalis sibi vendita, et sic dictus Tomas Pepur,
omnibus computatis, in octabis Sancti Benedicti⁵ anno 18 Ricardi
abbatis, vjs. Item idem Tomas Pepur emit ij vaccas de dicto elemosinario pro xvijs. Summa totalis debiti xxiijs. preter firmam magni
crofti, videlicet (anno 18) xxiijs. iiijd.

(ᵈ IN NECESSARIIS. In solutis pro una cella seculari ad omnia de novo,
iijs. viijd. Quere ante in folio tercio.)

(ᵈ Memorandum de meremio empto de Brigid' Martyn cum cariagio,
ixs. xd.)

[f. 39v.] Anno Ricardi Abbatis xvij°.⁶

(ᵈ JOHANNES BEYLDE. Memorandum quod Johannes Beylde, bocher,
debet fratri Willelmo Morton ad festum Apostolorum Petri et Pauli⁷
pro prato de Coksholme⁸ pro anno preterito xxiijs. iiijd. Idem Johannes
Beylde debet dicto fratri Willelmo Morton pro v acris prati in Swynys
medow, precium acre iijs., xvs. et mensura pertice, xvj pedes. Idem
Johannes Beylde debet xxvjs. viijd. dicto fratri Willelmo Morton ex
mituo, unde solvit ut inferius in ista parte folii ex transverso⁹ scripta.)

HAMONDE MEDOW. Memorandum quod anno Ricardi abbatis xviij° ad
Pascha, omnibus computatis, dictus Johannes Beylde debet medietatem
vituli et j caponem; in solutis pro viij rodis fodiendis in fovea juxta
viam ibidem in superiore parte prati elemosinarii, dando pro roda iijd.,
ijs.; item anno 18 pro renovacione vel mundacione ejusdem fossati, vjd.
Quere de fossato ad Muchylgappe in folio proximo.

FESTUM BEATE MARIE MAGDALENE.¹⁰ In una duodena servisie, xvd.;
in pane, iijd.; in una spada multonis in prima cena capellano capelle et
clericis mense jd. ob.; in die ad prandium: in ij ferculis grosse carnis,
(vd.); in ij caponibus, vjd.; in una auca, iiijd.; in uno porcello, vd.; in
una spada multonis, jd. ob.; in xij columbellis, iiijd. Ad cenam, in carne
multonis et carbage, ij caponum unius auce et unius porcelli, ijd. ob.;

¹ Presumably the respective wives of Pepper and Hinton.
² 25 Mar. 1455.
³ 6 Apr. 1455.
⁴ 16 Feb. 1454/5.
⁵ 28 Mar. 1456.
⁶ 1454–5.
⁷ 29 June.
⁸ Situated near the hospital of St. Leonard's at Westwood.
⁹ See below.
¹⁰ 22 July 1455.

in ij pulcinis, ij*d*.; in uno quarterio agni, ij*d*.; item in datis capellano Sancti T*home* martiris, quia non venit ad prandium propter jejunium Sancte Marie, iiij*d*. SUMMA iiij*s*. vij*d*. *ob*.

JOHANNES EGISTON. Memorandum quod frater Willelmus Morton, elemosinarius, vendidit unum equum grey coloris Johanni Egyston de Clopton pro uno quarterio frumenti et iiij*s*. ad proximum Natale Domini solvendis.

(ᵈ Frater¹ Willelmus Morton debet Johanni Beylde pro carne recepta ab eo pro camino tempore fratris Willelmi Markam infirmarii Burgi, xiij*s*. v*d*. Idem frater Willelmus Morton elemosinarius debet dicto Johanni Beylde pro carne ab eo recepta ad caminum tempore fratris Willelmi Melton infirmarii, xx*s*. j*d*. Idem elemosinarius debet dicto Johanni Beylde pro carne in Adventu pro pueris in subelemosinaria, videlicet per x dies scilicet, in die iij*d*., ij*s*. vj*d*. Idem elemosinarius debet dicto Johanni Beylde pro carne ab eo recepta pro hospitibus de Rampsey, (v*d*.) et Angnete Honnyng (iij*d*.), viij*d*. Idem elemosinarius debet dicto Johanni Beylde carnifici pro ij present*s* domino abbati unum ad Natale Domini et unum ad Pascha, xx*s*. Omnibus computatis neuter debet alteri, nisi medietatem vituli et unum caponem.)

[*f.40 r*.] [MISCELLANEOUS PAYMENTS.]²

(ᵈ In solutis pro succisione xxx peciarum quercinarum in circuitu vel urlyr de Sutton Wode propter Brygmylle de novo faciendum, xv*d*.; in cervisia, ij*d*.; in cariagio ad molendinum nichil quia per firmarium; in scapulacione dicti meremii [³   ]. In meremio empto de Roberto Mownselle, scilicet septem peciis quercinis videlicet prima pecia magna pro le Wat*ur*qhwele et aliis ibidem faciendis, due pecie pro straxsyll et quatuor alie pecie pro aliis faciendis ibidem, xj*s*.)⁴

RECEPTA PRO FOCALI SIVE LE CHECS VENDITIS.

[De] Johanne Martyn pro 4 carectatis, iiij*s*. iiij*d*., (solvit);⁵ de Johanne Tayl*ur* j carectata, xvj*d*. (solvit); de T*home* Habɯrgyl pro j carectata et dimidia, iiij*s*., (solvit). (A)⁶ De Roberto Brig', [pro] ij carectatis, ij*s*. iiij*d*., (debet); de [   ] Belle [pro] ij carectatis, ij*s*., (solvit); de uno scheperd pro uno toppe focalis, ix*d*., (solvit); de Johanne Eston pro una carectata, x(ᵈ viij)*d*., (debet); de filio Johannis Rowelle pro ij toppys focalis, xviij*d*., (solvit); de filio Johannis Yvysse pro ij toppis focalis, xvj*d*., (solvit); de Roberto Conqueste pro tribus parvis toppis focalis, viij*d*., (solvit).

---

¹ Upside down, afterwards deleted.
² 'Vacat' is written in the margin, by the side of each of the following cancelled entries.
³ Left blank.
⁴ Half the remainder of this folio is left blank.
⁵ In each case 'sol' is written in another hand above the line.
⁶ The compiler has separated the following groups of payments with the letters 'A' and 'B'. The former concerns fuel, the latter is a payment for wood-trimmings and the sale of boughs.

(B) Item de Roberto Brig' pro scapulacionibus et bowysse, xxij*d.* (debet.) SUMMA xxj*s.* vij*d.*[1]

[*f. 40v.*] *Anno Ricardi abbatis xvij°.*[2]

HOSPITALE.[3] In solutis pro emendacione portarum magne grangie ad hospitale Johanni Halle et T*ome* Heyd*s* per unum diem, x*d.*; item Ricardo fabro pro uno wyndyng' ponderante j libram iij quarteria, iij*d.* (d In solutis Johanni Halle et T*ome* Heyd*s* pro scapulacione tingnorum per unum diem, x*d.*; item in solutis dictis carpentariis clyvyng' splent*s* per unum diem, x*d.*, (satis vera est)).

HOSPITALE. In solutis Johanni Aspeschaw pro perforacione de v mille de sclatt*s* ob defectum venditoris, scilicet Johannis Kyrcby, quia ipse perforasset dictos sclatt*s* (d ij*s.* vj*d.*) in parte majoris summe, vide-licet, v*s.*

IN OFFICIO. Item in solutis dicto Johanni Aspeschaw pro se et tribus servientibus suis conductis (d per v dies,) viij*s.* in parte solucionis majoris summe pro le poyntyng' de vj rodis (super aulam) in officio et aliis defectibus ibidem emendatis super longam domum in officio ex utraque parte (per) vj dies, ij*s.* vj*d.*; item puero, scilicet filio suo Johanni, iiij*d.* Summa soluta ix*s.* x*d.* (d Item memorandum quod Johannes Aspescaw recepit pro opere ad hospitale per recognicionem propriam,) xlvij*s.*, unde x*s.*, pro opere super Sowter row; item postea xiij*s.* x*d.*; et sic neuter debet alteri set eque inter eos.

MUKHYL GAPPE. In solutis pro bina fodicione ibidem de x rodis fossati elemosinarii, ij*s.* vj*d.*

(d CARIAGIUM RICARDI PYND*ER*. In primis viij carectatis feni de crofto infra officium, xvj*d.*; item ij carectatis zabuli et iij carectatis calcis ab officio ad hospitale, xv*d.*; item iij carectatis (scafoldti*m*b*ur* et) tingno-rum de officio ad hospitale, ix*d.*; item iij carectatis feni de Hamond medow ad officium, ix*d.*; item anno xviij° incipiente iij carectatis zabuli de Newerk ad hospitale, xv*d.* Item idem elemosinarius emit xij eskeppas avenarum de Ricardo Pynder, (18*d.*))

Memorandum de vj*c* thak emptis de uno de Wytlisse propter Sowter row et hospitale, iij*s.* 4*d.* Memorandum quod Ricardus Pantr' solvit xx*d.* in parte solucionis majoris summe scilicet ij*s.* ij*d.* pro j acra in Cok*s*holme. Item Multon solvit xiij*d.* in casu consimili.

[*f. 41r.*] *Anno Ricardi abbatis xvij° finiente.*

CARIAGIUM T*OME* MOLTON ETC. In solutis T*ome* Molton et Willelmo Maydelette pro iij carectatis meremii pro scafold*s* ad hospitale, ix*d.*; item pro ij carectatis de sclatt*s* ab officio ad hospitale, vj*d.*; item

---

[1] The compiler of the account inserted all amounts due which amounted to 21*s.* 7*d.*, and then proceeded to mark eight items as paid and the other three as still owing.
[2] *1454-5.*   [3] St. Leonard's or the Spittle at Westwood.

j carectata rubie tyl' pro camino ibidem, iij*d*.; item pro iij carectatis
zabuli illuc, ix*d*.; item pro tribus carectatis zabuli de Newerk illuc, ix*d*.;
item iij carectatis terre rubie in villam, scilicet in Heygate, vj*d*.; item
pro cariagio unius carectate meremii de Westegate, ij*d*.; item j carectata
meremii de Cowgate ad officium, ij*d*.
Memorandum[1] de iij*s*. iij*d*. obstupatis pro j acra prati in Cok*s*holme.

([d] EMPCIO CALCIS PRO HOSPITALE. In solutis pro quatuor fodo*ur*sse
calcis emptis, unde ij fod*ur*sse propter hospitale et cum cariagio illuc,
iij*s*. ij*d*.)

CUSTUS IN VILLA HUC USQUE. Item ij fod*ur*sse propter messuagium, in
quo Henricus Colermaker manet, cum cariagio illuc, iij*s*., videlicet ad
Sowter row. Nota de factura novi tecti in tenemento in quo Henricus
Collermaker manet super Sowter Row.

Anno Ricardi abbatis xviij[mo] *incipiente.*

In solutis Roberto Bryg carpentario pro ([d] tota) carpentria novi tecti
ibidem continentis xvij copulas videlicet de le framyng illius operis
(per xiiij dies) quia meremium erat scapulatum antea ad manus ejus,
vj*s*. ij*d*.; item pro victualibus (et cervisia) eis datis in le reysyng' dicti
tecti, iiij*d*.; item Johanni Pippewelle et Johanni Pynchebec (juniori)
pro bemfyllyng ibidem per j diem, viij*d*.

NAYL' DE STAURO. Item in solutis pro mille latt*s*, vj*s*.; item pro latte
pynnys videlicet vj mille, xviij*d*.; item in solutis Johanni Aspeschaw
tegulatori pro opere tegulatoris videlicet iij rodis ibidem, xv*s*.; item
pro c parvis tegulis, vj*d*.; item in solutis pro perforacione de xv[c]
sclatt*s*, xv*d*.
Memorandum de xv*d*. receptis de Willelmo Morton seriante de ecclesia
pro veteri meremio.
Memorandum de xvij*d*. receptis pro veteri meremio vendito Henrico
Collermaker.
Memorandum de viij*d*., item viij*d*. de Johanne Skynner et aliis receptis
pro equis in Coksholme.

[*f. 41v.*] *Anno Ricardi abbatis xviij*° *incipiente.*[2]

SUTTON COMPOTUS. In solutis Roberto Brygg' carpentario pro traccione unius boverie ad Sutton in manerio ibidem, iiij*s*., in parte majoris
summe, scilicet v*s*.; et nota quod dictus Robertus cum *To*ma Heydys
erant in dicto opere per x dies.
Memorandum[3] quod dictus carpentarius fecisset unum cok copyl ibidem vel mayst*ur* copille; item ij schort sp*er*t*s* in fine occidentali dicti
[*sic*] domus; item alia opera ibidem, videlicet unum threyschold in ostio
ibidem grangie pro vento; item iij paria fenestrarum in coquina.
Memorandum[4] de iij bemysse iij sparr*s* fraccinis et uno pari dernys
(quercinis) emptis pro dicta domu, xxx*d*.; item ij paria [*sic*] stok*s* de
ferro, iiij*d*.; item unum threyschold et unum trasyn in domo calcis, iij*d*.

---

[1] In margin.   [2] *1455-6.*   [3] *In margin:* Nota.   [4] *In margin:* Nota in compoto.

Solucio fratris Willelmi Morton elemosinarii pro tunicis post festum Sancti Luce Ewangeliste[1] pro anno xvij° Ricardi abbatis. In primis fratri Willelmo Morton elemosinario, x*s.*; fratri Johanni Northoppe, v*s.*; item, ij*s.*; item, iij*s.*; et eque; fratri Willelmo Walmysforthe, x*s.*, in die Sancte Cecilie;[2] fratri Waltero Wermyngton, x*s.*, in die Sancte Barbare virginis;[3] item fratri Willelmo Leycet*ur*, qui fuit thesaurarius, vj*s.* viij*d.*

Memorandum quod frater Ricardus Bysle emit unum (square) pyylle de chyppisse de fratre Willelmo Morton elemosinario vij pedum squar' ix pedum altitudinis pro vj*s.*; et quoad solucionem dictus elemosinarius habebit iij*s.* iiij*d.* de solucione pro speciebus per viam stupacionis ad festum Purificacionis Beate Marie proxime sequens; item ij*s.* viij*d.* solvit alia vice et eque pro hac solucione.

Memorandum[4] quod frater Willelmus Leycet*ur* obstupavit vj*s.* viij*d.* de communibus fratris Willelmi Morton elemosinarii propter debitum dicti elemosinarii ad officium thesaurarii de anno xvij, videlicet xxiiij*s.* j*d. q.*, et debet xvij*s.* v*d. q.*; unde solvit vj*s.* viij*d.*; item xij*d.*, per viam obstupacionis facte per Robertum Crosse. Et dictus elemosinarius debet (*d* ante) dicto fratri Willelmo Leycet*ur* modo ix*s.* ix*d. q.*; unde solvit iij*s.* vj*d.* per redditum alneti dicti selerarii, et j libram cimini spectantem sive pertinentem officio elemosinarii; item pro una libra cere obstupanda contra dictum Willelmum Leycet*ur* ex quo fuit thesaurarius. Summa soluta 18*s.* 4*d.* et debentur 6*s.* j*d. q.*

[*f. 42r.*] *Anno domini Ricardi abbatis xviij° incipiente.*[5]

Debita que frater Willelmus (Morton) debet.

Domino Willelmo Exton priori, nichil; domino Willelmo Melton pro officio hostilarie pro 7 annis, scilicet 4*s.* per annum, 28*s.* (solvit); (*d* domino Willelmo Markham, Roberto Orwyn, iij*li.* viij*s.*, (solvit) (parum); domino Johanni Burneham, xiij*s.* iiij*d.*, quos solvit et equet; domino T*ome* Maxey [6   ]; domino Ricardo Harlton, lxix*s.* iij*d. q.*, (solvit); domino Willelmo Vfforde (nichil); domino Henrico Lynne, 4*s.* 4*d.*; domino Nicholao, (solvit); domino Willelmo Hontyngdon, (solvit); fratri Johanni Burrowh iiij*s.*; tamen iste debet pro capella et officio [magistri] operis[7] et aliis elemosinario, (solvit); fratri Johanni Ryalle, ij*s.* ij*d.* pro prato in Maxey medow (solvit); fratri Willelmo Burrowh, sacriste, l*s.*, pro anno xvij° de redditu assise; fratri Johanni Lesyngham, viij*s.* pro refectorio; fratri Roberto Notyngham, xxiiij*s.* j*d. q.*)

Memorandum quod iste solvit sibimet anno xix° incipiente, de communibus fratris Willelmi Morton, vj*s.* viij*d.*; modo debetur xvij*s.* v*d. q.*, tamen iste tesaurarius debet fratri Willelmo elemosinario pro officio [magistri] operis[7] xij*d.* (*d* per annum, et est aretro pro iij annis); item pro

---

[1] *18 Oct. 1455* (?). The almoner made these payments after the commencement of the 18th year of Abbot Richard in respect of his 17th year which ended about Michaelmas, 1455.
[2] *22 Nov.*   [3] *16 Dec.*
[4] Two paragraphs have been rearranged in accordance with a note made by the compiler of this account.
[5] *1455–6.*   [6] Left blank. *In margin:* parum.   [7] Master of the works.

fodicione lapidis per Ricardum Barbur, iiij*s*. Item idem frater Robertus
solvit sibimet iterum de communibus fratris Willelmi Morton vj*s*. viij*d*.
ad festum Pasche. Idem thesaurarius obstupavit vj*s*., quos pitanciarius
solveret elemosinario. Item elemosinarius solvit viij*d*. dicto fratri
Roberto [Notyngham] et equet.

FRATRI ROBERTO NOTYNGHAM ANNO XX INCIPIENTE.[1]

Elemosinarius debet xxiiij*s*. j*d*. *q*.; unde supradictus Robertus thesaurarius obstupavit penes dictum elemosinarium ad festum Michaelis, vj*s*.
viij*d*., de communibus dicti elemosinarii. Item dictus elemosinarius
solvit ad Johannem Coldwelle iiij*s*. pro dicto thesaurario. Idem
thesaurarius obstupavit pro ij libris cere xij*d*. Item idem Robertus
Notyngham thesaurarius obstupavit vj*s*. de redditibus quos pitanciarius
solveret elemosinario per annum. Item obstupavit vj*s*. viij*d*. ad festum
Pasche de communibus supradicti elemosinarii (et equet).

Item frater Robertus thesaurarius recepit pro anno xx Ricardi abbatis
in primis vj*s*. viij*d*., ad festum Michaelis xxj^mo incipiente; item 5
carectatas spinarum, precium carectate 6*d*.; item ij mille cooperture,
precium 13*s*. 4*d*. Item thesaurarius obstupavit vj*s*. quos pitanciarius
solveret elemosinario; item vij*d*. pro una libra cere, 29*s*. (et equet).

Anno[2] *Ricardi abbatis xvij ad festum Annunciacionis Beate Marie*.[3]

Johanna Gattele recepta erat inter sorores ad capellam Sancti Tome
Martiris, et dicta Johanna recepit de elemosinario anno xviij in festo
Advincule Sancti Petri,[4] ij*s*.; item per filium[5] suum, scilicet fratrem
Willelmum Byry, iij*s*. iiij*d*. et equet.

[*f. 42v.*] PASTON.[6] Rector[7] ibidem, dominus Johannes Hamurton, solvit
domino Willelmo Morton elemosinario, ut patet in fine septimi folii
precedentis, videlicet:—xix*li*. xvj*s*. vj*d*. per vices pro annis xv et xvj,
et sic debet clare pro dictis ij annis xxx*s*. ij*d*. Postea solvit in anno
xviij° Ricardi abbatis, scilicet feria quarta in ebdomada Palmarum,[8]
xxx*s*. ij*d*.; et sic equet pro ij annis. Item idem solvit eodem die de
anno tercio, xxxvj*s*. vj*d*.; et nota quod iste due ultime soluciones erant
simul in uno die scilicet feria quarta in ebdomada Palmarum per filium
Roberti Steynton. Item idem rector solvit ad festum Sancti Georgii,[9]
xl*s*.; (^d et sic debet modo pro duobus annis preteritis xxix*s*. ix*d*.) et
pro tercio anno cvj*s*. viij*d*.; ut patet in sexto folio ante per manum
proprium dicti rectoris; unde solvit infra Octabas Apostolorum Petri

---

[1] *1457–8.* [2] Footnote upside down.
[3] *25 Mar. 1455.* [4] *1 Aug. 1456.*
[5] The mother of William Gatley alias Borough, or Bury, is admitted into the sister house.
She appears to have received an annual fee of *5s. 4d.* The question arises whether any other
sisters were relatives of monks who had been born in the town. For further particulars
of the sisters see *Valor Ecclesiasticus*, translated in N.R.S. xii. 18. References to 'the
Sister House' appeared continually in Peterborough Cathedral registers up to the eighteenth
century. See also above, pp. xxviii–xxix.
[6] The date of this account is not stated at the head of the folio. It was apparently in
respect of the period 1456–9. See the payments therein referred to.
[7] See above, pp. 7, 66, 68. [8] *24 Mar. 1456.* [9] *23 Apr. 1456.*

et Pauli anno 18[1] pro anno xvij, xxvj*s*. v*d*. (^d viii*d*.). Item idem solvit anno xix pro anno xvj per Johannem Coldwel xxvj*s*. viij*d*., videlicet in crastino Concepcionis Beate Marie anno quo supra, scilicet xix^{mo} Ricardi abbatis;[2] item per Laurencium Toche in crastino Anunciationis Beate Marie,[3] xxiij*s*. iiij*d*.; item in camera abbatis, rectore de Fletton presente, xx*s*. in vigilia Philippi et Jacobi.[4] Modo debet xl*s*.; unde solvit per Laurencium Toche, vj*s*. viij*d*.; item per dictum Laurencium, xiij*s*. iiij*d*. tercio die ante Purificacionem Beate Marie[5] anno xx° Ricardi abbatis.

Item supradictus rector solvit xviij*s*., et elemosinarius condonavit ij*s*., pro diversis causis sibi allegatis ex parte dicti rectoris.

LAURENCIUS TOOCHE. Nuncius rectoris de Paston solvit feria tercia Pentecostes[6] xl*s*. ad Johannem Coldwel. Item dictus Laurencius solvit in crastino sancti Oswaldi[7] xxxiij*s*. iiij*d*. pro anno xviij Ricardi abbatis. Item pro eodem anno dictus Laurencius solvit in capella Trinitatis[8] xxxiij*s*. iiij*d*.; memorandum de falso grosso recepto. Item tercio Kal. May[9] idem Laurencius solvit iiij marcas anno xx pro anno [[10]   ]. Idem Laurencius solvit in Vigilia Sancti Barnabe anno xx°[11] pro anno [[10]   ] xliij*s*. iiij*d*.; item anno xxj in die Sancti Juliani episcopi,[12] xxvj*s*. viij*d*. pro 3 croppe; memorandum de iij falcis grossis receptis. Summa recepta de supradicto Laurencio, xj*li*. x*s*. pro iij annis, et debet xx*li*. x*s*., unde solvit receptori[13] domini Ricardi abbatis pro debito elemosinarii, ut patet alibi in computacione inter dictos elemosinarium et receptorem Ricardi abbatis videlicet:—iiij^{xx} quarteria brasii, precium quarterii, ij*s*. vj*d*., x*li*. Item idem Laurencius solvit x*s*.; item iiij Kal. May[14] l(^dj)x*s*., (^d ix*d*. *ob*.) Nota quod habuit j*d*. ad potum.[15] Memorandum de multis falsis denariis. Idem Laurencius solvit Sabbato infra octabas Corporis Christi anno xxj[16] pro anno [[10]   ] xl*s*., et debet 4*li*. (^d x*s*. 2*d*. *ob*.); unde solvit xx*s*., in Vigilia Symonis et Jude[17] per Robertum Morton; item xx*s*. anno xxij tempore regis et regine hic;[18] item per Willelmum Beylde, bocher, ut in carnibus, xx*s*.; item per Laurencium supradictum xx*s*. et eque.

SUMMA SOLUTA: 27*li*. (^d 19*s*. 9*d*. *ob*.)

[*f. 43r*.] *Anno domini Ricardi abbatis xvij° incipiente*.

DEBITA QUE DEBENTUR FRATRI WILLELMO MORTON ANNO QUO SUPRA. Dominus Ricardus Ayston abbas debet pro crosse [*sic*] de Weryngton et Roberto Brig' et croftis et elemosin' [[10]   ]; dominus Willelmus

---

[1] *6 July 1456.*   [2] *9 Dec. 1456.*   [3] *26 Mar. 1457.*   [4] *30 Apr. 1457.*
[5] *31 Jan. 1457/8.*   [6] *7 June 1457* (?).   [7] *6 Aug. 1457* (?).
[8] Payments were often made in chapels in the monastic church.
[9] *29 Apr. 1458.*   [10] Left blank.   [11] *10 June 1458.*   [12] *27 Jan. 1458/9.*
[13] Note the delivery or payment to the abbot's receiver of malt on account of sum due to the almoner, because of a debt due from the latter to the abbot.
[14] *28 Apr. 1459.*
[15] The almoner's debtor on making a payment is given a penny for a drink for himself, see back.   [16] *26 May 1459.*   [17] *27 Oct. 1459.*
[18] This royal visit during the year 1459-60 does not appear to have been recorded elsewhere in the Peterborough documents. It occurred probably after the battle of Bloreheath. There is a record of their visit to Croyland about this time.

Exton, prior, iij*s*. iiij*d*. ex quo fuit celerarius; item iij*s*. iiij*d*. solutos et non solvendos in aula minucionis; item (ᵈ iij*s*. iiij*d*.) (x*s*.) pro mensa dicti Willelmi Morton elemosinarii (et vicarii sui¹ per ij annos) in cursu primo post Pascha; (Item iij*s*. pro dimidio apro; item 8*d*. pro pane et servisia post Pascha ad Sutton); dominus T*omas* Depyng' pro officio celerarii,² iij*s*. iiij*d*. per annum per iiij annos; (ᵈ dominus Robertus Notyngham pro officio operis³ per iij annos xij*d*. per annum et 5*d*. pro fodicione); dominus Willelmus Spaldyng pro officio pitanciarii,⁴ vj*s*. (ᵈ per annum pro iij annis xviij*s*.); dominus Willelmus Melton ix*s*. pro fratre Johanne Wynwyk; dominus Johannes B*u*rrow junior⁵ pro capella Sancte Marie viij*d*. per annum per [⁶   ] annos; Willelmus Brasiar de Wysbeche (ᵈ vj*li*.) iiij*li*. pro brasio; item v*s*. pro breve; Johannes Hopkyn et Willelmus Hopkyn, c*s*. v marcas x*li*.; Ricardus Freman de Fodryngay, 7*s*.; Johannes Essam de eadem, iij*s*. j*d*.; Ricardus Mayhewhe de Deysb*u*rrow xxx*s*. de redditu assise ad capellam; Robertus Patynmak*er* de Burgo, xx*d*.; Willelmus Bentle, xxij*d*. *ob*. pro redditu septem acrarum quondam Reginaldi Donwyche; T*omas* Mo*ur*by de Croylond, iiij*d*., pro redditu j acre in Stybbyngg*s*, (solvit); Willelmus Payn de Burgo (ᵈ iiij*li*.), (xx*s*.), pro brasio (ᵈ inde solvit lx*s*.; iij*li*); (ᵈ Rector de Paston, vij*li*.) pro decima ibidem pro anno xvj°, (ut in folio ante). (ᵈ Idem rector debet pro decima) pro anno xvij°, (vide ex altera parte ante.)⁷ Dominus Ricardus Dycklon debet pro (ᵈ decima) (porcione) de Norb*u*rrow, x*s*. per annum pro [⁶   ] annis dimidio. (ᵈ Dominus⁸ Johannes Donsby, Rector de Owr'ton, debet pro xviij (ᵈ quarteriis) bussellis brasii, videlicet ij quarteriis, viij*s*. (iiij*d*.), unde solvit iij*s*. iiij*d*.; item ut de precio unius apri empti ibidem, v*s*., (solvit). (ᵈ Johannes⁹ Beylde bocher, x*s*., pro Swyns medow, citra v*s*. per antea solutos, (vacat)), unde solvit etc. et debet unum caponem et medietatem porci vel vituli. Johannes Colyn de Newerk debet (ᵈ iii)j*d*.

[*f. 43v*.] Petrus Lorr' et (ᵈ N   ) (Willelmus) Gedney de Wytheryngton (ᵈ 4*s*.; item 16*d*.) (in fine anni 17, ij*s*. iiij*d*.); item de eadem villa, Johannes Crosse, vij*s*. iiij*d*.

(a.) T*omas* Beylde de Walton debet iiij eskeppas frumenti et iij eskeppas brasii; Ricardus Eston de eadem, iij*s*. xj*d*.; Willelmus Pye de Paston, 7*s*. 6*d*.; T*homas* Eston pater debet (ut inferius) pro xj peciis meremii, iij*s*. Tomas Noblette (solvit); Jankyn Bern*er*de cum [⁶   ] fratre suo [⁶   ].

(b.) Willelmus Bernard de Gonthorp 4*s*. (ᵈ vel et) pro iij eskeppis brasii. Johannes Burges filius Ricardi B*u*rges, xxj*d*. Item Johannes

---

¹ The words in brackets were entered later above the line.
² Cellarer of the convent.   ³ Master of the works.
⁴ Pittancer.   ⁵ The warden of the Lady Chapel.
⁶ Left blank.   ⁷ Above, f. 42*v*., p. 76.
⁸ The cancellations were probably made after the memorandum had been entered in another compotus, or after the debtor had paid the whole or part of the amount due.
⁹ *In margin*: vacat.

Burges senior [   ]. Robertus Gronger, iij*s*. iiij*d*. Johannes Pypp-wel, 4ᶜ thac. Willelmus Arthorne de Eye pro ij eskeppis ciliginis, 14*d*. Johannes Colyngham (B*u*rrowhe) 12*d*. et plus.¹ Alicia Kelfole (Wytyl-sey), xij*d*. pro pomis. (ᵈ Frater Willelmus Wennam iij*d*. *ob*. (xv) unde ij*d*. ad Eld*u*rnale.) Johannes Roper de Wodston (ᵈ ij*s*.) vj*d*. (ᵈ Johannes Egyston de Clopton iiij*s*. pro equo.) (ᵈ Johannes Multon debet pro grissel amblar', v*s*., solvendos ad festum Lammesse anno xix domini Ricardi abbatis). Johannes Eston (Cast*u*r) pro focali, xviij*d*.

B*u*ROW. Johannes Wakyrle pro (ᵈ Paynsho) Cathetwhayte pro (ᵈ duobus annis); T*oma*s Eston pro uno beem, uno walplate, 7 sp*er*rys; Johannes Wryhte pro ij sp*er*rys et 7 h*er*dyll'. Johannes Bradbyry vel cum barba debet v*s*. iij*d*. de redditu, ut in anno xv et folio xxiij ante; idem debet de redditu in Comersgate.

WALTON. Symon Walleram debet de redditu assise ut patet postea. (ᵈ Johannes Incley iiij*s*. iiij*d*. anno xviij finiente.) Johannes Horne, iiij*d*.; Willelmus Belamy pro firma terre per ij annos, viij*s*. Willelmus Hawxby et Johannes Chaln*er* debent fratri Willelmo Morton ccccc rubias tylas vel wallyngtyl'; Willelmus Dawntre, x*d*.; (ᵈ Johannes Asp-schaw, xv*s*.)

[*f. 44r*.] *Anno Ricardi abbatis xviij incipiente*.²

CUSTUS IN B*u*RGO SUPER SOWT*ER* ROW. Memorandum de cariagio T*home* Multon ad messuagium super Sowt*er* Row in quo Henricus Collermak*er* manet. In primis [pro] ij carectatis meremii, scilicet (novi) tecti ibidem, (iiij*d*.;) item ij carectatis [de] sclatt*s* de hospitale illuc (vj*d*.;) j carectata sclatt*s* de officio illuc, (ij*d*.;) iij carectatis terre rubie illuc, (vj*d*.;) j carectata (terre) ad messuagium ibidem iuxta (ij*d*.;) j carectata zabuli illuc, (vj*d*.)

NECESSARIA. In una pecia de gartheweb (de bono canabo) empta ad Depyng' pro singulis equinis longitudinis xij virgarum et dimidie, viij*d*.

SARRACIO AD SUTTON. In solutis Roberto et Willelmo (ᵈ Elyngham) Ev*er*yngham (de Gretam) fratribus pro roda et dimidia quercus sarrate. Prima pecia continebat xx tabulas, secunda xv, tercia xj. Notandum de viginti scoor' foote pro roda, vj*s*.

JOHANNES SMYTHE DE WODCROFT. Memorandum quod Johannes Smythe de Wodcroft solvit elemosinario in die Sancti Clementis Pape³ vj*s*. viij*d*., et notandum quod iurabat quod debebat elemosinario pro tunc nisi xx*s*., unde solvit x*s*. in die Sancti Antonii;⁴ item viij*s*. in Dominica Ramis Palmarum⁵ (ᵈ viij*s*.) et debet ij*s*. de anno xvij; unde solvit xxij*d*., et debet ij*d*.

JOHANNES DRAP*ER*. Omnibus computatis inter fratrem Willelmum Morton et Johannem Draper in festo Sancti Nicholai.⁶

¹ Almost illegible.   ² *1455*.   ³ *23 Nov. 1455*.   ⁴ *17 Jan. 1456*.
⁵ *21 Mar. 1456*.   ⁶ *6 Dec*. The entry was not completed.

CLOPTON. ɸ In solutis Roberto Bryg' carpentario pro diversis emendatis in messuagio in quo Johannes Leygben nuper manebat, videlicet in occidentali latere grangie ibidem, scilicet le drawyng' in unius plaate longitudinis fere xxx pedum et item le drawyng' tocius illius Walsche illius partis cum vj novis coplysse tingnorum in tecto cum iiij post*s* (de) novo impositis (ᵈ vel de novo impositis) cum emendacione unius nedd*ur* govylle ibidem per ix dies cum T*homa* Heyd' adiuvante, iiij*s*., per manus Henrici Frer' collectoris; item pro mensa eorum iij*s*. (dicto collectori;) item in datis pro rewardo dicto Roberto carpentario, xvj*d*. pro labore suo transeundo de Helpston illuc et redeundo. Quere plus in principio quinti folii sequentis ad tale signum. q¹

[*f. 44v.*] *Anno Ricardi Assheton abbatis xviij incipiente.*²

CARIAGIUM ROBERTI CROSSE PRO ELEMOSINARIO.
In primis [in] ij carectatis calcis ad hospitale, scilicet ij fodursse, vj*d*.; item alia carectata de Heygate illuc, scilicet ij*c* rubie bryc vel walletyl' cum vij*c* lathysse, iij*d*.; item j carectata sclatt*s* ad hospitale, iij*d*.

IN BURGO. Item ij carectatis calcis ad messuagium Henrici Coller-make*r*, iiij*d*.

HAMOND MEDOW. In solutis pro mundacione sive renovacione de viij rodis quasi de novo factis anno precedente, vj*d*.

*Anno 18*³ *incipiente in Adventu.*

Nota bene. Memorandum quod ista computacio subscripta facta est pro anno xvij Ricardi abbatis.

SUTTON.⁴
(ᵈ In solutis T*home* Smythe pro uno pari [de] heyngl' et stok*s* pon-derantibus iiij libras dimidiam deliberato Roberto Mowncelle miller, ix*d*.; item Johanni Yvisse in pessulis snatchysse cum aliis ferramentis pro ostiis grangie ibidem, vj*li*., xij*d*.)

HOSPITALE. In solutis T*ome* Smyth pro ij ligaturis ferri pro nova aula ibidem (ponderantibus) v libras, x*d*.; item in solutis dicto fabro pro iij spyndyll' propter iiij faanysse cum vj claspys ferreis ponderantibus xiiij libras, ij*s*. iiij*d*.; item eidem fabro pro factura de le fanysse, iiij*d*.; item eidem fabro pro iij barr*s* ferreis pro una fenestra in le garrette versus austrum ponderantibus xvij libras, ij*s*. x*d*.

IN OFFICIO. Item eidem fabro pro iij ligaturis ferreis propter magnas portas iuxta fontem ponderantibus xij libras, ij*s*.; item eidem fabro pro uno pari catenarum uno haspe et ij stapyll'⁵ ponderantibus vj libras, xij*d*.

FERRURA EQUORUM. In solutis pro xx ferramentis equinis, ij*s*. vj*d*., pro xlv *r*emovyngg*s*, xv*d*.; item in froste nayl*s*, ij*d*.; in solutis pro una vanga ferrata, ij*d*.⁶

---

¹ See below, p. 87. This sign may be an Arabic 5.   ² *1455.*   ³ *1455.*
⁴ The following paragraph was deleted with the explanation: 'scribitur in compoto'.
⁵ Fetters for the prisoners in the jail.
⁶ At the foot of this page are the figures xv*s*. ij*d*.

[*f. 45r.*] *Anno xvij° incipiente anno domini Ricardi Aysshston abbatis xvij° incipiente.*[1]

Memorandum quod post computacionem inter fratrem Willelmum Morton elemosinarium et Johannem Kyrcby de Dodyngton [de] nova aula facta ad hospitale anno Ricardi abbatis xvij°, Johannes Kyrcby debet dicto elemosinario xvij*s*. viij*d*.; item x*c* sclatt*s*, (18*s*.) Item debet pro labore Johannis Coldewelle equitantis ad dictum Johannem pro defectu de sclatt*s*. Postea dictus Johannes Kyrcby vendebat domino Willelmo Morton v mille [de] sclatt*s* cum cariagio ad hospitale ad cooperiendum unum novum garrette ibidem in grosso, continentem iij rodas pro xxxvij*s*. vj*d*., et omnibus computatis dictus Johannes Kyrcby debet predicto elemosinario ix*c* sclatt*s* cum cariagio ad officium elemosinarii.

JOHANNES IRN*E*RDE, anno xviij° Ricardi abbatis, solvit xiij*s*. iiij*d*. (elemosinario,) feria vj ante Pasca,[2] et debet clare, iiij marcas (pro rectoria;) item iiij*li*. pro decima de Newp*a*rk; item pro certis reparacionibus [3   ;] item [3   ;] unde idem Johannes Irn*e*rde solvit in crastino Sancti Marci Ewangeliste[4] in presencia fratris Ricardi Bysle, vj*s*. viij*d*.; item per Nicholaum Smythe, xx*s*., Johanne Coldwel nuncio; item vj*s*. viij*d*. per hostilarium dicti Nicholai feria tercia in ebdomada Palmarum anno xix Ricardi abbatis.[5] Quere plus in [3   ]

WILLELMUS B*U*RROW SACRISTA. Memorandum quod in die Sancti Tome Apostoli anno xviij[6] frater Willelmus Morton elemosinarius solvit fratri Willelmo Burrowhe sacriste in parte solucionis de v marcis, xx*s*. de grossis, et unum nobile auri; item unum soorte de ficubus et racemis, precium xv*s*. (*d* viij*d*.), (quia Johannes [Coldewelle] famulus elemosinarii equitabat ad Norhamton propter illos;) item mille mille rubie tyle sive wallyng' tyle, xij*s*. Summa soluta liij*s*. viij*d*. et debet clare dicto sacriste, xiij*s*.; tamen supradictus elemosinarius habet sive debet obstupare contra supradictum sacristam x*s*. recipiendos de magistro Ricardo Dycklon, rectore ecclesie de Norb*u*row pro porcione ibidem. Idem elemosinarius solvit dicto sacriste anno xix° in previgilia Simonis et Jude,[7] xiij*s*. iiij*d*.; item Dominica quarta Adventus Domini,[8] x*s*., et ij quadrantes auri; item Sabbato Sexagesime,[9] vj*s*. viij*d*. per manus Johannis Coldewel; item pro focali Johanni Barb*u*r, (xx penykydd*s*, xx*d*.); item pro ficubus et racemis, xv*s*. (*d* iiij*d*.) Require plus in folio 17 sequente ad tale signum ⊠[10] SUMMA SECUNDA SOLUTA, 50*s*.

Memorandum quod Johannes Irn*e*rde petit allocacionem (*d* de xij*s*.) 16*d*. pro decima ij acrarum terre in Sowthfeld, ut in folio 1 ante;[11] item pro (decima) j acre prati, iiij*d*.; item pro decima alterius acre ibidem in Marram mett per rectorem Peykyrc, (4*d*.;) item iij*s*. iiij*d*. in reparacione ut in ostiis et magnis portis ad Maxey.

1 *1454.*
2 *26 Mar. 1456.*
3 Left blank.
4 *26 Apr. 1456.*
5 *12 Apr. 1457.*
6 *21 Dec. 1455.*
7 *26 Oct. 1456.*
8 *19 Dec. 1456.*
9 *26 Feb. 1457.*
10 See below, p. 111.
11 See above, pp. 25–26.

[*f. 45v.*] *Anno domini Ricardi Aysshston abbatis xviij°.*[1]

In vino empto (in die Natalis domini) de fratre Johanne Ryalle, sub-sacrista, videlicet ij lagenis (solvit) j potelle (solvit,) j quarte (solvit); item j quarte (solvit); item j potel (Oxney) et j pynte (solvit.)

FRUMENTUM. In solutis pro quatuor quarteriis emptis de balivo magistri Willelmi Rathe, precium quarterii frumenti iiij*s.*; item in solutis Johanni Egiston pro uno quarterio, iij*s.* iiij*d.*; item in solutis pro ij bussellis frumenti emptis in foro, xij*d.*

AVENE. In solutis Johanni Drap*er* pro iij esk*eppis* avenarum, vj*d.*; item pro ij esk*eppis* emptis per Johannem Coldewelle, iiij*d.*; item de Johanne Yvysse de Sutton [pro] iiij esk*eppis*, vj*d.*; item ij esk*eppis*, iiij*d. ob.*; item x esk*eppis*, xvj*d.*; item (ᵈi)j quarteriis et (ᵈ ij) iiij eskeppys de Ricardo Pyndar, xviij*d.*

PISE. In solutis pro uno esk*eppa* (iij peck*s*) pro gardino, iij*d. ob.*; item pro (ᵈ vj eskeppis) ij quarteriis de Petro Lorr*yer* iij*s.*; item j quarterio et iiij esk*eppis*, ij*s.* iiij*d.*; item j quarterio, xx*d.*

BREVE ad arestandum Johannem Baxst*er* pybak*er*, Willelmum Bowyar' de B*ur*go, Johannem Eyr' de Sutton, Johannem Irn*er*de de Yaxle, Johannem Jelyan de B*ur*go furb*ur*, xxx die Januarii[2] anno regni nostri xxxiiij, (30*li.*[3])

BASTONROPE. In solutis pro xxx bonchysse de bastonrope emptis de sacrista B*ur*gi, xx*d.*

NOTA. Memorandum quod T*omas* Noblette de Paston solvit elemo-sinario (pro anno xvij) xx*d.* de redditu, et stupavit iiij*d.* (male et iniuste,) solutos collectori de Wyryngton. Memorandum quod de iij esk*eppis* frumenti nisi 38 panes ponderantes lxx libras; item de eodem frumento secunda vice 46 panes ponderantes vˣˣvj libras. (ᵈ Summa de panibus, 84.) SUMMA de panibus iiij*ˣˣ* et iiij*ᵒʳ* ponderantes viij*ˣˣ*xvj libras.

Ricardus Clocsmythe (solvit)[4] ad festum Natalis domini (solvit) anno quo supra scilicet xviij debet elemosinario 28*s.* 4*d.*, unde solvit ij marcas et debet 20*d.* Item solvit postea vj*s.* per J*ohannem* Waldyng; item ix*s.* in ebdomada Pasche anno 19 pro anno 18.

Ebdomada prima, v esk*eppe* pisarum; ebdomada secunda, vj esk*eppe* dimidia; tercia, vj esk*eppe* dimidia; quarta [*cetera desunt.*]

[*f. 46r.*] *Anno domini Ricardi abbatis xviij.*[5]

SOLUCIO FRATRIS WILLELMI MORTON ELEMOSINARII PRO SPECIEBUS AD FESTUM PURIFICACIONIS.[6]
In primis fratribus Willelmo Morton, elemosinario, Waltero Wermyng-ton (solvit x*s.*,) T*home* Gosberkyrc (solvit x*s.*,) Johanni Northop (solvit xj*s.*,) Ricardo Bysle (solvit x*s.*,) Willelmo Melton, (solvit x*s.*,) Willelmo

---

Walmysf*ord* (solvit x*s*.,) Willelmo Byri (v*s*.,) Johanni Croylond (v*s*.,) Willelmo Ramsey cuilibet x*s*. [*sic*] SUMMA. c*s*.

COXHOLME ANNO XVIJ[1] [RECEPTA.]
Memorandum quod elemosinarius recipiebat de Johanne Beyl boch*er* (anno sexto decimo) pro Coxholme (23*s*. 4*d*.) et Swynsmedow (15*s*.). De ([d] Johanne) Toma Lewyn et T*oma* Molton pro j acra prati ibidem, ij*s*. ij*d*. (solverunt;)[2] de Johanne Sab*ur*to̧n et Willelmo Maydelette pro secunda acra ibidem ij*s*. ij*d*. (solverunt;) de Johanne Nafferton skynn*er* pro tercia acra ibidem, ij*s*. iij*d*. (solverunt); de Ricardo Fysch*er*' vel Ricardo Pantre pro iiij acra ibidem, ij*s*. ij*d*. (solverunt); de Roberto Crosse de Westegate pro v acra ibidem, ij*s*. ij*d*.; de Toma Townsende pro tribus rodis prati ibidem, xxj*d*. (solvit)

[SOLUCIONES.]
Et in deliberatis T*ome* Hab*ur*gylle tenenti elemosinarii (iij rode) ad cooperiendam unam domum de novo factam in Kowgate ad custus elemosinarii, quo ad magnum meremium, scilicet ij walleplat*s*, ([d]i)ij balk*s*, residuum vero reparacionis per dictum T*omam* Hab*ur*gyl, bark*er*; item in solutis pro falcacione ligacione cum schokyng' de mille et vj[c] garbis cooperture pro hospitale et tenantria ad Sutton, iij*s*. iiij*d*.; item in solutis uno de Fletton cum carectta sua cariando ibidem in Coxholme dictam coperturam ad unum cornerium prati, xvj*d*.; et in ij hominibus conductis pro le stackyng' (ejusdem) ibidem per j diem, viij*d*.; item in uno homine conducto cum batella sua ad cariandam dictam cooperturam ad feriam [*sic*] de Alownton, xx*d*.; item in solutis pro iiij carectatis scilicet dicte coperture ad Sutton,[3] xx*d*.

SWYNSMEDOW, ANNO RICARDI ABBATIS XVIJ.[4] De Johanne Pybaker, x*s*.

COLUMBARIUM ET MANGNA GRANGIA AD HOSPITALE, ANNO RICARDI ABBATIS XVI.
De vicario B*ur*gi et Willelmo Bowyȝar, xj*s*. viij*d*.

SPYTILLECROFTE,[5] ANNO XVI.
De Riçardo Pynd*ar* et Willelmo Sewale, xx*s*. Verte folium.

[*f. 46v.*] COLUMBARIUM AD HOSPITALE, ANNO RICARDI ABBATIS XVII.[4]
De vicario Burgi, vj*s*. viij*d*.

GRANGIA IBIDEM. De T*homa* Pep*ur*, boch*er*', vj*s*. viij*d*. anno xvij.

SPYTYLLECROFTE. De T*homa* Pep*ur*, boch*er*, xxiij*s*. iiij*d*. anno xvij.

Anno xviij[6]

SPYTYLCROFTE. De T*homa* Pep*ur*, xxiij*s*. iiij*d*.; item de eodem pro grangia ibidem, ut in anno precedente.

---

[1] *1454-5*.
[2] The accountant first entered the sum due and afterwards wrote *sol*' over the name of each person who paid and, in some cases, over the amount as well.
[3] Apparently reeds, cut in Coxholme for thatching, were taken by water to Alwalton hithe or ferry, and carted thence to Sutton.   [4] *1454-5*.
[5] The field near St. Leonard's hospital in the Spittle.   [6] *1455-6*.

COKKYSHOLME. De Henrico Kysby, (solvit); et Ricardo fratre suo, (solvit); et Johanne Parteney, 18*s*. 6*d*.; (solvit), et habent diem Sancti Martini; [*In margin*] solverunt.

A. Quere plus in 12 folio sequente.[1]

B. SWYNSMEDOW. De Johanne Aspeschawhe pro v acris ibidem, x*s*.

FALLAMHYRNE. De filio Johannis Saburton, (solvit), et Willelmo Tyler (solvit), iij*s*. 8*d*. pro et c*e*tera(?) unde solverunt iiij*d*. pro arra et debent iij*s*. iiij*d*., (solverunt.)

JOHANNES COLDEWELLE. Anno Ricardi abbatis xviij in die Sancte Prisce Virginis videlicet xv Kal. Februarii.[2]

Recepit de magistro suo, elemosinario, pro stipendio suo 4*s*. 6*d*. et eque pro tunc; item xv Kal. Marcii,[3] iiij*s*. vj*d*.; item (pridie) Idus Marcii,[4] iiij*s*. vj*d*.; item tercio Idus Aprilis,[5] iiij*s*. vj*d*.; item vij Idus May,[6] iiij*s*. vj*d*.; item viij Idus Junii,[7] 4*s*. 6*d*.; item 4 Nonas Julii,[8] [9   ] (solvit); item in festo Advincule Sancti Petri[10] (solvit;) in festo (A) (d Bertini) iiij*s*. vj*d*. (solvit,) Decollationis (B) Johannis Baptiste[11] (C); item Dominica ante festum Michaelis,[12] iiij*s*. vj*d*. (solvit;) item ix Kal. Novembris,[13] iiij*s*. vj*d*.; item xj Kal. Decembris,[14] iiij*s*. vj*d*.; item xiiij Kal. Januarii,[15] iiij*s*. vj*d*.; item pro viij ebdomadis ad festum Ermenilde[16] regine, ix*s*.; in crastino Gregorii,[17] iiij*s*. vj*d*.; item iiij Idus Aprilis,[18] iiij*s*. vj*d*.; item viij Idus May,[19] iiij*s*. vj*d*.; item Nonas Junii,[20] iiij*s*. vj*d*.; item v Nonas Julii,[21] iiij*s*. vj*d*.; item pridie Kal. Augusti,[22] iiij*s*. vj*d*.; item quinto Kal. Septembris,[23] iiij*s*. vj*d*.; item vij Kal. Octobris,[24] iiij*s*. vj*d*.; item x Kal. Novembris,[25] iiij*s*. vj*d*.; item xij Kal. Decembris[26] et die Nativitatis Domini,[27] ix*s*., scilicet de precio unius equi nigri; item in festo Gregorii,[28] xiij*s*. vj*d*., pro iij mensibus; item quinto Idus Aprilis,[29] iiij*s*. vj*d*.; Quere in 12 folio sequente ad tale ⊙.[30]

HODYS MEDOW. De Willelmo Sewale pro ij acris cum multis sellionibus ibidem, ij*s*. et habet diem festum Michaelis proximi; item debet xij*d*. pro Spitilcrofte; item uxor eius debet vij*d*. pro flaxlonde. Johannes Clark de Wodcroffte solvit vij*s*. in Sabbato Ramis Palmarum;[31] et debet ij*s*. de anno xvij Ricardi abbatis, unde solvit xxij*d*.; et debet ij*d*.

[*f. 47r.*] *Anno Ricardi abbatis xviij.*[32]

EBDOMADA SEXAGESIME ET MINUCIO TERCII PRIORIS; ITEM DOMINICA QUINQUAGESIME.[33]

DOMINICA. In aprina, ut in aliis annis precedentibus; item in uno

---

[1] The note marked A in the MS. is written in the margin opposite the last words of Coldwell's receipts—at n. 30. The reference is to the entries on p. 106.

[2] *18 Jan. 1456.*	[3] *16 Feb.*	[4] *14 Mar.*
[5] *11 Apr.*	[6] *9 May.*	[7] *6 June.*
[8] *4 July.*	[9] Blank.	[10] *1 Aug.*
[11] *29 Aug.*	[12] *26 Sept.*	[13] *24 Oct.*
[14] *21 Nov.*	[15] *19 Dec.*	[16] *13 Feb. 1457.*
[17] *13 Mar.*	[18] *10 Apr.*	[19] *8 May.*
[20] *5 June.*	[21] *3 July.*	[22] *31 July.*

[23] *28 Aug.* The word 'Augusti' (deleted) occurs in error in the MS.

[24] *25 Sept.*	[25] *23 Oct.*	[26] *20 Nov.*	[27] *25 Dec.*
[28] *12 Mar. 1458.*	[29] *9 Apr.*	[30] See below, p. 106.	
[31] *20 Mar. 1456* (?).	[32] *1455–6.*	[33] *7 Feb. 1456.*	

ferculo grossarum carnium cum una assacione ad prandium et alia assacione ad cenam, v*d*.; in ij aucis, viij*d*.; in carnibus vitulinis, viij*d*.; in wyldefowle ad cenam, vij*d*.: et in j pullet sive gallina, ij*d*.; feria secunda, in uno perfecto ferculo pro prandio et cena, v*d*.; in iiij capitibus vitulinis, vij*d*.; in uno capone cum iij gallinis, ix*d*.; ad cenam in uno sew, v*d*.; in (4) volatilibus, vj*d*.; feria tercia, in uno perfecto ferculo pro prandio et cena, v*d*.; in j porcello, v*d*.; in 8 volatilibus, vij*d*.; in pedibus vitulinis ad cenam, iiij*d*.; feria quarta, nichil.[1] Feria v, in ovis kolloppys, v*d*. *ob*.; in viij (volatilibus) teel', vij*d*. ad cenam; item eodem die ad prandium, in ij aucis expensis ad prandium, viij*d*.

DOMINICA QUINQUAGESIME. In uno pestelle porci cum capite vitulino, iiij*d*.; cum una assacione, j*d*. *ob*.; in volatilibus ad cenam, ij*d*. Memorandum quod iij anguille assate erant expense feria quarta ante, viij*d*.

VINUM. In vino empto in festo Apostolorum Petri et Pauli[2] de Johanne Tylly, videlicet iij lagenis v pynt*s*, precium lagene x*d*., iij*s*.

NOTA DE SOLUCIONE [PRO SIGILLACIONE] UNIUS BREVIS.
Memorandum quod Johannes Coldewelle solvebat ix*d*. pro sigillacione unius brevis, quando fuit Londoniis ante festum Purificacionis[3] in presencia Ricardi Pytt*s*.

Anno Ricardi abbatis 16.[4]

A. CUSTUS MURORUM SANCTI JOHANNIS BAPTISTE.
Fodicio [*sic*] vj carectatarum cum cariagio illuc, xij*d*.; in uno latomo conducto ad emendandum dictos muros in tribus locis in grosso, xvij*d*. De Willelmo Barb*ur* aque baiulatore pro una carectata, (*d* ij*s*. 3*d*.) xx*d*. solvit.[5]

B. CUSTUS IN OFFICIO.[6] In solutis Johanni Pyppewelle pro certis diversis defectibus emendatis in muris (gardini) Sancti Johannis Baptiste; item in consimili in muris (petrinis) gardini infra officium elemosinarii, iij*s*. v*d*.

TERRE RUBIE. Item in solutis Willelmo Belamy pro vj carectatis terre rubie ad supradictum opus, ix*d*.

RECEPTA AD SPYTYLCROFT. De To*ma* Hab*ur*gylle pro iiij carectatis focalis sibi venditis, vij*s*. 4*d*., (solvit); de Willelmo Davyntre pro una carectata, ij*s*. j*d*.; de Willelmo Clerk pro j carectata, ij*s*.; de To*ma* Pep*ur* pro j carectata, ij*s*. j*d*.; de Johanne Smythe famulo Johannis Stel pro

---

[1] The word 'nichil' is marked with dots for deletion.
[2] *29 June 1456.*   [3] *Before 2 Feb. 1455/6.*   [4] *1453–4.*
[5] *Marks over murorum and uno as well as at the beginning and end of this sentence indicate that its proper position is at the end of f. 47r.*
[6] The almoner's office was adjoining the eastern gate of the Monastic Close. Presumably his garden was the southern part of the original vineyard, where is now the garden of Archdeaconry House. The garden of St. John the Baptist was situated presumably in St. John's Close, the field on the eastern side of the modern Vineyard Road. See also note on p. 101.

j carectata, ijs. jd. (solvit); de Johanne Leggette pro j parva carectata, xijd., (solvit); de Johanne Kaker pro j carectata, xxd., (solvit); de Tendale scissore (pro carectata), xxvjd., (solvit).

[f. 47v.] *Anno Ricardi abbatis xviij.*[1]

SUTTON. In solutis Roberto Bryg' carpentario pro succisione meremii, scilicet iij bemysse, ij platts sive walleplats, ij wyffyrsse (precium vjd.), v tingnorum sive spartys per unum diem, vd.; in scapulacione dicti meremii cum iij tingnis de Roberto Conquest, precium iiijd. cum le framyng' per ix dies, (iijs.), scilicet ab uno homine; (memorandum de iij sparts emptis de Roberto Conquest, 4d.;) item in le reysyng' sive exaltacione dicti meremii sive tecti continentis xv coplysse, duobus carpentariis per unum diem, xd.; item in factura ij fenestrarum dictis carpentariis, vjd.; item in le drawyng' unius muri de camera supra stabulum ibidem per unum diem cum duobus hominibus, xijd. Idem carpentarius imposuit unum beeme in grangia ibidem. Summa vjs. vjd., unde Johannes Eyr' collector ibidem solvit dicto carpentario iiijs., et elemosinarius solvit residuum videlicet ijs. vjd.

Dominus Abbas debet fratri Willelmo Morton pro crofto continente x acras inter pratum Burgi et Newerk, videlicet xijs. per annum, sic per 4 annos et dimidium, liiijs. Idem dominus abbas recepit de elemosinario, videlicet fratre Willelmo Morton, xxs. versus Walsyngham[2] peregrinando. Idem dominus debet fratri predicto, xxs. implendo solucionem sacriste pro uno messuagio in Westgate. Idem dominus debet dicto elemosinario xxvs. pro lynyn yarne et una armilasa, scilicet a cloke. Idem dominus debet xls. pro uno hedge row ad lodgeyaate de Estwod'. Idem dominus debet iiijd. ex mutuo pro avic' [sic] etc.; idem dominus pro Crosse de Wyryngton, vjs.; item pro Johanne Bernerde, vs.; item pro Roberto Brig' carpentario ijs. Idem dominus debet fratri Willelmo Morton iiijli., videlicet pro omnibus fraccinis crescentibus in una fovea ex australi parte crofti elemosinarii ad capellam Beate Marie Magdelene, cum ccxl penykydds; item cum stowyng de omnibus salicibus et fraccinis iuxta et circa dictum capellam. Idem abbas debet dicto elemosinario pro una olla enea ponderante xliiij libras, precium unius libre ijd., vijs. iiijd. Idem abbas debet xxd. quos dictus elemosinarius solvit Johanne Craane.

Quere plus in ix folio sequente.[3]

Emma sive Emmota Gromchestur fuit facta ancilla sorarum[4] capelle Sancti Thome martiris, per consensum fratris Willelmi Morton elemosinarii, in festo Petri et Pauli anno quo supra.[5] Idem[4] Emma recepit de elemosinario, xijd.; item ijs.; item xijd.; item ijs.

RECEPTA. Memorandum de xxd. receptis de Johanne Eyyr juniore propter scapulaciones ibidem per eum venditas.

Memorandum de ij roll'[6] de meremio pro domo trahend cum uno poleyn de meremio, unum pykax de ferro ibidem ad Sutton.

---

[1] *1455–6.* [2] The abbot makes a pilgrimage to Walsingham.
[3] See p. 102. [4] *Sic.* [5] *29 June 1456.* [6] Roll, windlass.

[*f. 48r.*] *Anno Ricardi abbatis xviij.*[1]

CLOPTON. CUSTUS IBIDEM. (Item quere in quinto folio ante ad tale signum:—Ø)[2]

5. In solutis Johanni Bytrysche et T*home* Asselyn carpentariis conductis per iiij dies ad faciendum unum gabulum boriale unius solarii iuxta viam ibidem in quodam messuagio in quo Johannes Legbene nuper manebat, iij*s.*; in solutis pro splent*s* emtis de Willelmo Gardiner pro eodem opere, xij*d.*; item pro dawbyng' ibidem, xvj*d.*; item pro stramine cum cariagio illuc, xiiij*d.*; item Johanni Manton propter thakkyng' ibidem, cum serviente suo ibidem, scilicet emendando per loca per quatuor dies, xviij*d.*

NOTANDUM IN COMPOTO.
Item in ij bonchis bastonrope, ij*d.*; item pro lxiiij spyk*s*, iiij*d.*; item in stramine, xij*d.*; item thackyng' grangiam per vij dies, ij*s.* iiij*d.*; et servitoribus, viij*d.*; in solutis pro carpentria per iij [dies] domus ubi [Willelmus] Gardyn*er* manebat, iij*s.* iiij*d.*; stramen per Willelmum Gardyn*er* thackyng' per iij dies [3   ].

NAYL'. In solutis pro x^c grossis spyk' emptis pro B*r*igmylle, precium de c nayl' vj*d.*, v*s.*; item quod c nayl' de supradictis ponderant iiij libras dimidiam et dimidium quarteron. [*sic*]

HORSSE SCHON. In solutis pro ij duodenis emptis ad nundinas de Stan*ford*, xvij*d.*

SPAVEYN DE SORELLE IN TIBIIS POSTERIORIBUS.
In solutis cuidam scienti ad Owndylle, 6*d.*

CUSTUS IN BURGO. In emendacione unius serure in Howgate, ij*d.*, ubi Ricardus Crosse manet.

OFFICIUM CALX. In solutis (^d Johanni) Tome Thorppe et Johanni Aylston pro ij fod*ur*sse calcis, ij*s.* viij*d.*

RUBIE TYLE. Memorandum quod frater Willelmus Morton elemosinarius emebat per Johannem Coldewelle famulum suum v mille rubie tyle sive wallyngtyle ad Wygnale, precium [de] mille, iij*s.* viij*d.*, xviij*s.* iiij*d.*
Item Johannes B*er*newelle emebat xiiij^c rubie tyle ibidem pro dicto elemosinario, precium v*s.* Et in solutis dicto Johanni Bernwelle pro cariagio dicte rubie tyll', scilicet vj mille et iiij^c bryc de Wygnale ad Burgum per aquam, vj*s.* v*d.*; item in solutis cuidam de Fletton pro cariagio de xiiij^c cum carecta sua de Bulle yate ad officium elemosinarie, iiij*d. ob.*; (hospitale) item pro cariagio de mille rubie tyl' ad hospitale, propter le garrette ibidem.

Memorandum quod sacrista et magister operis habuerunt iiij mille pro xxiiij*s.*

[*f. 48v.*] *Anno domini Ricardi abbatis xviij.*[4]
Memorandum quod frater Willelmus Morton dedit Tome Morton erga ingressum suum in religionem ad Rampsey, videlicet:—in Translacione

---

[1] *1455-6.*   [2] See above, p. 80.   [3] Amount omitted.   [4] *1455-6.*

Sancti Martini episcopi[1] anno domini mcccclvj :—in primis ij paria de
strayl', (xjs. iid.); unum pannum de sago, (xs.) xiiij virgas;—alium
pannum de xiij virgis et dimidia, (xvs. viijd.); xij virgas stamini, (iiijs.);
ij uncias nigri serici, (xxd.); unam peliciam, (ijs. viijd.); unum bonum
covirlette greene, (vijs.); ij paria ocriarum, (ijs. ijd.); item xxs. iiijd.;
unam tunicam de nigro panno, (iiijs.); unam albam tunicam, (ijs. vjd.);
ij playts linie tele pro femoralibus, (xijd.); (item unam parvam cistam,
precium xijd.); vj Yrische skynnys blac ad penulandam unam almiciam,
(xviijd.); item [2   ] ulne [sic] de kanvasse pro ij kochowrs emptis de
Roberto Orwyn, [2   ]; (solvit); item in exhenniis [sic] domino abbati
de Rampsey, scilicet, vj caponibus ijs.; item in servisia, vjd.; item in
exhenniis domino priori ibidem ij caponibus, viijd.; in servisia, iiijd.;
item domino Johanni Glatton, in una olla servisie, iijd.; item ad unum
coclearium argenteum faciendum, iijs. iiijd.; item iijli. transiundo Oxo-
nias. SUMMA. vijli. xiiijs. 4d. [repeated in the margin]

SOLUCIO FRATRIS WILLELMI MORTON, ELEMOSINARII, AD FESTUM SANCTI
JOHANNIS BAPTISTE PRO LE O.
In primis dicto elemosinario, vjs. viijd.; item fratri Waltero, vjs. viijd.,
(solvit); item fratri Johanni Borowh, vjs. viijd., (solvit); item fratri
Willelmo Dey, vjs. viijd., (solvit); et fratri Roberto thesaurario iijs.
iiijd., (solvit); et equet pro hac solucione.

SOLUCIO FRATRIS WILLELMI MORTON PRO TUNICIS AD FESTUM SANCTI
LUCE EWANGELISTE PRO XVIII ANNO DOMINI RICARDI ABBATIS.[3] In
primis fratri Willelmo Morton, xs.; fratri Roberto Lythyngton, vjs.
viijd.; fratri Thome de Sancto Neoto ijs.; iiijs. viijd.; item vjs. viijd.;
fratri Willelmo Byry, 6s. 8d.; item iijs. iiijd.

PEYSKODDYS. In solutis Roberto Wryhtte de Gonthorp pro vj bussellis,
iiijd. Memorandum quod elemosinarius faciebat cariagium ad officium.
Memorandum de ijs. solutis Roberto Brigge anno Ricardi abbatis xix
incipiente[4] pro v diebus in opere carpentrie ad ponendum xxij tracinas
ad hospitale in le garret ibidem; item eidem pro aliis v diebus ibidem
ante (et ad) festum Omnium Sanctorum, ijs.
Memorandum quod Johannes Scarlette operatus est, ut dicit, per xvj
dies xviij tabulas in die Bricii episcopi,[5] xijd.; item Johanni Scarlet,
xijd.; Roberto Brigge cum famulo per dimidium diem, iiijd.
Quere plus in quarto folio sequente ad tale signum. Å[6]

[f. 49r.] Anno domini Ricardi abbatis xviij.[7]
NAYL'. In solutis pro ccc grossis spyks, xijd.; in xve splyntyng nayl',
(ijs. vjd.).

JOHANNES WALDYNG'. Memorandum quod debentur eidem Johanni
xixd. pro una camisia et candela. (solvuntur.)

CUSTUS FORINCECUS. In solutis generali capitulo pro iij annis, scilicet :—
obolum ad marcam, viijs. ixd.

---

[1] 4 July 1456.	[2] Left blank.	[3] 18 Oct. 1455 (?). [4] 1456-7.
[5] 13 Nov.	[6] See below, p. 95.	[7] 1455-6.

FALCACIO. In solutis Johanni Pyppewelle et Johanni Pynchebec pro falcacione unius acre et dimidie, ix*d*.; item Johanni Balle pro falcacione ij acrarum, [¹   ]; item Johanni Rop*er* pro iij acris et dimidia, [¹   ].

FENACIO. In solutis Ricardo Grawnte et aliis, x*d*.

CARIAGIUM. In solutis Ricardo Pynd*ar* pro vij carectatis, xxij*d*.; item eidem pro iiij carectatis, xvj*d*.

PORRETTIS emptis vj*d*., et in solutis pro plantacione Ricardo Grawnte et uxori ejusdem, 6*d*.

OBLACIO AD CAPELLAM BEATE MARIE MAGDALENE in vigilia et die,² xxj*d*. *ob*.

JANTACULUM SIVE PRANDIUM CUM SENA (UT POSTEA). In duobus ferculis grossarum carnium, videlicet:—bovinarum³ et ovinarum, v*d*. *ob*.; uno capone, (iiij*d*.); una gallina, uno porcello, vj*d*.; una auca, iiij*d*.; uno schold*ur*, uno breeste, [¹   ]; vj columbellis, (ij*d*.). Ad senam, in carne ovina pro uno sewh, ij pulcinis et v columbellis; item in pane, (iij*d*.); cervisia villana, videlicet:—duodena de optima cervisia, xv*d*.; et v lagenis de mediocre cervisia, ij*d*.; item in datis capellano capelle Sancti T*home* martiris, eo quod non fuit cum elemosinario in prandio propter ieiunium Beate Marie Virginis, v*d*. [*In margin*]⁴ Bysle, Walmysford, Stamford, J. Burrow, Wennam, Robertus Orwyn cum uxore, Ricardus Gregor*y*, Ricardus Grawnte.

NAYL' deliberati (ex mutuo) fratri Willelmo Borowh, sacriste, c de grossis spyk*s* (vj*d*.) ponderantes vj libras dimidiam (sol') [repeated five times]; item fratri Johanni Borowh cc splyntnayl' ponderantes iij libras, precium vj*d*.

Solucio fratris Willelmi Morton elemosinarii fratri Johanni B*ur*neham, refectorario, viij*s*.

Frumentum contra annum Ricardi abbatis xix emptum (ad Alwalton) pro distribucione pauperum in die Animarum,⁵ videlicet:—quatuor quarteria, xiiij*s*.

[*f. 49v.*] *Anno regni regis Henrici sexti post conquestum xxxv incipiente in crastino Decollacionis Sancti Johannis Baptiste et anno Ricardi abbatis xviij.*⁶

Memorandum quod Symon Walram (manens in Walton), nativus domini abbatis Burgi, inveniebat ij fidejussores fratri Willelmo Morton elemosinario Burgi, scilicet:—Johannem Burgesse de Gonthorppe et Robertum filium supradicti Symonis Walram pro debito de redditu assiso (duarum) acrarum terre arabilis jacentium ad capud ville de Dosthorppe versus Burgum Est et Weste wlgariter dictarum hyhedlond, cum alia (inquiratur quare per thesaurarium) acra ibidem jacente

¹ Left blank.   ² *21 and 22 July 1456.*
³ This explains the meaning of 'grosse carnes', e.g. beef and mutton.
⁴ Apparently the following monks and servants partook of the provisions described. ·
⁵ *2 Nov.*
⁶ *30 Aug. 1456.* The regnal years of Henry VI were normally reckoned from 1 Sept.; but cf. below, pp. 135, 168.

(in ij sellionibus); item dictam foreram et messuagium quondam Willelmi Hoode de Dostorppe, modo Willelmi Sand*ur*, reddendo per annum ij*d*. ij*s*., et habent diem solucionis festum Michaelis proximum.

STERBRIGE FEYR'. (Scribuntur in compoto). In solutis pro quatuor ryngg*s* cum quatuor bosysse; item ij bosysse, latchysse, crokys et snatchysse, pro ostiis ad hospitale, ad Ster'brigge feyr' emptis, xiiij*d*.

NECESSARIA. Item in una cuvella pro pisis adaquandis et aqua defferenda in aliis operibus necessariis pro officio, viij*d*.; item in solutis pro uno quarterio, videlicet:—xxx estrische bord*s*, xix*s*.; in cariagio per aquam usque ad Burgum per Johannem B*er*newel, vj*d*.; in expensis Johannis Coldewel equitantis pro supradictis emendis sive comparandis ad nundinas supradictas xviij*d*.[1]

PET*UR* BRIGE FEYR'.[2] In solutis pro v scafis emptis pro officio et subelemosinaria, x*d*.; in una serura empta, iij*d*.; in una ferrea furca fimaria pro stabulo, iij*d*.

ELY FEYRE. In (Ely) una situla, iiij*d*.; in solutis pro una cista, (pro T*o*m*a* Morton monacho), xij*d*.; in una corda ponderante ij libras dimidiam longitudinis viij virgarum, ij*d*. *ob*.; in una alia corda canabina ponderante j libram iij quarteria longitudinis xxiij virgarum, ij*d*.; in quatuor· capistris canabinis ponderantibus ij libras, ij*d*.; in ij magnis boc*s* [*sic*] et ryng*s*, (in compoto), pro ostiis, xvj*d*.; in iiij paribus sotilarum, xxij*d*.; in solutis pro ij magnis coffinis cum ij scotyll', xxj*d*.; (^d in xij tabulis quercinis longitudinis xj pedum latitudinis xvij inchis; item xj tabulis quercinis longitudinis x pedum latitudinis xiiij inchis, precium tabule, v*d*.;) item xxij tabule longitudinis iij pedum, precium tabule, j*d*. *q*.

Ricardus Horton habet vyneg*ur* potte. (^d Willelmus Norton habet j baskette. Frater Willelmus Walmisford habet hachette, flaket, kruette.) Margareta Kyng habet (unum saccum). Item Willelmus Payn securim et saccum. [*f. 5or*.] (^d Robertus[3] Conquest habet rydyng kope.) Frater Johannes Glynton habet unum pars*ur* (^d calcaria nostra).

Memorandum quod Margareta Balle solvit vj*s*. viij*d*. pro crofto juxta Schepkote et dicit quod debet nisi v*s*. pro alio crofto ibidem de anno xviij. Require plus ex altera parte istius folii.

[*f. 5or*.] *Anno regni regis Henrici sexti incipiente xxxv et anno domini Ricardi abbatis xviij finiente*.[4]

Memorandum quod in anno domini Ricardi Abbatis xiiij finiente ad festum Michaelis[5] frater Willelmus Morton elemosinarius debebat fratri Ricardo Harlton pro tunc thesaurario pro tribus annis preteritis lxj*s*. *ob*. *q*.; item pro ij annis sequentibus scilicet xv et sextodecimo[6] xlviij*s*.

---

[1] Stourbridge Fair.   [2] See above, p. 67.
[3] The following two paragraphs are written in continuation at the foot of f. 5or.
[4] *Sept. 1456*. The 18th year of Abbot Richard finished at Michaelmas 1456. The 35th year of Henry VI began on 1 Sept. 1456.
[5] *1452*.   [6] *1452–4*.

ij*d. ob.* Summa cix*s.* iij*d. q.*, unde dictus Willelmus Morton elemosinarius solvit pro thesaurario supradicto xl*s.* fratri Willelmo Spaldyng
pro tunc pitanciario. Item dictus frater Willelmus Morton solvit fratri
Ricardo Harlton ut in xviij virgis de Karse precium xv*s.*, una batella
sive navicula, xix*s.*, et uno equo nigri coloris, xviij*s.* Item xiiij quarteriis brasii precium quarterii ij*s.* viij*d.*, xxxvij*s.* iiij*d.* Item ut in v libris
cere precium de libra, vj*d.*, ij*s.* vj*d.* pro Willelmo Thorppe. Idem frater
Ricardus Harlton recepit de stipendio Willelmi Depyng' cantoris (per
viam detencionis) in capella beate Marie in monasterio Burgi, vj*s.* viij*d.*
quos solvisset fratri Willelmo Morton (elemosinario) pro redditu suo
aretro pro uno tenemento in Cowgate. Item frater Willelmus Morton
solvit v*d.* pro vino dato domino episcopo post reversionem suam de
Wallia, unde ij*d. ob.* pro fratre Ricardo Harlton. Item idem frater
Ricardus receptor recepit pro fratre Willelmo Morton elemosinario de
Ricardo Baate collectore elemosinarii ad Wermyngton ij quarteria
brasii, iiij*s.* viij*d.* Idem emit unum cabulle cum uno magno gunfo [*sic*]
ferreo, vj*s.* viij*d.* Item Willelmus Rodg*er* solvit dicto fratri Ricardo
Harlton pro dicto elemosinario. SUMMA soluta 7*li.* 10*s. obolum.*

Memorandum quod anno domini Ricardi abbatis xx^mo finiente elemosinarius debet dicto fratri Ricardo Harlton receptori abbatis x*li.* xvj*s.*
ij*d. ob. q.* unde supradictus receptor recepit per Laurencium Toche pro
dicto elemosinario, x*li.*

[*f. 50v.*] *Anno regni regis Henrici sexti xxxv et anno Ricardi abbatis xix
incipiente.*[1]

Memorandum quod Ricardus Pynd*er* fecit cariagium in carecta sua de
xxxj tabulis fraccinis et tabulis de wallenot treys, (iij*d.*). Tomas Pampe
cum carecta abbathie xv tabulas fraccinas et iij tabulas quercinas densas,
[*sic*] (ij*d.*). Ricardus Browny, secundus carectarius abbathie, xiij tabulas
fraccinas et unam peciam quercinam longitudinis quatuor pedum (ij*d.*).

Memorandum de tribus quercinis tracinis emptis in Westgate; item
alia vice T*omas* Pampe (j*d. ob.*) et Ricardus Browny (j*d. ob.*) cum ij
carectatis domini abbatis adduxerunt ad hospitale xiiij tabulas quercinas
longitudinis xij pedum; item vij tabulas quercinas longiores; item xx
tabulas quercinas longitudinis xj pedum emptas ad Ely; item cum
carecta abbatis ix tabulas quercinas bowyng, [   ] estrischebord*s* xv
ledg*s* 4 pedum et dimidii; item xxxvj ledg*s* quasi de ij pedibus et
dimidio et eo amplius; item ix ledg*s.*[2]

(^d W. PAYN (vacat). In meremio ab eo empto ad Tanholtte[3] pro Brigmylle scilicet xvj peciis quercinis, xx*s.* j*d.*); in extraxsione ejusdem de
fovea ibidem, vj*d.*; item pro quadracione de iiij^xx peciis, ij*s.* xj*d.*

MEREMIUM EMPTUM. (Scribitur in compoto.)
In solutis Ricardo Maddy pro (meremio scilicet) xij peciis quercinis
scapulatis, vj*s.* cum cariagio. (^d Vacat. Item in solutis Ricardo Knotte

---

[1] *1456.*   [2] A blank space.
[3] Near Eyebury, where the abbot's cattle were put out to graze.

de Stanford' xxs., (solvit), pro xxiiij peciis quercinis, videlicet xv
carectate. Item pro uno hedstok et una alia pecia quercina, (unde
solvuntur iiijd. pro arra; item 17s.).

Johannes Clark de Wodcrofte solvit elemosinario xxs. pro anno xviij[1]
([d] tamen debet (solvit) ijd. de anno xvij[2] ut in folio quinto ante scilicet
in fine.) MARGARETA BALLE solvebat ut ex altera parte istius folii; item
solvit anno xix Ricardi abbatis post Pascha,[3] vjs. viijd. (item iijs. iiijd.)
pro magno crofto ibidem et pro anno xviij[4] et notandum quod ad
festum proximum Michaelis videlicet anno xx Ricardi abbatis incipiente[5] debitum erit vjs. viijd. pro parvo crofto ibidem; item vs. pro
magno crofto ibidem, tamen debentur le wynturyng' et somuryng unius
bovis pro iij annis. Item solvit vjs. viijd. per Johannem Coldwel post
festum Michaelis anno xx[6] incipiente; item eodem anno, vjs. viijd.;
item, viijs.; et hic juravit quod debent nisi xijs. ad Pascha anno xxj
Ricardi abbatis.[7]
Quere plus in 24 folio sequente ad tale '24'.

[*f. 51r.*] *Anno Ricardi abbatis xix.*[8]
AVENE RECEPTE.

Memorandum quod Galfridus Kechelle comparabat unam equam bay
coloris (cum pullo suggente) de fratre Willelmo Morton elemosinario
pro quatuor quarteriis et quatuor eskeppis avenarum solvendis sive
deliberandis per ebdomadam ij eskeppis usque ad plenam solucionem
per primum diem Marcii proxime sequentem,[9] Johanne Draper juniore
fidejussore; et notandum quod fecerunt fidem levando manus dexteras
unde solverent ([d] ad) ante festum Omnium Sanctorum j quarterium;[10]
item ij eskeppas in festo Bricii;[11] item in Vigilia Concepcionis Beate
Marie[12] j quarterium; item j eskeppa cumulata; item anno xxj[13] incipiente iiij bussellos; item iiij bussellos dimidium. Modo debet ix
bussellos et dimidium, unde solvit ij eskeppas.

LINIA TELA. In solutis pro ij virgis sive una ulna et dimidia (undique)
de linia tela ad involvendum Johannem Ermytte[14] ad hospitale; item
tantum pro alio mortuo in (carcere),[15] xvjd.

FRUMENTUM. In solutis pro quattuor quarteriis pro distribucione (pauperum) in die Animarum,[16] xviijs.;[17] item pro iiij eskeppis frumenti
emptis in foro, xxijd.; item ij eskeppis in foro, xijd.

PISE. In solutis pro vj eskeppis pisarum, xvjd.; item pro v eskeppis,

---

[1] *1455–6.* [2] *1454–5.*
[3] *17 Apr. 1457.* [4] *1455–6.* [5] *29 Sept. 1457.*
[6] *1457–8.* [7] *25 Mar. 1459.* [8] *1456–7.*
[9] *1457.* [10] *1 Nov.* [11] *13 Nov.*
[12] *7 Dec.* [13] *Michaelmas 1458.*
[14] Did the hermit who lived in the cell adjoining the chapel of St. Mary Magdalene at
Newark spend his last days in St. Leonard's Spittle?
[15] Note that the almoner paid for the shroud of a man who died in the abbot's prison.
[16] *2 Nov.*
[17] Note this reference to the distribution of loaves amongst the poor on All Souls' Day,
2 Nov.

xij*d. ob.*; item pro iij quarteriis de Johanne Coldewelle, iiij*s.* ix*d.*; item pro v eskeppis, xij*d. ob.*; item pro ij bussellis, v*d.*

SOLUCIO ELEMOSINARII PRO SPECIEBUS AD FESTUM PURIFICACIONIS BEATE MARIE.[1] In primis fratribus Willelmo Morton et Willelmo Walmysford, xx*s.*; et fratri Roberto Notyngham thesaurario, iiij*li.* in officio suo et in presencia sacriste et aliorum; fratri Ricardo Bysley debentur (ᵈ iij*s.*) pro officio subelemosinarie.

SCOLARIBUS SIVE STUDENTIBUS OXON'. Debentur eisdem ad Nativitatem domini anno xix,[2] v*s.*, (solvit).

(Dimidia) decima soluta domino regi (in comitatu Narhamt*onie*), xlvj*s.* vj*d. ob.*; item (in comitatu Huntyngd*onie*), j*d. ob.*

Johannes Wakerley solvit per T*homam* Eston pro Cathetwayte in Vigilia Cecilie Virginis,[3] xiij*s.* iiij*d.* pro anno xvij[4] et debet residuum unde solvit (ᵈ in crastino Concepcionis Beate Marie[5]) per manus T*home* Eston xx*s.* et debet xix*s.* quos solvit per puellam suam et equet.

Johannes Wak*er*ley debet elemosinario pro anno xix[6] Ricardi abbatis, xxvj*s.* iiij*d.*, unde solvit per Johannem Kyrcby de Dodyngton xx*ᶜ* latt*s* cum cariagio, xj*s.*; item de dicto Johanne v*ᶜ* sappe latt*s*, xvj*d.* et Johannes Wakyrley debet pro anno xix, xiij*s.* x*d.* Item pro anno xx,[7] 26*s.* iiij*d.* unde solvit per Laurencium Webst*er* de Walton, xiij*s.* iiij*d.*; item anno supradicto in Vigilia Pentecostes,[8] xxvj*s.* v*d. ob.* et debet pro xx anno 6*d. ob.*; et memorandum de falso grosso cit*ra.*

Gonthorppe tenens ibidem (mulier) solvit iij*s.* pro anno xviij et equet.

[*f. 51v.*] *Anno Ricardi Abbatis xix.*

42 folio ante vide de ista materia clare ibidem de annis precedentibus.[9]

SOLUCIO FRATRI WILLELMO MELTON. In solutis fratri Willelmo Melton infirmario pro anno xviij domini Ricardi abbatis, videlicet anno xix dicti abbatis ut supra, et in vigilia Nativitatis Domini[10] per Johannem Coldewelle, xl*s.*; item in solutis dicto infirmario ut in dimidio apro sibi vendito, ij*s.* viij*d.*; item in solutis dicto infirmario, ut in carnibus de T*homa* Pep*ur* (et aliis) pro coquina, xxvij*s.* (iiij*d.*) Item idem elemosinarius solvit dicto infirmario in vigilia Pasche,[11] xl*s.* Idem elemosinarius solvit dicto infirmario postea (ᵈ xx*s.*) vj*s.* et equet pro anno xviij. Item idem elemosinarius (eodem die) statim incontinenter solvit dicto infirmario in camera sua propria xiiij*s.* pro anno xix; item xxvj*s.* viij*d.* ix Kal. Novembris[12] in propria camera dicti infirmarii post completorium; item in dicta camera in crastino Sancti Martini,[13] xiij*s.* iiij*d.* anno xx pro anno xix; item xxx*s.* in vigilia Sancti Antonii[14] in supradicta camera; item in previgilia Sancti Elphegi[15] episcopi, xx*s.*; item secunda die Augusti super altare Sancti Laurencii, xx*s.*, unde xij*s.* pro anno

[1] *2 Feb.* [2] *25 Dec. 1456.* [3] *21 Nov. 1456.*
[4] *1454-5.* [5] *9 Dec. 1456.* [6] *1456-7.*
[7] *1457-8.* [8] *20 May 1458.* [9] Lost, see above, p. xxxix.
[10] *24 Dec. 1456.* [11] *16 Apr. 1457.* [12] *24 Oct. 1457.*
[13] *12 Nov. 1457.* [14] *16 Jan. 1457/8.* [15] *17 Apr. 1458.*

xix et viij*s*. pro anno xx; item in die Sancti Laurencii[1] in camera camerarii post prandium, xx*s*.; item in crastino Sancti Bricii episcopi[2] anno Ricardi abbatis xxj statim post prandium in fenestra parlure in hostilaria, xl*s*. pro anno xx; item Tome coquo (pro infirmario), vj*s*. viij*d*.; item dicto coquo (pro infirmario) alia vice in camera prioris,[3] iij*s*. iiij*d*.; item ij*s*. pro supradicto infirmario; item in purificacione Beate Virginis,[4] iiij*s*. Tome coquo et 9*d*. Modo elemosinarius debet de anno vicesimo xxxj*s*. ix*d*., unde solvit in Vigilia Pasche[5] xx*s*.; item xj*s*. ix*d*. Sabbato infra Octabis Corporis Christi;[6] et sic equet pro anno xx.[7]

(Memorandum de 34 ferculis inter Natale et Quadragesimam, precium xvj*s*. ix*d*.)

Item supradictus elemosinarius in Vigilia Sancti Johannis Baptiste[8] solvit dicto infirmario pro anno xxj Ricardi abbatis, xxix*s*., videlicet super tabulam in aula hostilarie. Item elemosinarius solvit in Vigilia Sancti Laurencii[9] ix*s*. in camera dicti infirmarii; item xx*s*. pari modo in Vigilia Mathei Ewangeliste[10] in presencia Ricardi Grawnte; item xl*s*. in presencia fratris Tome Neede[11] in Vigilia Translacionis Sancti Martini;[12] item in die Translacionis Martini,[13] xviij*s*. et equet pro officio infirmarii:

(Memorandum[14] de ij*s*. solutis Tome coco pro carnibus; item sarratoribus, ij*s*. (quere alibi); item 9*s*. Tome coco)

[*f. 52r.*] *Anno Ricardi abbatis xix.*[15]

OBLACIONES: Clerico prioris, (2*s*.); Johanni Caker, (iiij*d*.); Willelmo refectorarie, (iiij*d*.); Johanni Dey, (iiij*d*.); Johanni Halle, (iiij*d*.); Thome Roceby, (iiij*d*.); Petro, (ij*d*.); et Willelmo, minucionis [*sic*], (ij*d*.); Tome gardinario, (ij*d*.); Waltero hostilarie, (ij*d*.); Thome, clerico camerarie (ij*d*.); Johanni Brevitori, (ij*d*.); clerico fratris Nicholai, scilicet Johanni Adam, (ij*d*.); clerico fratris Walteri Wermyngton, scilicet Thome Ay, (ij*d*.); iij servientibus in elemosinaria, videlicet Johanni Coldewelle, (ij*s*. v*d*.); Roberto Morton, (xij*d*.); et Johanni Qhwyte, (iij*d*.)

[SOLUCIO] PRIORI. In solutis domino Willelmo Exton priori pro mora sua[16] post Pascha, xl*s*.

Memorandum quod Johannes Tempylle et Henricus Palmer solverunt redditum unius quarterii. Item Johannes Barforde solvit xij*d*. pro firma ij acrarum et dimidie de anno xviij° et eque. Item Thomas Noblette solvit pro anno xviij° redditum pro cotagio in Paston, ij*s*. et equet.

---

[1] *10 Aug. 1458.*　　　　[2] *13 Nov. 1458.*

[3] Presumably the payment was made in the prior's chamber near the Cloister, and not in a separate lodging. Definite proof that the prior had a separate lodging on the north of the church, although this is suggested by later writers about the cathedral, is difficult to obtain.

[4] *2 Feb. 1458/9.*　　　[5] *24 Mar. 1458/9.*　　　[6] *26 May 1459.*

[7] *In the margin opposite to the words* in camera prioris.

[8] *23 June 1459.*　　　[9] *9 Aug. 1459.*

[10] *20 Sept. 1459.*　　　[11] Thomas of St. Neots.

[12] *Sic (3 July), but 10 Nov. is probably meant.*

[13] *Sic (4 July), but 11 Nov. is probably meant.*

[14] *Footnote deleted* quia alibi.　　　[15] *1456–7.*　　　[16] At Oxney Grange.

Katerina Pygge de Yaxle, iiij*s*. vj*d*.; Agnes Coteler, ij*s*. vj*d*. pro primo quarterio de anno 19 Ricardi abbatis. Johannes Incle solvit iij*s*. et debet (^d 16*d*.) iiij*s*. iiij*d*. Item Willelmus Glynton solvit xij*d*. de redditu assise. Petrus Lorr', ij*s*. pro anno septimodecimo.

(^d SCLATTS. In solutis Johanni Kyrcby, ((^d compot*um* anni preteriti); falsum est; in anno sequente), pro mille de sclatt*s* cum cariagio ad rectoriam de Maxey, unde v^c perforate et v^c non perforate, vij*s*. vj*d*.)

Memorandum quod Johannes filius Willelmi Belamy veniebat ad ele-mosinarium statim post festum Purificacionis Beate Marie anno quo supra scilicet xix^{mo} [1] et conduxit vij acras et dimidiam terre per iij annos sequentes, excepto aliquo firmario superveniente, (ad hospitale manere) reddendo annuatim sicut pater ejus ut patet in folio xxij° ante, scilicet, iiij*s*. per annum. Idem elemosinarius dimisit eidem unam aliam dimi-diam acram terre buttantem super Westwod jacentem inter ij balk*s* prope Botolsok pro iij*d*. per annum.

Memorandum quod Robertus Crosse accepit Hodys wong' ad firmam de elemosinario pro quatuor vel quinque annis ad voluntatem elemo-sinarii, si aliquis firmarius venerit ut supra in proxima dimissione antea scilicet Johannis Belamy, reddendo elemosinario annuatim, vj*s*.

(Memorandum quod ista dimissio erat circa Purificacionem Beate Marie.)

[*f. 52v.*] *Anno Ricardi abbatis xix°.*

(In compoto scribitur anno xviij).

À[2] In solutis Roberto Brigg pro v diebus in opere tabularum rabbyttyng pro cameris ad hospitale, xx*d*.

CUSTUS IN OFFICIO. Item eidem pro opere per iij dies, xv*d*.; item eidem pro ij diebus emendando le tumberrelle juxta fontem in officio, x*d*.

CUSTUS IN BURGO.
(Scribitur). In solutis dicto carpentario incipiendo unum parvum domum (cum camino), super Sowter Row, ubi Henricus Collermaker manet, per ij dies, x*d*.; item Roberto dicto carpentario operante super supradictum domum per vj dies, ij*s*. vj*d*., et famulo suo per j diem, iij*d*.; item Johanni Ravon carpentario et famulo suo adjuvanti in dicto opere et framyng aliam domum (de) xij coplys ibidem prope, super Sowter Row per vj dies, iiij*s*.; item dicto Roberto Brig cum famulo suo faciendo ij ostia propter duo tenementa super Sowter row cum una fenestra, ix*d*. Item quere plus in tercia linia sequente ad tale signum .3.

CUSTUS IN BURGO. THAK. In solutis uno de Wyttlyssey pro cccc coperture, iij*s*. et in cariagio de Boylȝata usque Sowter Row, Roberto Crosse.
(^d .3. In solutis Roberto Brig pro opere rabyttyng tabularum per iij dies ad hospitale, ij*s*. ij*d*.; item in solutis dicto carpentario et famulo suo pro consimili labore ibidem per totam primam ebdomadam post

---

[1] *2 Feb. 1456/7.*   [2] See above, p. 88.

Purificacionem (per Henricum Collermaker), iiij*s.*; item in obstupacione eidem, vj*d.*)

Sowter Row. Item in solutis dicto carpentario cum ij carpentariis sub ipso, per vj dies super Sowter Row emendando in diversis locis ibidem cum splentyng, vj*s.* vj*d.*; item in rewardo sibi, ij*d.*; et in cervisia dictis carpentario, tectori et servienti suo per vices, iiij*d.* Quere plus de ista materia in quarto folio sequente ad tale signum ⚏.[1]

SOWTER ROW, DRAWYNG OF THACKE & THACKYNG. In solutis Roberto Ionysse pro quinque diebus in opere thackyng, xix*d.*; Johanni Bytam xj dies drawyng et servyng in opere supradicto, xij*d.* in manibus et (ᵈ xvj)(30)*d.* per obstupacionem pro focale sibi vendito. Quere plus de materia in iij folio sequente ad tale signum +.[2]

(ᵈ Memorandum quod Robertus Brig debet in die Sancti Vincencii[3] pro Thoma Heyd*s*, xij*d.*; item 8*d.* (solvit).

[*f. 53r.*] *Anno Ricardi abbatis xix⁰.*

MINUCIO TERCII PRIORIS, VIDELICET, PRIMA TEMPORE NATALIS DOMINI DIE DOMINICA SCILICET IN OCTABIS SANCTI STEPHANI.[4] In ij aucis, viij*d.*; in iiij volatilibus, vij*d.*; feria secunda:—In uno porcello, vj*d.*; in aprina, anglice brawn,[5] pista de stauro et in pura farina; feria tercia:—In iiij gallinis, viij*d.*; in viij volatilibus, xiiij*d.*

SECUNDA MINUCIO POST NATALE. In iiij cuniculis[6] de stauro captis in cimiterio Sancti Johannis Baptiste et le Trenchys in officio; item in ij cuniculis emptis, v*d.* (iij*s.* ij*d.*)

EBDOMADA SEPTUAGESIME [*sic*] CUM DOMINICA QUINQUAGESIME.[7] In primis in die dominica[8] nisi iij capones pro magna appellacione; feria secunda: in uno ferculo grossarum carnium, v*d.*; in iiij capitibus vitulinis, vij*d.*; in carnibus vitulinis assatis, 7*d.*; (sena) in volatilibus cum grosso sowse, 7*d.*; feria tercia: in j ferculo, v*d.*; in carnibus vitulinis, 7*d.*; sena: in sew, iiij*d.*; feria v: in j ferculo, v*d.*; in carnibus porcinis salcatis propter collops cum ovis, v*d.*; in carnibus vitulinis assatis, 7*d.*; ad senam: in iij gallinis cum uno ferculo assatis (7*d.*) 8*d.*

DOMINICA QUINQUAGESIME.[9] In j pestel porcina cum uno capite vitulino, iij*d.*; in carnibus porcinis assatis, j*d. ob.*; ad cenam, in una gallina, ij*d.*

SOLUCIO SORORIBUS IN CAPELLA SANCTI THOME MARTIRIS. In primis priorisse, iij*s.* iiij*d.*; item Atheline Yve, iij*s.* iiij*d.*; item Johanna Gattele recepit per filium suum fratrem Willelmum Byry, iij*s.* iiij*d.*; item ij*s.* antea, ut patet in folio xj ante.[10] Memorandum quod elemosinarius solvit aliis sororibus ad omnia usque ad festum Sancti Nicholai[11] in anno xx Ricardi abbatis.

---

[1] See below, p. 100. [2] See below, p. 99. [3] *22 Jan.*
[4] *2 Jan. 1456/7.* [5] Note the translation of *aprina* = brawn.
[6] Rabbits taken in St. John's Close or graveyard and in the trenches in the close adjoining the almoner's office at the east side of the monastery.
[7] *13–19 (?), and 27 Feb. 1456/7.* [8] *13 Feb. (?)* [9] *27 Feb.*
[10] See above, p. 76. [11] *6 Dec. 1457.*

In forincecis. In solutis pro procurationibus[1] domino episcopo Lincolniensi pro ecclesia de Maxey, v*s. ob.*

Studentibus. In solutis eisdem per dominum Willelmum Rathe, teste fratre Johanne ([d] By) Pychele x*s.* Pasca.

Stanford Feyyr'. Nayl'.

In solutis pro c magnis clavis ponderantibus v libras dimidiam, viij*d.*; item c et dimidio comyn spyk*s,* c ponderantes iiij libras, viij*d.*; item ccc spyk*s,* c ponderantes iij libras dimidiam, xiij*d. ob.*; item ccc minoribus spyk*s,* c ponderantes iij libras quarterium, xiij*d. ob.*; item ccc splynt nayl', c ponderantes ij libras quarterium, ix*d.*; item ccc minoribus splynt nayl', vij*d. ob.*; item ij mille latte nayl', ij*s.* vj*d.,* mille ponderantes xj libras dimidiam; item mm minoribus lathe nayl', mille ponderantes v libras dimidiam, ij*s.*; item pro vj novis seruris cum clavibus, xviij*d.*; in uno pectino equino cum una ferrura pro una vanga, iiij*d.*; in expensis Johannis Coldewelle equitantis ad Stanford*iam* pro supradictis emendis, xij*d.*; item in cariagio, iij*d.*

[*f. 53v.*] *Anno Ricardi abbatis xix°.*

Require plus de vendicione focalis in decimo et xj foliis sequentibus.[2]
Ø. Johanni Stawnton, barbur, quasi carectata fraccina ([d] xvj*d.,* et solvet ad cariagium), (xiij*d.* et solvit per manus proprias); T*home* Spencer, sadler, quasi ij carectate, ij*s.* viij*d.,* (solvit[3]); Willelmo o the Fret*ur* xiij pecie fraccine, vj*d.,* (solvit); item Johanni Chaln*er* ([d] quasi) ij carectate fraccine, iij*s.* iiij*d.*; Johanni Ryette, webster, (solvit), pro xix penykydd*s* (salicum et fraccinorum) de trenchys, 2*s.* 5*d.*; T*home* Rowseby, (coquo), ([d] quasi) xij carectatis de salicibus et iiij carectatis fraccinorum cum alnis scilicet assepys [*sic*] cum eld*ri*sse in orto Sancti Johannis, xv*s.*; T*ome* Pep*ur* per Johannem Coldwelle vij item ([d] ix) kydd*s*; item eidem ix kydd*s*; Johanni Pybaker v penikydd*s,* (solvit); T*ome* Tounende xliiij penykydd*s,* iij*s.* v*d.* (solvit); Roberto Brig' et Johanni Bernarde, quasi carectata focalis, xiiij*d.* (solvit); Laurencio Webster xv kydd*s,* xv*d.* (solvit); item ij kydd*s* ex dono; item fratri Johanni Burrowh, magistro operis, [pro] centum tingnis, xx*s.*; item eidem dicto fratri Johanni xj[xx] tingnis precium pecie *ob. q.,* xiij*s.* ix*d.*; quere solucionem; Johanni Pynchebec seniori bona carectata pro xx*d.*; et habet diem usque festum Apostolorum Petri et Pauli, tamen elemosinarius habet unum plegghe scilicet ij virgas viridis panni, (solvit); Johanni Bykyrton xv peny-kydd*s*; item xxv kydd*s* (solvit); Waltero Whyte xv kydd*s*; item xlviij pro fratre Johanne Pychele; (parvus) Waltero Smythe x kydd*s* (solvit); item vj kydd*s,* solvit et equet; Symoni famulo Johannis Byk*ur*ton x kydd*s,* x*d.,* (solvit); Roberto Keyworthe xx kydd*s,* xx*d.*; unde solvit j*d.*; item xx*d.*; (quia postea;) ([d] item Johanni Ryette, webster, x kydd*s* per Johannem Coldwel (solvit); Johanni Medow, kydd*er,* xx kydd*s* salicum); (quia postea); Willelmo Joly, x kydd*s,* salicum, x*d.,* et solvit

---

[1] See pp. 44–45.   [2] See below, pp. 113–14.   [3] Repeated thrice.

ut in carectata feni pro veteribus muris faciendis (solvit); item Johanni Ryette x kydd*s*, (solvit);

Summa [¹   ]

Prime iij carectate, lxx pecie; quarta carectata, xl pecie; quinta, 35 pecie; sexta, 28; septima, 25; item de residuo, vj^{xx}v tingna.

[*f. 54r.*] *Anno xix domini Ricardi abbatis.*²

Johanni Medow xxx kydd*s* unde solvit videlicet per kyddyng de ciiij^{xx} xix fagott*s* or kydd*s*, xxij*d*. et (ᵈ debet viij*d*.) (solvit); Roberto Orwyn xxviij kydd*s*; item xv kydd*s*; Johanni Alownton xxx fagott*s* et habet Missom*ur* Day; debet xx*d*.; Johanni Roper de Wodston, xv kydd*s*, unde solvit vj*d*., et debet ix*d*.

MERSTLONDE PER JOHANNEM COLDWEL.

Henrico Kysby de Wodston xxiij kydd*s*, (solvit³); item tercia vice xxj; item xxiiij, unde solvit ij*s*. x*d*. et modo debet ij*s*. iiij*d*., (solvit³); item x*d*. pro borowschyp, modo debet xx*d*., (solvit); item Willelmo Morton xl kydd*s*, iij*s*. iiij*d*., habet Missom*ur* Day, et fecit fidem, (solvit³); Johanni Barb*ur*, leeche, xxvj [kydd*s*], ij*s*. ij*d*., quos solvit; famulo Johannis Stele poticar' xxij kydd*s*, (solvit); Johanni Hetyng xv kydd*s*, solvit xv*d*.; domino Willelmo Kysby x kydd*s*, x*d*., quos solvit; Johanni Drews seniori, (ᵈ xxxxvj) (xlviij) [kydd*s*], iiij*s*., (solvit); item xij kydd*s*, (solvit); et debet xij*d*., (solvit); T*ome* Hab*ur*gylle xxx kydd*s*; congnato T*ome* Wollasse, xv kydysse, et solvit xv*d*.; Johanni Codd*er* de Owr'ton xx kydd*s*, xx*d*., (solvit); Johanni Caker xvj kydd*s* fraxsini, item iiij kydd*s*, xviij*d*., (solvit); Willelmo Pyppewel xij kydd*s* salicum (⁴   ); (ᵈ Willelmo Davyntr' et T*ome* Townysende) Tome Sadler, xxvij kydd*s*, (ij*s*.).

Frater Johannes Burrowh debet fratri Willelmo Morton pro ij (mille) bryke [*sic*], xiij*s*. Item debet dicto Willelmo Morton (ᵈ x*s*.) pro x carectatis de salicibus, x*s*., unde solvit vj*s*. viij*d*. et debet iij*s*. iiij*d*. Idem frater Johannes debet dicto fratri Willelmo pro c sp*er*tis sive tignis, xx*s*. Idem debet dicto Willelmo Morton pro xjv (xx. 14*s*.) peciis fraccinis; item pro cotagio [in] Groplane, ij*s*. viij*d*.; item pro stagno in le Werkry leyton pro (ᵈ ij) 4 annis; item pro 8 eskeppis calcis; item pro lx red tyl'; item pro ccclx nayl', 8*d*. *ob*. [*In margin*: 17.5^{xx}]

Memorandum quod frater Willelmus Morton elemosinarius debet Ricardo Papley pro iij compotis factis, xxix*s*., unde solvit ix*s*.; item xiij*s*. iiij*d*. in schoppa Roberti Lowthe in sartrina; item vj*s*. viij*d*. Item elemo-sinarius solvit pro anno xix°, iij*s*. iiij*d*.; item iiij*s*., item xx*d*., item xx*d*., et equet.

[*f. 54v.*] *Anno xix Ricardi abbatis.*⁵

HOSPITALE. In solutis Johanni (Hobard), dyker, sive Long Jon, dykyng et settyng ad hospitale pro xxx(ij) rodis, ij*s*. j*d*.; item iiij*d*.; item xiij*d*.; item j*d*.; item xviij*d*.; item xij*d*.; item xviij*d*. per Willelmum clericum

---

¹ Left blank, but by dot notation, £4. 1*s*. 3*d*.   ² *1456–7.*   ³ Twice.
⁴ Not stated, but by dot notation as above, £1. 6*s*. 4*d*.   ⁵ *1456–7.*

extra villam per stupacionem; item per Johannem Challen*er*, xij*d*.;
item iij*s*. vj*d*.; (^d modo debentur dicto Johanni xij*d*., quousque fecerit
bonum finem de dicta fossacione; (solvit).)

BRIGMYLLE. (Vacat hic, quia allocatur alibi). (^d In solutis predicto
Johanni pro totali fossacione et mundacione fossarum circumquaque
ibidem, videlicet de lxxij rodis; in primis per Johannem Coldwel, v*s*.;
item per elemosinarium, v*s*.; item per elemosinarium, vj*s*.; item per
Robertum Conquest, ut in victualibus, vj*s*.)

HOSPITALE. (^d In solutis Johanni Haale latamo pro factura unius
gabule in le Garret versus austrum ad hospitale per vij dies, ij*s*. vij*d*.;
item Johanni servienti eidem per idem, ij*s*.; item Willelmo Schepey
pro alia gabula boriali ibidem in grosso facienda, ij*s*. viij*d*.)[1]

A. COWGATE. (Scribitur). Memorandum quod Johannes Som*ur*, tector
(cum servitoribus) fuit super aulam Johannis Dawntre et per medietatem alterius incete ibidem per 7 dies; item ubi T*homas* Hab*ur*gyl
manet per 5 dies; item per iij dies ubi N[icolaus] manet, cum serviente.
+[2] (^d Item in solutis supradicto Roberto Jonysse thack*er* pro labore
suo per v dies, ut supra, super Sowter row, xv*d*.; ij*s*. j*d*.; in solutis
Johanni Bytam servienti dicto coopertori per dictos v dies; item uxori
Johannis Bytam adjuvanti per v dies drawyng et strawyng per v dies,
xiij*d*.; item Roberto Jonysse pro ij diebus super Sowter row, x*d*.; in
officio per j diem, iiij*d*.; item Johanni Bytam, servienti ei per iij dies,
xij*d*.; item dicto Johanni Bytam propter bemfyllyng' unius partis domus
juxta T*omam* Smythe ibidem super Sowter row per ij dies, viij*d*.; in
solutis Johanni Schyngle pro fundamento petrino de novo facto ubi
Henricus Kollermaker manet, vj*d*., (solvit); item eidem, vij*d*., (solvit);
in solutis Johanni Bytam dawbyng ibidem in iij locis (ut) supra; item
Johanni Bytam secunda ebdomada Quadragesime trahenti thac pro
stabulo in officio cum aliis laboribus per iij dies, xij*d*.; item eidem
dawbyng super Sowter row per alios iij dies, xij*d*.; item Roberto
Jonysse operante super stabulum in officio per iiij dies et dimidium,
xxij*d*.; item Johanni Bytam servienti ei per idem, xvij*d*.; item Roberto
Jonys per j diem super stabulum, v*d*.; item Johanni Bytam xj*d*. et
Johanni Roper ix*d*. per ij dies hedgyng'; in solutis Roberto Jonys pro
ryggyng et cuttyng unius domus super Sowter row per unum diem
et dimidium cum uno serviente ei, xiiij*d*.; item dicto Roberto cum uno
serviente per iij dies in Bondgate ubi Ricardus Crosse nuper manebat,
ij*s*. j*d*. ob.; item dic [*sic*].)[3]

B. Item dictis operariis (scilicet Roberto Jonys cum serviente) per vj
dies in Cowgate, iiij*s*. vj*d*. ob.; Raton row (iij dies); Bongate per iij dies.

T*homas* Derby solvit in ebdomada Pasche anno quo supra scilicet xix
pro ij annis iij*s*. et debet pro anno xviij xviij*d*., ut supponitur.

---

[1] *Deleted with the note* scribitur (in compoto).　　　[2] See p. 96.
[3] Note the whole of the above items were deleted, presumably when they were entered
in the almoner's compotus.

[*f. 55r.*] *Anno Ricardi Abbatis xix⁰.*[1]

HOSPITALE. (Inquiratur de ista materia quale opus et ubi.) $\#$[2] In solutis Roberto Brig carpentario cum ij famulis per v dies, scilicet ultima ebdomada Februarii, iiij*s.* viij*d.*; item dicto Roberto cum uno famulo per iiij dies in ebdomada Cinerum,[3] iij*s.* 4*d.*; item prima ebdomada Quadragesime[4] per iiij dies cum uno famulo, iij*s.*; item secunda ebdomada Quadragesime[5] cum uno famulo, 4*s.* 6*d.*, unde xx*d.* per obstupacionem; item idem recepit pro seipso cum famulo tercia ebdomada Quadragesime,[6] 12*d.* (3*s.*); item idem recepit pro se et famulo suo 4 ebdomada Quadragesime,[7] 3*s.* 2*d.* (ᵈ et nota quod idem habet xvij*d.* receptos ad solvendum Ricardo filio Willelmi Wryhte de Stanford et Paulo Neeleson et non solvit); item 5 ebdomada Quadragesime,[8] ij*s.* vj*d.* scilicet in opere hostiorum et aliorum ad hospitale; item sexta ebdomada Quadragesime[9] dicto Roberto cum famulo per j diem et dimidiam, xj*d.*[10]

[CUSTUS IN OFFICIO]
(Vacat hic quia alibi scribitur). In solutis ij carpentariis Ricardo (Boydyl) de Stanfordia et socio suo (scilicet Paulo Nelson) pro meremio scapulato in officio per vj dies, iiij*s.* iiij*d.*; item eisdem per vj dies iiij*s.* vj*d.*; item eisdem per ij dies Ebdomada Pasche et Roberto Bryggh cum famulo, ij*s.* xj*d.* in dicto opere, videlicet in le Trenchis et orto Sancti Johannis Baptiste; item in solutis Roberto Brig' pro iij diebus scapulando meremium in le Trenchys, xv*d.*; item *Johanni* famulo suo per v dies, xx*d.*; item Ricardo Boydylle et Paulo Nelson per v dies capientes [*sic*] in die ix*d.*, iij*s.* ix*d.*

FORINCECA. In solutis Ricardo Haryngton cantori ex precepto prioris in festo Petri et Pauli,[11] x*d.*

NECESSARIA. In solutis pro uno ryppe pro herbis coligendis, ij*d. ob.* (ᵈ Memorandum quod Robertus Brig', carpentarius, mituatus est vj*s.* viij*d.*, et inde solvit xx*d.*, item xx*d.*, item xij*d.*, (14), modo debet xx*d.*, et pro T*homa* Heyd*s*, ij*s.* (solvit); modo debet ij*s.* vj*d.* (solvit), quos solvit.)

[*f. 55v.*] *Anno Ricardi abbatis xix⁰.*[12]

Vide principium istius materie sequentis in x folio sequente ante tale signum ⊙.[13]

⊙. (ᵈ In solutis Johanni Challener pro ccccccc plantulis fraccinis plantandis in orto Sancti Johannis Baptiste et in le Trenchys, xxj*d.*; item[14] in solutis fratri Johanni Burrowh pro ij carectatis de plantulis salicinis plantandis in supradictis locis; item in solutis Willelmo Martyn de

---

1 *1456–7.*
2 This sign '$\#$' is written before the paragraph, see above, p. 96.
3 *During the week from 28 Feb. to 5 Mar. 1456/7.*
4 *The week from 6 to 12 Mar. 1457.*   5 *The week from 13 to 19 Mar. 1457.*
6 *From 20 Mar.*   7 *From 27 Mar.*   8 *From 3 Apr.*
9 *From 10 Apr.*   10 A blank space of 1½ inches.
11 *29 June.*   12 *1456–7.*
13 *The following sentences were deleted with the note* scribitur alibi. Cf. p. 114.
14 *In the margin:* alibi.

Flete et Willelmo Rodger per ij ebdomadas primas Quadragesime plantyng sive settyng plantulas suprascriptas, iiijs.; item Willelmo Rodger et uno alio laborario (Johanni Bytam) tercia ebdomada Quadragesime, iijs. iiijd.; item Ricardo Mason et Johanni fratri suo et Johanni Sewalle (Agas) succidentibus fraccinos in orto Sancti Johannis Baptiste per ij dies, ijs. vjd.; item eisdem per quatuor dies succidentibus in le Trenchys, vs.; item Johanni Hoberd pro labore suo in plantacione per ij dies in locis suprascriptis, viijd. Item (scribitur) Willelmo Rodger pro quarta ebdomada Quadragesime, xxd. pro porcione de splynts de Trenchys in officio et settyng (de) staks in orto Sancti Johannis Baptiste; item Johanni Bytam pro consimili in dicto tempore, xijd.; item iiijd.; item Johanni Bytam 5 ebdomada Quadragesime succidendo spinas per 3 dies et per alios 3 dies in opere muri in gardino, xijd.; item patri suo Johanni Ropere succidendo et portando spinas per vj dies, xviijd.; item Johanni Hoberde copynng unius muri in gardino cum preparacione materie per vij dies, ijs. iiijd.; item Johanni Bytam portanti meremium de Trenchys in officium per vij dies cum aliis laboribus ibidem, ijs. iiijd.)

Quere plus de ista materia in secundo folio sequente ad tale signum 2.[1]

[*In margin*] (Scribitur alibi. Nota de succisione spinarum et cariagio de Trenchys in ortum Sancti Johannis et per quot dies; item de ij sepi [*sic*], prima unius partis siti[2] Sancti Johannis longitudinis cc et xx pedum, longitudo alterius sepis ibidem prope ibidem, videlicet, cc et xl pedum.)

PYNDER Ricardus Pynder emit de elemosinario unum hedghe row ad Fallam herne videlicet xvj carectatas spinarum cum srubb' ibidem, precium carectate, 8d.; et habet dies solucionis Fastyng gong' et Pasch unde solvit postea vjs. viijd.; item iijs. iiijd.; modo debet pro ij carectatis.

[*In margin*] Memorandum de ij carectatis spinarum, ultra 15 carectatas, non cariatas sed stant ibi quousque.

RICARDUS PYNDAR. Cariagium Ricardi Pynder. In primis ad hospitale iij carectate de calce, tracin' est strischburde, ixd.; (d item j carectata de conductu citra Burowbery salices ad officium, (iijd.)); item ij jaggs (iiijd.) de Sowter Row; item j carectata rubie tyl' ad hospitale (iijd.); item iij carectate arundinis de hospitale ad officium, viijd.; item iij parve carectate feni de Hamonds med' (viijd.); item vj carectate de Mukhyl gappe, xxiijd.; (d item viij carectate meremii quadrati de aqua in officium, xijd.; item per unum de Fletton vj carectate meremii de Trenchysse in officium, vjd.)

[PRO FOCALI VENDITO.]

Solvit xixd. per Johannem Halle cocum; pro focali vendito in orto Sancti Johannis, Willelmo Barbur, quasi iij carectatis; item Johanni Burle chyppys ut in secundo folio sequente, vs. (solvit); item iij carectatis de bows sive focalis 5s. ut in 4 folio sequente; item Ricardo

---

[1] See below, p. 104.

[2] This reference to the site of the original chapel of St. John the Baptist would appear to indicate that it was very near to the almoner's office at the east gate of the monastery.

Bladesmyth xvij peciis fraccinis pro tribulis et baculis, ut in [octavo] folio sequente, v*s.* ij*d.*

Memorandum quod Johanna Golsmyth fuit tenens elemosinarii per ij annos et dimidium reddendo per annum viij*s.*, xx*s.*; unde solvit, x*s.*; item vj*s.* viij*d.* Modo debet iij*s.* iiij*d.* Item solvit ij*s.*, et debet xvj*d.*; unde solvit xij*d.*

[*f. 56r.*] *Anno domini Ricardi Abbatis xix^mo* 1

CALX. In solutis pro iiij fodursse calcis Johanni Aylston, precium de fod*ur* xv*d.*, v*s.*; in cariagio ad officium [2   ]. (Vacat hic quia scribitur alibi.)

[WILLELMUS SCHEPEY]
Willelmus Schepey recepit de elemosinario pro muris petrinis ad Brig-mylle, vj*s.* viij*d.*; item iij*s.* iiij*d.* ibidem ad Brigmylle dominica tercia post Pascha; item iij*s.* iiij*d.* per proprium filium rec'; item xx*d.* per proprium filium in vigilia Pentecostes;3 item per proprium filium in crastino Sancti Botulphi,4 ij*s.*; item in vigilia Marie Magdalene,5 iiij*s.* ij*d.*; item in vigilia Advincule Sancti Petri,6 iiij*s.* iiij*d.*; item v*s.* in festum Mellonis episcopi.7
Summa soluta, xxx*s.* vj*d.*

Dominus Abbas debet fratri Willelmo Morton, xij*d.* quos dictus Willel-mus solvit Alicie Kyng pro abbate. Item frater Willelmus Morton solvit Willelmo (Lowthe,) j*d.*; item uxori Willelmi Craane, 6*s.* 8*d.*; item xx*s.*; item x*s.*; item iij*s.* iiij*d.*; item pro domino abbate fratri T*home* de Sancto Neoto, iij*s.* iiij*d.* (Vide de abbate in 9 folio precedente.)

SOLUCIO FRATRIS WILLELMI MORTON ELEMOSINARII PRO LEZ O AD FESTUM SANCTI JOHANNI BAPTISTE ANNO QUO SUPRA SCILICET XIX.8 In primis dicto elemosinario, vj*s.* viij*d.*; domino priori, x*s.*; fratri Ricardo Bysle, vj*s.* viij*d.*; fratri Johanni Borow, vj*s.* viij*d.* per stupacionem et pro meremio sibi vendito.

Nota quod Johannes Waldyng debet iiij*s.*, (solvit), vj*d.* (non solvit), pro Pewt*ur*rer' Plase; item pro firma calceti pro ij annis (*d* et dimidio) (16*d.*) ij*s.* viij*d.*; item xvj*s.* de redditu ubi manet pro ij terminis de anno xviij°; item xxiiij*s.* pro (iij) termino de redditu ubi manet, 37*s.* 2*d.*; unde solvit xxiiij*s.*; item vij*s.* ix*d.*; item xl*s.*; et debet ut patet inter debitores fratri Willelmo Morton; vide postea in folio quintodecimo in parte secunda.

Memorandum quod T*homas* Ryalle debet elemosinario pro Johanne Rose de Maxey xxij*s.* solvendos ad Pentecostem,9 xij*s.*, (solvit); item x*s.* ad festum Advincule Sancti Petri,10 (solvit).

(*d* Memorandum quod debentur Johanni Coldwelle xiij*s.* iiij*d.*, per fratrem Willelmum Morton, in previgilia Assencionis,11 (solvit).)

1 *1456–7.*	2 Left blank.	3 *4 June 1457.*
4 *18 June 1457.*	5 *21 July 1457.*	6 *31 July 1457.*
7 *22 Oct. 1457.*	8 *24 June 1457.*	9 *5 June 1457.*
10 *1 Aug. 1457.*	11 *24 May 1457.*	

[*f. 56v.*] *Anno domini Ricardi abbatis xix.*

[*In margin*] Vacat hic ista materia, quia melius alibi.

RICARDUS SMYTH CARPENTARIUS DE ABTHORPPE in previgilia Annunciacionis Beate Marie¹ concessit elemosinario obligari cum aliis duobus ad libitum fratris Willelmi Morton elemosinarii in xx*li.* ad faciendum molendinum Brigmylle vocatum, pro cxiij*s.* iiij*d.* infra quarterium proximum sequent*em* [*sic*] in omnibus cum (una camera et) uno ponte lingneo preter facturam murorum scilicet stonwerke etiam thakkyng, et dictus carpentarius transibit pro meremio eligendo cum aliis negociis dicto operi requirendis [*sic*] sive expediendis sumptibus suis propriis et elemosinarius inveniet omnimodam materiam.

Memorandum quod supradictus Ricardus carpentarius habuit pro arra et regardo per vices, 12*d.* Item memorandum de regardis aliorum quasi vj*s.* Item idem Ricardus carpentarius recepit de elemosinario prima vice pro stipendio suo in presencia Johannis Coldwelle, x*s.*; item xx*d.* juxta chyme in claustro; item eodem (per Johannem Coldwel), xx*d.*; item (per Johannem Coldwel), xiij*s.* iiij*d.*; item xx*s.*, in crastino Sancti Botulfi Abbatis;² omnia per tallium istuc [*sic*]; item in festo Sancte Marie Magdalene,³ xvj*s.* viij*d.*, (sine tallia); unde iiij*s.* per Johannem Eyr' collectorem de Sutton; item eodem die incontinenter, iij*s.* iiij*d.* Memorandum quod supradictus Ricardus recepit per talliam per vices iij*li.* xvj*s.* viij*d.*; item sine tallia Johann' Kydwel carpent', ij*s.* vj*d.*; item idem Ricardus recepit (ᵈ de Johanne Eyr'). Item elemosinarius solvit pro mensa dicti Ricardi cum sociis suis, tempore facture supradicti molendini, xlviij*s.* vj*d.* Roberto Conquest firmario manerii de Sutton.

Memorandum quod elemosinarius solvit Johanni Coldewel pro Sara Esex, xx*d.*; item dicto Johanni pro roba sua, v*s.*; item xx*d.* Agnes Draper mituata est xx*d.* de fratre Willelmo Morton, (solvit.)⁴

[*f. 57r.*] *Anno Ricardi abbatis xix.*⁵

SPYTYL CROFFTE cum dimidio sive medietate grangie ibidem usque Kandylmesse,⁶ de Tomas [*sic*] Pep*ur*, xxvj*s.* viij*d.*; Swyns medow de Johanne Aspeschaw, x*s.*; Fallam hirne de Willelmo Sewale de Westgate, iij*s.* viij*d.*; Hodys wong' cum ij acris prati de Roberto Crosse pro quatuor vel quinque annis per annum, vj*s.*; columbarium ad hospitale de vicario Burgi, vj*s.* viij*d.*; Coxholme [⁷   ]

Festum Marie Magdalene ad primam cenam, in una spada multonis pro capellano capelle Sancti T*ome* Matiris, (ij*d.*); in pane empto, ij*d.*; in cervisia villana; in una duodena de optima, xv*d.*; in v lagenis de mediocri cervisia, ij*d.*; in die ad prandium scilicet feria sexta, in anguillis pro uno jawge scilicet xv, (ij*d. ob.*); item iiij rostyng el, (iiij*d.*); in medde fysche, iiij*d.*; in uno quarterio salmonis, (iiij*d.*) cum capite; in rochysse (v*d. ob.*); in heryng, (ij*d.*); in dimidia libra amigdalorum, ij*d.*; in pipere, croco, et reysyngg*s* of Corawnse, j*d. ob.*; in oniowns, *ob.*

---

¹ *23 Mar.* 1456/7.   ² *18 June 1457.*   ³ *22 July 1457.*
⁴ Each sentence is marked 'Vacat'.   ⁵ *1456–7.*
⁶ *2 Feb.*   ⁷ Left blank.

[*Note in margin*] Fratres, Willelmus Melton, Walmysford, Stanford, Ryal, Pycheley, Wennam, Robertus Orwyn, cum uxore, Ricardus Papple. RECEPTA POMORUM. In receptis pro pomis venditis Agneti Hernes, scilicet viij eskeppis, xx*d.*, unde solvit [¹   ]

Noverint universi per presentes me Tomam Cuttlar nuper de Burgo Sancti Petri in comitatu North*amptonie* remisisse relaxasse [et] omnino pro me heredibus et executoribus meis in perpetuum quietum clamasse Abbati de Burgo predicto et fratri Willelmo Morton elemosinario ejusdem loci omnimodas acciones tam reales quam personales quas erga predictos abbatem et Willelmum Morton habeo habui seu quovismodo habere potui racione alicujus debiti querele (demande) sive alterius cujuscumque tituli a principio mundi usque in diem confeccionis presencium. In cujus rei testimonium huic presenti scripto sigillum meum apposui. Data apud Burgum supradictum iij die mensis Augusti anno regni regis Henrici Sexti post conquestum Anglie xxxv.²

IN FORINCECIS. In solutis Nicholao fabro pro potione dato prima vice Sorelle, iiij*d.*

MAWDE RAVON. Memorandum quod frater Willelmus Morton dimisit ad firmam Matilde Ravon unam vaccam rubeam usque ad principium proximi May reddendo iij*s.*, unde solvit xij*d.*; item lac duarum vaccarum sive vitulis per idem tempus pro xx*d.* Idem Matilda solvit xij*d.*; item in crastino Martini,³ xij*d.*; item xij*d.* in Vigilia Corporis Christi,⁴ xij*d.*

[*f. 57v.*] *Anno Ricardi abbatis xix.*⁵

2.⁶ (ᵈ In solutis Henrico Kysby pro cariagio de iiij carectatis meremii de Trenchys in officium, 6(vj)*d.*)

IN OFFICIO. (Scribitur.) (ᵈ In solutis Johanni Medow pro factura de vᶜiiijˣˣxix kydd*s*, v*s.* x*d.*); item Johanni Hobarde et socio suo Henrico in factura de novo unam partem [*sic*] orientalem unius muri de gardino in officio (scilicet xxij pedum) per vj dies., videlicet cum copyng ibidem similiter, iiij*s.*; item in stramine et feno emptis ad Lowhe cum cariagio, scilicet ij carectatarum in officium, xvij*d.*; item in arundine empta, videlicet iijᶜlx cum cariagio, vij*s.* v*d.*; item in le copyng ibidem in gardino de novo scilicet vj rodis, dando pro copyng' unius rode vj*d.* *ob.*, iij*s.* iij*d.* et in servisia, j*d.*; (ᵈ item in solutis diversis operariis pro portacione meremii scapulati ad aquam, (xv*d.*); item pro extraxcione de aqua simul cum cariagio in officium (scilicet) xvj carectatarum, videlicet Hugoni laborario (xv*d.*) et Ricardo Pyndar, ut in tercio folio ante in secunda parte folii, xij*d.* [*Note in margin*: Vacat hic quia scribitur alibi.]

JOHANNI BURLEY, VENDICIO FOCALIS. Johannes Burle emit de elemosinario unum pyle de chyppys pro v*s.*, unde solvit ij*s.* vj*d.*, et debet tantum prima Dominica Quadragesime,⁷ quos solvit et equet.

---

¹ Left blank.   ² *3 Aug. 1457.*   ³ *12 Nov.*   ⁴ *15 June.*
⁵ *1456–7.*   ⁶ See above, p. 101.   ⁷ *6 Mar. 1457.*

SOLUCIO FRATRIS WILLELMI MORTON ELEMOSINARII PRO TUNICIS post festum Luce Ewangeliste[1] et pro anno xix domini Ricardi abbatis. In primis dicto fratri Willelmo Morton, x*s*.; item fratri Johanni Pycheley, 15*d*.; item fratri T*ome* de Sancto Neoto, xl*d*.; item xl*d*.; item xl*d*.; item fratri Ricardo Bysley, x*s*.; receptos per Johannem Coppyng'; (^d item fratri Willelmo Wennam, x*s*.); 6*s*. 8*d*.; iij*s*. iiij*d*. pro officio sub-elemosinarie; item fratri Willelmo Byrry, x*s*.; et tesaurario, vj*s*. viij*d*.; item iij*s*. iiij*d*.

[*In margin*] Nota quod non solvit: recepit pro officio subelemosinarie vj*s*. viij*d*.

Willelmus Rest senior solvit elemosinario iij*s*. iiij*d*. pro longa forera prope Bondstyle cum sellione infra Coldham juxta vicariam Burgi anno xix^{mo} domini Ricardi Abbatis. Nota quod ista solucio maxime erat pro aysyamento intrandi per Coldham cum bestiis suis in vicariam tempore yemali set non estivali propter blada ibidem crescensia [*sic*].

BRIGMYLLE. A LUFFE BONE. Memorandum de cariagio per viam amoris ibidem anglice a luffe boone, videlicet x carectate, prima per Robertum Conquest, secundum per Johannem Eyr', tercium per Johannem Yvys, quarta per Robertum Wymys, quinta per Willelmum Blogwyn, sexta per Jacobum servientem rectoris de Cast*ur*, 7 per T*omam* Hontte, 8 per Willelmum Wymys et T*homam* Edows, 9 per Johannem Gronger de Eyl'worth, x per Ricardum Knythe de eadem.

[*f. 58r.*] *Anno domini Ricardi abbatis xix.*[2]

MAXSEY. (^d In solutis uno lathamo conducto ad emendandum (muros), (^d certas) sive diversas parcellas in grangia rectorie de Maxsey, (subtus le Walsche ibidem), xxij*d*.; item ad potum per vices, 4*d*.; item in solutis Johanni [³   ] pro v quarteriis calcis emptis et j bussello, iij*s*. v*d*.; item pro ij carectatis zabuli [³   ]; item Roberto sclatt*er* Stanfordie emendando ibidem per v dies in diversis locis, ij*s*. vj*d*.; item pro xx^c sclatte pynnys [³   ]; item pro mille sclatt*s* emptis de Johanne Kyrcby unde v^c non perforatis, cum cariagio, vij*s*. vj*d*.; latt*s* et latte nayl' cum aliis clavis de stauro. In solutis Johanni Aspschaw thegulatori operante super grangiam in rectoria ibidem, (iiij*s*. vj*d*.) in parte solucionis majoris summe (scilicet pro iij rodis mille sclat pynnys); item et pro perforacione de ccccc sclatt*s* [³   ])

[*In margin*] Memorandum de carpentria ibidem per ij dies, xij*d*.

SUTTON. In solutis Roberto Mownsylle pro falcacione de Brigmylle holme per ij annos [³   ] et in cariagio ejusdem usque Sottun [³   ]; item pro asportacione dicti thak de dicto holme ad carectas, vj*d*.

CAMERA IN INFIRMARIA. In solutis pro xlj foote in walplat*s*, iij*s*.; item pro xiij tignis, ij*s*. viij*d*. *ob*.; item pro xv libris dimidia in iij ancoris ferreis pro tribus beemys debilibus, ij*s*. vij*d*.; item pro tayl fete, [³   ]; in solutis Johanni Myller, (ix*d*.) et Stephano carpentario (cum Paulo

---

[1] *18 Oct. 1457 (?)*.   [2] *1456–7*.   [3] Left blank.

Nelson) pro operacione supradicti meremii ad supradictam cameram in diversis locis ibidem, iij*s*. vj*d*.; item pro iiij carectatis terre rubie, ix*d*.; item in solutis duobus latamis et uno servienti operantibus ibidem per ij dies et dimidiam, xx*d*., (scilicet pro fratre Johanne York) et magister operis solvit eis residuum. In ij fod*ur*s calcis et dimidio cum cariagio, iij*s*. viij*d*. *ob*.; item pro iij carectatis zabuli, xij*d*.; item Johanni Aspeschaw tylar cum aliis tribus adjuvantibus ibidem in grosso, ix*s*.; in iij*c* latt*s*, ij*s*. : in xv*c* latte nayl', xvj*d*., ij mille pynnys (8*d*.). Johanni Potter pro evacuacione et inundacione camerarum per ij dies, viij*d*. pro plast*ur*yng Johanni Aspschaw et filio, viij*d*.; item Willelmo Coper pro vj crestis, x*d*.; item pro ij mille sclatt*s* [¹   ]; item pro cariagio, v*s*. et in victualibus, viij*d*.

[*Note at foot of text*] Dominus abbas habet (*d*librum scilicet 'Speculum stultorum') quaternum de 4 foliis noviter scriptum de croniculis veteribus et novis.

[*f. 58v*.] *Anno domini Ricardi abbatis xix*º.²

28. SUTTON. JACOBUS PENYNGTON. THOMAS ROTLANDE ALIAS SMYTHE. (*d* In solutis T*ome* Smythe pro vj paribus heynglysse et stok*s* deliberatis Roberto Conqueste firmario de Sutton, xvj libris, xvj*d*., xxxij*d*.)

HOSPITALE. (*d* In solutis dicto fabro pro ij paribus magnis de heyngl' et stok*s*, ponderantibus xxxix libris pro ij ostiis (aule) ad hospitale, vj*s*. vj*d*.; item [³   ])

[*In margin*] 28 vide plus de ista materia in xxviij folio precedente; et item in penultimo folio libri ad tale signum ·Θ·⁴

IN OFFICIO (vacat quia scribitur alibi). Item pro j ligatura propter unum instrumentum vocatum Anglice a gy[   ] cum uno clasppe (retro) (*d* propter) le wyckette subtus le garrette in officio ponderante v libras, x*d*.; item in xxxij removyngg*s* calcarium equorum xij*d*.; item in v ferramentis equorum, vij*d*.; item pro ligacione cum ferramentis unius veteris situle ad fontem in officio, ij*d*.; item pro froste nayl' et emendacione ij vangarum, iij*d*.

⊚⁵ Johanni Coldwel pro stipendio suo (*d* Non. May,⁶ iiij*s*. vj*d*.; item pridie Non. J. vj*d*. iiij*s*.;) in crastino Sancti Johannis Baptiste,⁷ ix*s*.; item Dominica post Assumpcionem Beate Marie,⁸ ix*s*.

CLOPTON. In allocatis Johanni Hartte pro australi parte stabuli, xx*d*.; item in allocatis dicto Johanni pro australi parte grangie sue, iij*s*.

DOMINO ABBATI (VERSUS WALSYNGHAM) IN DIE ASSUMPCIONIS BEATE MARIE.⁹ Elemosinarius frater Willelmus Morton solvit per Robertum Morton xx*s*.

ROBERTUS RYDAR. In solutis eidem, dominica infra Octabis Sancti Oswaldi,¹⁰ xl*d*.

(*d* lynyn¹¹ cappe, Matilda Ravon habet lavare.)

---

¹ Left blank.   ² *1456–7*.   ³ Not continued.   ⁴ See above, p. 86, and below, p. 167.
⁵ See p. 84.   ⁶ *7 May 1457*.   ⁷ *25 June 1457*.
⁸ *21 Aug. 1457*.   ⁹ *15 Aug. 1457*.   ¹⁰ *7 Aug. 1457*.
¹¹ Note at foot of folio, afterwards deleted.

[*f. 59r.*] *Anno domini Ricardi abbatis xix^mo.*[1]

JAMYS PENYNGTON.
Memorandum quod elemosinarius debet Tome Rowsby coquo pro ij
minucionibus clare, iiij*s.* j*d.* Item idem elemosinarius debet dicto Tome
xiij*s.* iij*d.* pro carnibus per eum emptis pro coquina, ultra xiiij*s.* j*d.* per
talliam de carnibus receptis de Toma Pep*ur*. Item idem elemosinarius
debet dicto T*ome* coquo ut supra xiij*s.* iiij*d.*, pro fratre Willelmo M*er*kam
nuper infirmario. Summa xxx*s.* viij*d.*; unde dictus elemosinarius solvit
dicto T*ome* coquo, ut in focali sibi vendito, xv*s.*; item in denariis sibi
solutis in presencia Willelmi Jaxson, ix*s.* Modo debentur nisi vj*s.* viij*d.*

FRUMENTUM. (Vacat quia postea melius) ([d] In solutis Willelmo Haryson
de Alwalton pro iiij quarteriis frumenti (precium quarterii, iiij*s.* v*d.*)
contra diem Animarum,[2] xv*s.* (xvij*s.* viij*d.*) in anno xx domini Ricardi
abbatis.)

([d] IN OFFICIO. In solutis Ricardo Gregory pro ccclx garbis de potyng-
thak pro stabulo in officio, precium de c, vij*d.*, ij*s.* *ob.*; item eidem pro
factura de ij acris prati ad Mukhyl gappe, vj*d.*)

IN FORINCECIS. In solutis Morgon (Owyn) Walysman[3] pro fodicione
juxta foreram elemosinarii per vij loca prope Bond style, v*d.*

BRIGMYLLE. In solutis (Johanni Coldwel) pro sarracione de xij srobbe
bord*s* pro ij wat*ur* qwhel' ad Brigmylle, xvij*d.* Et nota quod dictus
Johannes prius solvit sarratori.

FORINCECA, (v*s.* iiij*d.*) In solutis pro equis mittendis [ad] (Oxon*iam*)
pro fratribus Henrico Burrowh et Johanne Malden in previgilia Sancti
Jacobi Apostoli[4] et in itinere eorum versus Oxoniam (xv. Kal. Decembris,[5] v*s.*; iiij*s.*)

MARRAM. T*homas* Gyl[ham] ibidem solvit xiij*s.* iiij*d.* et debet xiiij*d.* et
memorandum de grosso cum foramine. Nota quod in festo Sancti
Laurencii[6] erat solucio supra pro anno xviij.

PESSKODD*S*. In solutis Johanni Pye de Paston pro v bussellis, cum
cariagio ad Burgum, 8*d.*; item in solutis uxori Davy Brown pro uno
pek farine avenarum, ij*d.* *ob.* ([d] Frater Johannes Pychele promisit cum
juramento levando dexteram manum solvere xv*d.* pro Waltero Qhwyte
fratri Willelmo Morton; scilicet pro xv kydd*s* fraccinis ad proximum
festum Michaelis sequentem [*sic*] videlicet percipiendum de cameraria
sua modo ex parte domini abbatis; (condonatur).[7]

MAXEY. In solutis Roberto Brig laborante super grangiam de rectoria
ibidem per ij dies, xij*d.*

([d] Memorandum de lxj peciis quercinis in tenemento fratris Willelmi
Morton in Westgate, unde xviij pecie magne.)

[1] *1456–7.*   [2] *2 Nov. 1457.*   [3] Morgan Owen, a Welshman.
[4] *23 July 1457.*   [5] *17 Nov. 1457.*   [6] *10 Aug.*
[7] Repeated thrice.

[*f. 59v.*] *Anno domini Ricardi abbatis xix.*[1]

(^d IN NECESSARIIS. In solutis pro reparacione unius celle monachalis, v*d. ob.*)

OXNEY. In solutis fratri T*home* Kydde, gardiano de Oxney, pro anno Ricardi abbatis xvij et communibus ibidem, xxvj*s.* viij*d.* per priorem (recepta [*sic*]) in festo Nativitatis Beate Marie[2] anno xix°. Item frater Willelmus Morton elemosinarius solvit dicto gardiano in festo Michaelis[3] anno xx incipiente, vj*s.* viij*d.*, pro anno xix^{mo}. Item idem elemosinarius solvit dicto gardiano sibi solutos per manus Johannis clerici de Oxney, xiiij*s.*, quos dictus clericus debebat fratri Willelmo Morton elemosinario. Item idem elemosinarius concessit solvere priori pro dicto gardiano xxvj*s.* pro anno domini Ricardi abbatis vicesimo, et hic gardianus debet elemosinario iiij*d.*, (solvit); item xx*d.* pro redditu assise, (solvit.)[4] Item dictus frater Willelmus Morton elemosinarius solvit supradicto gardiano viij Kal. (^d Julii) Decembris,[5] xij*s.* super altare Sancti Laurencii post missam. Modo elemosinarius debet gardiano xij*s.* pro anno xxj Ricardi abbatis.[6]

Johannes Colyngham solvit iiij*d.* de redditu assiso [*sic*] pro anno xix pro j acra terre ad Fallam hyrne.

(^d WAXHOWS PONDE, (vacat). Ibi sunt vij pecie quercine scapulate cum signo de ij nyck*s*; item j beeme fraccina.)

[*f. 60r.*] *Anno domini Ricardi abbatis xx incipiente.*[7]

(^d In solutis (^d Johanni) (Willelmo) Rede pro vij mille dimidia (vel v^c) sclatt*s* ab eo emptis propter Brigmylle, precium de mille v*s.* vj*d.*, xiij*s.* iiij*d.*; xlj*s.* iij*d.*) (Vacat hic.)

Memorandum de ij pullis scilicet ij hors fool,[8] scilicet, uno bay coloris et j nigri coloris etatis xxvij ebdomadorum ad Natale domini anno quo supra emptis per fratrem Willelmum Morton de Johanne Coldwelle pro vj*s.* vj*d.*, solutis in manibus.

IN BURGO. In solutis Willelmo Pyppwelle pro iij libris sowd*ur* cum labore super Sowter Row, ubi Henricus Collermaker manet, in una guttera ibidem, 12*d.*

IN OFFICIO. In solutis pro iij fodyrsse calcis iij*s.* ix*d.*; in cariagio, vj*d.*, unde ij fod*ur*s et dimidium ad cameram in infirmaria.

IN FORINCECIS. In solutis pro uno jale cervisie iiij*d.* pro uno monacho de Abyngdon in octabis Dedicacionis.[9]

TANHOLT.[10] Memorandum quod in solutis pro meremio scapulato[11] ad Tanholt, Ricardo de Apthorp, Johanni Kydwelle et T*ome* Stranglyon per ij dies, iij*s.*, (in cervisia, j*d.*); item Stephano et Paulo Nelson

---

[1] *1456–7.*   [2] *8 Sept.*   [3] *29 Sept. 1457.*
[4] Thrice repeated.   [5] *24 Nov.*
[6] Half a folio was left blank for the insertion of further payments, which, however, were not recorded.   [7] *1457–8.*   [8] Horse foals.
[9] *5 Oct. 1457.* The dedication of Peterborough monastic church was on 28 Sept.
[10] The cattle farm of the monastery, near Eyebury.   [11] Trimmed timber.

scapulantibus (iiij pecias quercinas)¹ per unum diem ibidem, x*d*.; in cervisia, ij*d*.; item in cariagio de Tanholtte ad elemosinariam scilicet pro ij carectatis, xvj*d*., et in victualibus, iiij*d*.; item T*ome* Cowper, (16*d*.), et Roberto Wryhte de Fletton (18*d*.) pro aliis ij carectatis, ij*s*. x*d*.; etiam in rewardis Willelmo Reeste, Tome B*ur*bryg et aliis diversis adjuvantibus ad le jybbe sive le ferne, xij*d*., et in victualibus, 8*d*.

IN FORINCECIS. Memorandum quod Johannes B*ur*le emit iij carectata focalis in orto Sancti Johannis pro v*s*. vj*d*., unde solvet ij*s*. ix*d*. in festo Nativitatis domini (per Johannem Coldwel, anno xxj); item ij*s*. ix*d*.

Robertus Austorp emit ij stepyng fatt*s* de fratre Willelmo Morton pro v*s*. vj*d*., unde solvit ij*s*. et ix*d*.; et habet diem de residuo usque proximum Pascha.

FORINSECA.² In solutis ij studentibus in recessu eorum versus Oxoniam in festo Sancti Romani,³ x*s*.; et sic equet usque ad Pascha.

Memorandum de xvij*s*. iiij*d*. deliberatis Johanni Coldwel (Merstlonde, per vices)⁴ unde dictus Johannes solvit pro iiij (mille) [de] sclat nayl', iiij*s*.; item pro iij libris amigdali, ix*d*.; item pro cccc grossis spyk*s*, xviij*d*.; item pro cc mydyl spyk*s*, vj*d*.; item pro cc splynt nayl', v*d*. Idem Johannes solvit pro mylle stonys in plenam solucionem, vij*s*. ij*d*., ultra x*s*. per elemosinarium; item xij*d*.; omnibus computatis, predictus Johannes Coldwel debet xx*d*.

[*f. 60v.*] *Anno xx* [*domini abbatis Ricardi.*]⁵
Memorandum (ᵈ to owt*ur* ij fatt*s*; item) to clennysse ye sewer' at ye Cyst*er* howse; item to howse ye tymb*ur* in Westgate & in ye offysse; (ᵈ item to delyv[   ] fallyngg*s*; to (do) by) clowt led*ur* for Rob*er*d item sclat bastard for [H (?)] Palm*er*s pr*e*vy; (ᵈ item to holde kowr't*s*); item to kary chyppys from Sutton & owt of trenchyz w*ith* od*ur* tymb*ur*; (ᵈ item to make ij cowl'); item offe stelyng' offe rede in Coxholme, also bord*s* sclatt*s* & od*ur* thyngg*s* at Brigmylle stolne; (ᵈ item sclattyng' on ye Sowter Row); item to by baston roppe; item a ladd*ur* (ᵈ in Howgate) (at Sowter Row); item Agneti Honnyg tayle de debito, lv*s*., citra debitum de brasio, scilicet ix quarteriis iiij eskeppis, precium quarterii iiij*s*., (38*s*.), (ᵈ xl*s*.); unde solvit per vices, xxiij*s*. iiij*d*.

BRYGMYLLE. Memorandum quod in previgilia Omnium Sanctorum,⁶ omnibus computatis inter elemosinarium et Johannem [Coldewelle] famulum suum, videlicet, pro pane, (x*d*.), pro servisia, iij*d*.; ad Abthorp, in cervisia, (j*d*.); item in servisia ad Maxey, (j*d*.); Sutton, in servisia, j*d*.; Allewalton in prandio, (iij*d*.,); hic domi in o[   ] servisie pro priore, vij*d*.; in multone pro Johanne Honnyng, j*d*. *ob*.; in ij casiis, (iiij*d*.).

COWGATE. In solutis Hugoni de Walton pro labore per vj dies drawyng & strawyng, ij*s*. (ij*d*.).

¹ Trimming four pieces of oak.   ² This word is quite uncertain.
³ *23 Oct. 1457.*   ⁴ Marshland.   ⁵ *1457–8.*   ⁶ *30 Oct. 1457.*

COKKYSSE HOLME. Item in solutis ij carectariis de Fletton pro thak cariando de Coxholme in villam, xij*d*. Idem Johannes solvit Johanni Aspschaw [*sic*], xij*d*.

ELYFEYR'. Pro vj virgis de grey frese, iij*s*. iiij*d*.; in ij salcatis piss[   ] pro Ricardo Pitt*s*, xv*d*.; item pro fratre Roberto Notyngham, iiij*s*.; item pro roba dicti Johannis Coldwel pro ij terminis ante festum et in festo Michaelis anno xx incipiente, iij*s*. iiij*d*. SUMMA xviij*s*. vj*d*. *ob*. (*d* unde dictus Johannes recepit.)

[JOHANNES COLDWELLE.]
Idem Johannes solvit Johanni Potter, xviij*d*.; (vj*d*.; vj*d*.); item Johanni Som*ur* thakker, xij*d*.; (viij*d*.); item pro ocriis, vij*d*. cervisia, iiij*d*.; chyppis beryng, iiij*d*.; in pissibus, cervisia, metyng of lyme, iiij*d*; item ad Wermyngton, xj*d*. SUMMA xxiij*s*. vj*d*. *ob*., unde recepit xiij*s*. iiij*d*. Idem Johannes Coldwel solvit Willelmo M*e*rkande viij*d*., pro labore ad novam domum super Sowter Row. Idem Johannes Coldwel recepit iij*s*. iiij*d*.; item iiij*s*. de Willelmo Reede.

Johannes Incle solvit elemosinario, xvj*d*. et equet pro anno xix°.

Henricus Palmer solvit xiij*s*. iiij*d*., tempore Natalis domini pro anno quo supra scilicet xix, et modo debet vj*s*. viij*d*. pro tenementis suis, (solvit.)[1] Johannes Tempyl solvit xv*d*., de anno xx^mo. Johannes Barford solvit xij*d*. pro anno xix°. Willelmus Glynton solvit pro anno xix, xij*d*. Katerina Pyg solvit, ut supra, (pro) anno xix°, iiij*s*. vj*d*.

[*f. 61r.*] *Anno xx Ricardi abbatis ad festum* Thome *Apostoli*.[2]

SUTTON. In solutis Johanni (*d* Boman) Halyday, carpentario, viij*d*. pro scapulacione xviij tracinarum, ubi Johannes Boman manet.

SUTTON. In solutis ij carpentariis pro iiij tracinis de novo impositis cum naylyng on of bord*s* in le malt chawmb*ur* in manerio ad Sutton per ij dies et dimidium, x*d*.

MAXEY. CUSTUS DE ROSE PLACE SUPER CORNERIUM IBIDEM. In solutis pro cariagio de quatuor carectatis meremii scapulati ab officio illuc, iiij*s*.; et in victualibus et servisia illuc, viij*d*.; et in solutis Roberto Brig carpentario cum aliis ij carpentariis ibidem per xj dies, iiij*s*. iiij*d*.; item per Johannem Coldwelle, ij*s*.; item per elemosinarium, v*s*.; item iij*s*.; item in obstupacione pro veteri debito dicti Roberti Brig, elemosinario, ij*s*. vj*d*.; item pro c grossis spyk*s*, (v*d*.); item clx splent nal', [3   ]; item dicto Roberto Brig per ij dies splentyng ij gabull' ibidem et faciendo ij laddyrsse in ij guteris ibidem, x*d*.

IN RECTORIA. (*d* Item dicto Roberto carpentario per (*d* iiij) v dies in una hustrina in rectoria ibidem ponendo, j som*ur*tre et viij tracinas, omnia de novo, ij*s*. j*d*.

MEMORANDUM DE ROSE PLASE. Item Roberto firmario de Maxey pro splent*s* emptis pro Rose Plase, vij*d*.

---

[1] Four times repeated.   [2] *21 Dec. 1457*.   [3] Left blank.

In RECTORIA. (ᵈ Item in solutis pro uno pari de heynglys et stok*s* cum clave, vj*d*. pro ostio hustrine suprascripte cum tabulis quercinis de stauro officii.)

Anno xix°.¹ WERMYNGTON. In solutis pro ij carectatis spinarum emptis ultra Owndylle, cum cariagio ad Wermyngton, ij*s*.; et in una sepe mortua ibidem facienda juxta Awmeners lane vel Long lane continente (per estimacionem) xvj rodas cum stak*s* emptis ad idem opus, ij*s*.

Anno xx°. Item pro factura unius muri terrei continentis iij rodas, iiij*s*. vj*d*.

[*f. 61v.*]

(Summa soluta patet antea, scilicet in xvij folio,² C iij*s*. viij*d*.)

*Anno Ricardi Abbatis xx.*³

⊠ SACRISTA. De solucionibus fratri Willelmo Borowh, require antea folio 17,² (xvij). Item idem frater Willelmus Morton elemosinarius solvit dicto sacriste in Sabbato post Epiphaniam,⁴ x*s*.; item domino abbati, vj*s*. pro ficubus et racemis. Sacrista anno xx°.

SUMMA SOLUTA cxix*s*. viij*d*.; et ultra sacrista recepit per viam obstupacionis 27*s*. SUMMA TOTALIS [⁵   ].

In FORINCECIS. In focali vendito domino abbati subtus Estwoode ex utraque parte de lodge yaate ibidem, xl*s*.

In FORINSECIS. Item de Davy Browne pro alio hedge row ad vij acras terre elemosinarii ad M*er*chel stybbyngg*s*, xliij*s*. iiij*d*. et quatuor carectatis meremii⁶ ibidem, unde solvit xxj*s*. viij*d*. Item solvit residuum in ebdomada Pentecostes; item pro focali vendito (ad Parke kyrc,⁷ debet modo iiij*d*.) Johanni Draper de Newerk et Matilde Ravon, ij*s*. et 8*d*. (debet modo, 6*d*.); item de Johanne Potter pro focali ibidem sibi vendito ij*s*. (solvit) iiij*d*., (solvit), et solvit [⁵   ].

SOWTER ROW (scribitur in compoto anni xix.)
(ᵈ In solutis Johanni Halyday carpentario pro factura et emendacione de tribus ostiis ibidem cum fenestris et latchys, snatchys et hagoday[   ] ix*d*.)

Willelmus Sand*ur*, Johannes Incley, heres T*home* Boysse, Johanna Lynton, Symon Walram, Willelmus Leverysse de Wermyngton.

CALX. In solutis pro vij fodyrsse calcis Johanni Baker, unde iij fod*ur*s (v eskeppe) pro camera, precium de fodyr, xiiij*d*. cum cariagio, ix*s*. iiij*d*.; item Tome Thorppe pro iij fodyrsse calcis, ij*s*. vj*d*., et in cariagio ejusdem, vj*d*.

VINUM PRO CONVENTU. In solutis Johanni Tylly pro iiij lagenis vini; item pro vj pynt*s*, iiij*s*. vj*d*. dominica Pentecostes; item in festo

---

¹ *1456–7.*   ² See above, p. 81.   ³ *1457–8.*
⁴ *7 Jan. 1457/8.*   ⁵ Left blank.   ⁶ Four cartloads of timber.
⁷ The chapel of St. Mary Magdalene, Newark.

Apostolorum Petri et Pauli vinum emptum de fratre Johanne Ryalle, videlicet iij lagene j potell' et j quarte, iij*s*. ix*d*.

NECESSARIA. In solutis pro iiij mille [de] latte nayl', iiij*s*. (3*s*. 8*d*.); item pro mille de minoribus splynt naylys, 3*s*. 3*d*.

WODCROFTE. Johannes Smyth solvit pro anno xix v*s*. (elemosinario) (d Johanni Coldwel famulo elemosinarii); item solvit elemosinario, vj*s*. viij*d*., et debet viij*s*. (iiij*d*.), unde solvit v*s*. viij*d*., et debet ij*s*. vii[j*d*.]; unde Johannes Coldwel debet xx*d*. (solvit). Modo Johannes Smyth debet xij*d*.

[*f. 62r.*] *Anno domini Ricardi abbatis* xx°.[1]

MAXSEY. 26. Vide de ista materia in (d xx) 26 folio precedente ad tale signum 26.[2]
Robertus Smyth firmarius de Maxsey solvit elemosinario in festo Apostolorum Petri et Pauli[3] anno xx, pro anno xix^{mo}, iij*li*. xiij*s*. iiij*d*.; item in festo Sancti Oswaldi,[4] iiij*li*.; item anno xxj in festo Sancte Katerine,[5] iiij*li*. pro anno xix° et 7 croppe; modo debet viij*li*. vj*s*. viij*d*.; unde solvit in Cena Domini[6] iiij*li*.; hic debet 4*li*. 6*s*. 8*d*.; unde solvit in Translacione Sancti T*home* Martiris,[7] iiij marcas; item in octavis Sancti Oswaldi,[8] iiij marcas.

Memorandum de uno penytopense pro grosso, unde (x)xxxiij*s*. iiij*d*. pro anno xix^{mo} et septimo croppe; item xxx*s*. pro anno xx° et octavo croppe; item vj*s*. viij*d*.; item in Vigilia Reliquiarum,[9] iij*li*.; item in festo Sancti Antonii[10] abbatis anno xxij, iiij*li*.; similiter pro octavo croppe; item in Cena domini[11] (anno xxij), iiij*li*.; item solvit in crastino Translacionis Sancti Martini,[12] v*li*. viij*s*. iiij*d*. et xx*d*. condonatur et sic equet, pro viij croppe. Item idem Robertus solvit anno xxij finiente in festo Sanctorum Florentini Cosme et Damiani[13] iiij*li*. propter le ix croppe. Item anno xxiij° in festo Sancte Lucie virginis[14] solvit iiij*li*.; item in Cena domini[15] iiij*li*.; item in festo Apostolorum Petri et Pauli,[16] iiij*li*. Item idem solvit iij*li*. vj*s*. viij*d*.; item pro expensis dicti firmarii (40*d*.) versus Narhamton [*sic*] propter sequestracionem factam in rectoria de Maxsey; item propter le x croppe, iiij*li*. Item iiij die Novembris idem firmarius solvit iiij*li*.; item iiij*li*. in festo Annunciacionis Beate Marie anno regni regis Edwardi Quarti post conquestum secundo[17] et anno Ricardi abbatis xxiij [*sic*]. Item dictus Robertus solvit eodem anno infra Octabas Sancti Benedicti,[18] vij*li*. x*s*.; et equet preter reparacionem.

Memorandum de allocacione petenda pro uno cesteron; item pro vj carectatis albi straminis; item xvj*d*. pro Ricardo Honnyng; item tantum pro Roberto Morton; item pro una roba Roberto Hok' data, vj*s*. viij*d*.

---

[1] *1457–8*.   [2] See above, p. 67   [3] *29 June 1458*.   [4] *5 Aug. 1458*.
[5] *25 Nov. 1458*.   [6] *22 Mar. 1459*.   [7] *7 July 1459*.   [8] *12 Aug. 1459*.
[9] *20 Oct. 1459*.   [10] *17 Jan. 1459/60*.   [11] *10 Apr. 1460*.   [12] *5 July 1460*.
[13] *27 Sept*.   [14] *13 Dec. 1460*.   [15] *2 Apr. 1461*.   [16] *29 June 1461*.
[17] *25 Mar. 1462*.   [18] *28 Mar. 1462*.

[*f. 62v.*] *Anno Ricardi abbatis xix.*[1]

Vendicio focalis in le Trenchys.

In primis Martino sutori xv pecie fraccine pro x*d.*; (solvit, tamen debet iij*d.* pro ramelle.[2]) Ricardo Pantre iij grosse fraccine; item xvj parve, iiij*s.* iiij*d.*; (solvit[3] xij*d.*; item iij*s.* iiij*d.*) Ricardo Chawmeberleyne, (Webster), ij selliones in quibus sunt quasi vj carectate salicum, (pro viij*s.* vj*d.*), unde solvit (*d* ante cariagium) iij*s.* iiij*d.*, (*d* et habet diem de iiij*s.* usque festum Beate Virginis in Quadragesima,[4] et fecit fidem cum dextera [manu];) (et debet v*s.* ij*d.*, unde solvit ij*s.* viij*d.*; modo debet, ij*s.* vj*d.*) *Thome* carpentario de Wodston quasi iiij carectate sub murum orientalem gardini herbarum in elemosinaria, vj*s.* viij*d.*, (solvit.) Ricardo Bladesmythe, j peciam fraccinam pro baculis vj*d.*; (solvit.) (*d* Item Martino Sutori quasi) [*In margin*] Johanni Bytam, (unde solvit), j carectatam et dimidiam, iij*s.* (*d* viij*d.*) Johanni Drewsse juniori[5] vij carectate salicum, ix*s.* ij*d.*; (unde solvit iiij*s.*; item iij*s.* et debet ij*s.* ij*d.*)

Domino Johanni B*u*rrowh, magistro operum iij selliones, vij carectate x*s.*; (unde solvit vj*s.* viij*d.*)

Willelmo Morton serianto [*sic*] in abbathie vestiario iij carectate fraccinorum et salicum, v*s.* unde solvit 2*s.* 3*d.* (scilicet per mensam Willelmi et Willelmi), et solvet residuum ad proximam Purificacionem;[6] (solvit (*d* iij*s.* j*d.* et debet 22*d.*) totum ad festum Anunciationis Beate Marie;) [*in the margin*] solvit xxij*d.*

Item Johanni Bytam quasi ij carectate et dimidia salicum et fraccinorum pro v*s.*, et habet ij dies solucionis, primum ad mediam Quadragesimam,[7] secundum ad proximum Pentecostem,[8] et fecit fidem Roberto Morton levando manum; (solvit iij*s.* iiij*d.*; item iiij*d.*; j*d.*; et debet 15*d.*; unde solvit 8*d.* et 7*d.* et equet.)

Johanni Challener xxxvij pecie salicum quasi j carectata et dimidia pro ij*s.* iiij*d.* Idem Johannes habuit ij penykydd*s* ad emendacionem [*sic*] et habet diem solucionis festum Ermenilde Virginis;[9] (solvit.) Item ij mulieribus x penykydd*s* pro x*d.*; (solverunt.) [*In dot notation here,* £2. 7*s.* 2*d.*]

(*d* Johanni Schyngle latamo xv kydd*s* salicum et xv fraccinorum, ij*s.* vj*d.* unde solvit [10   ] et habet diem de residuo festum Anunciacionis Beate Marie,[11] et fecit fidem coram Willelmo Schelleford fidejussore.)

(*d* Memorandum quod Johannes Bytam debet ut supra iij*s.* pro focali et viij*d.* pro canabo, ut in fine sequentis folii ex altera parte.)

[*f. 63r.*] *Anno xix.*

Vendicio et succisio focalis. Johanni Barb*ur*, leche, xv penykydd*s*, unde solvit totum; (solvit.) Roberto Hosyar xvij penykydd*s*, unde

---

[1] *1456–7.*   [2] Brushwood.   [3] Repeated thrice.   [4] *25 Mar. 1457.*
[5] As to John Drews, senior, and John Drews, junior, see *Cal. Rot. Pat., 1461–7*, 180 (25 Mar. 1462). Grant to William Greneham . . . for his good service to the King's father [i.e. Richard, Duke of York] and the King [Edward IV] of the custody during minority and the marriage of John son and heir of John Drewe late of Peterborough, 'gentilman'.
[6] *2 Feb. 1457/8.*   [7] *12 Mar. 1457/8.*   [8] *21 May 1458.*   [9] *13 Feb. 1457/8.*
[10] Not stated.   [11] *25 Mar.*

solvit xvj*d*.; (solvit.) Johanni B*u*rle, fuller, xxv penykydd*s*. unde solvit ij*s*.; item x kydd*s*; (solvit.) Vicario Burgi unam sellionem quasi (*d* v) iiij carectate pro iij*s*. viij*d*.; (solvit.) Johanni Stawnton, berbur, xx penikydd*s* salicum; sacrista solvet ut alibi. Johanni Noox vj penykydd*s*, vij kydd*s*; (unde solvit 1*d*.) Johanni Snow iij penikydd*s*; (solvit). Johanni Yowng (*d* viij) ix penykydd*s* (salicum), iij fraccini kydd*s*, viij*d*. Johanni Snow 3 penykydd*s* salicini; (solvit j*d*.) Reginaldo Merbyri generoso (14 salicini et) xxij penykydd*s*, pro xx*d*.; (unde solvit xvij*d*. et debet, iij*d*.) Johanni Sucklyng vi (iij) carectate salicum et fraccinorum, xij*s*., unde solvit x*s*., et solvet ij*s*. ye nexte Lammesse, levando dexteram manum in presencia Roberti Bryg. Johanni Wentbrig, wever, iiij penykydd*s*; (solvit.) Domino Johanni Glynton, [¹   ] penykydd*s* salicini et fraccini. Domino Johanni Lesyngham (*d* quasi) vij carectate fraccine pro viij*s*. [*In dot notation, £1. 5s. 2d.*] Willelmo Foole (*d* quasi) unam carectatam salicum et fraccinorum pro xx*d*.; (solvit bene et fideliter.) Nota: require plus de ista materia in undecimo folio ante ad tale [signum].⊘²

In succisione cum kyddyng (scribitur alibi) de c kydd*s* (salicinis et fraccinis), xiiij*d*.; item in regardo, ij*d*.; item in solutis dictis operariis pro succisione et factura de xx kydd*s* salicinis (ij*d. ob.*) cum schredyng in uno calceto elemosinarii inter pratum elemosinarii et Snorshylle per ij dies, cuilibet capienti in die iij*d*., xij*d*.; (*d* in solutis Ricardo Mason et Johanni fratri suo et (Johanni) Sewalle succidentibus fraccinos in orto Sancti Johannis Baptiste contra lez Trenchys in officio per ij dies, ij*s*. iij*d*.); in solutis Willelmo de Yaxle et Willelmo (Martyn) de Flete pro succisione salicum et aliis operibus per v dies, iij*s*. iiij*d*.; item Willelmo (Martyn) de Flete per aliam ebdomadam, ij*s*.; item eidem et Willelmo alio per (primam) ebdomadam (Marcii) primo Willelmo, xix*d*.; item viij*d*. (ex mituo) secundo Willelmo; xvj*d*.; item in solutis Willelmo laborario per iij dies, x*d*., scilicet in ebdomada Cinerum;³ (*d* item Ricardo Mason, (10*d*.), et fratri suo, (10*d*.); et Johanni Sewale, (7*d*.); item Willelmo Martyn, (xxij*d*.); et Willelmo socio suo, (20*d*.) plantyng per ebdomadam primam Quadragesime.⁴) Require plus de ista materia in x folio ante ad tale signum. ☉²

In veteri meremio vendito Henrico Collermaker, viij*d*., (solvit); in focali vendito, scilicet veteri meremio Johanni Bytam super Sowter Row, vij*d*., (solvit.)

(*d* Memorandum quod supradictus Johannes Bytam debet pro canabo sibi vendito, 8*d*.)

[*f. 63v.*] *Anno domini Ricardi abbatis xix, quadriduum ante Purificacionem.*
SARRACIO PROPTER HOSPITALE.
In solutis ij sarratoribus Stanf*o*rdie pro et cetera in sequente, 5*s*. 3*d*. videlicet pro xxiiij karffys in estrischeb*u*rd*s*, ij*s*.; item dictis operariis pro sarracione de ledg*s* pro ostiis et fenestris ad hospitale et stothysse

---

¹ Left blank.   ² See above, pp. 97, 100.
³ *28 Feb.–5 Mar. 1456/7.*   ⁴ *7–12 Mar. 1456/7.*

per iiij dies, iij*s*. iij*d*.; item in solutis dictis sarratoribus per ij dies et dimidium pro opere consimili (propter hospitale), ij*s*. vj*d*.; et ad potum, ij*d*. (scribitur in compoto.)

Anno xx°. Emma Gromchest*ur* recepit de elemosinario, xij*d*.; item ij*s*.; item xij*d*.

Anno xx *domini Ricardi abbatis.*

Solucio fratris Willelmi Morton elemosinarii pro speciebus. In primis dicto elemosinario, x*s*.; item fratri Ricardo Bysley, iij*s*. iiij*d*.; item xx*d*.; item xx*d*.; item Roberto Columbyn, xl*d*.; fratri Willelmo Byry, vj*s*. viij*d*.; item xx*d*.; (nota hic); fratri T*home* de Sancto Neoto, vj*s*. viij*d*.; item iij*s*.; iiij*s*.; fratri Ricardo Oxford (d juniori) tercio priori, v*s*.; item v*s*.; fratri Johanni Borowh, magistro operis, x*s*., ut in obstupacione; fratri Willelmo Melton, x*s*., in cameraria.

(Solucio per elemosinarium pro officio Crucis[1]) fratri Henrico Lynne, (ij*s*. ij*d*.); item pro speciebus, x*s*. in capella noviciorum (in festo Vedasti et Amandi);[2] fratri Willelmo Depyng (Cley), xx*d*.; (item T*home* de Sancto Neoto), xx*d*.; item xx*d*.; item xx*d*.; xx*d*.; et equet; fratri W[altero] Wennam, viij*s*.; item ij*s*.; item ij*s*.; modo elemosinarius debet iiij*s*. pro omnibus (solvit), aretro feria v Cena domini[3] anno xx, quos solvit feria secunda Pentecostes[4] (d omnia) pro anno xix.

[*In margin*] Nota de solucione vj*s*. facta pro officio subelemosinarie aretro pro anno xix et eque pro omnibus debitis illius anni.

Memorandum quod Incle solvit vj*s*. de suo debito, et debet xvj*d*. pro anno xix.

(d Johanna Goldsmythe debet xvj*d*. de redditu, ut in fine noni folii ante.)

(d Vendicio focalis (quia antea). Pro focali vendito Davy Brown, mercer, ij*s*. anno xx°,) (solvit.)

Memorandum quod omnibus computatis inter fratrem Willelmum Morton et Johannem Coldwel, Sabbato in medio Quadragesime[5] dictus frater debet Johanni ij*s*. viij*d*. *ob*.

Fratri Tome de Sancto Neoto solvitur pro vicaria elemosinarii in choro in primis post Pascha,[6] v*s*.; item alia vice dicto Tome per manus fratris Willelmi Rampsey, ij*s*. iiij*d*.; item alia vice, scilicet, in dominica ante Adventum,[7] xx*d*., per manus proprias, et equet pro anno xx.

(d Flowr', Almawnds, Spyse. Memorandum de j pastey in custodia pe [*sic*].) Memorandum loqui Johanni Evysle pro papiro croniculari. (d Johannes Burle debet ij*s*. vj*d*.; solvit Johanni Coldwel.)

[*f. 64r.*] *Anno Ricardi Abbatis* xx° *incipiente.*

Brygmylle. (d In solutis Johanni Potter pro fodicione de xxx carectatis cley pro rammyng de Brigmylle; item Roberto Conquest pro

---

[1] The office of Warden of the altar of Holy Cross.
[2] *6 Feb. 1457/8.* [3] *30 Mar. 1458.* [4] *22 May 1458.*
[5] *11 Mar. 1457/8.* [6] *2 Apr. 1458.* [7] *26 Nov. 1458.*

cariagio ejusdem ad Brigmylle, vj*s*.; item dicto Roberto pro cariagio de quatuor carectatis libere petre de Bernak quarrera ad pontem et pro fundo de le for' bay ibidem, iiij*s*.); item Roberto Conquest pro mensa Johannis Halyday carpentarii per iij dies, vj*d*.; (*d* item dicto Roberto pro una carectata, scilicet mille [de] latt*s*, ccc sclatt*s* et xxxj crest*s* de Stanford et Eston usque Brigmylle, xviij*d*.; item pro mensa carpentariorum in factura de dicto Brigmylle per [¹   ] septimanas, xlviij*s*. vj*d*.

Memorandum de uno equo vendito, Sorelle nomine, pro viij*s*. ad nundinas Stanford*ie*; item de alio empto (ibidem) bay coloris pro xiiij*s*. viij*d*.; item pro expensis [²   ]

WILLELMUS RAMSEY. Memorandum quod elemosinarius solvit fratri Willelmo Rampsey x*d*., pro caponibus suis.

(*d* RICARDUS GRAWNTE,³ anno xxj, recepit de elemosinario pro diversis laboribus in gardino per (*d* 4) 5 dies, x*d*.; item xij*d*.; item 4*d*.; item pro 17 dies, ij*s*. x*d*.; item 5 dies, x*d*.; item 18 dies, iij*s*.)

FRUMENTUM. In solutis Johanni Haryson de Alownton [*sic*] pro iiij quarteriis frumenti pro die Animarum,⁴ xvij*s*. viij*d*.)

PISE. In quatuor et sex eskeppis per Johannem Coldwel emptis, ij*s*. j*d*.; item iiij bussellis, xj*d*.; item vj bussellis, xvij*d*.; item v eskeppis, xvj*d*.; item ij eskeppis, vj*d*.; item vij eskeppis, xx*d*.; item ij eskeppis, vj*d*.

AVENE. In solutis pro xij eskeppis, ij*s*. j*d*.

MEMORANDUM quod Robertus Conqueste fatetur quod debet elemosinario pro firma sua pro ij annis et ij quarteriis, vij*li*. Item idem fatetur quod debet xl*s*. pro T*h*oma Prio*ur*, patre suo.

[*f. 64v.*] *Anno Ricardi abbatis* xx.⁵

Principium istius materie in folio 17 ante.⁶

Symon Walram debet pro una forera (duarum acrarum) ad capud (ville) de Dosthorppe, ut antea in folio xvij° unde solvit, xij*d*., et debet anno xxj finiente, xx*d*.⁷

Johannes Bernwelle manens super Raton row debet elemosinario ij*s*. ex mituo, (solvit); item pro redditu ubi Willelmus Rodger manet, x*s*.; item pro iiij annis ibidem super Raton row de redditu, xx(xij)*s*. Nota dampnum quod fecit in prima domo per ignem condonatur, unde solvit 16*d*. per cariagium de 4 mille latt*s*; item xij*d*.; item vj*s*. [*In margin*] Nota quod etc. de x*s*. solutis versus T*h*omam Coke de perantea (solvit). Memorandum quod T*h*omas Rosby vel coquus⁸ xxx die Marcii jurabat solvere fratri Willelmo Morton elemosinario anno quo supra pro supradicto Johanne Bernewelle xxxij*s*. infra duos annos, scilicet iiij*s*. per quarterium, unde solvit anno xxj in festo Sancti Johannis Baptiste,⁹

---

¹ Number of weeks not inserted.   ² Not stated.
³ This paragraph was deleted with a note above the surname Grawnte, scribitur [in compoto].
⁴ *2 Nov. 1457.*   ⁵ *1457–8.*
⁶ See above, p. 89.   ⁷ A blank space follows.
⁸ Rowsby, the infirmary cook, see pp. 20, 54, &c.   ⁹ *24 June 1459.*

(totum solvit.) Item dictus Johannes Barnewel debet anno 23 finiente xxs., unde solvit ijs. per Johannem Barf[orde]

STAWNFOR FEYR'.[1] In solutis pro ij^c grossis spiks, viijd.; item pro cc midil spyx, vjd.; item cccc splynte nayll', viijd.; item viij (mille) [de] latte nayl', vijs. vjd.; item pro xv^c lattysse longitudinis trium pedum, precium de c, vjd. q., viijs., et in cariagio, xjd.; (^d item pro xxij paribus de heynglys et stoks, (ponderantibus lxxx libras propter hospitale) pro hostiis et fenestris ixs. et in cariagio, 3d.; (vacat hic); item pro expensis Johannis Coldwel famuli elemosinarii, et pro cariagio, xxd.)

Willelmus Rodger debet pro uno cotagio super Raton row pro iij annis, anno Ricardi abbatis xx finiente, unde solvit vjs. viijd.

[SUCCISIO MEREMII]
In succisione ij carectatarum meremii in Bongate cum cariagio ad officium, viijd.

[MORTUI IN CARCERE] In solutis pro iiij ulnis de kanvas pro ij mortuis in carcere,[2] precium ulne, iiijd. ob. q.; xixd.

(^d Memorandum to schrede appyltres in Bondgate; also te (do) H. Palmer yarde [sic])

(^d Sacrista habet librum feodarium;[3] item c de grossis spyks, solvit).

[f. 65r.] Anno Ricardi abbatis xx.[4]

Memorandum de ostio cimiterii ad hospitale emendando cum aliis faciendis ibidem; item de muro cotagii juxta Tomam Rowsby; (^d et muris Sancti Johannis); item de curiis tenendis; item de cotagio dimittendo ad Gonthorp.

SUTTON. Item de domo Johannis Durram; item de una hustrina (Tome Rothewel); item ubi Fayreday manet; (^d item de corticibus vendendis ad Suttonwode) et meremio ibidem (pro xvjs. solvendis ad festum Michaelis et)

Item de terris supervidendis et pratis in Maxsey felds et Norburrow; item de (^d baston rope, Garthe web, sclatts emendis; item zabulo; item de fagetts ad Oxney); item de pencione scholarum, xs., (solvit); (^d item sororibus capelle, (solvit);) item propter mundare seweram ibidem. (^d Item memorandum loqui Roberto Jonysse propter quot dies ipse et alii fuerunt super Sowter row; item per quot dies Johannes Somur tector fuit super domos in Cowgate vel alibi); item cariagium de ij (mille) [de] sclatts; (^d item sellyng offe bars (pro xvjs.). Inquiratur per quot dies Johannes Aspschaw fuit super Sowter row et quantum de empcione); obligacio in custodia Ricardi Pappley deliberanda. Memorandum (^d de obba[5] pro vino in Holondia). De libro materie placiti inter elemosinarium et vicarium de Maxsey [qui] est in custodia vicarii de Burgo Sancti Petri.[6]

---

[1] Stamford fair.   [2] Prisoners dying in the abbot's prison.
[3] Is this a reference to The Book of Fees of Henry of Pytchley, N.R.S., vol. ii?
[4] 1457-8.   [5] Beaker.
[6] See the different accounts of the proceedings for the deprivation of the vicar of Maxey which are printed on pp. 43-45, 58-59 above. What has become of this record?

RICARDO BARBUR MORTUO. Alicia uxor ejus(dem ^d) promisit solvere xiijs. iiijd. de redditu fratri Willelmo Morton elemosinario, in die Sancti Georgii Martiris[1] post Pascha anno quo supra, scilicet xx, videlicet ad festum Sancti Johannis Baptiste proxime sequens, x(^dx)d.; [in margin Nota quod solvit xd.]; ad festum Michaelis anno Ricardi abbatis xxj incipiente, xxd.; ad Natale Domini, xxd.; ad Pascha, xxd.; ad festum Sancti Johannis Baptiste, xxd.; ad festum Michaelis anno Ricardi abbatis, si per tantum tempus vixerit, xxijº, xxd.; ad Natale domini, xxd.; item ad Pascha, xxd.; item ad festum Johannis Baptiste, xxd. Et ad istas soluciones fideliter solvendas fecit fidem supradicta Alicia levando dexteram, (item juravit super librum osculando dictum librum,[2]) in presencia fratris Willelmi Morton elemosinarii et Johannis Coldwel.

[f. 65v.] Anno Ricardi abbatis xxº.[3]

IN FORINCECIS.
In solutis clerico Ricardi Pytts pro brevibus et materia de Wyllybrok, anno ut supra, et cum rewardo, iiijs. jd.

IN NECESSARIIS, MEREMIUM.
In solutis Johanni Aspshaw pro xx peciis quercinis, xvs., et in cariagio, xiiijd.; in solutis pro lx peciis meremii scapulatis emptis in Westgate, xxvijs.

CUSTUS IN BURGO. (Scribitur in compoto.)
In solutis pro viij carectatis terre rubie pro domo Tome Haburgyl in Cowgaate, ijs.; item Henrico Mason, cum uno serviente sibi emendando muros ibidem per iiij dies (dimidium) capientes [sic] in die ixd., iijs. iiijd., et in servisia, jd.; item pro splentyng et dawbyng unius gabuli ibidem, in grosso, xviijd.; item Johanni Ravon carpentario pro framyng de xij coplysse cum novis taylfets (cum ij fenestris perfectis, iijs. 4d.; item pro cariagio meremii scapulati illuc, 4d.) (^d et splentyng unius gabuli ibidem in grosso.)

SCLATTS. Item Willelmo Rede pro mille [de] sclatts cum cariagio illuc, viijs. iiijd.; item pro iij carectatis zabuli illuc, 18d.; item (^d latts,) latthysse nayl' (^d et) crest' et calx de stauro; item Johanni Aspschaw pro lat pynnys, videlicet iij mille ccccc, xiiijd.; item dicto Johanni pro ij rodis et uno quarterio de novo sclattyng, xs.; item dicto Johanni pro poyntyng ibidem, xvjd.[4]

SCLATTS. Item dicto Willelmo pro ij mille sclatts cum cariagio.

HOSPITALE. Item pro j carectata terre rubie pro ostio cimiterii ad hospitale, 2d.; item Henrico Mason, cum uno serviente, per ij dies emendando supra dictum ostium, xviijd.

---

[1] On 23 Apr. 1458 the widow swore to pay the almoner 13s. 4d. on account of her late husband's debt, by quarterly instalments of 20d. on the dates thereafter mentioned if she should survive. The first instalment was of 10d., as she made a first payment of 10d. Eight further payments of 20d. were promised, which seems to be one too many.
[2] By 'Kissing the book'.   [3] 1457-8.
[4] In the left-hand margin, a line is drawn from the words Custus in Burgo to cariagio with the note: 'Vacat quia in anno xixº.'

IN NECESSARIIS. In solutis Johanni Meyre, (potter), pro lx creests cum cariagio, precium pecie, jd. q., vjs. iijd.; unde in voltis, xxd.

Johannes Beene solvit xjd. Item memorandum quod Johannes Coldwel solvit xviijd. receptos de uxore Johannis Pyk' pro Johanne, ut supra.

PETRUS LORR' solvit ijs. viijd. pro ij annis Sabbato ante Rogacionem;[1] tamen vide de ipso antea utrum debet vel non.

RUBIE TYLE. In solutis Johanni Coldwel pro mille rubiis tyl', vjs.; item dicto Johanni pro copyyng in certis locis in le urlyr de Sutton wode, viijd.

LONDONIE. Predictus Willelmus Morton commonachus abbatis de Peturborowh reddit Johanni Humfrey de London, erynmonger, iijli., quas Johannes Wynwych' concessit Johanni Hatherley de London' erynmonger, cum predictus Humfrey primo tempore aprentitus [est] cum convencione, et quas Johannes monachus concessit ei; et bona Johannis Wynwic venerunt ad manus Willelmi Morton.

CUSTUS IN BURGO. Memorandum de ijs. iiijd. solutis per Willelmum Morton pro sepibus et clausuris factis in Bondgate.

[f. 66r.] *Anno xix Ricardi abbatis.*

JOHANNES BELAMY FECIT CARIAGIUM DE COXSHOLME.
In primis xij carectatas de thak (et) coopertura ad hospitale unde ij carectate de hospitale ad Cowgate; item ad Cowgate vj carectate; item ad Sowter row vij carectate; item ad Raton row j carectata scilicet c garbe; item ad Bondgate una carectata, videlicet c garbe. SUMMA SOLUTA Johanni Belamy pro xxvj (iii) carectatis, vjs. 8d.

Item dicto Johanni Belamy pro una carectata de chyppys ad cameram, iijd.; item, anno xx, pro iiij carectatis terre rubie, viijd. ad messuagium Tome Haburgyl; item pro una carectata coperture deliberata fratri Johanni Pychele, hostilario, iijd. Item memorandum quod dictus hostilarius habuit ij carectatas ultra, per Johannem Sucklyng anno domini Ricardi abbatis xix°.

Anno Ricardi abbatis vicessimo.

IN OFFICIO. In solutis pro porrettis emptis, vijd.; item pro plantacione earum in gardino, vijd.

(d JOHANNES ASPSCHAW. Memorandum quod computatum est inter fratrem Willelmum Morton elemosinarium et Johannem Aspeschaw in festo Sancti Johannis Baptiste,[2] videlicet pro Haburgylle plase in Cowgate et Cuttlar plase ita quod dictus Johannes satisfecit elemosinario de debito, scilicet xiijs. iiijd., et sic equet in predicto festo scilicet Sancti Johannis inter eos pro omnibus materiis preteritis.)

(d JOHANNES COLDWEL. Memorandum quod allocantur Johanni Coldwelle in crastino Sancti Johannis Baptiste, videlicet pro olla servisie, (vd.); item jd. pro Stranglion; item propter baston rope Johanni Harte

---

[1] *6 May 1458.*   [2] *24 June 1458.*

de Clopton, ij*d.*; item v*d.* solutis Johanni Aspeschaw; item vj*d.* Ricardo Pynd*ar* pro cariagio carectate meremii de Tanholte; item vj*d. ob.* pro sotularibus Roberti Mort*on*; item pro porrettis, iiij*d.*; item ij*d.* pro cervisia data carectariis ad Eston; item ij*d.* ad Stanford; item ij*d.* ad Depyng'; item pro cervisia hic dom', *ob.*; item pro vino dato Roberto et Anne Conquest et Roberto Morton, vj*d.*; item versus Robertum Morton in Holond, tempore infirmitatis, viij*d.*; item pro cc latt*s*, xviij*d.*; item dicto Johanni pro stipendio suo in crastino Sancti Johannis Baptiste[1] ix*s.*, ut alibi antea.)

Rector de Marram solvit per Johannem Coldwel, x*s.*, et debet iij*s.* et uxor Roberti Belcyse solvit pro iij fraccinis ad Marram, v*s.* viij*d.*; Johanna Goldsmythe, xij*d.*

IN FORINCECIS. In solutis Ricardo Haryngton, cantori, in festo Petri et Pauli,[2] ex precepto prioris, viij*d.*

SOLUCIO PRO LE O AD FESTUM SANCTI JOHANNIS BAPTISTE.
In primis fratri Willelmo Morton, elemosinario, (solvit); item fratri Henrico Lynne, vj*s.* viij*d.* (solvit[3]); item fratri Willelmo Byry, vj*s.* viij*d.*, (solvit[4]); item fratri Tome de Sancto Neoto vj*s.* viij*d.* (solvit[4]); et thesaurario in manibus (solvit[4]), iij*s.* iiij*d.*, (solvit) et sic pro anno vicesimo Ricardi abbatis.

JOHANNI ASPSCHAW,[5] (8*s.* 8*d.*) [pro domo] ubi T*homas* Hab*ur*gyl manet, [pro domo] Agnetis Kotlar et pro camera in infirmaria. (d Johannes Ravon recepit ij*s.*) Tomas Stranglyon recepit pro domo Agnetis Kotlar et camera cum grangia, vj*s.* viij*d.* Henricus Mason cum serviente, (d xx*d.*; 18*d.*); 18*d.*

[*f. 66v.*] *Anno domini Ricardi abbatis* xx°.[6]

Memorandum de Johanne Malthows,[7] serviente cum Toma Browh, in familia ducis Eboraci.

COMPUTACIO ET ALLOCACIO ELEMOSINARII AD JOHANNEM COLDWEL, (MERSTLONDE), VII IDUS JUNII.

In primis in ferrura unius equi, ij*d.*; item in servisia sive potu ad Eston, j*d.*; in casio empto, iij*d. ob.*; item in oblitis (non) computatis in media Quadragesime ultima preterita, iiij*d. ob.*; item in cervisia data Johanni Colchest*ur*[8], j*d.* in carcere; item in cervisia data carectariis venientibus de Tanholt *ob.*; item in humanitate exhibita Johanni Malthows de familia ducis Eboraci,[9] j*d. ob.*; item in solutis carectariis venientibus de Tanholt, xvj*d.*

---

[1] *25 June.*   [2] *29 June.*   [3] Four times repeated.   [4] Twice.
[5] The following contemporary notes are added at the foot of f. 66r. with a different pen. They relate apparently to the work of different local tradesmen in repairing two houses forming part of the almoner's estate and a chamber in the farmery.
[6] *1457-8.*
[7] Note the payment made by John Coldwell, the almoner's servant, below.
[8] Beer given to a prisoner in the abbot's jail.
[9] Presumably one of the household servants at Fotheringhay castle.

SUTTON WODE. In solutis pro xxviij rodysse hedgyng, precium rode, jd. ob., iijs. vjd.; et in solutis pro succisione unius acre et (ᵈ unius rode) ibidem Ricardo Mason et Johanni fratri suo per iij dies, iijs., et in cervisia, ijd.; item propter le dressyng et preparacionem ad venditionem et ad cariagium, Willelmo Blogwyn et Johanni Ivysse, ijs. viijd.

MEREMIUM IBIDEM. Memorandum de lvij majoribus sperrysse ibidem; et de lxxj minoribus sperrs, item de xxxvij tracinis ibidem inventis; item de peciis parvis, scilicet xvij pro un' to-falle, ubi Johannes Yvisse manet. Item sunt ibidem alie pecie, scilicet bone tracine, xv. Item Willelmus Blogwyn custos ibidem solvit elemosinario pro chets ibidem venditis; prima vice, xxs.; secunda vice, iijs.; item viijs.; item ixs.; item viijs.

Memorandum¹ quot pecie deliberate erant Johanni Eyr' et alibi, ut patet inferius.

NOTA. Memorandum de xvjs., (solvit), recipiendis de Toma Habyrgyl barkar, (solvit), pro corticibus sibi venditis, videlicet ad festum Michaelis proximum, viijs. (solvit) et ad Nativitatem domini, viijs., unde solvit, prima vice post mortem, per manus Tome Hanwod totum.

MEREMIUM DELIBERATUM. Memorandum quod Johannes Eyr' habuit viij sperris; Johannes Corbette, iiij tracinas; Tomas Rowelle, xlij sparrys; Robertus Conquest, iij plow beemys. Memorandum de ix carectatis meremii de Sutton wod ad officium, dando pro carectata xd., vijs. vjd.

Johannes, sutor abbathye, debet elemosinario de redditu pro vj quarteriis, (xs. vjd.), unde solvit vijs. per Johannem Coldwelle, et debet iijs. vjd., quos solvit, videlicet in ocriis et sotularibus.²

HOSPITALE (post magnum ventum). In cariagio unius carectate(ᵈzabuli), (calcis), de officio illuc, iiijd.; et Ricardo Edgyston sclatter cum filio suo per iij dies et dimidium, capientes in die ixd., ijs. vijd. ob.

Matilda Edynam recepit de elemosinario iijs. ex mutuo, in Conversione Sancti Pauli,³ et habet diem proximum Missomur; item ipsa recepit arram,⁴ scilicet jd. pro una olla enea ponderante 28 libras, si defecerit in solucione.

Ricardus Cowston recepit de elemosinario xiiijd.; 6d.; xd.

Frater Ricardus Bysle recepit iiijd. ex mituo de elemosinario.

Stranglyon recepit de elemosinario xijs. vjd.; item 8d.; 4d.; xd.; vd.

[Johannes] Asppeschaw recepit de elemosinario xiijs. iiijd. ultra xxs. pro meremio, unde vs. ex mituo. Idem recepit iiijd.; xijd.; xijd.; 8d.; 8d.; 4d.; 16d.; 4d.⁵

[f. 67r.] *Anno domini Ricardi abbatis xxº et die Sancti Swytuni episcopi.*⁶

IN OFFICIO. In solutis pro emendacione murorum Sancti Johannis

---

¹ Written in the margin.
³ *25 Jan. 1457/8.*
⁵ *In margin:* 10li. 7s. 4d.

² *In margin:* Vacat modo quia solvit.
⁴ Earnest money for a copper pot.
⁶ *2 July 1458.*

Baptiste[1] hoc anno Johanni Pypwelle, in primis per Johannem Cold-welle, xvj*d*.; item per elemosinarium, xx*d*.; item iiij*d*.

IN NECESSARIIS. BASTON ROPE. In solutis pro ij bonchez de baston rope, ij*d*.; item pro iiij duodenis baston rop, xxxj*d*.

IN FORINCECIS. In solutis Ricardo Gregory pro emendacione unius fenestre ad capellam Beate Marie Magdalene, propter nimium ventum,[2] iij*s*. iiij*d*.

Festo Sancte Marie Magdalene, hoc anno contingente in Sabbato.[3]

In primis in una duodena cervisie, xv*d*.; in albo pane, iij*d*.; in grene pissibus, iij*d*.; in xv rochys, iij*d*. *ob.*; in anguillis pro uno sewhe vel jawge, j*d*. *ob.* et in stok fysche pro eadem, j*d*.; item pro uno samowne trowte, viij*d*.; ij crabb', ij*d*.; lx wylkys, j*d*.; item in speciebus, scilicet, croco et pipere, ij*d*. SUMMA iij*s*. iiij*d*. Orwyn[4] cum uxore, et capellano, Melton, Pychele, Ryal, T*homas* de Sancto Neoto, dominus Willelmus Travesse.

RICARDUS GRAWNTE. In solutis dicto Ricardo pro labore in gardino et aliis laboribus per xvj dies ante et post festum Sancti Tome martiris, scilicet, Translationem,[5] ij*s*. viij*d*.; item per v dies, scilicet, feriales post festum Sancti Oswaldi,[6] x*d*.; et in regardo sibi dato, ij*d*.; item dicto Ricardo per Johannem Coldewel et pro dicto Johanne Coldwel per v dies, quando supradictus Johannes fuit in Holondia[7] et ad Lynne in negociis suis propriis, x*d*.; item alia vice per vij dies et dimidium, xv*d*.; item per ij dies et dimidium, v*d*.; item [per] v dies, x*d*.; item per ix dies, xviij*d*.; item per v dies, x*d*.; item per vij dies, xiiij*d*.; per 9 dies, 18*d*.; per v dies, x*d*.

In solutis pro pessecodd*s*, scilicet v eskeppis, ix*d*.; et pro uno pecke et j potel farine (avenarum, iij*d*.)

Frater Johannes Pycheley recepit de elemosinario xx*d*. in parte majoris summe, videlicet iiij*s*. de redditu assise pertinente ad officium hostilarie. Item dictus frater Johannes recepit alia vice, iiij*d*.; item alia vice, xij*d*.; item xij*d*., et equet.

Anno xxj*mo* incipiente. Item memorandum quod elemosinarius sol-vit scolaribus vj*d*., pro dicto fratre Johanne hostilario. Item idem

---

[1] Can it be assumed from these payments that the original parochial chapel of St. John the Baptist in the vill of Burgh was situated on the northern side of the east gate of the monastery, and that when the new parish church was built in the middle of the Market Place out of materials taken from the old parish chapel and the nave of St. Thomas's chapel on the north side of the west gate of the monastery (see N.R.S. ix. 219–22), the site of the former parish chapel was added to the almoner's office at the east gate of the monastery? There has always been considerable doubt as to the actual site of the original chapel. In this account-book there are numerous references to the walls, the garden, and the cemetery of St. John the Baptist. See pp. 33, 55, and 101.

[2] The Park kirk in Newark, damaged by a gale.

[3] The date of the feast was Saturday, 2 July 1458.

[4] The names of these lay tenants and officers of the almoner and of certain monks are written in the left margin, opposite to the list of provisions purchased for the feast, in which, presumably, they participated.

[5] *29 June to 6 July* and *8–15 July, 1458.*   [6] *7–11 Aug. 1458.*

[7] The Holland division of Lincolnshire.

elemosinarius dedit dicto Johanni Pychele iiij*d*. ad potum. Item dictus elemosinarius inveniebat sibi, scilicet hostilario in Vigilia et in festo Omnium Sanctorum xvij dimidium pownd*s* candelarum cere; et nota quod vastum candelarum fuit vj*d*. Item dictus Johannes hostilarius habuit de elemosinario x*c* garbas cooperture, vj*s*. viij*d*. Item elemosinarius solvit xij*d*. pro cariagio in Bondgaate juxta T*omam* Rowsby. Item elemosinarius solvit Willelmo Ploman, tectori, cum uno serviente, pro 9 diebus, 3*s*. 5*d*.; item dicto Willelmo, ij*s*. x*d*.; item sui [*sic*] servienti, xvij*d*.; item dicto coopertori, xj*d*., et servienti, v*d*.; item pro terra rubea ad ryggandum, iiij*d*.; item postea pro thakkyng cum ryggyng, xxj*d*. Anno xxij dictus elemosinarius solvit fratri hostilario, xij*d*. ad Nativitatem Domini. Item, eodem anno, scilicet tercia die May solvit Paulo carpentario pro opere suo juxta T*homam* Rowsby per iiij dies, xv*d*.; et pro uno post quercino et ij tey balk*s* cum alio meremio ibidem, xv*d*. Quere plus in quarto folio sequente.[1]

Nota quod grangia elemosinarii ad Gonthorp reparata fuit per dominum T*homam* Depyng doctorem anno Ricardi Ayheston abbatis secundo.[2] Summa exspensarum ibidem xvj*li*. xvj*s*. vij*d*. *ob*. Et memorandum quod habuit subsidium in anno precedente, ut patet in compoto, videlicet, vj*li*.

[*f. 67v.*] *Anno domini Ricardi abbatis* xx*mo* *ad festum Advincule Sancti Petri*.[3]

FALLAM HERNE. De Ricardo Pyndar pro Fallam hyrne cum ij acris prati ad Hodys wong pertinentibus, v*s*., solvendos ad festum Bartholomei[4] vel vij dies proxime sequentes, et festum Nativitatis Domini proxime sequentem [*sic*].

HODYS WONG. De Roberto Crosse pro Hodys wong, ut antea in folio xvij in fine prime partis folii,[5] vj*s*.; debet modo v*s*. iiij*d*. (Memorandum[6] quod Willelmus Sand*ur* vastavit ibidem cum equis tet*ur*yng.)

SWYNS MEDOW. De Johanne Asppeschaw et Toma Hab*ur*gylle, x*s*., (solverunt.)

CUSTUS [AD] HOSPITALE. In solutis Johanni Benette et Johanni filio suo hedgyng per vij dies, capientes [*sic*] in die, vj*d*., iij*s*. vj*d*.; item ad potum, ij*d*. Et nota faciebant xxviij rodas.

SPYTYL CROFFTE. In solutis Ricardo Cowston pro falcacione de [7   ] acris ibidem; item pro fenacione ejusdem, ij*s*.; et in cariagio de xij carectatis feni ibidem in grangiam ibidem, ij*s*. ij*d*.

RECEPTA. Et in receptis de Willelmo Rydar pro feno sibi vendito, scilicet ij jagg*s*, iij*s*. viij*d*., (solvit); item de Willelmo Beyld pro j carectata, ij*s*. vij*d*., (solvit); item de Willelmo Lucas pro ij jagg*s*, iij*s*.

COXHOLME. In falcacione, Roberto Keyworth (falcando) et alio, iiij*s*.

---

[1] See below, p. 128.   [2] *1439–40*.   [3] *1 Aug. 1458*.
[4] *24–31 Aug. 1458*.   [5] See p. 95.
[6] It is not clear whether this note of damage refers to Hod*'s wong* or S*winesmeadow*.
[7] Left blank.

vij*d*.; et in solutis uxori Johannis Bytam pro ligacione de iiij mille (ccc) garbis, vj*s*. 2*d*.; et in cariagio ad hospitale de v*c* per T*omam* Copar, ix*d*.; item Johanni Ven*ur* pro cariagio de xij*c* in croftum sacriste juxta Coxholme cum cariagio de xxij*c* ad le Boyl yaate,[1] omnia per aquam, ij*s*.; et in servisia, 2*d*.; in receptis pro ij*c* venditis Johanni Dawntre pro vacca sua, xvj*d*.; item in receptis de Roberto per[sona] de Wodston pro una acra sibi vendita, ij*s*. et nota [quod] ipse habuit vij*c* et lx (magnas) garbas de illa acra. Memorandum de falcacione ut supra; item de ligacione supra; item pro cariagio (cum biga) cum le stackyng per ij dies et dimidium cum victualibus, iij*s*.; item pro cariagio per aquam ut supra.

[*In the margin*] Fratri Roberto, thesaurario, xx*c*; fratri Johanni Pychele, x*c*; fratri Willelmo Depyng custodi Sancte Crucis, 4*c*; Johanni Dawntr*e* ij*c*; ad hospitale, v*c* et in cariagio supra.

oc borde, latth*s*, canvasse, wax, almand*s*, seff*er*on, lock*s*, j lepe et scotyll' nigrum pannum, bodghe, sadylle, bridyl, garthe web.

[*f. 68r.*] *Anno domini Ricardi abbatis* xx *ad festum Sancti Laurencii.*[2]

Thomas Molton computavit (pro se et Willelmo Maydelette) cum elemosinario pro diversis materiis sequentibus.

In primis pro iiij carectatis terre rubie ad Sowter row, viij*d*.; item ibidem alia vice [pro] ij carectatis terre rubie, iiij*d*.; item in Cowgate pro ryggyng ibidem ix carectate terre, xviij*d*.; item [pro] iiij carectatis zabuli, unde prima ad hospitale, secunda ad Cowgate, tercia pro camera in infirmaria, quarta in officio, xviij; item pro vj carectatis fimi usque Swynys medow, iij*d*.; item pro iij carectatis feni de Hamond medow, x*d*.; item j carectata feni de Non hylle, iiij*d*.; item pro cariagio de xij carectatis feni de Spytyl croffte ad grangiam ibidem, ij*s*. ij*d*.; item pro xj carectatis terre rubie per dictum T*homam* Molton et Willelmum Bowyar', unde viij carectate ad Sowter row, ij carectate ad murum cimiterii ad hospitale, j carectata ad stabulum in officio, xiij*d*.; ultra xiij*d*. pertinentes Willelmo Bowyar'.

Willelmus Maydelette et T*homas* Moltun solverunt pro secundo herbagio (de anno xix) de Coksholme, ij*s*.

Frater Johannes Burneham recepit v*s*. de elemosinario per Robertum Morton in parte solucionis majoris summe, scilicet viij*s*. pro refectoraria, et debet iij*s*., quos solvit et equet.

STERBRYDGE FEYR'. In solutis pro iiij (mille) latt*s*, longitudinis v pedum precium xviij*s*.; item pro vj bodgy skynnys, ij*s*. vj*d*.; item pro uno quarteron croci, ij*s*. iij*d*.; item pro 4 libris (3 quarter') cere, precium unius libre vj*d*., ij*s*. iiij*d*.; item pro iiij libris amigdalarum, precium libre iij*d*., xij*d*.; (item pro uno speculo, iij*d*.); item pro ij virgis dimidia blac offe lyr', vij*s*. vj*d*.; item xx ulnis de canvasse, scilicet brodboske, viij*s*.

---

[1] Bull gate, the hithe on the north bank of the river on the east side of the town bridge.
[2] *10 Aug. 1458.*

ij*d*.; item pro una cella monachali cum freno, v*s*. vj*d*.; item pro iij scotyll', vj*d*.; et pro cariagio usque Burgum per aquam, xxij*d*.; item in exspensis unius equitantis illuc ad emendum supradicta, xx*d*.

CUSTUS IN OFFICIO. In solutis Johanni Aspeschaw, sclatt*er*, cum filio suo conductis per viij dies ad emendandum certos defectus super le garrette (et in officio) capientes [*sic*] in die ix*d*., vj*s*.; item Ricardo Edgyston cum filio suo in predictis locis per v dies capientes ut supra, iij*s*. ix*d*.

IN OFFICIO. In solutis Johanni Hubbok et socio suo conductis per quatuor dies ad scapulandum meremium, iij*s*. iiij*d*.; item dicto carpentario per vj dies scapulando, v*s*.

(*d* Johannes Coldewel debet elemosinario, xxij*d*. (solvit); omnibus computatis Johannes Halle, coquus, debet elemosinario pro focale, 8*d*.)

[*f*. *68v*.] *Anno regni regis Henrici sexti xxxvij et anno domini Ricardi abbatis Burgi, xxj incipiente*.[1]

ZABULUM IN OFFICIO; ITEM AD HOSPITALE. In solutis pro fodicione zabuli per v dies, xij*d*.; item Willelmo Lucasse et aliis pro cariagio de iiij carectatis, xx*d*.; item pro cariagio de aliis 4 carectatis, unde quatuor ad hospitale et iiij ad officium, xx*d*.

SOLUCIO FRATRIS WILLELMI MORTON ELEMOSINARII PRO TUNICIS POST FESTUM SANCTI LUCE EWANGELISTE.

In primis dicto elemosinario, x*s*.; item fratri Willelmo Ramsey, x*s*., pro fratre Johanne Ryppon, (3*s*. 4*d*.; item vj*s*. viij*d*.); item fratri (*d* Ricardo Oxford juniori) Johanni Hylle, x*s*., (solvit); item fratri Johanni Glynton, x*s*., (solvit ad Willelmum Ramsey[2]), et thesaurario, vj*s*. viij*d*.; et equet pro anno xx°.

Nota quod Johannes Waldyng, mercer, solvit elemosinario, ad festum Michaelis anno quo supra, scilicet xxj incipiente, xl*s*., et debet modo nisi v*s*. vj*d*. pro omnibus materiis habitis per antea.

Thomas Cowper de Fletton recepit pro cariagio (meremii) cum equis trahentibus fraccinos in (*d* le) orto Sancti Johannis et de dicto loco per carectam suam in officium, xvj*d*., in Vigilia Omnium Sanctorum anno quo supra; item dicto Tome pro consimile labore, in die Animarum post nonas, vj*d*.; item, alia vice, xv*d*. pro simili labore, et cum iij fleyk*s* sive h*er*dyll' factis.

ELY FEYR'. In solutis pro xxvij b*ur*dys quercinis, vij*s*. xj*d*.; in cariagio, viij*d*.; in uno pari ocriarum, ij*s*.; in uno long trowh pro elemosina conservanda in refectoria, iij*d*.

Robertus Conquest anno xxj° solvit ad curiam, pro anno xx° Ricardi abbatis, xiij*s*. iiij*d*. pro Bacon et Malyns thynk. Item (nota quod) non est allocandum Johanni Eyr'; item ij*s*. x*d*. pro prima multura molendini, unde xviij*d*. soluti domine de Thornaw; item xx*s*.; item x*s*.; item

---

[1] *1458–9*.
[2] See footnote below, p. 165.

vjs. viijd. (pro Johanne Yve); item vjs. viijd., (pro Willelmo Blogwyn); item pro Willelmo Geffron xvjs. xd.; item pro Roberto Mowncelle, vijs. Nota 4*li*. 6d. receptos, et debet [¹   ]; unde solvit [¹   ]; item per Johannem Yvys vjs. iiijd. Item Robertus Conquest solvit pro Bacon et Malynsthink pro anno xxj xiijs. iiijd.; item pro Roberto Godfrey xijs. pro anno xx; item tantum pro anno xxj°; item iijs. iiijd. pro Willelmo Blogwyn de anno 21; item anno xxij in Cena Domini xxs., sed inquiratur pro quibus.

Item per Johannem Rowelle, 8s., anno 23 in Vigilia Andree apostoli;² item pro eodem, xiijs.; item pro Toma Rowelle, xviijs.; item pro aliis, ijs. iiijd.; item de Roberto Fayreday, xjs. viijd.; item de Willelmo Netterde, iijs.; item jd. de Willelmo Mil' pro redditu assise; item pro Roberto Fayreday, ut in una equa, vs. et ij porcis, vs.; item xxs. pro Johanne Eyr' et Toma Waryn.
Require plus in folio xvij sequente ad tale signum |Λ.³

SCLATTS. In solutis Willelmo Rede sclatter pro ij mille sclatts, xs.; item Tome Cowper de Fletton pro cariagio tercie partis de Kyrcby felde ad officium, ijs.

[*f. 69r.*] *Anno regni regis Henrici Sexti xxxvij et anno domini Ricardi abbatis xxj in crastino Animarum.*⁴

DEBITORES FRATRI WILLELMO MORTON ELEMOSINARIO. In primis Thomas Barker, vjd., (solvit); (ᵈ Johannes Waldyng alias Fletcher, xiijs. ijd. de anno xix°; item pro anno xx totum redditum. Debet⁵ vs. vjd.) Willelmus Payn debet (ᵈ xxs.) Robertus Patynmaker debet 20d.

RICARDUS CROSSE. Johannes Pynchebec junior debet pro Ricardo Crosse, (ᵈ ijs. vjd.,) iiijs. Ricardus Crosse debet, ijs. vjd.
Thomas Pepur (bocher) debet pro focali, Flaxlond et Spytil croft cum grangia, xiijs. iijd.
Willelmus Reede, bocher, debet de redditu iiijs., (solvit.)
Johannes, sutor abbathie debet (ᵈ iijs. vjd.), ut in fine tercii folii ante, tamen et equet.
Johannes Beene debet de veteri anno vjs., unde solvit ijs. vjd. Idem Johannes debet de anno xx iijs., (solvit.)
Johannes Dawntr' debet de anno xx iijs., (solvit); item pro cc fodur, xvjd.
Ricardus Cowston omnibus computatis debet [¹   ]
(ᵈ Johanna Lynton debet pro ij annis et ultra [¹   ])
Thomas Spencer, sadler, debet pro xxvij kydds, ijs.; (item pro focali); unde solvit [¹   ].
Ricardus Chawmberleyn, textor, debet (ᵈ pro xxvij kydds) ijs. vjd. pro focali.
(ᵈ Johannes Bytam debet, ut in fine septimi folii ante, (pro focali), iijs.; item 8d. pro canabo (solvit).)

---

¹ Left blank.　　　² *29 Nov. 1460.*　　　³ See below, p. 156.
⁴ *3 Nov. 1458.*　　　⁵ Repeated in margin.

Willelmus Morton, (ecclesie), debet pro focali xxij*d*.; item pro redditu ad proximum Pascha xj quarteria. Johannes Archar' [   ]. Johannes Bernwelle debet ut in v folio ante. Willelmus Rodger pari modo in v folio. Johannes Whyte, berkar, debet [¹   ] Agnes Hernesse debet pro pomis xx*d*., unde solvit in cervisia 5*d*. Johannes Chalner debet v° wallyng tyle; [item] pro focali. Johannes Nox pro uxore sua, iij*s*. iiij*d*.; item pro focali. Johannes Yonghe, viij*d*. pro (x) kydd*s*, (solvit). Johannes Eston de Cast*ur* xviij*d*. pro focali unde solvit [¹   .] Ricardus Bladsmyth debet xvij*d*. Johannes Burley debet v*s*. vj*d*. (solvit ij*s*.) ut in x folio ante. Tom*as* Hab*ur*gylle debet (fere in oblivione) pro xxx kydd*s*, ij*s*. vj*d*. (solvit omnia²); item pro focali ad Ospitale. Margareta Austhorp (debet) ij*s*. ix*d*., vide quo modo in folio x ante. Willelmus Reeste debet pro grangia in Westgate, iij*s*. iiij*d*. Memorandum de una fenestra lapidea vel petrina ibidem; item de una alia fenestra ad Newerk.

[*f. 69v.*] *Anno regni regis Henrici Sexti xxxvij et anno domini Ricardi abbatis xxj.*³

ADHUC DEBITORES FRATRI WILLELMO MORTON.

(ᵈ Martinus sutor debet pro focali iij*d*.; item pro redditu.) Johannes Drews junior debet ij*s*. ij*d*. pro focali. Johannes Alownton, sutor, debet pro xxx kydd*s*, unde solvit x*d*. (per sotulares); item x*d*. Modo debet x*d*. Willelmus Bowyar*e* debet pro grangia ad hospitale, v*s*., unde solvit pro cariagio.

(ᵈ Johannes Som*ur*sette (coquus) debet pro una forera in Bondfeld, ij*s*.) Johannes Socklyng, j*s*. pro focali. (ᵈ Johannes Inckle debet pro ij toftis ij*s*. ix*d*. (solvit); item pro terra arabile iij*s*. iiij*d*. citra anticum debitum, scilicet 16*d*.,) (solvit). Johannes Waldyng, mercer, debet v*s*. vj*d*. de anno xx; item (ᵈ 8) 16*s*. anno xxj; item 16*d*. (ᵈ Agnes Hostylar debet viij*s*. T*homas* Coper pro Swyns medow anno xxij, x*s*.)

FLETTON. (ᵈ Thomas Cowper de Fletton debet ij*s*. ex mituo usque Quadragesimam proximam; item xviij*s*., ut in iij folio sequente.)

Willelmus Dawntre [debet] pro carectata focalis, ij*s*. j*d*.; Willelmus Woode (clerke) pro alia carectata focalis, ij*s*. ij*d*.; Willelmus Sewalle pro prato ad Hod*s* medow et aliis, iij*s*.; uxor ejus debet 8*d*. pro Flaxlonde; Ricardus Pynd*ar*, [   ]; Robertus Crosse, [   ]; Alicia Barb*ur* debet, ut in quinto filio ante.⁴ Willelmus Lucasse debet iij*s*., ut in tercio folio ante.⁵ Willelmus Craane debet pro iij vaccis; item pro j acra et dimidia terre 8*d*. per annum, sic per 9 annos, [.] Johannes Pyppewel debet pro ccc thak, ij*s*.

NOTA. Memorandum quod fratres qui occupaverunt (in) officium subsacristie debent fratri Willelmo Morton elemosinario pro iij acris dimidia terre ad Fallam herne iiij*d*. per annum de redditu assiso

---

¹ Left blank.   ² Repeated in margin.   ³ *1458-9*.   ⁴ See p. 118.   ⁵ See p. 123.

continuando jam per multos annos videlicet per [¹   ] annos. Item qui
occupaverunt in officio celerarie debent predicto fratri Willelmo Morton pro j libra cinini ij*d*. per annum. Item Nicholaus Eston de Cast*ur*
debet pari modo pro j *lb*. ij*d*. per annum; modo aretro per [¹   ]
annos [¹   ].

Memorandum quod invenitur in compoto elemosinarii de anno ix,
(x et xj^mo) domini Henrici de Owrton abbatis: Et de j libra cimini de
celerar' conventus. B. Et de j libra recepta de Willelmo Budde pro
tenemento, quondam Johannis Cordelle de Castr*e*, situato inter tenementum dicti Johannis, quod dictus Willelmus Budde modo tenet, et
tenementum Symonis Pewys. Item anno viij dicti abbatis invenitur in
compoto elemosinarii: A. Et de j libra cimini de Willelmo Budde.

Nota. Anno domini Nicholai abbatis primo secundo et tercio invenitur quod Tomas Budde capellanus solvebat predictam libram cimini.
Item nota, in registro elemosinarii,² quod Radulphus Palmer de Castr*e*
tenet in feodo unum messuagium in eadem villa et reddit per annum
pro omnibus serviciis j libram cimini. Illud idem messuagium tenet
modo Johannes Cordel et jacet inter tenementum Symonis Pewys de
Rampsey et tenementum Johannis Cordelle. Item inquiratur de illo
dicto Pewys quia in uno anno scribitur Powys.

Anno Johannis abbatis xvij Nicholaus Eston primo solvebat post
Johannem Eston patrem suum supradictam libram cimini.

[*f. 70r.*] *Anno Ricardi abbatis xxij^do tercio Idus May.*³

[JOHANNES PYCHELEY] De fratre Johanne Pycheley, vide antea in
quarto folio⁴ scilicet in prima parte fere in fine.

In splent*s* emptis, vj*d*.; in clavis ferreis emptis, iij*d*.; et in splentyng
unius gabule, juxta T*homam* Rowsby (xv*d*.), ut in quarto folio ante
cum aliis operibus;⁴ item in solutis pro c et septem garbis coperture,
(cum cariagio), emptis per dictum fratrem Johannem Pychele, xv*d*.;
item Willelmo Coopertori pro emendacione de ij foraminibus per
carpentarium facta, ij*d*.; item servienti propter strawyng et drawyng
ibidem, [¹   ]; item pro nova serura ad hostium aule ibidem, iij*d*.
ob.; item in datis eidem fratri Johanni Pychele in Translacione Sancti
Benedicti,⁵ xx*d*.; item in solutis Ricardo Paple pro factura compoti
supradicti fratris Johannis, vij*d*.; item in solutis Paulo carpentario
propter und*ur* settyng cotagii, ubi Willelmus Foole manet, x*d*.; item
dicto fratri Johanni propter solvere pro iij carectatis terre rubie, vij*d*.;
(latamo⁶ iiij*s*. per manus fratris Johannis Pycheley.)

Item Tome Multon pro iij carectatis terre rubie in Westgate, iij*d*.; item
Henrico Mason, xiij*d*., pro emendacione unius parietis, ubi Johannes
Benet nuper manebat; item dicto⁷ fratri Johanni, xij*d*., pro expensis
versus Dowsdale; item Paulo carpentario, iiij*s*. ix*d*. propter totalem

¹ Left blank.   ² This register has not been traced.
³ *13 May 1460*.   ⁴ See p. 123.   ⁵ *11 July 1460*.
⁶ This last payment is recorded in the margin of the folio.
⁷ This second group of payments also related to transactions with the said brother John
[of Pytchley].

emendacionem veteris tecti ubi Willelmus Foole manet. Item memorandum de meremio dato per elemosinarium ad dictum opus cum clavis, rope, wattlyng; item in solutis firmario de le Low¹ pro cxxiiij garbis cooperture, (ᵈ xviij*d*.,) 3*s*.; et in cariagio ejusdem ad cotagium ubi Willelmus Foole manet, cum meremio elemosinarii de illo loco ad elemosinariam, iiij*d*.; item dicto fratri Johanni ad solvendum pro thacke et ceteris, xx*d*.; et uxori T*ome* Starr' trahendo et serviendo tectori per iiij dies et dimidium [ᵈ ix*d*.] 8*d*.; item in solutis Willelmo Lucaz pro meremio ad unum par de dor' dernysse faciendum (in Westgate), vj*d*.; item dicto fratri anno 24 feria 4 post festum Sancti Bartholomei² (per vices), xiiij*s*. viij*d*.³

(ᵈ MEMORANDUM quod Willelmus Belamy abducit cccc red tyl' ad Westgate, ad ingnor*anciam* elemosinarii.)

Sacrista debet ccccc redde tyl' vel wallyng tyl'. Sacrista debet vj lepysse calcis (solvit fere).

Magister operis debet pro iiij eskeppis calcis et xl rubias tyl'.

Celerarius (Lecet*ur*) debet xjˣˣ rubias tyl'. Uxor Ricardi Horton debet cclxxiij rubias tyl'. Celerarius, scilicet frater Willelmus Lecet*ur*, debet fratri Willelmo Morton elemosinario pro v tabulis quercinis, xv*d*., (20*d*.).

[*f. 70v.*] *Anno regni regis Henrici sexti post conquestum, xxxvij et domini Ricardi abbatis xxj, scilicet, ad festum* Tome *Apostoli.*⁴

Memorandum quod frater Willelmus Morton elemosinarius emit unam libram cere, (v*d*.), de fratre Ricardo Bysley diliberandam per subsacristam; item alias (tres) libras pro fratre T*homa* de Sancto Neoto pro xiiij*d*., unde una libra ad festum Purificacionis Beate Marie⁵ proximum per subsacristam, vel.

JOHANNES CLERK DE WODCROFFT. Memorandum quod Johannes Coldewel solvit in Nativitate domini, anno quo supra pro Johanne Clark de Wodcrofte, x*s*. Item dictus Johannes [Coldewelle] solveret ad festum Purificacionis Beate Marie proximum sequens, alios x*s*. pro dicto Johanne Clerk. Item dictus Johannes Coldwel solvit xx*d*. pro dicto Johanne Clerk de debito antiquo. Modo Johannes Clerk debet 12*d*. de debito antiquo, (solvit); item solvit xx*s*. x*d*., ut in quinto folio sequente,⁶ et equet pro anno xxj°.

WILLELMUS BEYLDE, BOCHER. In solutis dicto Willelmo pro primo present ad Natale Domini x*s*. vj*d*.; item pro alio ad Pascha, xj*s*. (ᵈ vj*d*.) scilicet in vigilia Pentecostes.⁷ Summa xxj*s*. vj*d*.

SOLUCIO FRATRI WILLELMO DEPYNG, CRUCIS CUSTODI. Elemosinarius solvit pro annis scilicet xxᵐᵒ et xxj° ccccl garbas de thacke, precium de c, viij*d*., ij*s*. xj*d*. Item idem elemosinarius solvit dicto custodi,

---

¹ The farmer of Low Grange, which belonged to the chamberlain's department in the monastery.
² In the reign of Edward IV, 25 Aug. 1462.
³ A blank space follows about 1¼ inches in depth. ⁴ *21 Dec. 1458.*
⁵ *2 Feb. 1458/9.* ⁶ See p. 137. ⁷ *12 May 1459.*

scilicet, fratri Willelmo Depyng, (Cley),¹ xij*d*. et dictus elemosinarius debet v*d*.

THOMAS ROWSBY, (COKE).² Memorandum quod omnibus computatis elemosinarius debet dicto Tome de debito antiquo, vj*s*. viij*d*., scilicet, pro fratre Willelmo Markam, (infirmario); item pro minucione ante Nativitatem Domini et prima minucione post Nativitatem domini et ebdomada xxᵐᵒ, unde recepit vj*s*. viij*d*. per duas vices. Modo elemosinarius debet dicto coquo 8*s*. j*d*.; (ᵈ de quibus solvit.)

Summa xiiij*s*. ix*d*., unde elemosinarius solvit (ᵈ vij*d*. pro Dominica Quinquagesime, tamen nota de istis 7*d*. solutis in manibus allocati erant in iij linea supra, scilicet in 8*s*. j*d*.); iiij*s*. ix*d*. secundo Sabbato Quadragesime.³

Nota hic,⁴ 4*d*. pro factura avenarum in farinam.

NOTA. Johanna Dawntre solvit xij*d*. pro primo quarterio anni xxjⁱ Ricardi abbatis. Item Willelmus Glynton, 12*d*. (solvit de redditu assise). Item Henricus Yaryngton, iij*s*. iiij*d*., pro primo quarterio, ut supra. Johannes Barford solvit xij*d*.

NOTA. Prior clamat recipere de elemosinario ij nobilia xl*d*.; item vj*s*. 8*d*. pro webbe plumbi fratris Ricardi Stanf*ordie*, et xiij*s*. iiij*d*. pro gardiano de Oxney, scilicet, T*homa* Depyng'.

[*f. 71r.*] *Anno Ricardi Abbatis xxj ad festum Juliani Episcopi.*⁵
Vide plus de ista materia satis clare in folio xxxviij ante.⁶
38. ROBERTUS CONQUEST. Memorandum quod Robertus Conquest solvit pro firma de Sutton pro primo quarterio anni supradicti, scilicet xxj, videlicet viij*s*. x*d*.; et vij*s*. pro mensa Roberti Morton, millar; (ᵈ item in obstupacione pro Brigmylle, vij*s*. vj*d*.) Item dictus Robertus solvit pro secundo quarterio, xv*s*. x*d*. Item dictus Robertus solvit tercio Idus Augusti ut in cariagio de viij carectatis petrarum lib*eratarum*, xx*d*.; item xiiij*s*. ij*d*. in denerir' [*sic*] videlicet grossis. Item solvit pro quarterio termino et ultimo anni, xiiij*s*. iiij*d*.; item xviij*d*., in obstupacionibus pro redditu soluto domino de Thornaw; et equet pro anno xxj.

Item anno xxij Ricardi abbatis, Robertus Conquest solvit in Cena Domini⁷ xv*s*. x*d*., pro primo quarterio anni vicesimi secundi; et hic nota de vj denariis falsis. Item idem Robertus solvit xv*s*. x*d*. pro secundo quarterio. Item idem Robertus solvit xxxj*s*. viij*d*. pro aliis ij terminis et equet pro hoc anno xxij°. Item idem Robertus Conquest solvit xv*s*. ix*d*. pro primo quarterio anni xxiij. Item idem solvit pro aliis iij terminis xlvij*s*. vi*d*. et equet pro anno xxiij°.
Item idem Robertus solvit xxxj*s*. viij*d*. pro medietate anni . . . .⁸

---

¹ Cf. p. 115 : William Deeping seems to have had the alternative name of Clay—presumably his surname before he entered religion.
² Farmery cook.
³ The year is not stated.
⁵ *27 Jan. 1458/9.*
⁷ *10 Apr. 1460.*
⁴ In margin.
⁶ See p. 63.
⁸ Half a folio left blank.

Robertus Conquest habet le iryn goiowne cum le brasse de uno fine de le axstre de Brygmylle.

[*f. 71v.*] *Anno regni regis Henrici Sexti post conquestum xxxvij et anno Ricardi abbatis xxj ad festum Purificacionis.*[1]

SOLUCIO ELEMOSINARII AD FESTUM PURIFICACIONIS BEATE MARIE. In primis domino priori pro (se) et fratribus Henrico B*u*rrow, (nuper mortuo), et Willelmo Wennam, (nuper mortuo), xl*s*., (solvit); fratri Willelmo Morton elemosinario, x*s*., (solvit); fratribus T*home* Ramsey et Ricardo Bysle, vj*s*. viij*d*.; item tantum, (scilicet 6*s*. 8*d*.), secundo Sabbato Quadragesime;[2] item vj*s*. viij*d*. in Vigilia Pasche,[3] et equet; fratri Willelmo Walmysforde, x*s*., (solvit); item fratri Willelmo Stan-*fordie*, x*s*., (solvit); fratri Waltero de Wermyngton, (solvit xl*d*.; item vj*s*. viij*d*.)

FRUMENTUM. In solutis Willelmo Payn pro ij quarteriis frumenti precium quarterii [4   ]; item pro aliis ij quarteriis emptis in foro pro die Animarum[5] [4   ].

PISE. In solutis pro j quarterio pisarum empto in foro, ij*s*. primo Sabbato Quadragesime;[6] item in solutis pro alio quarterio empto de Willelmo Belamy, ij*s*.; item pro ij eskeppis pisarum emptis in foro quarto Sabbato Quadragesime,[7] v*d*. *ob*.; et in ij eskeppis in Sabbato ante dominicam Passionis,[8] vj*d*.

AVENE. In solutis pro ij eskeppis avenarum emptis in foro, iiij*d*.

IN VASIS CIRCULANDIS IN OFFICIO. In solutis Benedicto Coper pro ix ligaturis sive hopys pro iiij vasis emendandis et circulandis, x*d*.

SOLUCIO PRO CERVISIA RECEPTA PER VICES DE ET CETERIS, X KAL. APRILIS SCILICET IN DIE PARASSEUES.[9] Servisia empta de Katerina Orwyn, videlicet, xvij tankard*s*, precium amfre,[10] v*d*., vij*s*. j*d*.

MEMORANDUM quod Johannes Coldwelle debet fratri Willelmo Morton elemosinario, in primis pro (d Johanne Cast*ur*) Roberto Gardyner, (v*s*.); Johanne Clerk de Wodcroffte, Johanne Burley, (d Johanne Tempylle, 3*s*. 9*d*.) (solvit); unde solvit pro Roberto Gardyner viij*s*. ad Nativitatem domini anno Ricardi abbatis xxj ut supra; item in Cena domini ad ostium refectorie, iij*s*. iiij*d*. (pro quo scilicet Willelmo Br*ew*ster), ut patet in albo libro.[11]

[*f. 72r.*] *Anno Ricardi abbatis xxj^{mo} et viij Idus Marcii.*[12]
In solutis pro ij^c grossis spyk*s*, 8*d*.; item pro comyn spyk*s*. 3^c, ix*d*.; item iiij mille splynt nayl', ut in folio sequente, vj*s*. iiij*d*.; item pro clowtnayl', 9*d*.; item pro iij seris, xiij*d*.; item pro viij paribus heynglys cum stok', ponderantibus xiij libras, xvij*d*. per Johannem Coldewel.

---

[1] *2 Feb. 1458/9.*	[2] *17 Feb. 1458/9.*	[3] *24 Mar. 1458/9.*
[4] Left blank.	[5] *2 Nov.*	
[6] *10 Feb. 1458/9.*	[7] *3 Mar. 1458/9.*	[8] *10 Mar. 1458/9.*
[9] *23 Mar. 1458/9.*	[10] Amphora.	
[11] The almoner's white book has not been discovered.		[12] *8 Mar. 1458/9.*

132 THE BOOK OF WILLIAM MORTON

Per Thomam Cooper recepta ad hospitale. Memorandum quod (ᵈ vendidit) Thomas Cowper de Fletton emit de elemosinario vj carectatas feni 4 Idus Marcii¹ pro xviijs. Memorandum quod ista solucio fiet per cariagium cum carecta sua infra annum, capiente per diem xiiijd. sine victualibus, unde solvit ut per cariagium de ccc arundinibus in Coxsholme ad aquam et post, vjd.

Allocantur. (ᵈ Item vij carectate (terre rubie) ad domum nuper in tenura Agnetis Cotelar' et ubi Thomas Haburgylle berkar (nuper manebat) in Cowgate, xd.). Item² dicto Tome propter dawbyng in supradictis locis per ij dies, viijd. (non allocatur); item pro cariagio de ij fodours calcis ad hospitale, iiijd. (non allocatur); item pro cariagio de aliis ij fodowrs calcis ad officium, ijd.; item in solutis pro cariagio de j fodur calcis ab officio ad Sutton cum remeacione cum veteri meremio, xiiijd. ((ᵈ non) allocatur); item pro cariagio de xiijᶜ et xl sclatts de Estonfeld ad grangiam decime vel elemosinarii in dominio ad Gonthorppe, (ᵈ vs.) ijs. iiijd., ((ᵈ non) allocatur); item pro factura de iij quarteriis brasii, 15d.; item cariagium de iij jaggs feni de Hamond medow ad officium, vjd.; item de Mukhylle gap v carectate feni ad officium, xviijd.; item iiij carectate de Fallam hyrne ad hospitale, xiiijd.

Orwyn. Item v carectate feni de prato juxta Stony Pytts videlicet Swyns medow unde prima carectata Roberto Orwyn, secunda domino Johanni Burneham, tercia ad hospitale, quarta ad officium, quinta Tome Cooper de Fletton, xiiijd.; item vj carectate terre rubie ad messuagium ubi Janyn manet (ᵈ vjd.) xvd. (allocatur); item ij in officium, vd.; item pro cariagio de xv carectatis feni de croffts in grangiam ibidem ad hospitale, ijs. vjd.; item pro traxcione meremii de aqua cum cariagio in officium per vj horas, vd.; item, (inquiratur bene), pro cariagio de ij carectatis cooperture de hospitali ad cotagium, ubi Johannes Bernewel manet super Raton row, vjd. ((ᵈ non) allocatur, inquiratur); item pro una carectata terre rubie illuc, ijd. ob.; item pro alia carectata terre rubie ad domum Johannis Palmer in Comersgate, ijd. ob.; item pro iiij carectatis terre rubie usque [domum ubi] Janyn Berkar manet, vijd.; item pro cariagio de petra veluta, scilicet v carectatis, vjd. (non allocatur, inquiratur); item iij carectatis terre illuc, vjd.

Quere plus de cariagio dicti Thome Cowper in 6 folio sequente ad tale signum 6.³

[f. 72v.] Anno regni regis Henrici sexti post conquestum xxxvij.

Canapeum (album) (frater Willelmus Morton iterum habet) longitudinis ij virgarum sive sex pedum latitudinis x virgarum. Frater Willelmus Ramsey mituatus est de fratre Willelmo Morton cum aliis rebus, videlicet, j parvam cistam cum clave, j bibliam, j auroram.

Custus in Burgo. In uno latamo cum suo serviente conducto ad

¹ 12 Mar. 1458/9.
² In the margin beside the following entry: non allocatur.
³ See below, p. 142. In the left-hand bottom margin the sum £2. 3s. 2d. is written in dot notation.

emendandum le goote sewer' super Chapelle row, ubi Ricardus Clok-smyth nuper manebat, ix*d*.; in calce, zabulo et rubiis tyl', omnia de stauro officii; item in terra rubia cum cariagio illuc, vj*d*.; item, alia vice, alio latamo cum suo serviente pro uno muro emendando ibidem.

TOMAS RAMSEY. In solutis fratri Tome de Sancto Neoto vicario elemosinarii, iij*s*. iiij*d*., xj Kal. May;[1] item alia vice, vj*s*.; item in Translacione Sancti (Martini),[2] ij*s*. vj*d*. scilicet anno xxij.

VINUM.[3] In solutis Johanni Tylly pro vino dato conventui, videlicet die Pentecostes iiij lagene et dimidia, iij*s*. ix*d*.

VINUM. Iterum datum conventui, videlicet in festo Assumpcionis Beate Marie[4] (emptum de sub-sacrista) iiij lagene quar[terium], precium lagene, x*d*., iij*s*. vj*d*. *ob*. Nota quod subsacrista solvit elemosinario hic pro pipere de redditu assise pro iij acris et dimidia ad Fallam hyrne.

24. Margareta Balle solvit ut patet in folio xxiiij ante.[5] Item ipsa solvit anno quo supra scilicet xxj°, pro anno xix, iij*s*., videlicet in Vigilia [Sancti] Dunstani episcopi[6]; item in octabis Assumpcionis Beate Marie,[7] ix*s*.; item dicta Margareta in octabis Martini episcopi[8] per filium Johannis Dey in capitulo, scilicet, in anno xxij° Ricardi abbatis solvit vj*s*. viij*d*., et hic vel modo debet [9   ], unde solvit x*s*., videlicet vj Idus May[10] anno vicesimo secundo, pro anno, scilicet xx. Item dicta Margareta solvit, per manus Roberti Morton, anno xxiiij Ricardi abbatis incipiente in festo Symonis et Jude,[11] x*s*., pro anno [9   ], modo debet [9   ]; unde solvit, ut in viij playt*s* de linia tela, precium iij*s*. iiij*d*.; item vj*s*. viij*d*., super le trowhe de petra ad ostium feni in officio, in v ebdomada Quadragesime[12] anno Ricardi abbatis xxiiij; et nota quod juravit hic quod debet nisi vj*s*. viij*d*., ad proxima Pascha, et postea solvit.

[*f. 73r.*] *Anno regni regis Henrici sexti post conquestum xxxvij et anno domini Ricardi abbatis xxj* [*in*] *vigilia Sancti Donstani.*[6]

In solutis pro vj ulnis (dimidia) de Kendale, precium ulne v*d*., (ij*s*. viij*d*. *ob*.); item propter wat*u*ryng et le scheryng (cum) teynt*u*ryng, 2*d*.; item propter facturam unius toge ad Robertum Morton, vij*d*.; item in solutis propter le lynyng ejusdem toge, xv*d*. SUMMA. iiij*s*. viij*d*. *ob*.

SUTTON. In solutis pro fodicione cum cariagio de [9   ] carectatis terre rubie pro una gabula, [9   ]; in uno fowd*ur* calcis empto, xv*d*.; et in cariagio ad Sutton pro diversis defectibus in manerio ibidem emendandis, x*d*.; et in zabulo empto, [9   ] (vacat).

SOLUCIO FRATRIS WILLELMI MORTON ELEMOSINARII PRO LE OOZ AD FESTUM SANCTI JOHANNIS BAPTISTE ANNO QUO SUPRA.
In primis fratri Willelmo Morton, elemosinario, vj*s*. viij*d*.; item fratri

---

[1] *21 Apr.*
[2] *4 July 1460.*
[3] *In margin:* Tercio idus May, *i.e. 13 May.*
[4] *15 Aug.*
[5] See above, p. 92.
[6] *18 May 1459.*
[7] *22 Aug. 1459.*
[8] *18 Nov. 1459.*
[9] Left blank.
[10] *10 May 1460.*
[11] *28 Oct. 1461.*
[12] *5-10 Apr. 1462.*

Willelmo Byry, vj*s*. vj*d*.; item fratri T*ome* de Sancto Neoto, x*s*. (*d* viij*d*.);
item fratri Waltero Wermyngton, vj*s*. viij*d*.; (*d* thesaurario in plenam
solucionem et in manibus, iij*s*. iiij*d*.)

In forinsecis. In solutis Ricardo Scharppe cantori in die Sancti
Oswaldi[1] ex precepto prioris, 4*d*.; in solutis pro ij virgis linie tele,
videlicet elne broode sive latitudinis quinque quarteriorum pro uno
paupere, mortuo in carcere (18 Kal. Julii[2] anno quo supra), vij*d*.;
item ad subsidium generalis capituli, obolum ad marke, viij*s*. viij*d*.
ob. di. q'.

Festum Sancte Marie Magdalene[3] hoc anno contigit in dominica
(et minucio tercii prioris)
Ad cenam nichil; in pane, j*d*.; in una duodena cervisie, xv*d*.; in tribus
aucis, (xj*d*.); in ij pestellis porci, (iij*d*.); in ij porcellis, (x*d*.); in v farssyd
pulcinis, (vj*d*.); in sew ad cenam, iij*d*.; in multone assato, (ij*d*.); feria
secunda, in diversis, x*d*.; feria tercia, in ij porcellis cum carne vitulina,
x*d*.; in ovis et pane, j*d*. *ob*. Summa, iiij*s*. viij*d*. *ob*.

Necessaria. In duobus manitergiis pro mandato puerorum in locutorio, iiij*d*.

Molendinarius. Johannes Drury de West Depyng solvit pro firma
de Brigmylle anno quo supra, videlicet pro termino inter Pascha et
festum Sancti Johannis Baptiste, x*s*. Item vj Kal. Februarii[4] solvit pro
ij terminis sequentibus, xx*s*. Memorandum de 3 cop*ur* pens et aliis.
Item Stephanus filius dicti Johannis Drur*y* solvit per manus Roberti
Conquest xviij*s*. vj*d*.; et in obstupacione pro redditu soluto domino
de Thornawh, xviij*d*. pro Brigmylle et debent modo ad Nativitatem
domini anno xxiij Ricardi abbatis, xx*s*., unde solvit xiij*s*. iiij*d*.; et nota
de obolo; item viij*s*.; item ut de precio cooperture crescentis in le dame
molendini, iij*s*. iiij*d*. (sine fidejussore suo); item x*s*.; item x*s*. ad curiam
post Pentecostem anno 24; item xv*s*. in argento et in cccccccc cooperture
pro domibus ad Sutton, v*s*.

[*f. 73v.*] *Anno regni regis Henrici Sexti xxxvij^{mo}, et anno Ricardi abbatis
xxj.*[5]

Rector de Paston. Xv die Julii[6] rector de Paston veniebat ad elemosinarium in capella minucionis, et promittebat solvere fratri Willelmo
Morton, elemosinario, viij*li*. vj*s*. viij*d*., v quarteria boni frumenti, v
quarteria pisarum et quatuor quarteria avenarum, videlicet pro totali
parte decime pertinentis ad officium elemosinarie in parochia de Paston,
unde solvit totum granum; item viij*li*.; et debet vj*s*. viij*d*.; unde condonantur iij*s*. iiij*d*., et debet clare iij*s*. iiij*d*.

Anno xxij rector de Paston in principio Autumpni emit de elemosinario
totalem porcionem suam decime ibidem in parochia de Paston pro xvij
marcis, unde solvit v quarteria frumenti, precium xx*s*.; iiij quarteria

---

[1] *5 Aug. 1459.*   [2] *14 June 1459.*   [3] *22 July 1459.*
[4] *27 Jan.*   [5] *1458-9.*   [6] *15 July.*

avenarum, precium v*s*. iiij*d*.; v quarteria pisarum x*s*.; item iiij*li*.; item c*s*., et debet modo xj*s*. iiij*d*.; item iij*s*. iiij*d*., pro anno preterito.

NECESSARIA. In solutis Johanni Amerose de Ryssele pro vij^{xx} xij creest*s*, xij*s*. iij*d*. Et preteria memorandum de istis suprascriptis vij^{xx} xij creest*s* fuerat bona carectata.

NAYL' NECESSARIA. In solutis pro iiij mille splyntnayl' emptis de Johanne Coldwelle, precium de mille, xix*d*., vj*s*. iiij*d*.; unde solvit iiij*s*. vij*d*., et debentur dicto Johanni, xxj*d*,

MEMORANDUM DE FORERA LONGA JUXTA LONGAM FORERAM VICARII BURGI PROPE BONDE STYLE.
In solutis pro prima arura ejusdem, viij*d*.; item pro secunda arura cum seminacione et totali harpicacione, (cum rollyng) ejusdem, x*d*.; item pro v eskeppis et dimidia ordii emptis ad villam de Farsedde,[1] xxij*d*.; in sarculacione, nichil; in falcacione, ligacione et preparacione ad carectam, ix*d*.; in cariagio ejusdem, videlicet de cccc et viij garbis cum lez rakyngg*s*, scilicet ij carectate, v*d*.; in trituracione, ventilacione et cribracione de quatuor quarteriis, xij*d*.; item propter brasium inde factum, xx*d*.

Willelmus Sand*ur* solvit elemosinario ix*s*. pro xxxvij acris terre jacentibus in lez Stibbyng*s*, et ad finem messuagii sui in Dosthorppe, videlicet ex parte australi et debet, xviij*d*., unde solvit per estimacionem totum per Johannem filium suum.

PISE. Anno xxij, ebdomada prima, 7 eskeppe; ebdomada secunda 5 eskeppe et dimidia; ebdomada tercia [2   ] eskeppe [2   ].

Memorandum quod frater Willelmus Morton mituatus est de fratre Willelmo Rampsey xiij*s*. iiij*d*. (solvit), quando frater T*omas* Morton, monachus de Ramsey, primo transiebat ad Oxford, unde solvit iij*s*. iiij*d*.; item 3*s*. 4*d*.; item vj*s*. viij*d*., et equet.

[*f. 74r*.] *Anno regni regis Henrici Sexti xxxviij* [*incipiente pen*]*ultimo die Augusti* (. . . *Baptiste*),[3] *et anno domini Ricardi abbatis xxj.*

CLOPTON. In solutis Johanni Hubboc et socio (suo) carpentariis pro factura unius novi domus, longitudinis xxj pedum per (^{d} xx) 17 dies (^{d} viij*s*. iiij*d*.) 7*s*. j*d*.; item puero Petro Burton, 16*d*.; item in solutis dictis carpentariis propter le reysyng dicte domus per iij dies cum puero Petro, iij*s*.; item supradictis carpentariis propter le drawyng aule T*ome* Wryhte ibidem per iij dies, ij*s*. viij*d*.; item xij*d*. uxori Johannis Hertte pro mensa illorum per supradictos iij dies.

ELEMOSINARIA. In medicamine pro equis hoc anno [4   ].

CUSTUS IN BURGO. DUO CARPENTARII CUM PUERO PER V DIES. Item in solutis supradictis carpentariis, pro exaltacione unius som*ur*pese, cum tracinis et tabulis, cum factura unius hostii gradibus novis, et aliis

---

[1] Farcet, Hunts.   [2] Left blank.
[3] *30 Aug. 1459*: cf. p. 89. From here to the end of the book the tops of the pages are badly stained by water. In many cases the date heading is now only partly legible and in a few places some lines of the text are also illegible.
[4] Not stated.

defectibus ibidem emendatis, ubi Janyn Fusȝarde manet in Cowgate, capientes [*sic*] in grosso, iiij*s*. ij*d*.; et puero x*d*.; item pro parvis heynglysse et stok*s* pro fenestris ibidem, ij*d*. *ob*.; item pro factura de le schoppe wyndow Johanni carpentario, vj*d*.

IN BURGO. In uno scanno meremii facto, ubi Johannes Palmer manet in Comersgate, vj*d*.

IN OFFICIO. In solutis supradictis carpentariis pro veteri meremio de certis copulis deponendis de furno infra officium cum nova carpentria certi meremii ibidem per 3 dies, ij*s*. vj*d*.; et puero Petro, vj*d*.; item eisdem ibidem per ij dies, ij*s*.; item eisdem pro factura unius trappedo*ur* et ostii aule per j diem, xij*d*.; item eisdem pro divisione facta in stabulo pro equis et emendacione unius racke, xij*d*.

IN OFFICIO SCILICET in solutis Ricardo Edgyston sclat*ter* pro bemfyllyng' et xv*c* latte pynnysse cum aliis parvis laboribus ibidem, xv*d*.; item eidem Ricardo pro sclattyng de ij rodysse ibidem super le bakhows, ix*s*.

Anno xxij Ricardi abbatis in Quadragesima.

Ricardus Grawnte recepit de elemosinario pro succisione et portacione spinarum in le Trenchys, xviij*d*.; item pro labore in gardino in Quadragesima per ix dies et dimidium, 19*d*.

NOTA. Johanni Hubboc xvij dies dimidium, (7*s*. 3*d*. *ob*.); item Johanni Cowper per x dies, (4*s*. 2*d*.); item Petro Burton per xiiij dies (2*s*. 4*d*.)

[*f. 74v.*] *Anno regni regis Henrici* [*sexti*] *post conquestum xxxviij.*[1]

SUTTON. In solutis Ricardo Edgyston et famulo suo (et uni puero), sclattarsse, propter emendacionem camere occidentalis in manerio ibidem, (*d* per) et in aliis locis diversis per iij dies, iij*s*. x*d*.; item pro factura unius nove fumerelle in aula ibidem Johanni carpentario per ij dies, x*d*.; item pro ferramentis, [²   ]; in solutis pro una carectata straminis ordei Roberto Conquest, pro messuagio ubi Robertus Godfrey manet, vij*d*.; item uno coopertori per ii dies, x*d*.; item dicto Roberto Godfrey pro stramine et suo labore ibidem, xiiij*d*.; item propter hedgyng, xij*d*.

SOLUCIO FRATRIS WILLELMI MORTON ELEMOSINARII PRO TUNICIS AD FESTUM SANCTI LUCE EWANGELISTE PRO ANNO XX DOMINI RICARDI ABBATIS.

In primis elemosinario, x*s*.; fratri Waltero Wermyngton, x*s*.; (unde solvitur nobile; item iij*s*. iiij*d*.; et equet); fratri Willelmo Byry, x*s*. (*d* 5*s*.), v*s*.; item v*s*. et equet); fratri Willelmo Ramsey, x*s*.; (3*s*. 4*d*.; item 6*s*. 8*d*., et equet hic); item thesaurario in manibus, unum nobile auri et equet pro hoc solucione.

NOTA HIC. Memorandum quod Johannes Coryo*ur*,[3] super Sowter Row, solvit elemosinario pro cotagio ibidem, ij*s*.; item solvit per Johannem Corveser vel Sowter, ij*s*.; et debet pro anno xx v*s*., unde

---

[1] *1459–60:* rest obliterated by damp. [²] Left blank. [3] Currier.

solvit ij*s*. per supradictum Johannem; item per eundem Johannem, xvj*d*.; item, per eundem, unum par ocriarum novarum, xiiij*d*.; (solvit 18*s*. pro 16*s*.)[1] Memorandum quod omnibus computatis inter predictos, anno xxiiij Ricardi abbatis finiente, dictus Johannes Coryo*ur* debet fratri Willelmo Morton, elemosinario, xxij*s*. per suam propriam confessionem, tamen [de] summa suprascripta soluta fuit 18*s*. et Johannes Corio*ur* computavit et dicit nisi 16*s*., unde solvit per Johannem Sowter ij paria ocriarum, scilicet, primum par pro fratre Gylberto, secundum pro fratre Morton, precium ij*s*.; item vawmpeyyng paris ocriarum, vj*d*., et debet xix*s*. vj*d*.; unde solvit [   ].

NOTA. Johannes Ryalle frater noster mituatus est ij*s*. viij*d*. (solvit); Agnes Draper, xvj*d*.; in solutis Willelmo Mason pro opere ubi J[anyn] Fyssarde manet, xij*d*.; item Johannes Hubboc carpentarius cum sociis suis ad Cloppton, 3*s*. Nota bene hic. ([d] Item Ricardus Sclatter super le bachows in officio, 4*s*.)

NOTA. Johannes Wakerle solvit pro anno xxj Ricardi abbatis, xx*s*. et debet (clare) vj*s*. ([d] iiij*d*.,) x*d*. *ob*.; unde solvit per Ricardum filium suum, vj*s*.; modo debet x*d*. *ob*. Item solvit pro anno xxij, xx*s*. et debet clare vij*s*. ij*d*. *ob*.; unde solvit iij*s*. iiij*d*.; item iij*s*. Modo debet x*d*. *ob*.

[*f. 75r*.] [*Anno regni regis Henrici sexti post conquestum xxxviij*,[2]] . . . *viij Kal. Decembris*.[3]

SOLUCIONES AD WODCROFFTE. Johannes Clerk, alias vocatus Johannes Smythe de Wodcroft, solvit elemosinario, xxj*s*. vj*d*.; tamen dictus Johannes post solucionem quasi per horam iterum veniebat dicto elemosinario et iterum peciit, viij*d*., quos elemosinarius ei solvit et sinit abhire in pace. Item iterum postea venit et peciit grossum erga annum futurum.

SOLUCIO FRATRIS WILLELMI MORTON ELEMOSINARII PRO SPECIEBUS AD PURIFICACIONEM BEATE MARIE[4] ANNO XXIJ. Elemosinario suprascripto, x*s*.; fratri Waltero [Wermyngton], unde solvit iij*s*. iiij*d*.; item 3*s*. 4*d*.; fratri Willelmo Byry, v*s*., [in die] Agnetis secundo;[5] item iij*s*.; item ij*s*.; et equet; fratri Willelmo Ramsey, x*s*. in manibus, 17 Kal. Februarii;[6] fratri T*ome* de Sancto Neoto pro fratre Willelmo Walm*esford*, x*s*., solutos in manibus in die Agnetis secundo; fratri T*ome* de Sancto (Neoto) pro se ipso, v*s*.; item v*s*. et equet; fratri Johanni Ryppon, x*s*. 3 Kal. Marcii,[7] ante prandium prope cimbam[8] in claustro; fratri Johanni B*urrow* juniori, per T*omam* Neede,[9] x*s*., solutos in manibus in die Agnetis secundo; item domino priori, xx*s*. per manus fratris Willelmi Ramsey in grossis et dimidio ([d] fratri) nobile auri.

OBLACIONES. Clerico prioris, ij*s*.; item pro infirmario, xiiij*d*.; item puero prioris, ij*d*.; servienti fratris Walteri Wermyngton ij; servienti fratris Ricardi Oxford senioris, ij*d*.; Roberto o the fret*ur*, iiij*d*.;

---

[1] Written in the margin.   [2] Partly obliterated by the damp.
[3] *24 Nov. 1459*.   [4] *2 Feb. 1459/60*.
[5] *28 Jan. 1459/60*.   [6] *16 Jan. 1459/60*.
[7] *28 Feb. 1459/60*.   [8] The reliquary (or bell: cf. p. 103) in the cloister.
[9] Brother Thomas of St. Neots.

Johanni Caker, 4*d*.; seriantibus minucionis, viij*d*.; T*ome* Rowsby, vj*d*.; Johanni Bytam, ij*d*.; Johanni Halle, iiij*d*.; Jacobo, ij*d*.; Ricardo Sterr', ij*d*.; Waltero Qhwyt, ij*d*.; Willelmo Stoxley, ij*d*.; (Roberto) Kolde Owreton, j*d*.; Johanni Clendon, et T*ome* Halle, iiij*d*.; servientibus sacriste, scilicet (*d* duobus) iij, ix*d*.; servientibus magistri operum, Willelmo Pypwelle, (iij*d*.) et Stephano Carpentario (ij*d*.), et puero, j*d*.; Roberto Morton, xij*d*.; Tome Burowhbrig,[1] vj*d*.; servienti thesaurarii [[2]   ]; Johanni Coldwelle, ij*s*.; clerico camerarii, ij*d*.; focario, ij*d*. [*In margin*] Nihil quia tes*aurarius* non dedit servientibus elemosinarii.

Nota ij present*es* de Willelmo Beylde bocher. In solutis dicto Willelmo pro primo present ad Natale Domini, xj*s*., tamen habuit nimis multum per sex denarios, vide in quinto folio precedente,[3] Johanne Coldwelle teste.

Henricus Palmer solvit pro anno xxj° et primo quarterio anni xxij ad festum Nativitatis domini xviij*s*. et iiij*d*.; et stupavit xiiij*d*. pro ocriis Ricardi Tayllo*ur*; item viij*d*. pro mensa Pauli Nelson carpentarii.

Henricus Colermaker solvit iij*s*. iiij*d*. pro primo quarterio anni suprascripti. Margareta Beene solvit iij*s*. prima ebdomada Quadragesime anno quo supra.

[*f. 7*v.] *Anno regni regis Henrici sexti post Conquestum xxxviij et anno xxj Ricardi abbatis 4* [. . .] #.[4]

NOTA. Robertus Boswelle senior debet (elemosinario) pro Pewterer' plase per (unum) annum xvj*s*. et ad minus pro uno quarterio anni, iiij*s*., (solvit,) unde solvit iiij*s*.; item idem solvit pro proxima celda[5] ibidem, ij*s*. viij*d*.

NOTA. Robertus Boswelle junior debet elemosinario pro alia domo ibidem juxta, pro iij (4) terminis et ad minus pro [   ] termino, [[2]   ].

NOTA. Johannes Boswelle, frater Roberti Boswel junioris, debet elemosinario ad festum Annunciacionis Beate Marie[6] anno Ricardi abbatis xxj^{mo} pro quatuor terminis, pro alia domo ibidem, xvj*s*,; unde solvit prima vice iij*s*.; item secunda vice, feria quinta, in ebdomada Pasche v*s*. in presencia Roberti Morton et Tome B*ur*rowbrig; item alia vice, iij*s*. iiij*d*.; item ij*s*. viij*d*.; item anno Ricardi abbatis xxiiij in festo Sancti Gregorii,[7] ij*s*.; item in Vigilia Trinitatis[8] obilum auri.

Johannes Coldwelle (debet)[9] fratri Willelmo Morton elemosinario anno quo supra scilicet xxj. In primis p[ro] Johanne Cast*ur* nuper de Maxsey, [[2]   ]; Roberto Gardyner, [[2]   ]; Willelmo Br*e*wster, [[2]   ]; Johanne Burley, 3*s*. 6*d*.; Roberto Spencer, x*d*.; Ricardo Webster, 2*s*. 6*d*.; Johanne Drews, 2*s*. 2*d*.; Ricardo Bladesmyth, 17*d*.

---

[1] Boroughbury.   [2] Left blank.   [3] See above, p. 129.
[4] Cross-reference apparently lost.   [5] *Selda*, a shop or stall.
[6] *25 Mar. 1459*.   [7] *12 Mar. 1461/2*.   [8] *19 June 1462*.
[9] *Debet* is inserted here above the line, but it is not certain whether John Coldwell is debtor in each case. He appears to have collected these amounts from the person named and to owe them to the almoner William Morton. See, however, the substituted paragraph on p. 140 below.

Johanne Eston de Cast*ur* debet pro focali, (^d xij) x*d*.; Johanne Hontte de Cast*ur* pro veteri meremio sibi vendito ad Brigmylle, xvj*d*. (Quere^I istam materiam in folio sequenti melius.)

SOLUCIO FRATRIS WILLELMI MORTON, ELEMOSINARII PRO LE OOZ AD FESTUM SANCTI JOHANNIS BAPTISTE[2] ANNO DOMINI RICARDI ABBATIS XXIJ.
Fratri Waltero Wermington, vj*s*. viij*d*.; fratri Willelmo Morton, elemosinario, vj*s*. viij*d*.; fratri Roberto Lyderon, vj*s*. viij*d*.; fratri T*ome* de Sancto Neoto, vj*s*. viij*d*.; (^d fratri Roberto, thesaurario, iij*s*. iiij*d*.); fratri Willelmo Byry, iij*s*. iiij*d*. et equet pro hac solucione.

VINUM EMPTUM PRO CONVENTU IN DIE PENTECOSTES.
De Johanne Tylly, scilicet iiij lagenis citra iij quarteriis deliberatis ad Oxney pro sex fratribus commorantibus ibidem, precium lagene x*d*., iij*s*. xj*d*.; item in festo Apostolorum Petri et Pauli de eodem Johanne iiij lagenis et dimidia, iij*s*. ix*d*.

In solutis pro uno pyckesse empto de Agnete Pynchebec, vij*d*.

Johannes Chalner recepit de elemosinario pro plantacione de x^c plantularum fraccinarum, in trenchy[s], iij*s*. Item [cetera desunt]

[*f. 76r.*] *Anno regni regis Henrici 38, et anno Ricardi abbatis* [xxij],[3] *xij Kal. May.*[4]

Frater T*omas* de Sancto Neoto recepit de elemosinario pro vicaria sua, v*s*.; item alia vice, videlicet [5   ]. Memorandum quod Johannes Bernylle clericus Ricardi Pytt*s* recepit de elemosinario, xix*d*. pro uno breve (ad) exequendum contra T*omam* Bakon vicarium etc. Item memorandum quod elemosinarius solvit Willelmo Gervysse, videlicet homini domini regis ex precepto domini abbatis, ij*s*.

PRIOR. In solutis ei pro mora sua post Pascha per elemosinarium, xl*s*.; item pro cursu suo in Autumno [5   ].

OXNEY. Frater T*omas* Depyng, gardianus ibidem, recepit per manus fratris Willelmi Byry de elemosinaria, iij*s*. iiij*d*., scilicet xiij Kal. May;[6] scriberetur alibi; (item 3*s*. 4*d*. in choro); item iij*s*. iiij*d*. in Translacione Sancti Martini;[7] item eodem die, iiij*s*.; et pro officio Infirmarie, viij*s*. viij*d*.

Robertus Crosse de Westgate solvit elemosinario pro Hodys wong, vj*s*. viij*d*.; item alia vice, scilicet in crastino Phylyppys et Jacobi,[8] vj*s*.; et debet ad festum Michaelis[9] anno xxij finiente pro ij annis, xij*s*. unde solvit [cetera desunt]

NOTA BENE. It is to haffe in mynd y*a*t ye covent celerer' *&* Roberde Crosse of Burrow haffe in lytylle Coldam, ye sowthe heede offe ye awmenersse loonde ther*e*, with a balc perteyneyng in ye mydd*s* to ye forseyde awmener*e*. Nota also a new evydense offe ye for'seyde: Roberde Crosse specifythe y*a*t ye leynkythe offe ye for*e*syde loonde or

---

1 In the margin.   2 *24 June 1460.*
3 Almost obliterated by the damp.   4 *20 Apr. 1460.*   5 Left blank.
6 *19 Apr. 1460.*   7 *4 July 1460.*   8 *2 May 1460.*   9 *29 Sept. 1460.*

ell' ye sowthe heede is xx mette yardys or ell' lx foote, with ye walle
& ye dyke sowthward. Nota also it is (to) know yat alle Roberde Crosse
eldar evidense specifythe no leynkyth yeroffe.

CUSTUS IN OFFICIO. In solutis Paulo carpentario propter le trappedor'
emendandum, le longpresse cum aliis operibus in magna camera post
recessum regis et regine per iij dies,[1] xvd.; item dicto Paulo Nelson
carpentario pro scapulacione tingnorum, factura unius vange nove, et
emendacione unius fenestre super Chapel Row per v dies, ijs. jd.; item
dicto Paulo pro scapulacione meremii infra officium per ij dies, xd.

IN BURGO. Item dicto carpentario faciente lez dernys cum ostio et
fenestra, ubi Janyn manet, per v dies, ijs. jd.; item dicto Paulo, ubi
Johannes Boswel manet, emendando unum paale, et item operando in
sewera sororum ibidem per iiij dies, xxd.

[f. 76v.] *Anno Ricardi abbatis xxij in crastino sancti* [   ]*stani Augusti.*
Johannes Coldwelle[2] debet fratri Willelmo Morton, in primis pro Ely
Feyr', xjd. item pro ordio empto de Roberto Gardyner, scilicet iij
quarteria, vs. Idem debet pro Stephano Gardiner, iiijs. viijd., (solvit);
item pro Johanne Burle, iijs. vjd.; Roberto Spencer, xd., (solvit);
Ricardo Webster, ijs. vjd., (solvit); Johanne Drewysse, ijs. ijd.; Ricardo
Bladdesmythe, xvijd., (solvit); Johanne Hontte de Castur, xvd., (solvit).
Idem debet pro redditu super Chapel row, vs., (solvit); idem Johannes
solvit pro maltte makyng pro Willelmo brewster de Maxsey, ijs. xjd.,
(solvit). Memorandum quod supradictus Johannes solvit nunc ultra in
crossis [sic] viijs. vijd. Idem debet pro Johanne Eston de Castur, 12d.;
item ijs. pro magna sellione super Beyche anno xxiij in crastino Sancti
Botulfi.[3] Idem Johannes Coldwel solvit pro Johanne Castur, 4s. xd.
Idem Johannes Merstlonde vel Coldwel solvit pro schoppa vs. Idem
Johannes debet vc latnayls.

Frater Willelmus Morton debet Johanni Coldwel in primis de debito
antiquo, xxjd., (solvit); item pro uno gladio, ijs., (solvit); item pro j
arcu, xiiijd., (solvit); item pro j salette, ijs. vjd., (solvit); item pro
sprotte, ijs. vijd., (solvit); item pro clowt leddur, ixd., (solvit); item
pro avellanis xvd. (solvit).[4]

Tabule quercine quatuor cum aliis emptis de fratre Toma de Sancto
Neoto, xiijd. Calx v fowdur, 7s. jd., unde ad grangiam de Gonthorp
totum citra staurum officii.

SUBCIDIUM. In solutis generali capitulo hoc anno, scilicet, jd. ad libram,
iijs. xd. ob.

NOTA. Johannes Schynggey (vel Kydman) recepit de elemosinario,
ijs. iiijd. in Vigilia Pentecostes;[5] item xijd.; item in uno regardo sibi
dato pro suo bono labore ubi Janyn manet.

---

[1] Note the reference to the royal visit in 1459 (cf. pp. 77, 156).
[2] An incomplete note of these transactions is inserted above on p. 138.
[3] *18 June 1461.*   [4] One third of this folio is left blank.   [5] *31 May 1460.*

[*f. 77r.*] [*Title obliterated by damp . . . anno domini Ricardi abbatis*]
xxij°.¹

CUSTUS GRANGIE DE GONTHORP. In solutis T*ome* Inglond pro cariagio
unius carectate meremii scapulati ab officio illuc, ix*d.*; item T*ome* Copar
de Fletton pro (cariagio de sex) (ᵈ 13 carectatis calcis, zabuli, quinque)
scalis cum magno meremio latt*s*, creest*s*, uno hyrdyl, scafolde tymb*ur*
ad Gonthorp; item post reparacionem ibidem factam reducendo scalas
et alia, scilicet leepys, scafol tymb*ur*, etc., scilicet xiij carectatas, viij*s.* vj*d.*

In solutis Johanni Hubbok carpentario cum suo aprenticio per (ᵈ ix)
17 dies completos (ᵈ in Vigilia Assumpcionis beate Marie,)² capientes
[*sic*] in die ix*d.* (ᵈ vj, ix,) unde rece[pit] v*s.*; item, alia vice, ij*s.*; item
ij*s.*, per Robertum Morton; item iij*s.* ix*d.*

SUMMA soluta tribus carpentariis pro tota carpentria ibidem, 19*s.* 5*d.*,
et in potu, 7*d.*

(ᵈ Item in solutis Paulo Nelson carpentario in supradicto opere per vij
dies in Vigilia Assumpcionis beate Marie, capienti in die v*d.*, ij*s.* ix*d.*;
item pro vij diebus ij*s.* xj*d.*; item x*d.*

[SCLATTYNG.] In solutis Willelmo Rodger, sclatt*er*, propter sclattyng
de viij rodis (et ij rodas poyntyng*e*, ij*s.* iiij*d.*), capienti pro roda iiij*s.* vj*d.*,
xxxvj*s.*; item in solutis supradicto Willelmo Rodger emendando ibidem
per diversa loca et crestando residuum per viij dies capienti in die v*d.*,
3*s.* 4*d.*; unde recepit xij*d.*; item xij*d.* per Johannem Hylle; item xvj*d.*;
item, xij*d.*; item eidem pro viij mille sclatte pynnys, ij*s.* viij*d.*; item pro
latt pynnys vij mille, ijs. iiij*d.*; item dicto Willelmo Rodger, xij*d.*; (item,
xij*d.*; item pro perforacione de xxᶜ sclattys, xx*d.*); item in solutis
Johanni Hylle, laborario, adjuvante supradictum Willelmum sclatt*er*,
per xxj dies, capienti in die, iiij*d.* unde recepit prima vice, xij*d.*; item
xviij*d.* et equet in Vigilia Assumpcionis Beate Marie;³ item per vj dies,
ij*s.*; item per vj dies, ij*s.*; item per vj dies, ij*s.* in Vigilia Nativitatis
Beate Marie;⁴ item iiij*d.*; item ij*s.* iiij*d.*

In solutis Willelmo Batteche cum suo famulo sclatters. In primis xx*d.*;
item ij*s.*; item Johanni Styvo*ur*, iiij*s.* vj*d.* pro mensa illorum per 3
ebdomadas; item dicto Willelmo, iij*s.* iiij*d.*

CALX. In solutis Johanni Growtte et Thome Colyn pro v fowd*ur*s
calcis, precium de fowd*ur* xiiij*d.*, vj*s.*; unde iij fowd*ur*s ad Gonthorp,
et ij fowd*ur*s in officio; et in solutis pro cariagio de supradictis iij
fowd*ur*s ad ut supra, ij*s.*; item pro aliis ij fowd*ur*s in officio, iiij*d.* Nota
in calce viij fowdyrs cum cariagio illuc, xvj*s.*

ZABULUM. In solutis pro vj carectatis zabuli cum fodicione et cariagio
illuc, vj*s.*

TERRA RUBIA. In solutis pro iij carectatis terre rubie propter bemfyllyng et alia facienda, ix*d.*

Petrus Lorr' solvit per proximum suum, pro anno xxij, xvj*d.*, videlicet
Robertum Reffeson.

¹ *1459–60.*   ² *14 Aug. 1460.*   ³ *14 Aug.*   ⁴ *7 Sept.*

Meremium emptum de Johanne Steu*ur*, scilicet 27 tingna cum uno bono walle plate, iiij*s*. viij*d*.

LAT NAYL'. 4 mille, 4*s*. 8*d*.; una longa scapha, 3*d*.; latpynnys 4 mille, xvj*d*., (solvit.)

[*f. 77v*.] *Anno regni regis Henrici sexti post conquestum 39, et anno Ricardi Abbatis xxij in crastino Lamberti episcopi*[1]

6[2] TOMAS COWPER. In solutis dicto Tome pro cariagio de xiij carectatis, ut in principio istius folii, videlicet ad Gonthorppe et de Gonthorp, viij*s*. vj*d*., ((ᵈnon) allocatur[3]); item dicto T*ome* per ij dies cariando fenum ad hospitale, scilicet xviij jagg*s* feni, ij*s*. iiij*d*.; item dicto Tome pro v parvis carectatis feni de crofto ad hospitale in magnam grangiam ibidem, vij*d*.; item pro ij carectatis straminis de domo Willelmi Craane ad ofuellum[4] novum faciendum in officio, iiij*d*.; item[5] pro cariagio de iij carectatis de sclatt*s* emptis ad Eston feelde,[6] unde ij carectate ad grangiam de Gonthorp et j in officium, iiij*s*.; item pro una carectata veteris meremii de Cowgate in officium, iij*d*. SUMMA xvj*s*.

MINUCIO (TERCII PRIORIS) TEMPORE NATALIS DOMINI, ANNO RICARDI ABBATIS XXIIJ.
Dominica in ij aucis, (8*d*.), et uno porcello, (5*d*.); feria secunda in carne vitulina, (7*d*.); et iiij volatilibus, (4*d*.); feria 3 in quatuor bake kofyns cum dimidia eskeppa farine, xiiij*d ob*., et in speciebus, iij*d*.; in ij aucis, 8*d*.; in uno porcello, 5*d*.; in ij caponibus et ij gallinis, x*d*.; in 4 volatilibus, viij*d*.; in sagina pro fryt*ur*s, iiij*d*.; in ovis, (2*d*.); in speciebus supra.

Laurencius Tooche, anno Ricardi abbatis xxiiij, solvit pro decima grangie de Gonthorp, videlicet, de anno Ricardi abbatis xxiij,[7] in primis xx*s*.; xl*s*.; iij nobilia auri, xx*s*., exceptis ij*d*.; item xx*s*.; item x*s*.; item xvj*s*. viij*d*.; item xxvj*s*. viij*d*.; et in variacione, xl*s*.

Willelmus Payne debet fratri Willelmo Morton, elemosinario vij quarteria brasii et j eskeppa, videlicet in le Cummys, et promisit solvere ante proximum Natale Domini.

Willelmus Neve solvit per vices vj*s*.; et memorandum quod ipse jurabat, anno 23 incipiente, quod ipse debet 6*s*., et postea solvit iij*s*. in capella Sancti Laurencii; item iij*s*. in ebdomada Pasche anno 24.[8]

[*f. 78r*.] *Anno regni regis Henrici Sexti post conquestum 39, et anno domini Ricardi Ayheston abbatis xxiij incipiente.*[7]

CUSTUS IN OFFICIO. In solutis Willelmo Rodger sclatter operanti in officio per iiij dies, capienti in die v*d*., xx*d*.; item per ij dies, x*d*.; in solutis Johanni Hylle laborario, servienti supradicto Willelmo, per idem tempus, xvj*d*.; in solutis eidem per ij dies, viij*d*.

---

[1] *18 Sept. 1460.*
[2] A special sign, see p. 132.
[3] Note in margin.
[4] *In margin:* hovellum.
[5] *The remainder of this paragraph is marked with a note in the margin:* (ᵈnon) allocatur.
[6] Colly Weston slates. [7] *1460-1.* [8] *Easter, 18 Apr. 1462.*

CUSTUS INFIRMARII IN REPARACIONIBUS. In solutis Willelmo Rodger sclattyng et poyntyng, ubi Willelmus Aldows manet in Heygat, per vij dies (ᵈ et dimidium xijd. *ob.*); item ijs. xjd.; et in cervisia, jd.; item in solutis Johanni Hylle servienti dicto Willelmo per idem tempus (ᵈ xd.; item xxd.); ijs. 4d.; in solutis supradicto Willelmo Rodger splyntyng et dawbyng in uno cotagio ad Martyn bryg¹ per iiij dies cum uno serviente, ijs.

SACRISTA. In solutis fratri Willelmo Borow sacriste pro officio elemo-sinarie, xiijs. iiijd. per manus domini abbatis receptoris. Item sacrista stupavit viijs. penes Willelmum Morton (servienti), quos dictus Willel-mus Morton (in vestiario) solvisset fratri Willelmo Morton (monacho) elemosinario Burgi. Item sacrista obstupavit xxxiijs., quos solveret infirmario.

PRIOR. In solutis domino Willelmo Exston priori, xxs. per manus domini abbatis receptoris; nota in perdicione; item in solutis Willelmo Rodger sclattyng le schoppe² ex parte boriali ostii capelle Sancti T*ome* Martiris per vij dies; item Johanni Hylle per idem.

SOLUCIO FRATRIS WILLELMI MORTON ELEMOSINARII PRO TUNICIS AD FESTUM LUCE EWANGELISTE.
Domino Willelmo Exston priori, xxs.; fratri Waltero [de Wermington], iijs. iiijd.; item fratri Willelmo elemosinario, xs.; et fratri Willelmo Ramsey, xs.; et equet.

Calx viva³ empta de Henrico Tarry, scilicet iiij fod*ur*s et dimidium pro ixs.; et in cariagio in officium, xijd. Item nota quod dictus Henricus jurabat. [cetera desunt].⁴

(ᵈ Willelmus Rodger recepit 3s. 4d. non computatos)

[*f. 78v.*] *Anno regni regis Henrici Sexti post conquestum 39, et anno Ricardi Abbatis xxiij, videlicet in festo Sancte Cecilie virginis.*⁵

In solutis Paulo Nelson carpentario pro labore carpentrie, ubi Johannes Boswel manet (*a*),⁶ per (*c*) xiij dies, et (*b*) in una schoppa ibidem prope; item dicto carpentario ubi Henricus (*b*) Palmer et (*a*) Johannes Stoxle manent per iiij dies removendo unum murum terrenum cum splent*s* factis et aliis operibus ibidem, xxd.; item dicto Paulo carpentario, ubi Henricus Yaryngton manet, operando ibidem unam novam gutteram per iiij dies.

Willelmus Rodger sclatter [pro] sclattyng, ubi Johannes Boswel manet, et super unam schoppam ex parte boriali ostii capelle Sancti T*ome* Martiris per [⁷   ] dies; item dicto sclatter pro sclattyng, ubi Henricus

¹ Martin's Bridge carried the footpath over the common sewer from Barnard's Cross in Westgate to Swan's Pool in Howgate (Midgate).
² Note the almoner's shop in Long Causeway, on the north side of the main entry to the nave of the chapel of St. Thomas the Martyr from the town.
³ Quicklime.
⁴ The following note is written at the foot of this folio.   ⁵ *22 Nov. 1460.*
⁶ These letters were inserted above the line to indicate that the phrases should be re-arranged in the order *a, b, c*.
⁷ Left blank.

Yaryngton [manet], et ibidem juxta, per [¹   ] dies; Johanni Hylle servienti dicto sclatter per eosdem dies.

IN OFFICIO. Item dicto Willelmo, sclatter, et Johanni Hylle servienti ei per [¹   ] dies, super le garrette in officio, et le long hows ibidem; item Willelmo plummer facienti unam gutteram de novo, ubi Henricus Yarryngton manet, xij*d*. et propter sowd*ur*, xij*d*., et pro plumbo; item Willelmo Reeste mundanti seweram ad Cyst*ur* hows, per vices, vj*d*.; in solutis Willelmo Rede sclatter pro xv*c* sclatt*s*, viij*s*. iij*d*.; item dicto Willelmo, alia vice, pro [¹   ] et pro cariagio, [¹   ]

[FORINSECA.] In uno equo conducto (per vij dies) pro scolaribus versus Oxoniam, ij*s*. iiij*d*.; item in expensis Tome Borowbrig redeuntis cum ij equis de Oxonia ad Burgum post octabas Martini,² ij*s*. viij*d*.

Willelmus Rodger sclatter cum Johanne Hylle sibi servienti fuerunt cum elemosinario postquam venerunt de grangia pro decima elemosinarii ad Gonthorp, videlicet in Vigilia Lamberti episcopi usque fere (ᵈ medium) finem Adventus Domini³ in diversis reparacionibus et laboribus in Burgo.

FALLAM HYRNE. Johannes Halle solvit pro gramine ibidem, iij*s*. iiij*d*., videlicet pro anno xxij⁴ Ricardi abbatis.

NOTA. (ᵈ Halywat*ur* stooppe deliberatur camere fratris Willelmi Lecet*ur*).

NOTA. Frater Willelmus Walmsford mituatus est, 12*d*. in die Sancti Vincencii⁵ ad solvendum medicum.

NOTA. Willelmus Rodger mituatus est 12*d*. de elemosinario 13 Kal. Februarii,⁶ Willelmo Reeste teste.

Willelmus Rodger (et Johannes Hylle) fuerunt cum elemosinario per lx dies ad festum Nicholi⁷ [*sic*].

[*f. 79r.*] *Anno domini Ricardi Aystton abbatis xxiij ad festum Concepcionis Beate Marie Virginis.*⁸

IN FORINCECIS. In solutis Willelmo Sand*ur* juniori et Ricardo Barker pro factura et fodicione unius fossati ad Lodghe yaate subtus Estwoode continente xxviij rodas, in latitudine fere v pedum, (et) in profunditate iij pedum, dando pro roda, ij*d*., iiij*s*. viij*d*.; et in rewardo illis, ij*d*.

MARRAM. Symon Wyberd ibidem venit et cepit (circa festum Sancti Andree⁹) de elemosinario unum toftum (in M*ar*ram) cum una sellione terre arabilis pro viij*d*. per annum, et nota quod habet reparacionem clausur'.

WODCROFT. Johannes Clerk ibidem solvit pro anno xxij°, vj*s*. viij*d*.; et debet elemosinario, 13*s*.; unde solvit iiij*s*.; item xiiij*s*. Modo debet pro anno 23, xv*s*. iiij*d*.; unde solvit x*s*.; item per filium suum, Johannem Godeale, ix*s*.

---

¹ Left blank.
⁴ *1459–60.*
⁷ *6 Dec.*

² *18 Nov. 1460.*
⁵ *22 Jan.*
⁸ *8 Dec. 1460.*

³ *From 16 Sept. to 24 Dec. 1460.*
⁶ *20 Jan.*
⁹ *30 Nov. 1460.*

FORINSECA. Item in solutis supradicto Willelmo Sand*ur* juniori pro fodicione de xiiij rodis in uno fossato ad Fallam hyrne subtus Westwod, roda continente in latitudine, (the breede), vij pedes, in profunditate, iij pedes et ij pedes in fundo, dando pro roda iij*d.*, iij*s.* vj*d.*

Anno domini Ricardi abbatis xxiij°

SOLUCIO FRATRIS WILLELMI MORTON, ELEMOSINARII PRO SPECIEBUS AD FESTUM PURIFICACIONIS BEATE MARIE[1]

In primis supradicto fratri Willelmo Morton elemosinario, x*s.*; fratri Waltero Wermyngton,[2] solvit et equet pro omnibus materiis; fratri Willelmo Bery, ij*s.*; item viij*s.*; fratri T*ome* Borowh, 5*s.*; item in claustro, 5*s.*; fratri T*ome* Croyland, solvitur fratri Johanni Baston, x*s.* et equet; fratri Georgio x*s.* in presencia [³   ]; fratri Roberto B*ur*rowh x*s.* (solvit) in claustro; fratri Johanni Burnam (x*s.*[4]); unde solvi x*s.*; fratri Edmundo Offord (x*s.*), item x*s.*; item fratri Roberto, thesaurario, x*s.* in manibus, et equet pro anno xxxiij° [*sic*] pro hac solucione.

NECESSARIA. In solutis pro ij tribulis emptis de T*oma* fabro manente super Sowter Row, xiiij*d.*, (non solvit.)

Doctrinale traditur fratri Johanni Ryalle in festo Agathe Virginis[5] ex mituo.

Johannes Rowsyng intravit in cotagium elemosinarii in Howgaate septimo Kal. Februarii,[6] anno ut supra, reddendo per annum, v*s.*

Robertus Baker solvit pro primo quarterio anni xxxiij [*sic*] iiij*s.* vj*d.*; item Willelmus Reede, bocher, iiij*s.* pro anno xxij°; Isabella Colermaker, iij*s.* iiij*d.* pro primo quarterio; Willelmus Glynton, xij*d.*

T*omas* Noblette solvit pro tenemento elemosinarii in Paston cum iij acris terre in campis ibidem per exsecutores suos pro iij annis, vj*s.* et debent pro redditu (2*s.*) et reparacione.

[*f. 79v.*] Anno regni regis Henrici Sexti xxxix et anno Ricardi abbatis xxiij, Quinto Kal. Marcii.[7]

NOTA. Plantacio pisarum, vocatarum hasty peysyn, v et quarto Kal. Marcii parvum post plenilinium.[8]

Iij celle allocantur cum frenis, cropis, et peyt*rell'*; furati sunt.[9] Cella cum

---

[1] *2 Feb. 1460/1.*
[2] Although the amount x*s.* does not appear opposite the next three names, it is obvious that the compiler of the account intended to insert it by the side of each name. He has only entered the instalments actually paid, and in some cases the place in the monastery where payment was made or the name of the person receiving an instalment on behalf of the person entitled thereto.
[3] Not completed.
[4] Above his name.
[5] *5 Feb. 1460/1.*
[6] *26 Jan. 1460/1.*
[7] *25 Feb. 1460/1.*
[8] A short time after the full moon.
[9] Note the horses with saddles and bridles belonging to the almoner, which were requisitioned and were stolen or lost at the battle of St. Albans in 1461. This occurred when the victorious Lancastrian forces marched south along the original site of the Great North Road through Sutton, after the battle of Wakefield, where Richard, duke of York, was killed. He was buried afterwards in Fotheringhay church. Some historians have stated that Peterborough itself was sacked on this occasion, and there is a record of loss

freno empta de Willelmo Stokysley, sexto Kal. Marcii,[1] ij*s*. iiij*d*.; cella cum freno empta de T*oma* Ay, xviij*d*.; ([d] cella cum freno T*ome* de Burbryg, propter cellam et frenum perditos ad bellum Sancti Albani.) (Vacat quia dictus Tomas vendidit Magistro Willelmo Rathe.) Equus (bay), cum cella et apparatu cum freno, de providencia Roberti Morton; equus (albus), cum cella debili et freno, emptus de Johanne Bytam, precii iij*s*. iiij*d*.; equus (bay), cum cella debili et freno, emptus de Roberto coquine abbatis, iij*s*. v*d*.; equus (doonne), cum cella debili et freno, emptus de Jacobo coquine abbatis, iij*s*. (Johannes Estas habet.[2])

Custus in Burgo. In solutis iij hominibus de Fletton conductis per unum diem ad faciendum unum murum terrenum gardini fructuum (in Howgate), longitudinis xxiij pedum, xij*d*.; in potu, j*d*.; et in carectata feni ad idem, ij*s*.

Memorandum qualiter Johannes Brodleg' pariter scripcit Roberto Staffe clerico venienti cum fratre Johanne Malden et fratre Johanne Glynton de Oxonia.

Nota bene. Mayst*ur* John Dauyson p*ar*son of Walpole & Fleete Har*e*gate.

Hospitale. In solutis Willelmo sclatt*er* pro emendacione unius foraminis supra altare ad hospitale, iij*d*.

In Burgo. In ij latamis cum uno serviente conductis per vj dies ad emendandum occidentalem gabulam domus ubi (in quo) sorores capelle manent vij*s*. (6*d*.); in cervisia, j*d*.; item pro asportacione materie ab orto, ubi Johannes Stoxle manet, in viam ad emendandum calcetum ibidem, vj*d*.; item pro una scala ferrata in opere ibidem.

Clopton. Et in reparacione facta per Willelmum Hart ex parte australi aule sue ad Clopton, xx*d*.

Fratri Johanni Pychele. In solutis dicto fratri v*s*., in parte solucionis majoris summe de x*s*. ad distribuendum pauperibus, et in datis eidem (ad potum), iiij*d*.; item postea (ad potum), viij*d*.; item alia vice, viij*d*., versus Dows*d*ale; item xx*d*. ad lard*ur* corner; item ij*s*. per proprium parvum puerum; item per eundem, viij*d*.; item xij*d*.; item v*s*. versus Walsyngham; item xx*d*. pro pane puerorum in mensa; item iiij*d*. pro volta; item j par sotularum precii vij*d*.; item vj*d*. versus Seyngylsold;[3] item ij*s*. xj*d*.; et equet pro omnibus materiis in anno xxiij domini Ricardi abbatis; item v*d*. ultra ad potum; item ([d] xvj*d*.; item xij*d*.); vj*s*. per vices.

([d] Johanni[4] Craane, 3 Non. May,[5] 4 Kal. Junii[6]). Henricus Palmer solvit xxvj*s*. viij*d*. pro anno xxij Ricardi abbatis et (quod) debet, nota bene, vi*s*. 8*d*.; T*omas* Elys de Marram.

of rent through devastated and unoccupied Peterborough houses in the account of the receiver of the vill of Burgh in 1461–2.
[1] *24 Feb.*   [2] This note above the line refers to the dun horse only.
[3] Singlesole, the grange of the pittancer. [4] *Deleted with a note above the line: quia alibi.*
[5] *5 May.*   [6] *29 May.*

Sp*er*lyng, viij^{xx} expenduntur in prima ebdomada Quadragesime; item 8^{xx}; item secunda [ebdomada] ccc.

[*f. 80r.*] *Anno domini Ricardi abbatis xxiij, xj Kal. May.*[1]

MARRAM. Ricardus Smythe solvit fratri Willelmo Morton elemosinario, videlicet, de precio v quarteriorum brasii venditi et deliberati cuidam mulieri ibidem ad Marram, precium quarterii iij*s*. viij*d*., xx*s*. ij*d*.; unde ipsa solvit dicto elemosinario in primis xxij*d*.; item vj*s*. viij*d*.; modo ipsa debet elemosinario, xj*s*. viij*d*.; unde solvit alia vice xj*s*. iiij*d*.; et condonantur iiij*d*.; et equet. Memorandum quod supradictus Ricardus debet. Inquiratur de rectore ibidem.

OBLACIO AD CAPELLAM BEATE MARIE MAGDALENE. Hoc anno, xvj*d*.; et in exspensis pro sociis recreandis in camino ex curiositate etc., iij*s*.

MAXSEY. In exspensis elemosinarii per diversas vices pro terra arabili et prato querendo in campis et pratis pertinentibus ad (rectoriam de) Maxsey, ij*s*. vj*d*.

SOLUCIO FRATRIS WILLELMI MORTON ELEMOSINARII PRO LE O AD FESTUM SANCTI JOHANNIS BAPTISTE. In primis fratri Willelmo elemosinario, vj*s*. viij*d*.; fratri Waltero Wermyngton, vj*s*. viij*d*., (solvit); fratri Willelmo Bery, vj*s*. viij*d*., (solvit); unde recepit iij*s*. iiij*d*.; item tantum alia vice; fratri Johanni Malden, iij*s*. iiij*d*., (solvit); fratri Ricardo Oxford seniori, vj*s*. viij*d*., (solvit.)

NOTA. Frater Willelmus Lecet*ur* debet fratri Willelmo Morton infirmario [*sic*] vj*s*. viij*d*. pro appellacionibus, ex quo idem frater Willelmus Leycet*ur* fuit celerarius conventus anno Ricardi abbatis xxij.

Idem frater Willelmus Lecet*ur*, (celerarius), debet dicto fratri Willelmo Morton (elemosinario) propter le Holt*s* celerarii, scilicet iij*s*. iiij*d*. per annum, aretro per [2] annos. Item debet (celerarius) pro [2] libras cimini per [2] annos [2].

SUBSACRISTA. Idem debet pro officio subsacristie per annum iij uncias piperis aretro per [2] annos [2]; idem debet xj^{xx} rubie tyl' vel wallyng tyl'; idem debet pro v tabulis quercinis, xx*d*. ut in folio x precedenti.

NOTA. Frater Willelmus Ramsey de(bet) fratri Willelmo Morton (^{d} iiij libras et) dimidiam (libram) cere pro officio subsacristie; item pro iij acris et dimidia terre ad Fallam h*er*ne de precio iij unciarum piperis, iiij*d*. Item idem debet fratri Willelmo Morton, vj*s*. viij*d*., (solvit), pro appellacionibus in anno Ricardi abbatis xxiij; item pro alneto suo pro ij annis; item pro appellacione anno 24, vj*s*. viij*d*.

Memorandum de reparacione facienda in rectoria de Maxsey videlicet de omnimoda materia cum cariagio et cetera; item de glasyng *and* leedyng ibidem.

---

[1] *21 Apr. 1461.*   [2] Left blank.

NOTA. Memorandum de certis parcellis prati ad Marram dimittendis, videlicet ij acre et dimidia etc. cum certis proficuis ibidem, scilicet hedgrows, pertres[1] cum aliis vendendis; item de cera ibidem.

Frer*e* T*omas* Grype de Stan*fordia* natus in Croxston et ordinis minorum. Frer*e* T*omas* Walys de Ludgate natus in (d Flete strete) Norwyche ordinis predicatorum.

[*f. 80v.*] *Anno domini Ricardi abbatis xxiij* [*in vigilia Sancti Jacobi apostoli*[2]] CUSTUS IN BURGO. In solutis Johanni Rockle carpentario pro tota carpentria unius aree facte cum tracinis et tabulis in coquina Johannis Helme, taylo*ur*, (cum novis gradibus et ij hostiis factis ibidem omnia de novo), continentis per unam partem fere xiiij pedes et per aliam partem x pedes (heyngyll' et stok*s* de stauro), v*s.*; et in cervisia, j*d.*; item in tabulis emptis ad dictum opus, iij*s.*

Cockysholme (15*s.*) cum v acris in Swyns med, (8*s.*), venduntur[3] T*ome* Cooper de Fletton et aliis duobus ibidem pro xxiij*s.*, et habent dies solucionis proximos etc. unde supradicti solverunt v*s.*; item v*s.*; item v*s.*

SPYTYLCROFFTE. Venditur Ricardo Murcote bocher', pro xiiij*s.* iiij*d.*

FALLAM HYRNE. Ricardo Pyndar pro iij*s.* iiij*d.*, solvit.

Muchyl gap *and* Nonhylle ad opus officii.

HODYS WONG *and* ij acre medow ibidem, Roberto Crosse.

Le iij acr*es* frisce, juxta le xl acr*es* prati, venduntur Laurencio Wevar pro xvj*d.*, unde solvit [4   ].

IN FORINCECIS. In solutis pro procuratoribus generalis concilii Lononiis xiiij*d.* receptis per vicarium Burgi, Johannem Haar*e*[5] nomine.

MAXSEY. T*omas* Kyllam de Maxsey promisit fratri Willelmo Morton elemosinario ad colligendam decimam in iij campis, videlicet le West felde inter ecclesiam et Maxsey, item le Sowt felde, item le North felde, (pro x*s.*). Item le Est felde Johannes Schyrwyn colliget pro viij*s.* Memorandum quod T*omas* Kyllam recepit per manus Roberti Morton, iij*s.*; item alia vice per eundem Robertum Morton, ij*s.*; item iij*s.* per manus elemosinarii.

Johannes Scherwyn recepit [6   ].

Robertus Morton recepit ad solvendum aliis, vij*s.* iiij*d.* per vices; (item 8*d.*); item xx*d.*; item 6*s.* 8*d.*

NOTA. For to make ye hey y*at* is notte soolde at Maxsey, *and* al so for ye cariage *and* howsyng.

NOTA. Ootemeele makyng.

NOTA. Item frater T*omas* Grype suspicatur quod frater Ricardus Schropsberi recepit de uxore Ricardi Horton [7   ].

---

[1] Pear-trees.   [2] *24 July 1461.* Almost illegible.
[3] Sale of grass-keep, or grazing rights for the season.   [4] Left blank.
[5] The vicar of Peterborough, John Hare, collects and pays Morton's contribution for the proctors at the Canterbury Convocation in London.
[6] Not stated.   [7] Amount not recorded.

Nota. Johannes Drews senior cepit domum, in quo Johannes Barne-wel manet, pro sorore sua, (erga festum Michaelis proximum), red-dendo per annum viijs.

Nota. De fratre Willelmo Eton de Norhamton'.

[f. 81r.] Anno domini Ricardi abbatis xxiij in vigilia Sancti Jacobi Apostoli.[1]
Nota. Custus [   ]. Johannes Estas recepit de fratre Willelmo Morton elemosinario xvs.; (item 2s.); ad ordinanda et emenda diversa requirenda propter cariagium decime Rectorie de Maxsey. (d Item Robertus Morton recepit viijd. [2] eadem de causa.) In primis predictus Johannes solvit pro uno cartte body (cum cart laddur), omnia de novo, iiijs. Item idem solvit pro apparatu, vel collers, trayts, cum aliis, pro quatuor equis carectariis; item pro le thylle hors, vjs. Item idem solvit pro uno carte rope, xd.; item pro factura de ij lyne pynnys, ijd.; item pro j corio de qwhyte leddur, viijd.; item pro viij carte clowts, viijd.; item [pro] ij hurtyrsse, 4d.; item pro adipe, jd. ob.; item pro xxij clowt nayl', j ob.; item pro schoyng, 5[d.]; item iiijd. in aliis.

Ricardus Honnyng recepit xijd.; item ijs.; item iiijd. per Robertum Morton; item iijs. iiijd.; et equet. Item idem recepit pro trituracione de [3   ] quarteriis frumenti (d xd.,) xxd.; item xvjd.; item vjd. per Robertum Morton; item xijd. per eundem; item ijs.; item iiijs.; item viijd.

Soluciones. In carne, vd.; in candelis Parisie, jd. ob.; in butiro et ovis, ijd.; in lacte, iijd.; in sale, jd. ob.; in farina avenarum, jd. ob.; in regardo uxori Tome Kyllam, xd.; (d item vjd. per Robertum Morton.)

(A) Maxsey. Reparacio magne grangie ibidem in rectoria.
In primis in solutis pro xijc sclatts, cum cariagio, 8s. 8d.; in latts vc, ijs. xjd.; in iiij mille pynnis, xvjd.; in v mille nayl', vs. xd.; in calce de stauro officii; (in zabulo, xvjd.); in solutis Willelmo Batche operante ibidem per vj dies et dimidium capienti in die, vjd., iijs. iijd.; item eidem per vj dies, iijs.; item Roberto Palle per iij dies et dimidium, xiiijd.; item dicto Roberto per vj dies, ijs.; item Willelmo Rodger, sclatter, pro poyntyng de vj rodis super magnam grangiam in (dicta) rectoria ibidem, roda ad xviijd., ixs.; item pro mensa dicti Willelmi, xxjd.; item in solutis dicto Willelmo, iijs.; item dicto Willelmo Rodger, ijs., per manus Willelmi Aldows, (d ijs.). Modo elemosinarius debet Willelmo Rodger, vs. iijd. pro supradicto opere; item pro opere trium dierum, xviijd.; unde dictus elemosinarius solvit xvd.; et sic remanent pro obstupacionibus propter redditum Willelmi Rodger, vs. vjd.

(B) Prior. Dominus Ricardus Harlton recepit per manus capellani sui de elemosinario v Kal. Septembris[4] pro cursu suo ad Pascha pre-teritum xxvjs. viijd., et hic elemosinarius debet priori xiijs. iiijd.; item pro cursu prioris in Autumpno [5   ].

1 24 July 1461.   2 Omitted.   3 Quantity not stated.
4 28 Aug.   5 Not completed.

MAXSEY. In solutis pro 4 petris plumbi pro cansella ecclesie de Maxsey [¹   ]; item pro xiij libris de sowdyr, iij*s*. iij*d*.; item Willelmo plummer conducto per v dies, capienti in die viij*d*., ad emendandum multos defectus canselle² ibidem, iij*s*. iiij*d*.; et in cervisia, ij*d*.

Nota quod Robertus Smyth solvisset 10*li*. [*sic*] in festo Sancti Oswaldi.

Memorandum ad mittendum Johanni Brow; item balivo de Schefford; item pro cariagio foragii et cooperture; item de eskeppa cum pomis.

Memorandum de caligis mittendis Roberto Morton, precii xvj*d*., feria 4 proxima.

T*homas* Cowper recepit de elemosinario xij*d*., ex mituo.

[*f. 81v.*] [*Anno³ domini Ricardi abbatis xxiij*]

In solutis fratri Willelmo Ramsey in primis in pane, xvj*d*.; in cervisia, x*d*.; in vino, xviij*d*.; in carne bovina et ovina, v*d*.; in ij caponibus, vij*d*.; in uno porcello, iiij*d. ob*. Ad cenam; in uno sew, videlicet in carne ovina, v*d*.; in iiij pulcinis, iiij*d*.; in iij spadis multonum, vij*d*.; in uno capone, viij*d*.

IN DIE SANCTI OSWALDI.⁴

Ad prandium, in ij salcatis pissibus, ij*s*. vj*d*.; in uno dentrice, xj*d*.; in viij perchys, x*d*.; in rochys de cervicio; in anguillis piscibus, x*d*.; in iij tenchys, iij*d*.; in amigdalo, scilicet j libra [⁵   ]; in solutis pro roba T*ome* coci, ij*s*. iiij*d*.; in secunda roba pro secundo coquo, ij*s*. vj*d*.; in una tunica pro secundo coquo, vj*d. ob*. Memorandum quod frater Willelmus Morton solvit v*s*. pro parte sua, et officium celerarii, et frater Willelmus Ramsey residuum.

Memorandum ad ordinandum pro domo Johannis Whyte super Raton Row; item pro thackyng in villa et ad hospitale, (ᵈ item propter unum cuttyng saw) computare cum Roberto Baate et alio, fowyng of ye comon sewer', rydyng for sylvyr, goyng to Eld*ur*nale.

Memorandum quod isti confratres commederunt cum priore ad Oxney ante et post festum Nativitatis Beate Marie Virginis.⁶

Die dominica, fratres Willelmus Morton, Willelmus Walmys*ford*, Oxford⁷ junior; feria 2, Johannes Hylle, T*homas* B*ur*rowh; feria 3, Baston, Nicholaus; feria 5, frater T*omas* Neede.⁸

Dominica secunda, Notyngham, Pychele, Malden, Ramsey; festo Nativitatis, Magni officiarii; feria 5, Johannes Pychele (2),⁹ Willelmus Bery.

Dominica 3, Sacrista et Subsacrista (2); feria secunda, Willelmus Morton (2); feria 3, Johannes Lesyngham, Henricus Lynne; feria quinta, Johannes Burrowh, Willelmus Spaldyng, Baston (2).

---

¹ Cost not stated.
² The almoner as rector pays for repairs to the chancel of Maxey church.
³ Heading obliterated by the damp.
⁴ *5 Aug. 1461.*   ⁵ Not inserted.   ⁶ *8 Sept. 1461.*
⁷ Richard.   ⁸ Of St. Neots, Hunts.
⁹ If a monk had his meal with the prior at Oxney on more than one occasion during the period, this was noted by a number written above his name.

Dominica 4, Stawnford, Sacrista (2), Notyngham (2), Henricus Lynne (2), Malden (2), Ramsey (2); feria secunda, Elemosinarius, Nicholaus; feria 3, Johannes B*ur*nam, Johannes B*ur*row senior, Willelmus Depyng (senior); feria quinta, Willelmus Walmysford (2), Baston (3), Celerarius (3), Malden (3).

JANTACULUM GILBERTI WALYSSE. Anno domini Ricardi abbatis xxiiij et in festo Cecilie virginis.[1]

In pane, vj*d.*; in cervisia, ix*d.*; in ij caponibus et ij aucis de Holondia;[2] in uno porcello empto in foro, vj*d.*; in grossis carnibus,[3] iiij*d.* Ad cenam: In carne multonum cum le fu, iij*d.*; in speciebus, j*d.*; in una spada multonis, j*d. ob.*; in igne et candela, ij*d.*

JANTACULUM WILLELMI WALYSSE. Anno domini Ricardi abbatis xxv, xj Kal. Decembris.[4]

In pane et cervisia, vij*d.*; in uno ferculo grossarum carnium, iij*d.*; in uno capone, j gallina, iiij pulcinis, j auca, et j porcello, de dono patris Willelmi Walysse.[5] Ad cenam: In uno sew cum speciebus, igne et candela, 5*d.*
[*In margin afterwards cancelled*] 3*li.* 14*s.* 9*d.*

[*f. 82r.*] *Anno regni regis Edwardi Quarti primo.*[6]

DEPYNG FEYR'. In solutis pro v*c* grossis spyk*s* emptis, xxj*d.*; item in v*c* midyl spyk*s* emptis, xv*d.*; item in solutis pro una absconsa, ij*d. ob.*

STAWNFORDE FEYR'. [In] ccc grossis spyk*s*, xij*d.*; v*c* mydylspyk*s*, xv*d.*; iij mille lat nayl', 3*s.*; item pro uno ferramento pro uno lato tribulo, ij*d.*

Memorandum de messuagio dimittendo ad Marram (Nota bene); item de reparacione ibidem facienda cum aliis rebus; item de sewera communi super Chapel row et de aliis faciendis, ut in parte altera precedentis; item de Henrico Palmer, cum materiis suis et indentura declaranda in capitulo.

Memorandum quod, computo habito inter fratrem Ricardum Harlton receptorem domini et fratrem Willelmum Morton elemosinarium per tempus ij annorum, idem (debet) per billam indentatam, vij*li.* viij*s.* iij*d.*, ad quos oneratur de vj*li.* vj*s.* tam pro Jaale sylv*er*, (30*s.*), quam pro firma pasture de Cathewayt,[7] (33*s.*) pro ij annis supradictis terminatis ad festum Michaelis xxxviij°.[8] SUMMA DEBITI:—13*li.* 14*s.* 3*d.*

De quibus allocantur ei x*li.*, ut in precio iiij*xx* quarteriorum brasii emptorum de eodem et liberatorum receptori per manus Laurencii Toche. Et debet clare in dicto crastino Michaelis anno xxxviij lxxiiij*s.* iij*d.*

Memorandum quod, consimili computo habito inter dictum receptorem et Nicholaum subsacristam a festo Michaelis anno xxxvj usque

---

[1] 22 *Nov. 1461.*
[2] Holland, Lincs.
[3] i.e. beef and mutton; see above, p. 89.
[4] *21 Nov. 1462.*
[5] A gift from the father of William Wallis.
[6] Heading and part of first line obliterated by damp. As to date, see below, p. 156.
[7] In Paston.
[8] Two years ending on 29 Sept. 1459.

festum Michaelis xxxviij, scilicet pro ij annis, videlicet per annum xvjs. viijd., xxxiijs. iiijd.

De quibus allocatur ei pro vino liberato,[1] ut patet per billam vel talliam etc.

NOTA DE WILLELMO ALDOUS. Memorandum quod computacio habita inter fratrem Willelmum Morton et Willelmum Aldows pro ij annis preteritis anno quo supra, et in die Quatuor Coronatorum,[2] dictus Willelmus Aldous de xls. debitis W(illelmo) Morton elemosinario. Predictus Willelmus Aldous solvit xxijs. iiijd.; et debet xvijs. viijd. unde solvit [cetera desunt]

SOLUCIO FRATRIS WILLELMI MORTON ELEMOSINARII PRO TUNICIS AD FESTUM SANCTI LUCE EWANGELISTE. Anno regni regis Edwardi ut supra.[3]

In primis dicto elemosinario, xs.; fratri Waltero Wermyngton, 6s. 8d.; fratri Ricardo Bysley, (d 40d., 20d.), xs., (solvit); fratri Johanni Ryalle, xs., (solvit), et equet; (d fratri Tome Croylande); fratri Johanni Tylly, vjs. viijd.; unde solvit xvjd., item vs. iiijd., et equet pro hac solucione.

EDMUNDUS LANGLE. RICARDUS PLANTAGINETTE.[4]

[f. 82v.][5]

[In solutis . . . W. Sandur] et aliis laborantibus [in communi sewera ad] capellam Sancti Tome Martiris, iijs.; item Johanni Downe, ijs.; item socio dicti Johannis, xviijd.; item xijd.; item in plenam solucionem, vs.; et in cervisia per vices, iiijd.

SOLUCIO FRATRIS WILLELMI MORTON ELEMOSINARIO PRO SPECIEBUS AD FESTUM PURIFICACIONIS BEATE MARIE ANNO QUO SUPRA.

1.[6] In primis supradicto elemosinario, xs.
2. Item fratri Waltero Wermyngton, [7   ].
3, 4. Item fratri Ricardo Oxford, (solvit), et fratri (d Johanni Tylly) Nicholao, vs.; item vs.; et equet.
5. Item fratri Willelmo Bery, iijs. iiijd.; item iijs. iiijd.; item iijs. 4d.
6, 7. Item fratri Johanni Baston et Tome Croyland unde receperunt, xs.
8. Item fratri Edmondo Lynne, iijs. iiijd.; item iiijs. vijd.; item ijs. jd.; et equet.
9. Item fratri Johanni Pychele, xs.; unde frater Thomas Nede[8] recepit totum; et equet.
10. Item fratri Johanni Ryppon, (xs.); unde solvit 3s. 4d.; item, (d per Robertum Morton), vjs. viijd.
7. Sorores capelle cum ancilla, videlicet cuilibet xxd., xiijs. iiijd.

---

[1] An allowance for wine supplied to the abbot's receiver by Nicholas, the sub-sacrist.
[2] 8 Nov. 1459.   [3] 18 Oct. 1461.
[4] Written at the foot of the folio without further comment.
[5] Title and first two lines obliterated by damp.
[6] The figures were inserted by the writer of the original text.
[7] The amount paid was omitted.   [8] Of St. Neots.

CUSTUS IN RECTORIA, MAXSEY. In solutis pro xiij tabulis quercinis emptis de Johanne Halle, longitudinis xiiij pedum [et] latitudinis xj inchys, precium, iiijs. vjd.; item in solutis ij carpentariis conductis per viij dies ad faciendum ij mangna hostia pro grangia magna ad Maxey in rectoria ibidem, iiijs.; in ij sarratoribus conductis per vj horas, ixd.; in meremio et clavis de stauro officii; item in solutis predictis carpentariis, scilicet Johanni Hubbok cum apprenticio suo conductis per vj dies ad emendandum alia ostia cum aliis defectibus in supradicta rectoria, 3s. 6d.; item Rogero Schyggey pro opere petrino ibidem per vj dies, ijs. vjd.[1]

MARRAM. Memorandum de respons[ione] danda uno de Thorney erga dominicam proximam etc. Item Johannes Downe solvet xviijd. elemosinario in festo Sancti Thome apostoli[2] proximi; item de apro emendo; item quo modo Ricardus Burges abstulit fraccinos cum spinis, et de domo ruinosa.

[f. 83r.] Anno regni regis Edwardi quarti post conquestum . . . . et Ricardi abbatis xxiij . . .[3]

Tomas Cowper petit allocacionem [pro materiis subscriptis. In primis videlicet pro] cariagio spinarum scilicet j carectate [sic] de officio ad Cowgate [vjd.]; item j carectata feni de hospitali ad Bondgate, iijd.; item j carectata de thacke de Snorshylle ad hospitale, vjd.; item ij carectate feni de Muckehil gap ad officium, viijd.; item ij carectate de sclatts de Eston-on-the-hylle ad rectoriam de Maxsey (d iijs.), ijs. viijd.; item pro iiij carectatis calcis de officio ad supradictam rectoriam, 4s. 8d.; item pro vj carectatis terre rubie ad unam gabulam perficiendam faciendam [sic] ubi Johannes Stoxley manet, juxta le Cystur hows, xijd.; item pro una carectata iiij quarteriorum frumenti pro die animarum[4] de Loolam myll' ad Burgum, xiiijd.; item pro cariagio magnarum portarum pro magna grangia rectorie de Maxsey, xviijd. SUMMA:— xijs. viijd., et est soluta.

Quinto die Aprilis, sequens computacio facta est.

Tomas Cooper iterum petit allocacionem pro materiis sequentibus. In primis pro ij carectatis thacke de officio ad Prestgate, iiijd.; item pro cariagio iij carectatarum thacke de hospitali ad Prestgate, xjd.; item 3 carectatis terre rubie ad Prestgate pro ryggyng ibidem, vjd.; item ij carectatis thacke de hospitale [ad domum] ubi Janyn Berkar manet, vjd.; item viij carectatis terre rubie ad messuagium ubi Henricus Palmer manebat super Chapel row, xvjd. ultra vj carectatas terre rubie illuc per Tomam Molton, illuc, vjd.; item pro cariagio de vj carectatis fimi ab illo loco extra villam, vjd.; item pro cariagio de ij carectatis pisarum de Maxsey ad officium pro distribucione[5] pauperum in Quadragesima,

---

1 One-third of page left blank.   2 21 Dec.
3 Title obliterated by damp.   4 2 Nov.
5 One of the few records of the gift of food to the poor, by the almoner.

(^d v*s*.) ij*s*. vij*d*. SUMMA est soluta (^d et *Tomas* Coper debet elemosinario, x*d*.; item j eskeppam ordei, (5*d*.) et j eskeppam crappys (2*d*.)).[1]

Memorandum ad ordinandum pro tenemento pro Stoxleys place et aliis diversis locis; item pro uno tectore.

(^d CRANE. Item Johanne[2] Craane v*s*. iij*d*. ex mituo sine die, unde solvit 3*s*. 8*d*.; et debet 19*d*.; item dicte Johanne ij*s*. versus Styleton; item xij*d*.)

NOTA. Robertus Reffson de [3   ] solvit pro uno tofto in Paston et iij acris terre in campis ibidem, 16*d*. Robertus Crosse solvit vj*s*., anno ut supra, tempore Nativitatis Domini, pro Hod*s* wong, et debet pro ij annis; Nota Willelmus Glynton solvit xij*d*. Willelmus Ryheston de Wermyngton solvit xij*d*. MARRAM. Congnato rectoris ibidem, 3*s*. 4*d*. Greene gyngyr, w*i*th ye potte wey:—a libram et dimidiam.
Treakyl *and* ye potte wey:—dimidiam libram et dimidium quarteron.

[*f. 83v.*][4] *Tomas* Rowsby petit et habet [allocacionem pro sequentibus materiis. In primis] pro ultimo quarterio videlicet [ante (^d . . .) Michaelis festum] anno Ricardi abbatis xxiij finiente (pro carnibus), vj*s*. viij*d*. Item petit pro proximo quarterio sequente (pro carnibus), v*s*. viij*d*. Item petit pro medietate stipendii sui pro ij annis preteritis, xiij*s*. iiij*d*. Item petit x*s*. pro fratre Willelmo Marcam. Item petit ij*s*., v*s*., solutos dicto coquo pro festo Sancti Laurencii[5] scilicet anno xxij Ricardi abbatis. Item idem petit xvj*d*. pro festo Laurencii anno xxiij[6] Ricardi abbatis ultra iiij*s*. solutos dicto coquo per antea; item pro una medietate unius fryyng panne, vj*d*.; item propter heryng[7] *and* sowyng de Longge hedlonde, xiiij*d*.; item ij*s*. pro carnibus emptis pro famulis in aula minucionis per iij ebdomadas in Adventu; item pro (iiij) caponibus pro appellacione magna, viij*d*.; item pro carnibus grossis emptis pro jantaculo Gylberti pueri elemosinarii, iiij*d*.; item pro cena, iiij*d*., scilicet pro spada multonis et carne pro uno sew; item ij apron cloy'is [*sic*] pro ij festis sancti Laurencii preteritis, viij*d*.; item (pro) Willelmo Brasyar pro emendacione olle et uno axhe, ij*d*. Item petit xiiij*d*. pro fratre Willelmo Depyng' infirmo[8] (in controversia vel dubio.)

SUMMA xliiij*s*. x*d*., et est soluta, exceptis xiiij*d*., ut supra in dubiis.

T*h*omas Rowsby petit pro diversis carnibus emptis et oblitis in titulo precedente pro operariis, xj*d*. *ob*.; item pro stipendio suo, ij*s*. vj*d*., (solvit), pro primo quarterio de anno Ricardi abbatis xxiiij; item pro secundo quarterio, xx*d*.; item pro medietate vituli, ij*s*. viij*d*.[9]

In uno equo conducto de Willelmo Man per ij dies pro fratre Edmondo Lynne equitante propter ordinem sacerdocii 4 et 3 Idus Marcii[10] anno quo supra, scilicet 24 Ricardi abbatis, viij*d*.

---

[1] A blank space of 1 inch.
[3] His address was not inserted.
[4] Title and first line destroyed by damp.
[5] *10 Aug. 1460.*
[7] Harrowing.
[9] One inch left blank.

[2] Payments to Joan.

[6] *10 Aug. 1461.*
[8] A sick monk.
[10] *12 and 13 Mar. 1461/2.*

Necessaria. In solutis T*ome* Segraffe de Donyngton pro una roda et dimidia de tabulis quercinis ab eo emptis, xiiij*s*. viij*d*.

Oneratur a fratre Willelmo Melton quod uxor Jacobi solvet argentum vel piper.

Johannes Galantte solvit infra triduum post festum Purificacionis Beate Marie anno quo supra, ij*s*. v*d*.

[*f. 84r.*]¹

WILLELMUS CRAANE. Memorandum quod computatione [habita inter fratrem Willelmum Morton elemosinarium et] Willelmum Craane dictus Willelmus Craane [debet supradicto] elemosinario, in primis pro una acra j roda et dimidia terre ad le Parke Yaate de Burgo pro x annis, v*s*. x*d*.; item pro firma vaccarum duarum per iij annos, xviij*s*. (12); item pro iiij eskeppis brasii, ij*s*.; item ij*s*. ex mutuo. SUMMA. xxj*s*. x*d*.

Frater Willelmus Morton debet Willelmo Craane pro materiis subscriptis. In primis dicto Willelmo Crane per iij dies circa albos spinos imponendos, xij*d*.; item pro iij acris falcandis ad Fallam h*er*ne, xv*d*.; item [pro] medietate de Cock*s* holme falcanda, ij*s*. vj*d*.; item pro ij acris falcandis in Hamond medow, x*d*.; item pro iij acris et dimidia falcandis ad Mockehyl gappe, xvij*d*.; item pro longa forera falcanda, vj*d*.; item pro iiij quarteriis brasii de novo factis et cum renovacione iij quarteriorum brasii, ij*s*.; item pro uno canvasse, ij*s*.; item pro vij porcellis, iij*s*.

Omnibus computatis in crastino Ascencionis² Willelmus Craane debet fratri Willelmo Morton elemosinario, viij*s*. vj*d*., scilicet anno quo supra. Et Johanna uxor ejus debet xix*d*.; xij*d*.; et j porcum. Idem [*sic*] Johanna debet elemosinario pro ij quarteriis ordii dradge, 32*d*.³

Relicta T*ome* Derby solvit elemosinario in xviij die Februarii, xviij*d*., anno quo supra; et debet pro ij annis, iij*s*.

Johannes Barford solvit elemosinario xxij*d*. pro anno xxiij Ricardi abbatis.

[*f. 84v.*]⁴   *xxiiij*

RECEPTUM PRO PRATO DECIME RECTORIE MAXEY.⁵

In primis Johannes [Clyvr*e* (?)] solvit in lagena olei] ij*s*. vj*d*. et debet v*d*. *ob*. Item Ricardus Andrew de Marram solvit vj*s*. Item rector de Marram debet iiij*s*. Item Ricardus Smythe debet; inquiratur. Item Ricardus Morton de West Depyng' solvit vij*s*. Item Robertus Gedney per cariagium solvit xv*d*. Item Johannes Scherwyn de Depyng' solvit viij*s*. et debet iiij*s*., (solvit). [*In margin*] debet 4*s*., solvit. Johannes Bern*er*de solveret v*d*. *ob*. pro ij acris; inquiratur. T*omas* Cast*ur* pro

---

¹ First lines partly obliterated by damp.   ² *15 May 1461 or 28 May 1462.*
³ Two inches blank.   ⁴ Title and first line obliterated by damp.
⁵ In margin. *Debet* is written in the margin by the side of each entry save four.

prato prope Saxpole, iijs. iiijd. Johannes Clarke pro vij acris decime prati (d xviij) xxjd. et ij cocks feni, 4d. Item Willelmus Brian vs. pro decima prati, (solvit.) Item Stephanus Gardiner vjd. pro prato. Summa (d 42) 44s. vel xliiijs.

Memorandum quod Ricardus Honnyng debet fratri Willelmo Morton, vs.; item iijs. solutos Johanne Craane pro vij porcellis.

Nota. Johanna uxor Johannis Clerk de Maxsey debet fratri Willelmo Morton pro barly straw, vs. Require plus in secundo folio sequente.¹

Nota quod elemosinarius solvit ad festum Annunciacionis xlvjs. viijd. pro medietate decime.

In forincecis. In solutis uno laborario coligenti fimum ante diversa ostia tenantrie elemosinarii in Burgo ante adventum domini regis Edwardi,² iijd.; item in solutis ij carectariis pro cariagio dicti fimi extra villam per ij dies, vs. iiijd.; item dictis carectariis pro cariagio fimi de diversis locis super Chapel Row et alibi scilicet Cystur howus prima vice, ijs.

Custus in Burgo. In solutis Johanni Thacker de Hydur Owreton³ thackyng ubi Janyn et Ricardus Cowston manent per vij dies, ijs. xjd.; et servienti ei xxjd.; item supradictis operariis thackyng ij cotagia in Prestegate per xij dies et ryggyng ibidem similiter, viijs.

Frater Robertus Borowh. Custos sancte crucis⁴ recepit de elemo-sinario, ijs. ijd.

[f. 85r.] *Anno regni regis Edwardi post conquestum quarti primo, Ricardi abbatis xxiiij.*

Robertus Conquest. (Solvit in folio xvij precedente ad tale signum •IΛ•⁵) Item idem collector Robertus Conquest solvit alia vice videlicet per Symonem Taylour de Castur, vs. Item Willelmus Blogwyn solvit vjs. viijd. Item obstupavit vjs. viijd. pro bosco supervidendo, scilicet de Sutton pro stipendio suo per ij annos preteritos, videlicet annos xxij et xxiij. Item Johannes Yvisse solvit in Kal. Marcii⁶ anno quo supra, xvs. Item idem collector solvit per Robertum Mowncel, vijs.; item per Robertum Mowncel, vijs.; item per Tomam Rowelle, xviijs.; item per Willelmum Myller, vjs. viijd.; item per Willelmum Clerk le Nettardde⁷ ibidem, iijs. xjd.; item per Johannem Yvys, iijli. xiijs. iiijd.; et residuum condonatur, scilicet, plus quam xxviijs.

Item [solvit] pro Symone Taylour de Castur per manus Jacobi magistri sui anno Ricardi abbatis xxvo in festo Sancti Botulfi,⁸ vs. Item Robertus Conquest solvit pro Willelmo Wymysche de Castur, vs. et dictus Willelmus debet vs. Item [solvit] pro Johanne Lay de Castur, xijd. de redditu assise. Item memorandum de Johanne Rowelle, quo modo

---

¹ p. 159.   ² Visit to Peterborough by Edward IV.
³ Hither Orton or Orton Longueville, Hunts.
⁴ The warden of the altar of Holy Cross in the monastic church had a separate estate in the vill of Burgh.
⁵ See p. 126.   ⁶ *1 Mar. 1461/2.*   ⁷ Neat-herd.   ⁸ *17 June 1463.*

satisfecit pro debito suo, ut patet in quarto folio sequente.[1] Item Robertus Conquest solvit pro Roberto Mowncylle, vij*s*. per manus Johannis Coldwelle. Item T*omas* Myller de Alwalton solvit fratri Willelmo Morton pro dicto Roberto Mowncylle ut de precio unius albi geldyng' cum debili freno et cella.

[*f. 85v*.][2] In solutis [3 . . . con]ductis ad faciend*um* un*um* [4 . . . et came-ram] in coquina, ubi Henricus Palm*er* nuper manebat super Chapel row, per viij dies, ij*s*. viij*d*.; item viij*d*.; item eisdem per alios viij dies ibidem, (in aliis operibus,) ij*s*. viij*d*.; item viij*d*.; item eisdem per vij dies et dimidium ibidem splentyng' et faciendo ostia, scanna et emen-dando fenestras iij*s*. j*d*. *ob*.; item suo aprenticio per predictos (d x)xxiij dies et dimidium, nisi ij*s*., quia non potuit bene liborare [*sic*] propter infirmitatem.

MARRAM. Item dicto carpentario per 5 dies in opere de Marram, 4*d*., item xx*d*.; item xij*d*.; item (per) x dies idus May,[5] ij*s*.; item supradicto Johanni Hubbok pro factura magnarum portarum cum le wyndo*ur* nove grangie ibidem per v dies, 2*s*. 3*d*. *ob*.; item fabro, ut in secundo folio sequente;[6] item ij sarratoribus. (d In solutis Willelmo Rodg*er* et Johanni Bytam sclattyng ubi Johannes Merstlond manet super Chapel row per j diem et dimidium.)

[CHAPEL Row] In solutis Rogero Schyngle propter dawbyng' super Chapel row erga adventum Johannis Coldwel et Johannis Fullar ibidem continuando per xv dies, v*s*.; item Willelmo Palm*er* et aliis adiuvantibus supradictum Rogerum, iij*s*. ix*d*.; item in evacuacione unius latrine ibidem, et elargando eam, ij*s*.

MARRAM. Item predicto Rogero pro uno muro lapidio et fundamento unius grangie ibidem altitudinis iij pedum et in circuitu vj rode [*sic*] de novo facto in xiij diebus, capienti in die vj*d*., vj*s*. vj*d*.; et in terra rubia fodienda carianda adaquand' et preparanda pro supradicto muro lapideo; et item propter dawbyng tocius grangie ibidem, 2*s*. 8*d*.; item in solutis vj laborariis dawbyng ibidem per vij dies et dimidium, xl*s*.

In iiij stawnchons emptis, iiij*d*.

RECEPTA GRANGIE RECTORIE DE MAXSEY. In primis v quarteria et j eskeppa frumenti; item j quarterium et vij eskeppe ciliginis; item lxxvj ordei, item viij quarteria et iiij eskeppe de dradghe korne (quart' (d 8) 16*d*.) item iiij quarteria crappysse (quart' 4*d*.): item xiiij quarteria pisarum et ij eskeppe; item j quarterium avenarum; item propter le chaffe, iiij*s*.; item pro xv (15) carectatis barlistraw venditis, precium carectate, vij*d*., x*s*.; item x carectatis straminis in factura brasii, scilicet frumenti, ciliginis et ordei; item pro v carectatis straminis pisarum, iiij*s*. iiij*d*.

MEMORANDUM quod Ricardus Honnyng solvit xvj*s*. vj*d*. *ob*. pro

[1] See p. 161.
[3] Almost a whole line illegible through damp.
[4] About four words illegible.
[2] Heading obliterated by damp.
[5] *15 May*.
[6] p. 161.

trituracione de lxvj quarteriis iiij eskeppis frumenti, ciliginis ordii et pisarum.

Memorandum de Roberto Stoon de Thorney et cetera.

Memorandum quod Willelmus o sandle primo intravit ad festum Annunciacionis Beate Marie[1] anno Edwardi secundo. [*f. 86r., foot*] Iste Willelmus o sandle alias dictus Willelmus Tapyser intravit in scoppam elemosinarii iuxta ostium capelle Sancti T*home* Martiris ad Anunciacionem Beate Marie, ut antea.

[*f. 86r.*][2]

In solutis fratri T*ome* de Sancto Neoto [3   ] xx*s.* videlicet ad emendas vaccas propter seynggys [3 . . . Item dicto Tome] ij*s.* viij*d.* pro primo quarterio vicarie sue in choro, tamen inde condonavit vj*d.* ad vinum; item dicto fratri Tome pro iij quarteriis vicarie sue, (solvit) et equet.

[OXNEY] In solutis domino Willelmo Leyce*tur*, priori, pro mora sua post Pascha, xx*s.*, per manus fratris Johannis Glynton rece*ptoris*.
In solutis fratri Willelmo Stanford et fratri Johanni Crowland pro clericis suis, vj*s.* viij*d.*

[VINUM PRO CONVENTU]
In vino empto in festo Pasche de Nicholao Smythe pro conventu, videlicet iij lagenis et dimidia, iij*s.* vj*d.* (solvit.)

[SCHOLARES AD OXONIAM]
In solutis fratri Johanni Malden, ex precepto domini abbatis et prio[ris][4] iij*s.* de pensione scolarum ad solvendum pro camera et aliis consuetudinibus in collegio Cantuar*iensi* Oxonie, videlicet:—pro uno integro (anno) ad ultimum Pascha plenarie completo.

[DEBITA FRATRIS WILLELMI MORTON, ELEMOSINARII.]
Frater Willelmus Morton debet fratri Johanni Pychele xiij*s.* iiij*d.*, ex mituo; unde dictus Johannes recepit, iij*s.*; item iij*s.*; item 3*s.* 4*d.*; (d item j libram cere; (6*d.*)) item xx*d.*; ij*s.* viij*d.*, et equet, tamen dictus Johannes debet unam libram cere, vel vj*d.* Frater Willelmus Morton debet fratri Waltero xiij*s.* iiij*d.*, ex solucione Pasche, anno ut supra, unde solvit xiij*s.* iiij*d.*, et equet pro hac solucione. Frater Willelmus Morton debet fratri Johanni Glynton xiij*s.* iiij*d.* de solucione Pasche, anno quo supra, unde solvit ij nobilia, et equet. Frater Willelmus Morton debet fratri Georgio, vj*s.* viij*d.*, de solucione Pasche, anno ut supra, unde solvit, viij*d.*

SOLUCIO ELEMOSINARII PRO LE O AD FESTUM SANCTI JOHANNIS BAPTISTE, ANNO QUO SUPRA.
In primis dicto elemosinario vj*s.* viij*d.*; fratri Waltero [5   ]; fratri R*oberto* Lytington, vj*s.* viij*d.*, per Nicholaum; fratri Willelmo Bery, vj*s.* viij*d.* per seipsum, et (d thesaurario) fratri Nicholao, iij*s.* iiij*d.*

---

[1] *25 Mar.*
[3] Illegible through damp.
[4] The MS. reads pio.

[2] Title destroyed by damp.
[5] Blank space

[*f. 86v.*]¹

CALX. [In solutis Johanni Baker de Reyche pro uno fowdyr de calce] in officio, x [. . . item Johanni Baker de le Reyche] pro alio fowd*ur* cum cariagio 18*d.* Item dicto Johanni pro [duobus fowd*ur*] cum cariagio ad messuagium, ubi W*illelmus* Aldous nuper manebat in Hythegate (ᵈ xx*d.*) ij*s.* iiij*d.*

Memorandum de xxv*s.* iij*d.* receptis de Nicholao Smythe pro fratre suo T*homa* Smyth.

NOTA. Ricardus Honnyg' debet, ex mituo de elemosinario, v*s.*, anno quo supra ad festum Sancti Johannis Baptiste;² item ij quarteria ordii vel vj*s.* viij*d.*; item xviij*d.* solutos pro porcellis. Item idem Ricardus debet fratri Willelmo Morton, nuper³ elemosinario, pro vj quarteriis brasii, xv*s.*; unde dictus Ricardus solvet ad proximum Martymesse, vij*s.*; et ad festum Pasche sequent', viij*s.* Require in secundo folio precedente.⁴

TYLE. Johannes Bak*er* de Reyche recepit de elemosinario pro 12ᶜ bryke, 7*s.*; (unde in Cowgate vjᶜ.)

Tomas Gebon, natus in Wictofte in Holondia, recepit de elemosinario anno quo supra Dominica ante festum Apostolorum Petri et Pauli,⁵ ij*s.* et viij*d.*, preter victualia, et lectum; et hic vel modo elemosinarius debet dicto T*ome* xix*d.*; unde solvit ij*d.*; item 4*d.*; item 3*d.*; item Dominica ante festum Sancti Bartholomei⁶ omnibus computatis T*omas* Gebon debet elemosinario, vj*d.*⁷

SOLUCIO FRATRIS W*ILLELMI* MORTON PRO TUNICIS et pro anno Ricardi abbatis 24 finiente.⁸

In primis fratri Waltero W*ermington* x*s.*; item fratri Willelmo Morton, x*s.*; item fratri Johanni Pycheley, x*s.*; item fratri (ᵈ Johanni Ryalle, x*s.*;) Henrico Lynne, x*s.*; item fratri Nicholao, pro fratre Roberto Lydyngton, vj*s.* viij*d.*; (solvit) et equet.

(ᵈ Memorandum de galonbotel; item pyynte gowrd;) item de 40*d.* in expensis tempore sequestracionis.

Nota de xx elne [*sic*] et ij pedes [*sic*] de lynyn clothe; item in alia pecia iiij virgarum et plus.

Memorandum de reparacione facienda et ij carectatis spinarum, ubi Willelmus Aldo*us* fuit.

SAWYNG' for ye yat*s* atte Marram, etiam a wynde do*ur*.

B. MEMORANDUM propter emendar' [*sic*] clausuram ad hospitale.

C. Henricus Palm*er* debet de redditu xxvj*s.* viij*d.*; item pro Johanne filio suo, vj*s.* viij*d.*; item pro reparacione [⁹]; item x*li.* per indenturam.

---

¹ Title and first lines obliterated by damp.　　² *24 June 1462.*
³ Note the retirement of William Morton from the office of almoner.
⁴ See p. 156.　　⁵ *27 June 1462.*　　⁶ *22 Aug. 1462.*
⁷ Almost illegible.　　⁸ *1462.*　　⁹ Not stated.

A. Memorandum de thackyng' per Willelmum Gyl' ad hospitale (Marram) et Oxney per concilium Johannis Coope.

D. Nota de adquisicione unius levii pro Johanne Clerk de Wodcrofte, pro xxv*s*.

E. Memorandum de uno levio adquirendo contra Johannem Burges.

Loquendum est Johanni Schyngey, quia ipse loquitur contra Johannam in diversis locis.

[*f. 87r.*] *Anno regni regis Edwardi post conquestum* [. . . *et anno Ricardi abbatis*] *xxiv.*[1]

(4ᶜ latt*s*, 25ᶜ py*n*nys, 3 mill' nayl')[2] [   ] Byta*m* servienti dicto sclatt*er* per xix [   ]; (ᵈ item Willelmo Rodg*er* operante ubi Johannes Merstlonde manet super Chapel row per ij dies super coquinam ibidem, xij*d*.)

Memorandum de iij*s*. viij*d*. in obstupacione pro redditu, et dictus Willelmus Rodg*er* debet elemosinario; item Willelmo Rodg*er* facienti, videlicet plast*u*ryng' ij areas in ij cameris, ubi Willelmus Ald*ous* nuper manebat, cum uno serviente per iij dies, capientes in die viij*d*., ij*s*. Quere plus in folio proxime sequenti ad tale signum ☉[3]

Tʜᴏᴍᴀꜱ Cᴏᴘᴇʀ ʀᴇᴄᴇᴘɪᴛ ᴅᴇ ᴇʟᴇᴍᴏꜱɪɴᴀʀɪᴏ ᴘʀᴏ ᴏᴘᴇʀɪʙᴜꜱ, ᴜᴛ ꜱᴇϙᴜɪᴛᴜʀ: In primis pro cariagio feni ad hospitale de crofto in grangiam, scilicet xvij carectate ij*s*. iiij*d*.; item pro cariagio de crofto infra officium, videlicet vij carectate viij*d*.; item de tribus carectatis, una cum splent*s*, et ij cum stothysse alio meremio pro muris grangie ibidem, (ad Marram,)[2] xviij*d*.; item pro una carectata zabuli in Hythegate, iiij*d*.; et una carectata terre rubie, ij*d*.; item pro iiij eskeppis de peysgᶜodd*s* vj*d*.; item dicto To*me* Coper, cariando petras velutas emendando viam, per j diem, into Cokk*s* holme, xvj*d*.; item dicto To*me* cariando thacke per iij dies de Cokk*s* holme, videlicet ad officium vijᶜ; item ad messuagium infirmarii in Hythegate vijᶜ; item ad tria cotagia infirmarii ad M*a*rtyn brig 8ᶜ, iij*s*. vj*d*.

Fᴇꜱᴛᴜᴍ Sᴀɴᴄᴛɪ Lᴀᴜʀᴇɴᴄɪɪ.[4] In pane, servisia, j quarte mellis, (4*d*.;) quarteron piperis, (3*d*. *ob*.;) in croco, (4*d*.;) in j quarteron reysyngg*s* corans, (3*d*.;) clows, (3*d*.;) mac*s*, (3*d*.;) j quarteron sawnd*u*rs, (4*d*.;) iij libris amigdalarum, (9*d*.)

In 3 ferculis grossarum carnium, (9*d*.;) in vij caponibus, (xx*d*.;) in iij aucis, (xj*d*.;) in ij porcellis, (x*d*.;) in vij pulcinis, farsyd, (7*d*.;) in carne pro supradictis, ij*d*. *ob*.; in lacte, carne porc*ina* pro secundo potagio, vj*d*.; in carne cum le sew ad cenam v*d*.; item pro vij pulcinis, vij*d*., unde ij pulcini pro v stageriis.

[*f. 87v.*] *Anno regni regis Edwardi Quarti post conquestum secundo et* [*anno Ricardi abbatis*] *xxiiij.*[5]

Memorandum quod isti confratres commederunt cum priore anno suprascripto.

---

[1] Title and the first two lines almost obliterated by the damp.
[2] In the margin.   [3] See the special sign on p. 161.   [4] *10 Aug. 1462.*
[5] Title almost obliterated by the damp.

(^d Dominica), feria secunda, fratres Willelmus Ufford, T*omas* Seyn Nedde, Johannes Croyland; feria 3, Stan*ford*, Pycheley, Ufford (2),[1] Johannes B*ur*row, Spald*yng*; feria quinta, Frater Henricus Lynne.

Dominica secunda, elemosinarius, thesaurarius, camerarius, celerarius; feria 3, Lesyngham, Walm*ysford*, Lyderon, Baston, Nicholaus; feria 5, Pycheley (2), Ox*ford*, et 3 prior (2), Johannes Borowh (2).

Dominica 3, Morton (2), Notyngham (2), Malden (2), Ramsey (2), T*homas* Borow; feria secunda Baston (2), Sen Neede (2), feria quinta Baston (3), Seyneed[2] (3), Henricus Lynne (2), Melton.

Dominica quarta, Sacrista, frater Johannes Gentte; feria secunda, Pychele (3), Spaldyng (2), feria 3, Yoork; feria v, (B*ur*neham,) Walms-*ford*, Notyngam (3), Johannes Borow (3), Nicol[aus,] Johannes Croylande.

FABER. Robertus Stokton fecit elemosinario in primis, ferramenta pro grangia nova elemosinarii ad Marram, videlicet:—ij hopys, ij plat*s*, ij goions, j haspe, et ij stapill', ponderantes vij libras dimidiam, x*d. ob. q.*

J*ohannes* Wakyrle solvit xix*s*. viij*d.* pro Cathethwayte et alio pro anno ut supra, et debet vj*s*. viij*d.*, (solvit;) item x*d. ob.* de vetere debito.

Willelmus Sand*ur* solvit fratri Willelmo Morton pro omnibus debitis terrarum elemosinarii, et fecit eque pro anno 24 Ricardi Abbatis.

T*homas* Lambe, scissor et tenens elemosinarii super Sow*ter* row, solvit fratri Willelmo Morton elemosinario xx*d*., et debet pro [3   ] annis et [3   ] quarteriis.

[*f. 88r.*] [*Anno domini Ricardi abbatis*] *xxiiij, pridie Non. Septembri*[4]

[*Note in margin*] ☉[5] Vide in folio precedente de ista materia. In solutis [Johanni Hubbok carpentario operante in hythegate ubi] Willelmus Aldous nuper manebat, pro opere carpentrie per unum diem, videlicet in una gabula de le Thakkyd How*us* juxta le Brewerne ibidem, vj*d.*; item Willelmo Rodg*er* splentyng et dawbyng ibidem per 4 dies cum uno serviente per ij dies, ij*s*. vj*d*.[6]

Johanna Dykyl, serviens Johannis Wakyrle, debet elemosinario de redditu [7   ] Johannes Torolde, serviens Laurencii Toche, debet elemosinario de redditu [7   ].

[*f. 88v.*] [*Anno domini Ricardi abbatis xxv*].[4]

Memorandum quod Johannes Rowelle de Sutton solvit elemosinario per vices per recognicionem Roberti Conquest xxxiiij*s*.; item per reparacionem, videlicet faciendo et imponendo unum par de d*or* dern*s* ad Malyns place, et obturando aliud ostium ibidem, et faciendo aliud pro ostio stabuli in dominio per vj dies, ij*s*. Et sic dictus Johannes

[1] See above, p. 150, note 9.
[2] St. Neots.
[3] Number omitted.
[4] Title almost obliterated by the damp.
[5] Special sign, see above, p. 160.
[6] Three-quarters of this folio was left blank, and the following note was written at the foot.
[7] Amount not stated.

A 9832   M

Rowelle debet clare fratri Willelmo Morton nuper elemosinario xxxix*s*., unde solvit x quarteria ordei, precium quarterii ij*s*., xx*s*.; et debet 19*s*. solvendos ad proxima festa ventura, videlicet Michaelis et Martini,[1] per duas equales porciones, Johanne Gron*ger* uno fidejussore et T*homa* Rothewel alio fidejussore, levando dexteram manum in presencia Roberti Conquest, unde solverat x*s*. et debet ix*s*.; unde solverat, iiij*s*., unde 3 falsi denarii. Item solverat v*s*. et equet.

Johannes Corbette debet fratri Willelmo Morton, nuper elemosinario, redditum pro ij annis, videlicet per annum iij*s*. (ᵈ iv*d*.) (4*d*.), vj*d*. (8*d*.); unde solvit per reparacionem, iij*s*. Idem Johannes Corbette debet de vetere debito, xvj*d*. Idem Johannes Corbette debet vj*s*. ij*d*. de redditu assise pro T*homa* Warynsthynk, unde solvit, ut in uno quarterio et iiij eskeppis brasii, iij*s*. vj*d*. Item solvit, ut in precio unius vacce, vij*s*. ij*d*. Modo debet vj*d*. [*In margin*] Robertus M*orton* recepit brasium, nota quantum.

Johannes Yvisse debet fratri W*illelmo* M*orton*, nuper elemosinario vij marcas et iij*s*. iiij*d*. ultra certas pecunias de tempore Johannis Eyr'. ([*In margin*] Nota quod in oblivione hic pro 3 annis 4*s*. 6*d*. non computatis, videlicet 18*d*. per annum;) unde solvit ut in factura unius muri petrini, (scilicet ij rodas [*sic*] et dimidiam,) et alterius terrei unius camini in coquina (scilicet ij paria splen3at*s*) et alie parcelle cum cariagio iiij carectatarum cooperture de Brigmylle, vj*s*. viij*d*., unde solvit iij*li*. xiij*s*. iiij*d*., per Andream Fullar de Walmysford, et residuum condonatur.

[*f. 89r*.] [*Anno domini Ricardi abbatis vicesimo quinto*].[2]

Willelmus [³   vj*s*. viij*d*.] fratri Willelmo Morton nuper elemosinario, videlicet in dominica prima Quadragesime,[4] et debet iij*s*. iiij*d*. quos dictus Johannes solvet dominica medie Quadragesime proxime futura,[5] quod factum est et equet.

Johannes Smythe de Wodcrofte solvit fratri Willelmo Morton, xvij*s*. vi*d*., item xij*d*., in tribus (casiis), et obstupavit xviij*d*., quos dictus Johannes solvit domino de Wodcrofte pro redditu assiso pro iij annis, videlicet:—vj*d*. per annum; et notandum quod obstupavit annuatim sic per antea et quietus abiit.

Custus in Burgo. In solutis T*ome* Cowp*er* pro tribus carectatis terre rubie pro ryggyng' ad messuagium in Hythegate.[6]

Johannes Barford solvit xij*d*. pro iij acris in Stybbyngg*s*; item x*d*. de *Johanne* Barford.

Johannes Wygston solvit xviij*d*. pro iij acris, nuper in tenura T*ome* Derby et debet [⁷   ].

Frater Ricardus Harlton recepit de fratre Willelmo Morton, per manus Johannis Halden,[8] elemosinarii, 23*s*. 2*d*.; et neuter debet alteri.

---

[1] *29 Sept. and 11 Nov.*
[2] Title destroyed by damp.
[3] Illegible.
[4] *27 Feb. 1463.*
[5] *20 Mar. 1463.*
[6] One half folio blank.
[7] Amount not stated.
[8] Note the name of the new almoner.

[*f. 89v.*] [*Anno domini Ricardi abbatis vicesimo quinto*].[1]

NOTA. Rogerus Yoong' et Dalad sawar' deliberabunt fratri Willelmo Morton [le juyn poleyn] in octabis Sancti Johannis Baptiste et ad hoc Johannes Dalad' fecit fidem levando dexteram manum Rogero Yong et fratri Willelmo Morton. Et ita fecerunt tarde, tamen [cetera desunt].

NOTA. Robertus Morton recepit ix*s*. de fratre Willelmo Morton ad emendum vj porcos in foro in crastino Sancti Johannis Baptiste.[2] Item alia vice recepit perantea de dicto fratre ad reparandum ad Fleete Hargate vj*s*. viij*d.* Item dictus Robertus recepit x*s*. de fratre Willelmo Morton propter brasium emendum[3].

Memorandum quod anno Ricardi abbatis 28 [*sic*] incipiente frater Willelmus Morton debet *Roberto* Morton in primis per talliam [cetera desunt].

[*f. 90r.*] [*Anno regni regis Edwardi quarti post conquestum secundo et anno domini Ricardi abbatis vicesimo quinto.*][4]

Advincule Sancti Petri[5] . . ..

Thomas Rowsby [[6] . . . coquus], vel pet*ere* de fratre Willelmo Morton infirmario[7] alicujus racione neque Johannes Palle nisi vj*d.*, quia dictus infirmarius solvit fratri Willelmo Ramsey celerario et Johanni Glendon v*d.* de stipendio dicti Johannis Palle. Item dictus celerarius obstupavit iiij*d.* solvendos dicto infirmario pro uno dressyng knyffe empto per infirmarium pro coquina.

FORINCECA RECEPTA. In receptis pro uno vetere (eque) lavacro ponderante iiij libras dimidiam et iiij parvis candelabris factis xx*d.*; item pro sex plat*er*sse et ij potyg*er*sse de veteri plectro ponderantibus xv libras ij*s*. vj*d.*

A.[8] In (*d* mutacione) vasorum empcione, videlicet:—ix plat*er*sse, vij potyg*er*sse, iiij sawc*er*sse ponderantes xxvj libras, precium libre iij*d.*, vij*s*.

(*d* Garcio coquine Johannes de Irlonde recepit de fratre Willelmo Morton, infirmario, iiij*d.* in presencia et in schoppa Roberti Lowthe in sartrina in Vigilia Assumpcionis Beate Marie[9] anno quo supra.)

B. In ij candelabris novis emptis ponderantibus fere v quarterons, viij*d.*

In solutis domino Johanni Reede (cantori) capellano et cantori, vj*d.*; In solutis pro iiij paribus de hengyll' (et stok*s*) pro hatchysse et fenestris ponderantibus vj libras, xj*d.*

[PLECTRUM] Memorandum quod frater Willelmus Morton emit xliij libras de novo plectro, precium x*s*. ix*d.*, unde erant j magnus plato*er*

---

[1] Title obliterated as before mentioned.
[2] *25 June.*
[3] Half this folio has been left blank.
[4] Title obliterated.   [5] *1463(?).*   [6] Illegible.
[7] Note William Morton's new office as infirmarer.
[8] The compiler has inserted the letters A and B before the two following paragraphs.
[9] *14 Aug.*

sive o charg*er*, xij comyn plat*er*s, xij potig*er*s, viij sawcers pro camera
sua; item j saltte salar *et* j d*r*inckyngpotte.

In solutis pro ix platarsse vij potyg*er*sse et iiij^or sawc*er*sse, omnia nova
[*sic*] ponder*antibus* xxviij libras, precium vij*s*. vij*d*., hoc est precium de
una libra, iij*d. q.*

[*f. 90v.*] Anno¹ *regni regis Edwardi quarti post conquestum* [   ]. *In*²
festo Assumpcionis Beate Marie Virginis.

Frater Willelmus Walmysford debet fratri Willelmo Morton pro officio
refectorij ij*s*. de redditu ad officium elemosinarie; item ij*s*. ad infir-
mariam; item pro ij staminis novis, ij*s*. vj*d*.; item xvj*d*. solutos barbitonsori. Item debet pro spectaculis, vj*d*.; item pro (^d clave ostii capelle
Sancti Laurencii;) item pro coperculo nucis nig*ri*³ videlicet ij ownc*s* et
dimidia ponder*antibus* [cetera desunt]

Vicarius de Stanggrownde, dominus Johannes Bevelle; item dominus
Stephanus Grobbe, natus in Maxsey.

Memorandum quod isti confratres co*m*mederunt cum priore, scilicet
fratre W*illelmo* Leycet*ur*, in cursu suo apud Oxney anno regni regis,
ut supra, In primis:—

DOMINICA infra Octavas Assumpcionis Beate Marie⁴:—fratres Willelmus Offord, Malden, Glynton, Ramsey; feria secunda:—Johannes
Baston, Willelmus Spald*ing*; feria v:—frater Johannes Borow senior,
frater Willelmus Depyng*e* senior.

Dominica secunda:—Frater Johannes Hylle, Frater Johannes Mors;
feria secunda:—fratres Willelmus Melton, Morton, Glynton (2); feria
tercia:—nemo; feria quinta:—(^d Willelmus Melton) Johannes Burnham, Walmysford, Willelmus Borowh senior, Johannes Pychele, Willelmus Ramsey (2); feria sexta:—Melton, Morton, Willelmus B*u*rrowh
senior, Johannes Ryalle, Glynton, Willelmus Ramsey.

In festo Nativitatis:—Prior cum officiariis suis.

Dominica tercia:—Fratres Robertus Notyngam, Johannes Baston (2);
feria secunda:—Willelmus Morton (2), Johannes Glynton (3); feria
3:—Ufford (2); feria 4:—frater Willelmus Morton; feria quinta:—
Johannes Borow senior, Henricus Lynne, Glynton (4).

Dominica 4:—Willelmus Offord (3), Pycheley (2); feria secunda:—
Oxford, Johannes Borow senior, Willelmus Ramsey, Willelmus Kydde
[   ]; feria 5:—Notingam, Johannes Borow senior, Hylle, Baston.

[*f. 91r.*] Anno regni⁵ *regis Edwardi Quarti post conquestum iij*° [   ]
In solutis ^r   ].

*Anno 26 Ricardi Abbatis.*⁶
In solutis dicto Priori prout supra.

---

¹ Almost indecipherable.   ² *15 Aug. 1463*; this is written in the margin.
³ The MS. may be read mgⁱ, i.e. nutmeg.   ⁴ *21 Aug. 1463.*
⁵ Title partially obliterated.   ⁶ *1463-4.*

Anno 26 dicti Abbatis. Memorandum quod isti commederunt cum priore.[1]

DOMINICA INFRA OCTAVAS ASSUMPCIONIS MARIE[2]:—Frater Johannes Pychele, Willelmus Ufforde, Henricus Lyn; feria secunda:—Willelmus Morton, Willelmus Stawnforde, Johannes Baston; feria 3:—Willelmus Spal*dyng*, Edmundus Lynne.[3]

DOMINICA SECUNDA:—Notyngam, Johannes Burg senior, Nicholaus, Ryppon; feria secunda:—Johannes Burg senior (2), Bery; feria 3:—Ryppon (2); feria v:—York, Willelmus Ufford (2), Willelmus Depyng*e* senior.

DOMINICA TERCIA:—Pychele (2), Oxford; feria secunda:—Lydygton, Notyngam (2); feria 3:—Nemo; feria 5:—Stanford (2), Lynne, Ryal, Baston (2), Byry (2).

DOMINICA 4:—Walm*ysford*, Ufford (3), Ryppon (3), Thornb*ery*;[4] feria secunda:—Willelmus Depyng (2), Nicholaus (2), Croyland, (d Ed*mundus* Lynne); feria 3:—Mor, Notynggam, Johannes Burrow senior (3), Edm*undus* Lynne (2).

Anno domini Ricardi abbatis 29.[5]

PET*UR*BRYGHE FEYR*E*[6]

In solutis pro uno pari de bodi*trayts* et alio pari de for*trayts*, xij*d.*; item pro j bac rope et iiij *trayte* pypys, iiij*d.*; item pro iiij paribus plow *trayts* et ij capistris canbinis, vij*d.*; item pro vj carte clowt^s, vj*d.*; item

---

[1] Note the names of the prior, obedientiaries, and monks in holy orders of the monastery, who were present in the chapter-house on 18 July 1471, at the beginning of the proceedings for the election of a successor to Richard Ashton the abbot, who had resigned his abbacy. The members of the convent then present nominated the following senior monks to undertake on their behalf any necessary business in connexion with the election. Their names were Henry Lynn, William Wansford, John Hill, and Nicholas Overton. The election was held in the chapter-house on 22 July 1471, the abbot elected being William de Ramsey. The following is the list of the prior and 37 monks of the said monastery, of the order and rule of St. Benedict expressly professed therein and in holy orders, forming and acting as the convent congregated as a chapter with no absentees, none other being entitled to a voice in the election of abbot. [See *The Book of Roger Bird*, ff. 70*v.* and 71, printed Dugdale, *Monasticon*, i. 363, n.b.]

Dom John Malden, prior and president; John York, an elder in the farmery; William Wansford, the same; William Burgh (see below); Robert Liddington; Robert Nottingham, sub-prior; John Pytchley, warden of Oxney; Richard Oxford, sub-almoner; John Burgh, precentor; William Spalding, infirmarer; Henry Lynn by William Burgh, his proxy; John Hall, cellarer; John Hill, third claustral prior; John Baston, chamberlain; Nicholas Overton, master of the works and pittancer; John Glinton, sacrist; William Bury, fourth claustral prior; William Ramsey, receiver and seneschal (steward); Robert Burgh, scholar; John Croyland, refectorer (or fraterer); John Ripon, great almoner; Thomas Burgh, hostiller (guest master); John Morys; John Gent, scholar; Edmund Lynn; George Burgh, sub-sacrist; John Tylly; Thomas London, warden of the altar of holy cross; Gilbert Holbeach; John Lincoln; Thomas Pinchbeck; William Newark; John Croyland, scholar; Richard Moulton, prior's chaplain; William Holbeach; Geoffrey Lynn; and William Shelford. It will be noted that the majority of the monks come from towns and villages in the eastern counties. [2] *19 Aug. 1464.*

[3] A monk not mentioned previously. [4] Another new monk.

[5] *1466-7.*

[6] Peterborough Bridge Fair held on or about the feast of St. Matthew the Apostle under a charter of Henry VI dated 1439. See Gunton, 51-52, 165-6. The date of the fair this year would be in the week commencing 21 Sept. 1466.

c clowte nayl', ij*d*.; item pro c horsschonayl', ij*d*. *ob*.; item in j pectine equino.[1]

[*f. 91v.*] ... Item W. Cook xvj*s*. viij*d*. . . . .[2]

SUTTON[3] . . . . . . [   ] Morton [   ] Roberti Conquest[4] [   ] per iiij^or annos v marcas viij*d*. Item idem [debet] fratri Willelmo M*o*rton de tempore Johannis Eyr*e* colle*c*toris ibidem (^d xvi*s*. x*d*.), xxvj*s*. x*d*., preter lookesylv*er*, unde solvit per manus sui tenentis, in presencia senescalli et receptoris, xxxiij*s*. iiij*d*.

Anno Ricardi abbatis xxvij° incipiente.[5]

Item Johannes Geffron solvit supradicto Willelmo Morton, per manus fratris Johannis Glynton residuum exceptis lookesylv*er* et wynesylv*er* condonatis et [*cetera desunt*].

Anno Ricardi abbatis 29.[6]

EYE. FALCACIO, FENACIO ET LIGACIO IN EST MEDOW DE EYE.
In solutis iij falcatoribus per iij dies falcando [*sic*] ibidem, 4*s*. 6*d*.; item quinque fenatoribus per j diem et dimidium, cuilibet, iij*d*. in die, xxij*d*. *ob*.

(^d Cast*ur* Cowrte tenta ad Peykyrc 13 Kal. Julii)[7] iij Nonas Julii.[8] Robertus Morton mituatus est de fratre Willelmo Morton magnam securim et xxiiij ova.[9]

[*f. 92r.*][10] In solutis Johanni Hubboc carpentario pro vij peciis [   ] meremii emptis de Roberto Morton viij*d*.; item in solutis dicto car-pentario pro emendacione nove hovelle ad Oxney, una nova scala ad optimum de novo facta, tribus aliis scalis emendatis, splenting in parvo stabulo ibidem, factura de le splent yaate cum emendacione ibidem; item in solutis dicto carpentario pro factura de quatuor (4) lectis unde ij in dormitorio et alii ij subtus in volta,[11] et emendacione de le syl*our* cum evacuacione fimi ibidem supra erga adventum domini Abbatis et prioris ante festum Nativitatis Beate Marie[12] per 4 dies, xij*d*.; item dicto carpentario pro tribus raft*ers* factis [13   ]; item dicto carpentario pro scapulacione meremii scilicet:—xj peciarum quercinarum et factura unius cheer' [*sic*] columbarii ibidem per v dies xv*d*.; in tabulis quercinis emptis ad idem ij*s*.; in clavis, iij*d*.; in meremio propter le nete rak. [*cetera desunt*.][14]

---

[1] Horse comb.
[2] Three or four lines at the top of this folio were obliterated by damp.
[3] In the margin.
[4] Towards the end of the manuscript the damage done by the damp at the head of each page is greater.
[5] *1464.*   [6] *1466-7.*
[7] *19 June.* Half a folio left blank for the record of this court which was not inserted.
[8] This note is entered at the foot of the folio.
[9] A large axe and 24 eggs.
[10] The first three lines are effaced by the damp.
[11] An interesting reference to the building presumably of the grange at Oxney.
[12] *8 Sept.*   [13] Left blank.   [14] The lower half of this folio is left blank.

[*f. 92v.*]¹ pro

haspys et stapyl', iij*d*. [........ .....] equorum, xiij*d*.; item
pro schoyng', secundo anno, iiij*d*.; item pro [ ] cum pertinenciis,
xvij*d*.; item pro uno wymbyl, j*d*.; item pro fly propter le clock, iiij*d*.;
item ferrura unius bokette, ij*d*.; item pro lock*s* et keyys, xv*d*.; item pro
iij halt*ur* ryngg*s*, iiij*d*.; item pro vj bokyll' pro womb roopys, ij*d*.;
item pro ij t*ur*rett*s*, ij*d*.

ANNO SECUNDO. 3 togwyttys ferreis, renovacione nove [*sic*] vomeris,
poyntyng plowhyrn*s*, ij stroppis stelyng, secur' potte, heyngyll', hopyng
kart nave, emendacione ij strok*s* for schoyng', 3*s*. 4*d*.

NOTA. OXNEY, *Anno Ricardi abbatis xxvij*.²

STAWNFORD FEYRS. In solutis pro iiij colersse equinis, ij*s*. iiij*d*.; in
solutis pro vj*c* grossis spyk*s*, ij*s*.; item viij*c* mydylspik*s*, xx*d*.; item
latte nayle, x*c*, xj*d*. (*d* item pro uno walette, in exspensis, x*d*.) item ij*c*
clowtnayl', iij*d*. item xij cartte clowtysse, xj*d*.; in j walette v*d*., in
expensis x*d*.

STER'BRIGE FEYR':—In solutis pro xviij virgis pro clerico, coquo,
gardinario, videlicet:—must*er*de de velers, xviij*s*.; item pro garcione
coquine iiij virge, ij*s*. viij*d*.; item alia virga, viij*d*.; item iiij warppe de
salso lynghe, (4*s*. 8*d*.) viij*d*.; item pro tribus ber'lepys, ij*s*. viij*d*.; item
pro ij magn' scotyll', vj*d*.; item pro ij parvis scotyll', cum ij precedentibus; in uno senevect',³ xiiij*d*.; item in cold weyht'⁴ pro veteri et novo
auro ponderando, xij*d*.; item pro vj tribulis⁵ et vangis non ferratis,
vj*d*.; item in exspensis pro cariagio, vj*d*.; item pro le schoyng' unius
equi, iij*d*.

BURROW FER'⁶ In j bolte sek clothe, iiij*s*. vj*d*.; in tribus p*er*sorsse, j*d*.;
in j libra piperis, xiij*d*.; in j quarterio saffron, ij*s*. viij*d*. Item [ ]*s*.

[*f. 93r.*] FRUMENTUM⁷ [⁸]

CILIGO [⁸] quarteria et [ ] T*ome* Smyth, ij eskeppe; Johanni
Reffson, (*d* ij) 4 busselli; Johanni Browne seniori, iiij busselli, xx*d*.;
Johanni Browne juniori, ij busselli, x*d*.; T*ome* Browne, ij busselli;
Johanni Wyllyamson, ij busselli, (solvit;) Margarete Olyv*er*, j bussellus
[⁹], 5*s*. 8*d*.

ORDIUM¹⁰ [ ]

PISE [⁸] quarteria et [ ] eskeppe, unde Johanni Alyn iiij eskeppe,
xvj*d*.; item Tome Fylyp, viij eskeppe; item uxore sue iiij eskeppe; item
Willelmo Colyn, [ ]; item Margar*ete* Wynwyc, [ ]; item Johanni
Deynys ij eskeppe, 8*d*.; item T*ome* Brown, ij eskeppe, 8*d*., (solvit);
item T*ome* Smyth, iij eskeppe, xij*d*.; item Johanni Reffson, ij eskeppe.

---

¹ Three or four lines at the head of this folio are partially effaced by damp.
² *1464–5*. ³ Query *cenevecterio*, a barrow? ⁴ Gold weights.
⁵ Six forks and shovels not bound with iron. ⁶ Peterborough Fair.
⁷ No title at the heading of this folio. ⁸ Quantity not entered.
⁹ Total not entered. ¹⁰ No entries.

Anno domini Ricardi abbatis xxix in ebdomada Pasche[1]

Frater Willelmus Morton et frater Johannes Pychele computaverunt pro ij annis, scilicet anno 27 et anno 28 Ricardi Abbatis et supradictus frater Johannes Pychele infirmarius debet fratri Willelmo Morton[2] gardiano de Oxney, pro prefatis ij annis ij*s*. iiij*d*., (solvit); et Robertus Morton, xv*d*. quos solvit.

[*f. 93v.*] Mutacio[3] annorum regni regis Henrici Sexti post conquestum in (pre)vigilia Sancti Egidii.[4] Item mutacio annorum domini Ricardi Ayheston abbatis in die Sancti Michaelis archangeli.[5]

Oxney.[6]

SUTTON. Receptum ibidem 12*li*. 19*s*. 4*d*.

Unde idem sacrista solvit x*s*.; item iij*s*. per viam obstupacionis de redditu assise pro j messuagio in le Marketstede solvendo Alredo Rolston, ultra ij*s*., solutos dicto Alredo per prefatum gardianum per viam obstupacionis de redditu assise unius cotagii in Howgate de Burgo solvendo supradicto gardiano pro ij annis iam preteritis. Item sacrista scilicet Johannes G[entte] solvit x*s*. per Robertum Morton; item per dictum Robertum x*s*.[7]

[8] Frater Willelmus Burrowh nuper celerarius debet fratri Willelmo Morton, gardiano de Oxney, xxxv*s*.; unde solvit v*s*. x*d*.; item unam unciam cerici nigri, x*d*. Item solvit vij*s*. et iiij*d*. Modo debet xx*s*.

[*f. 94r.*] [*Written on a small piece of vellum stitched into the end of the book*] Willelmus Morton elemosinarius solvit sacriste per Johannem Pye, ij*s*. iij*d*.; item per Willelmum Bernerde seniorem, iij*s*. iiij*d*.; item per Robertum Samon, xx*d*.; item per Johannem Penel, xxij*d*.; (pro j quarterio pis') item per Johannem Barnard seniorem, xx*d*.; item per Johannem Crosse de Weryngton, iij*s*. vj*d*.; item per Robertum Palmer de Maxey, vij*s*. de redditu; item per Saram Esex, iij*s*. iiij*d*.; item per Willelmum Reede, bocher, iiij*s*.; item vij eskeppas ciliginis precii ij*s*. xj*d*.; item xiiij quarteria pisarum (ex parte abbatis) xxvij*s*.; item iiij quarteria iiij bussellos precium quarterii, ij*s*. iij*d*., x*s*. vj*d*.; item per Magistrum Ricardum Dyclon, xx*s*.; item vij creests, precium xij*d*.; item xvij*d*. pro Johanne Pye propter iiij eskeppas brasii; item x*d*. pro ij eskeppis brasii de predicto Johanne Pye; item per Johannem Penel pro carectata straminis ordei vj*d*.; item ut in uno magno cabyl de canabo et uno hooke ferreo; item per Johannem Penel pro j quarterio ordei, ij*s*.; item ij*s*. vj*d*. per Willelmum Depynge. Idem sacrista reddit, ut in decima grangie de Paston [cetera desunt].

[*f. 94v.*] Johanni Egiston xx*d*. in factura grangie; item eidem xij*d*. pro cariagio thac; item viij*d*. splents. Amen.

---

[1] *29 Mar. 1467.*
[2] Note that William Morton has been transferred from his office as Infirmarer to the wardenship of Oxney.
[3] On two small slips attached to this folio.   [4] *30 Aug.*   [5] *29 Sept.*
[6] Written on folio 93*v*. itself.
[7] Half a page left blank.
[8] It is difficult to determine of which account the following entries are a continuation.

1 Prima pecia longitudinis vj pedum vj inchis, latitudinis ix pedum viij inchis dim' xj burdys [*sic*].[1]

7 Alia pecia longitudinis vj pedum, latitudinis xij pedum ix inchis xiij burdis iij^{xx} xvj pedum 6 inchis.

3 Alia pecia longitudinis xij pedum, latitudinis vij pedum x inchis, x tabule iiij^{xx} xviij pedum.

2 Alia pecia longitudinis xj pedum viij inchis, latitudinis viij pedum 9 inchis, x tabule iiij^{xx} xix pedum 6 inchis.

6 Alia pecia longitudinis viij pedum, latitudinis x pedum et ij inchys xij tabule iiij^{xx} iiij pedum.

5 Alia pecia longitudinis vij pedum, latitudinis xj pedum ij inchys xij tabule iij^{xx} xix pedum 4 inchys.

4 Alia pecia longitudinis v pedum 7 inchis, latitudinis xij pedum, xiij tabule iij^{xx} ix pedum 4 inchis.

8 Alia pecia longitudinis viij pedum latitudinis xij pedum, xiiij tabule v^{xx} xij pedum summa xxxiij^{xx} xv pedum.

⎰Pecia Willelmi Walmysford continet vj^{xx} xij pedes
⎱Pecia fraccina continet v^{xx} x pedes.

ij pecie pro leggs xxvj pedum.

Pecia pro monyell continet xl pedum vj inchis. In 2 magnis thel [*sic*] 28 pedes; in 4 theel 27 pedes.

[FINIS]

---

[1] The following measurements were written out of order upside down. To whom this timber belonged is not clear. Possibly it was used in the building of the barn for which John Egiston received the amounts mentioned in the note at the head of this scrap of vellum.

SELECT GLOSSARY

ABBREVIATIONS

A.   *Two Fifteenth Century Cookery Books*, ed. T. Austin (Early English Text Society, 1888)—where recipes or other references to items of food may be found.
O.E.D. *The Oxford English Dictionary.*
S.   L. F. Salzman, *Building in England* (Oxford, 1952).

I. LATIN

Classical Latin words (when used in their classical sense) are given in italics; words marked with an asterisk are not to be found either in Lewis and Short's *Latin Dictionary* or in J. H. Baxter and C. Johnson's *Medieval Latin Word-List* (Oxford, 1934). Some page references are supplied for words whose meaning is doubtful. The nom. sing. of nouns is given except where otherwise stated. Some minor variants of spelling (*-ng-* for *-g-* as in *tingnum*; *-e* and *-ae*; *c* and *t*, &c.) have been ignored: the form given is that most commonly used by Morton. Most of the trade-names are identified in the index.

accomodo: lend.
affurator: assessor of fines.
allecia: herring.
allocacio: allowance (in accounts).
alloco: allow.
alnetum: alder-grove.
amigdala, -um: almond (cf. A. index).
anguilla: eel.
apprecio: purchase.
*aprina: brawn (cf. p. 96, A. index, and O.E.D. s.v. 'brawn').
arconium: mow, stack, heap of corn (cf. English glossary and above, p. 11; also O.E.D., s.v. 'mow').
arculum: hoop (part of bell-ringing mechanism, cf. p. 5).
armilasa: cloak.
arra: earnest-money, pledge.
*assabilis: roastable.
assacio, asso: roast.
auca: goose.
*aurora: literally 'dawn': here a 'glory' (ornament of gilded rays) or something of the kind, 132.

barbitonsor: barber.
bigarius: carter.
boveria, -aria: byre.
bussellus: bushel.
butirum: butter.

*calcetum: causeway.
caminus: chimney (commonly both hearth, etc., and chimney, S. 97 ff.).
camisia: shirt.
*canabinus, canbinus: hempen.
canabus, canapeum: hemp.
*cansella: chancel.
capistrum: halter.
carecta: cart.
carectata: cart-load.

Carniprivium: Lent (specifically applied to Septuagesima or Sexagesima Sunday or to the first days of Lent).
caseum or *-eus*, casium, -ius: cheese.[1]
catena: chain.
cenevecterium: barrow (cf. S. 353).
cerura (for *serura*): lock.
cervisia (*servisia*): beer.
ciminum: cumin.
cista, sista: box.
coclearium: spoon.
*cofnus (coffinus): leap, basket.
colerium, colerum: horse-collar.
conduco: hire.
cooperio, coperio; coopertura, coopertura: thatch or roof (S. 223 ff.).
coopertor: thatcher or roofer.
*copbularius: probably a cobbler[2], 17.
copula: couple (see English Glossary, s.v. 'copil').
cortex: bark.
cresto: fix ridge-pieces.
*cribracio: sieving (from *cribro*, sieve).
crocus: saffron.
*curialiter (texti): curiously (woven), 18.
*curialibus (abl. pl.): probably dainties ('fit for a lord'), 13.
*cuvella, (*cupula*): a small vat.

dagarrum: dagger.
decorticatus: deprived of bark, peeled.
dentrix: pike.
duodena: dozen.

eskeppa: skep, basket, dry measure.
exhennium (*xenium*): present.

falcacio: mowing.
falco: mow.
familia: household.
famulus: servant.
femoralia: breeches.

---

[1] The nom. 'casium' occurs on p. 9; 'caseus' and 'casius' were the normal forms.
[2] Or 'coupler' = leash-maker or the like.

*fenator: haymaker (cf. Ducange, *Glossarium*, s.v.).
ferculum: dish (food).
ferrura (equorum): shoeing (of horses).
fimus, -um: dung, manure.
firma: farm (see pp. xxxiii–xxxiv).
firmarius: farmer.
focale: fuel.
fodicio: digging.
forera: headland.
fossatum: ditch.
*fraccinus, fraxsinus (*fraxinus*): ash-tree.
frena: reins.
*fricsum (frixum): something fried.
friscus: fresh, uncultivated, fallow.
furca: fork.
furfur: bran.
*furnicio (furnatio): baking, 9, 10.

gabulum: gable.
gallina: chicken, hen.
garba: sheaf (of corn).
gardinum: garden.
generosus: gentleman, servant of good birth.
glutinum: glue.
grossus: groat (4*d.*).
in grosso: in sum, in toto.
gunfus: hook of a hinge.
gutter, gutera: gutter, drain.

harpicacio: harrowing.
*hercie (nom. pl.) et reddicio: possibly candles and candle wax, 2–3.[1]
histrio: player, minstrel.
*hovellum, ofuellum: hovel, shed (apparently back-formation from M.E. hovel).
hustrina: *see* ustrina.

*informarius: informer, 27.

jantaculum (*jentaculum*): breakfast.
juvenca: heifer.

lagena: gallon.
latamus, lathamus, latomus: mason (cf. S. 1 ff.).
*levii (gen.): *unidentified*, 160 (bis).[2]
libero: deliver, pay.
ligacio: binding.
linia tela: linen cloth.
litera: litter, straw.
locio: washing.

manutergium, *manitergium: towel.
minucio: bloodletting.

ex mituo, mutuo: mutually.
multo: sheep, mutton.

naparia: cloth, linen, etc.
nobile: noble (gold coin).
nundine: fair.

obstupacio: stopping (of money or payment).
obstupo: stop (as above).
obturo: stop up, close.
ocrie, *ocree*: boots (possibly also gaiters).
olla: pot, jar.

*paleum (*palea*): chaff.
parlura: parlour.
pastellus: pasty.[3]
pecia: piece, plank.
penula: hood.
pertica: perch (measure of land).
pessulus, -um: bolt.
petra libera; *-veluta: freestone; *unidentified* type of stone (S. 124, 138).
*pilio (pilium): cap.
piper: pepper.
pisa: pea.
pissis (*piscis*): fish.
*pista: *unidentified* (food: possibly flour or something like potted meat), 96.
pistura: grinding.
polex (pollex): inch.
porcellus: little pig.
porrettum: leek.
potagium: pottage, broth.
potus: drink.
*prebenda:[4] provender.
procurasia: procuration.
providencia: provisions.
pulcinus: chicken.

quisquiliae: waste (equivalent of 'chyppys' on p. 36).

racemus: raisin.
*ramelle (*ramale*): branches, lopping.
reddicio: see hercie.
redditus assise, assisus: assised, i.e. customary, fixed rent.
roda: rod or rood (measure of land or of wood, cf. *O.E.D.* s.v. 'rood').
*ryggo: ridge (cf. English Glossary, s.v. 'ryggyng').

s- *often for* c- (as in senevecterium, sera, sitacio, etc.).
*sagina, *sagine (abl., p. 23): fat, lard.
sagum: say (woollen material).

---

[1] The context establishes that these are candles or quantities of candle wax. 'Hercie' may be connected with 'hercia', a candle-frame, but that exact meaning is impossible here; 'reddicio' might be drippings or candle-ends, melted for re-use, or 'renders', gifts or payments in wax.
[2] The context suggests some kind of legal instrument. The reading 'lenii' is not impossible.
[3] For medieval pasties see *The Goodman of Paris*, transl. E. Power (London, 1928), index, s.v. 'Pasty'.   [4] The MS. reads 'prebend'' (f. 22r), possibly for 'prebend*atu*'.

salciamentum: sauce.
sarculacio: hoeing.
sarracio: sawing.
sarro: saw.
sartrina: sartry, tailor's shop or workroom.
scafa, scapha: bowl.
scannum: bench or stool.
scapulacio: trimming.
schoppa, scoppa: shop.
sella, *cella: saddle.
sellio: measure of ploughland.
serviens: servant, serjeant.
*singulum (*cingulum*): belt.
situla: bucket, vessel.
solarium: solar, upper room (S. 197).
sorbilis: fresh (of eggs).
*spada multonis (spalda): shoulder of mutton.
species: spice.[1]
staminum: linsey-woolsey.
stannum = roda (measure of wood).
staurum: stock, store.
*stipo, *stupo: stop (cf. obstupo).
stipula, stramen: straw.
*stupacio: stopping.
superlectulum: coverlet.
sutor: cobbler.

tabula: board, plank.
tallia, *-ium: tally (see p. xli).
tasca: task-work, piece-work.
tegulator: tiler.
*tegulatum: tiling.

terra rubia: red earth (for mortar: cf. S. 152).
textor: weaver.
thegule rubie: red tiles, i.e. bricks (cf. S. 140 ff., and English Glossary, s.v. 'ty' ').
tignum: beam, spar.
*tinccio: dyeing.
traccio, traxcio: drawing (p. 132; but the meaning on p. 74 is apparently 'constructing': cf. English Glossary, s.v. 'drawyng').
*tracina: probably a back-formation from 'trason' (see English Glossary, s.v. 'tracynsse'), 19, 88, 91, 101, etc.
trituracio: threshing.
triturator: thresher.
trituro: thresh.
*tustata (barba-): *unidentified*, 17, 19, 28, 34, 37, 46.[2]

ulna: ell.
uncia: ounce.
ustrina, hustrina: kiln (cf. S. 151).

vanga: spade.
ventilabrum: winnowing-fork.
ventilacio: winnowing.
virga: yard.
vitulinus: veal.
vomer: ploughshare.

zabulum (*sabulum*): sand.
zinsiber (*zingiber*): ginger.

II. ENGLISH

All words, unless otherwise stated, are to be found in the *O.E.D.*, under the first modern form shown; the exceptions are marked with a dagger. Words for which this book gives an earlier date than those found in *O.E.D.* are marked with an asterisk. Page references are supplied for both. Plurals are sometimes given by Morton with an -*s*, sometimes with -*sse*; the latter variants have normally been ignored in this glossary.

annes: anise, aniseed.
†apron cloy'is: *unidentified* (some kind of food), 154.
†assepys, ayhepecs: ash-piece(s) or planks (cf. S. 251), 3, 97.
axstre: ax-tree, axle-tree (of a wheel).

bac, bak hows: bake house.
*bac rope: back-rope, backband (of a horse), 165.
balc: balk (of land).
balk; *tey balk: balk, beam; tie-beam, 123.
*barelle sope: barrel soap (soap packed in a barrel), 6.

*baston, bast, roope, rop, rope, roppe: bast rope (e.g. for scaffolding: cf. S. 319), 31, 34–5, 109, etc.
†bat*ur*yng: battering (bevelling prior to piercing slates, S. 234), 2.
beemfyllyng, bemfillyng, bemfyllyng: beamfilling (daubing of the wattling between the beams in making a plaster wall, S. 157).
beenke: bink, bench.
berkar: barker, tanner.
ber' lepys: bearleap(s), carrying basket.
blanket, -tte: blanket (white or undyed woollen stuff for clothing).

[1] For the use of spices in medieval cooking (of which there is much evidence in Morton's book) see W. E. Mead, *The English Medieval Feast* (London, 1931), pp. 72–8.

[2] The word occurs exclusively in the nickname of John the carpenter 'cum barba tustata'. Ducange gives 'tusto' as meaning to beat or shake; alternatively, it might be connected with *tostus*, past part. of *torreo*—hence 'scorched-beard'. Neither gives a very clear sense; and the reading seems in every case clearly to be 'tustata' not 'tuftata', tufted, which would be more intelligible. The reading 'tuscata' is possible. But it is hard enough at the best of times to reconstruct a private nickname.

bocher: butcher.
bodghe, bodgy: budge (fur).
bodi-trayts: *see* **trayts**.
bokyll': buckle.
bolte, boltys: bolt(s), roll of cloth (of fixed length).
borowschyp: borrowship, borrowage (surety).
boturasse: buttress.
brenlet: brandlet. brandreth, tripod (for cooking).
†**brennyngs**: *unidentified* (evidently a type of calf), 39.
brodboske: broad busk (linen fabric: broad as in broad cloth).
burdenayl': *see* **nails**.
*****buttyng**: abutting, 26.

cabulle, cabyl, -ylle: cable.
cade, cadys: cade(s), cask.
carbage: *see* **garbage**.
carte clowts, cartte clowtysse: cart-clout(s) (iron plate to protect axle-tree).
cesteron: cistern.
chyppisse, chyppys: chip(s), shaving(s).
chyppysse & offalle: chips and offal, shavings and scraps (of wood).
clowes, clows: cloves.
clowt leddur: clout-leather (for mending shoes).
clowtnayle: *see* **nails**.
comin, comon, comyn: common.
copil, -ille, coplys, copyl: couple, pair of rafters (S. 210 ff.).
copur pens: copper pennies.[1]
copynng, copyyng: coping (placing a coping or crest on top of a wall to throw off rain: cf. S. 89), 101, 104, 119.
cowle: cowl (a large vessel for water, etc.).
crappys: crap(s) (probably buckwheat).
crokys: crook(s), hook (here probably the iron hooks on which a door hangs).

dame: dam (of mill stream).
darns, derns, dernys; dor'-; -lyntel', -ll': durn(s), doorpost, framework of a door; door durns; durn lintel.
doocer: dosser (ornamental cloth or hanging).
dradge, dradghe korne: dredge, dredge corn (mixed corn, especially oats and barley).
draffe: draff, refuse.
†**drawyng'**: apparently in the sense of constructing (cf. Latin Glossary, s.v. 'traccio'), 80.
*****drawyng & strawyng**: drawing and strawing (straightening and preparing

straw for thatching, S. 224 f.), 99, 109, 128.

estrische bords, -burds, est strisch burde: estrich or Baltic boards (S. 245).
evysse borde: eaves-boards.

faanysse, fanysse: vane(s), weathercock (cf. S. 235 f.).
farsyd, farssyd: farced, stuffed, spiced.
Fastyng gong': Fastingong, Shrove Tuesday.
ferne: fern (verne), pulley or windlass (S. 324).
flaket: flacket, flask.
*****fly (propter le clock)**: fly (speed regulating device in a clock), 167.[2]
fodder, fodour, fodowrs, fodur, fodyr, -sse, foodur, fowdur, fowdyr: fother, load (here generally of lime; a fother of lead was about a ton, S. 122).
fortrayts: *see* **trayts**.
fowel: presumably fuel, 2.
fowyng: fow(ing), clean, cleanse.
frayl, freyl: frail (basket for figs and raisins; hence a measure).
frese: frieze (coarse woollen cloth).
froste nayle: *see* **nails**.
froyse: froise (a kind of omelette or pancake).
fryturs: fritters (cf. A. index and pp. 73–4).
fu: *unidentified* (certainly food, possibly offal), 151.
fumerel, -lle, fymerell': femerell, smoke vent or louvre (S. 219 ff.).
*****furyng**: furring (nailing on extra pieces of timber, S. 305 and n. 8), 2.
fyhesce, fysche: fish.

galyngale: galingale (cypress root).
garbage, carbage: garbage, giblets (A. index, and pp. 9, 72).
*****garthe web, -bbe**: garth-web, girth-web (material for saddle-girth), 34, 79, 117, 124.
goions, goiowne: gudgeon(s), metal pivot.
govylle, govyl mow: *see* **mow**.
gowrd: gourd (bottle or cup).
greyns: grains of Paradise (A. index).
groncell': groundsel, ground sill (timber foundation, ground-plate).
*****guttur bords, -pecs**: gutter-boards (S. 266), 2.

haache, hache, hatche, hatchysse: hatch(es), small gate.
*****hagoday**: haggaday, ring (handle for raising latch on a door, S. 299), 111.
hallyng: halling, tapestry or painted cloth.

---

[1] Not in the modern sense—there were no copper coins in fifteenth-century England. These were probably forged silver pennies made of copper with a fine coating of silver.

[2] The earliest reference given in *O.E.D.* (s.v. 'fly', sb.² 5b) for this meaning is 1599. But in the later Middle Ages the use of the fly (fan or wheel) as a speed-regulating device was certainly known—especially, from the late fourteenth century, in the striking-mechanism (J. D. Robertson, *The Evolution of Clockwork*, London, 1931, pp. 10 ff.).

halywatur stooppe: holy-water stop, stoup.

har syffe: hair-sieve.

*__**hasty peysyn**__*: hasty peas (early peas), 145.

*__**haukyd ster'**__*: hawked, spotted, streaked steer, 6.

hedpense: head-pence, poll tax.

*__**hedstock**__*: headstock (apparently the main beam in any construction, especially the thick beam from which a bell was hung), 92.

henglis, heyngl', heynglys, heyngyll': hingle, hinge (cf. S. 297).

herdlys, herdyll', hyrdl', hyrdyl: hurdle(s) (for scaffolding, etc., S. 320).

hopys: hoop(s).

hurtyrsse: hurter(s) (shoulder of axle or strengthening piece on it).

†**incete**: part of a roof, probably a gable (cf. 'inschydes', gables, S. 213), 99.

†**ja(a)le**: evidently a liquid measure, 21, 108.

†**jaale sylver, jalez**: *unidentified* (a payment of some kind, possibly connected with the abbey jail), 28, 151.

*__**jaggs**__*: jag(s), load (of hay), 101, 123, 132, 142.

jardyns: jordan almonds.

†**jawge**: *unidentified* (some kind of food: 'sewhe vel jawge'), 103, 122.

*__**jybbe**__*: jib, pulley, 109.[1]

karse: kersey (coarse, narrow stuff, perhaps originally from Kersey, Suffolk).

kart nave: probably nave or hub of a cart wheel, 167.

*__**katt'**__*: possibly catch(es), 34.

*__**kochowrs**__*: coucher(s), possibly for couch (a table cloth), 88.

kydds;† kydder; kyddyng: kid(s), faggot; maker of faggots, 97; binding faggots.

lathe, lathys, lat, -s, latt, latte, latts lattys: lath (S. 240–1: see also *nails* and *pins*).

lechis: leach(es) (slice of meat or dish of sliced meat and other ingredients).

ledgs, leggs: ledge (of a door).

leepysse, lepe, lepys; lepfulle: leap, basket; basketful (cf. p. 36, where about 25 leaps are equivalent to a cartload; cf. also S. 354).

†**lookesylver**: payment in commutation of Christmas food rent, 166.[2]

lover, loversse: louver(s), smoke-vent (S. 219 ff.).

lymmys (barow-): probably limbs (legs and handles) of a wheelbarrow, 16.

lyne pynnys: see *pins*.

lynghe: ling.

lyng' rope: *see* **wody roope**.

lyr', blac offe lyr': black of lyre (a kind of cloth, originally from Lire in Brabant).

lytster: litster, dyer.

macs: mace.

*__**mantyll', mantylpese**__*: mantel-piece (i.e. mantel-tree: cf. S. 101–2), 19, 34.

measure: †**knockyd-**, *__**strikyd, strikyn**__*: straiked, stricken measure (level, as opposed to heaped), 10, 15.

mette yardys: meteyard(s), measuring (or measured) yard (cf. S. 506).

*__**meyse**__*: mease (measure for herrings), 8.

mokeforc: muck-fork, dung-fork.

monyell: monial, mullion.

mow; govil, govyl, -lle -: mow, heap of corn; *either* gavel (unbound corn) *or* gavel corn (i.e. corn put aside to pay gavel, tax, rent or dues: cf. O.E.D. s.v. 'gavel', sb.[2], 1 and sb.[1], 3).

musterde de velers: musterdevillers (mixed grey woollen cloth, originally from Montivilliers, Normandy).

nails (see also *pins*, **spiks**): *__**burdenayl'**__*: board nail(s) (S. 306), 64.

*__**clowtenal', -nayl', clowtnayl', -le**__*: clout nail(s) (flat-headed nail for nailing iron to wood, S. 311–12), 36, 149, etc.

*__**froste nayl'**__*: frost nail(s) (nail in shoe— here horseshoe—to prevent slipping in frosty weather), 80, 106.

lat, lathe, latte, latthysse nal', nayl', nayll': lathnail(s) (for roofing, S. 310).

†**splent, splynt, -e, -yng, *stowryng vel splentyng'**,[3] **nal', nayl', -ys, nayll'**: splint, stowering nails, stud-nail(s), 36, 89, 117, 131, 135.

†**nerfis ad le schafte**: possibly nerves (in the sense of thongs or fetters) for the shaft of a church tower, 5.[4]

nete rak: neat, cattle rack (frame to hold fodder, like a manger).

notmug': nutmeg.

offalle: *see* **chyppysse**.

orgeyse: orgays, organ ling (fish).

---

[1] The context 'jybbe sive le ferne' leaves no doubt about the meaning, although the O.E.D. gives no reference for this kind of jib before 1764 (and then as the projecting arm of a crane).

[2] Cf. N. Neilson, *Customary Rents* (Oxford Studies in Social and Legal History, ed. P. Vinogradoff, ii, 1919), pp. 30–2.

[3] 'Stowryng vel splentyng' nayle' (p. 36) seems to indicate the identity of the two kinds, which is suggested by Mr. Salzman (p. 307).

[4] For this sense of shaft (which seems to be demanded by the context), see O.E.D., s.v. 'shaft', sb.[2] 4d (the definition given is 'spire', but the extracts quoted suggest a broader meaning, i.e. any kind of tower).

paale: pale (stake) or paling.

parsur, persorsse: piercer(s) (awl or the like, S. 345).

†penikydds, peny-: evidently a pennyworth of kids or faggots (cf. especially pp. 113–14), 81, 86, 97, 113–14.

pentes, -sse, pentysse: pentice, penthouse.

pestel (porci): pestle (probably ham or haunch of pig).

peytrell': peitrel (breast-plate of a horse).

pins: †lathe, lat, -tt, -tte, pynns, pynnys: lath-nails (q.v.), 2, 18, 51, 118, 136, 141, 142.

lyne pynnys: lin-pin(s), linch-pin.

*sclatte pynnys: slate-pins (S. 234–5), 141.

plegghe: pledge.

plowhyrns: plough-iron(s) (any iron part of plough).

plowtrayts: see trayts.

polen, poleyn: pulley (S. 323 ff.).

potel, -ell, -elle: pottle, half-gallon.

*potiger, potigers, potygersse: pottinger(s), porringer, 20, 164.

potyngthac: see thatch.

poynts: point(s) (fastening of cord in clothes, equivalent to modern button).

purlyn: purlin (beam supporting rafters, S. 198, 213 ff., and see diagram facing p. 196).

pyckesse, pykax: pickaxe.

*quernehowse: quern-house (for grinding corn), 3.

rabbyttyng, rabyttyng: rabbeting (making rabbets or grooves, or fitting boards together by means of a rabbet).

rak, -kke: see nete rak.

reedyng': redding (red ochre).

reysyngg', -s, reysyngs, corans, of Corawnse, of Corinth, korawns: raisins of Corinth, currants.

rostyng el: roasting eel.

*ryggyng: ridging (laying straw for thatching, S. 224; or making the ridge of a roof), 16, 99, 123–4, etc.

ryyng: reeing (cleaning and sifting winnowed corn).

salette: sallet, headpiece (in armour).

sappe latts: sap lath(s) (laths of the outer, sappy wood of oak, and possibly also laths made of deal, S. 240–1, 248).

*sawndurs: saunders, Alexanders (horseparsley), 6, 160.

schafte: see nerfis.

*sclat, sclatte, sclatts; sclatter, -arsse; *sclattyng; †sclatts bastard; *sclatte hows, -howsysse: slate(s), 2, etc.;

slater(s); slating, 2, etc.; slate(s) bastard (S. 233), 109; slate house(s) (house with slate roof), 51, 61.

scotyll': scuttle, basket.

sek clothe: sackcloth.

sew, sewhe: sew, pottage, broth (A. index).

sewtte: suet.

†seynggys: unidentified (possibly a proper name), 158.

snac', snatchys: snatch(es), hasp, catch or fastening (for door or window, S. 299).

somyrsse; somurpese; somurtre: summer, wall-plate (S. 197 ff.); summerpiece; summer-tree.

soorte, sorte: sort (measure or weight of figs and raisins).

sowdur: solder.

†sowlebacs: probably sole base, i.e. sill, 3, 19.

*sowsydde; *sowsyng': soused (pickled); sousing, 23, 43.

sparrs, sparrys, sperr, sperris, spertys, speyr, -rr': spar(s) or speer (screen, cf. p. 45 and S. 260).

sperlyng: sparling (fish).

midil, midyl, mydyl, spiks, spyk', spyks, spyx: middle spike(s) (general purpose nails, S. 304 f.).

splent, splents: splint (stake in wattle wall).

*splentyng, splyntyng: splinting (constructing with splints or laths), 55, 96, 110, 128, 161, 166.

†sprotte: either sprot, sprat (fish) or (as seems more likely from the context) a weapon or piece of armour, possibly a dagger (not in O.E.D.), 140.

srobbe, srubb': shrub, scrubwood.

stapill', stapyl': staple.

*steel', stel': stile (vertical bar of wooden framing—here rung of ladder), 64.

stoks: stock(s)—but in what sense uncertain (always in association with hinges; possibly stock locks).

stothysse: stud(s) (upright post in wattle house, S. 197, 206, etc.).

strayl': strail, blanket.

straxsyll: unidentified (a timber piece in the mechanism of a water-mill), 72.

sylour: cellar.[1]

†taylfeete, taylfets: apparently short pieces of wood attached to the feet of rafters: equivalent to timber for 'furyng'' (q.v. and cf. p. 2), 2, 118.

*teturyng: tethering, 123.

*teynturyng: tentering (stretching cloth after it has been milled), 133.

thac, thacke, thak; -cker; -kkyd; -ckyng, -kkyng; potyngthac, -ak: thack, thatch (thatch or any kind of roofing, S.

---

[1] The entry on p. 166 ('emendacione de le sylour cum evacuacione fimi ibidem') demands this interpretation, although the form itself rather suggests a celure, a canopy or bedhanging.

223 ff.);[1] thatcher, roofer; thatched; thatching; possibly poting thatch, 9, 43, 46, 107.[2]

thect': possibly thatch, 2.

*theel, thel: theal, plank, 169.

think, thynk, tink (Bacons-, Malyns-, etc.): possibly thing in the sense of possession.[3]

thylle hors: thill-horse (shaft horse or wheeler in a team).

*togwyttys: tugwithy (-ies) (a withy to attach the swingle-tree to head of plough, cart, etc.), 167.

toppe, -is, -ys: top(s), basket (of figs and raisins in *O.E.D.*, but here of fuel: cf. p. 74).

†tracynsse, trasyn: trason(s), joist (cross-beam between summers, S. 215, 520; cf. 'transom' in *O.E.D.*), 52, 74.

travysse: travis(es) (shoeing shed) or traverse (screen)—probably the latter, 19.

trayts; †trayte pypys; †bodi trayts; †fortrayts; †plow trayts: trace(s), 149, 165.

trowh, trowhe: trough.

*tumberrelle: tumbrel (counterpoise beam for raising well-bucket, 95).

turretts: torret(s) (ring, e.g. in horse's harness, through which reins pass: cf. S. 303).

tyl', tyle (*red or walling*); **walletyl'**: tile(s), brick (red brick) (S. 140 ff., 144).

tylds, tyyld, tyylde: tild(s), joint (normally each of four cuts into which a quarter of beef may be divided; here used also of pork).

undur settyng: underpinning (especially of timber house, S. 202 and n.).

valyng, wallyng: walling.

vaumpeyyng: vamping (shoes).

*vivysse: vives, glanders (cf. pp. 34, 37–8 and nn.).

†walheschysse, walsche: walsh(es), lean-to (*English Dialect Dictionary* gives 'walsh' as occurring in Lincs.; the context confirms this interpretation), 15, 80, 105.

walleplaate, walleplate, walleplats, walplate, walplatis, walplats: wall-plate(s) (S. 197 ff.).

warppe: warp (quantity of fish—usually four).

*webbe (plumbi): web, sheet (of lead), 36, 130.

*wody roope (baste sive lyng' rope): presumably woody, fibrous rope (the gloss identifies it with bast rope, q.v., and 'lyng' ' rope, which cannot be identified), 34.[4]

womb roopys: womb-rope(s) (belly-band of rope).

*wyche: wych-elm, 2, 4.[5]

wyffyrsse, wyfrysse, wyfurs; †wyfurbems; †wyfur pecs: wiver(s) (long beam of wood), 2, 51, 86.

wymbyl: wimble (gimlet, S. 345).

wynbems: wind-beam(s) (collar beam of roof, S. 211).

*wynde dour, wyndour: wind-door, windore, window or shutters (S. 256 ff.), 157, 159.

wyndyng, -ggs: winding(s) (of iron; coiled metal).

†wynesylver: rent in commutation of labour performed in vineyard, 166.[6]

y-: often for modern *g-* or *th-*.

---

[1] Mr. Salzman points out (p. 225) that the common phrase 'c thac' normally means a hundredweight of thatch; but the entry on p. 129 above ('cccc garbas de thacke'—cf. also p. 119) suggests a possible alternative rendering—a hundred sheaves of thatch.

[2] 'Potyngthac' is a mystery. It might be connected with *English Dialect Dictionary*, 'pote', 16: 'a broad piece of wood used by thatchers to open old thatch and thrust in the new straw'—in which case it would seem to be 'poting', i.e. 'poking thatch', new thatch used to repair defects in old.

[3] Bacon's think and Malyn's think were clearly small holdings which had at one time belonged to men of those names (pp. 48, 65, 125–6; and 'Malyns place', p. 161). For field names ending in ME. *thing* in Northants., see J. E. B. Gover, A. Mawer, and F. M. Stenton, *The Place-Names of Northamptonshire* (Cambridge, 1933), p. 270.

[4] 'Lyng' ' looks like 'ling', heather; bast rope was fibrous and woody, but seems hardly likely to have been made of heather (more recently it has been made of lime-wood—of which 'ling' ' might just possibly be a corruption, though an unlikely one—but it seems doubtful if it was made of lime in Morton's day).
Mr. Salzman has pointed out to me that the fact that 'wody roope' was glossed by Morton suggests that the phrase was a very local one.

[5] *O.E.D.* gives no reference earlier than 1626, but the *Promptorium Parvulorum* (*c.* 1440) gives the equivalence wych=ulmus.

[6] Neilson, op. cit., pp. 58–9.

INDEX OF PLACES AND PERSONS

All places are in Northamptonshire unless otherwise stated. Minor names in Peterborough (except those of well-defined hamlets) will be found under 'Peterborough', and other minor names, when they can be certainly identified, under the towns and villages where they occur. Cross-references are given except for those in Peterborough.

The label 'abbot' or 'monk' after a name indicates an abbot or monk of Peterborough Abbey.

Surnames at this date were still fluid, and the same man may be described either by his trade (e.g. Thomas Coke) or by his family name (Thomas Roceby). All the references in such a case are collected under the surname most commonly used with cross-references from the aliases. Trade names not given in this Index will be found in the Index of Subjects, under 'Trades'.

Doubtful identifications have been avoided where possible; but they are sometimes indicated by a cross-reference in brackets, e.g. Beyl . . . (cf. Bocher).

An asterisk denotes more than one mention to the page; a dagger, that the word or trade name is to be found in the glossary.

A

Abingdon, Abyngdon (Berks.), 108.

Abthorp, Abthorppe, see Apethorpe.

Acre, Acon (Palestine), 47.

Adam, John, 94.

Agas, see Sewale.

Ailsworth, Eyl'worthe, Eylesworth, 58n, 105.

Aldous, Aldows, William, 143, 149, 152, 159–61.

Aldwinkle, Aldewynkille, Alwyncle, Alwynkyl, 22, 27*, 62.

Almoner's Lane, see Warmington.

Alnwick, William, bishop of Lincoln, xii–xvii.

Alownton, John (cobbler), 98, 127.

Alwalton, Alownton (Hunts.), xx, 89, 107, 109, 116, 157; ferry at, 83*.

Alwarde, J., 49; W., 50.

Alwyncle, Alwynkyl, see Aldwinkle.

Alyn, John, 167.

Amerose, John, 135.

Andrew, abbot, xx.

Andrew, Richard, 155.

Apethorpe, Abthorp, Abthorppe, Apthorp, 103, 108, 109.

Archar, John, 127.

Armeston, Richard, 58.

Arthorne, William, 79.

Ashton, Ayheston, Ayston, Richard, monk, abbot, xiii–xvii, xviii, xln, *and passim*; register of, xi.

Aspschaw, Aspeschawhe, Asppeschaw, John (slater) 73, 74, 79, 84, 103, 110, 118*, 120, 121, 123; payments to,
52, 74; repairs done by, 66, 73*, 105, 106*, 117, 119, 120*, 125; John, his son, 66, 73, 106, 125.

Asselyn, Thomas (carpenter), 87.

Austhorp, Austhorppe, Austorp, Austorppe, Awsthorp, Margaret, 127; Robert, 53, 109; William (clerk), 42, 64, 65.

Avenam, John, 63.

Ay, John, 64; Richard, 52; Richard, son of John (almoner's servant), xxxin, 64*; Thomas (clerk), 59, 94, 146.

Ayheston, Ayston, see Ashton.

Ayleton, J., 50.

Aylston, John, 87, 102.

B

Baate, Bate, Richard, 50*, 91, 150.

Baconthink, Baconthynk, Bakonsthynk see Sutton.

Bacster, Baxster, alias Coke, Cooke, Pybaker, John (baker), 13, 64, 82, 83 (cf. Baker).

Bacyl, Bakyl, Ralph, 26, 50.

Baker, John, 111, 159; Robert, 145 (cf. Bacster).

Bakon, Thomas, vicar of Maxey, xxxiv, 43–45, 58, 59, 97, 117*, 139.

Balle, John, 53, 89; John, senior, 18; Margaret, 90, 92, 133; Thomas, 3, 7, 49; his wife, 7.

Baly, Bayly, John (almoner's servant), xxxin, xlii, 39; Thomas, 4.

Barba tustata, Johannes cum, see Bradbyry.

Barbur, Alice, 118*, 127; John, 81; John (leach), 98, 113; Peter, 22, 46; Richard, 76, 118; William, 85, 101.

Barford, Barforde, John, 94, 110, 117, 130, 155, 162.

Barkbe, Richard (magister), 58.

Barker, Hugh, 18; Richard, 144; Thomas, 126; *see also* Berkar.

Barnack, Bernak, xxxvii*n*, 51, 116.

Barnack, Bernak, John, monk, 42.

Barnard, Bernard, Bernarde, Bernerde, Jankyn, 78; his brother, 78; John, 15, 16, 34, 86, 97, 155; John, junior, 35, 36; John, senior, 35, 168; John, of Paston, 36; John, brother of William, 35; William, 36; William, of Gunthorpe, 78; William, junior, 35, 36, 38, 47; William, senior, 35, 36, 168.

Barnard's, Barnax Cross, *see* Peterborough.

Barnwell, Barnewel, Barnewelle, Bernewelle, Bernwelle, John, 56, 66, 87, 90, 116, 117, 127, 132*.

Basse, Basset, Thomas, 4, 5.

Baston, John, monk, 22, 33, 145, 150–2, 161*, 164*, 165*, chamberlain, 165*n*.

Batche, Batteche, William (slater), 141, 149.

Bate, *see* Baate.

Bawnce, Bawns, Henry, 28*; Robert (clerk), 26.

Baxster, *see* Bacster.

Bayly, *see* Baly.

Been, Beene, John, 60, 119, 126; Margaret, 138.

Belamy, John, junior, 17, 24; John, son of William, 95*, 119; William, 57*, 79, 85, 95, 129, 131.

Belcyse, Robert, 120; his wife, 120.

Belle, Davy, 52; (? Davy), 72.

Belsize, Belasyse, manor of, 1.

Benedict, abbot, xx.

Benet, Benette, John (cooper), 49, 123, 128; his son, 123.

Benetholde, *see* Sutton.

Bentle, William, 78.

†Berkar, Janyn, 132, 153; *and see* Fusȝarde, Janyn; *see also* Barker.

Bernak, *see* Barnack.

Bernard, Bernarde, Bernerde, *see* Barnard.

Bernewelle, Bernwelle, *see* Barnwell.

Bernylle, John (clerk), 118, 139.

Bery, *see* Bury.

Bevelle, John, vicar of Stanground, 164.

Beyche, 140.

Beyl, Beyld, Beylde, John (thresher), 11, 16, 37*, *and see* John; John (butcher), xxxv, 6, 26, 60*, 71*, 72, 77, 78, 83

(cf. Bocher); John, junior, 38; John, of Walton, 35, 36; John, alias Wryhete, 22, 38; Robert, alias Wryte, 11; Thomas, 11*, 15*, 16, 56*; Thomas of Walton, 36, 78; William (butcher), 123, 129, 138.

Bird, Roger, *see Subject Index under* Book.

Bisley, Bysle, Bysley, Bysly, Richard, monk, 22*, 75, 81, 82, 89*, 93, 102, 105, 115, 121, 129, 131, 152.

Bladdesmythe, Bladesmyth, Bladesmythe, Bladsmyth, Richard, 101, 102, 113, 127, 138, 140.

Blogwyn, William, custodian of Sutton Wood, 24, 48, 105, 121*, 126*, 156*.

Blome, Richard, 53.

Bloreheath (Staffs.), battle of, 77*n*.

Bocher, John, 62 (cf. Beyl).

Bolton, John (clerk), 17, 26, 53.

Boman, John, 110.

Bondfeld (probably in Peterborough), 127.

Borough, Borow, Borowh, Borowhe, Borrow, Burrough, Burrow, Burrowh, Burrowhe (Peterborough), George, monk, subsacrist, 165*n*, *and see* George; Henry, monk, 107, 131; John, monk, 25, 75, 88, 89, 98, 100, 102, 113, 115, 150, 161*, steward, 23, master of the works, 97, 113, 115, precentor, 165*n*; John, junior, monk, 137, possibly warden of the Lady Chapel, 78*; John, senior, monk, xv, 151, 164, 165*; Robert, monk, 145, 165*n*, warden of the altar of Holy Cross, 156*; Thomas, monk, 145, 150, 161, hostiller, 165*n*; William, monk, xiv, xv, xvii*, 88, 165*n*, steward, xvii, 53, 54*n*, sacrist, xliv, 69, 75, 81, 89, 111*, 143, cellarer, 168; sister of, 58; William, senior, monk, 164*.

Borowbrig, Burbryg, Burowhbrig, Burrowbrig, Thomas, 109, 138*, 144, 146.

Boswelle, John, 138, 140, 143*; Robert, junior, brother of John, 138; Robert, senior, 138.

Botolph Bridge, Botilbrige, Botylbrige (Hunts.), 32*.

Bowyar, Bowyȝar, William, 82, 83, 124, 127.

Boydyl, Boydylle, Richard, son of William Wryhte (carpenter), 100*.

Boys, Boysse, Thomas, 35, 49, 111.

Bradbyry, John, sometimes 'cum barba tustata' (carpenter), 17*, 19, 28, 30, 34, 37, 45, 46, 65, 79.

Brasier, Brasyar, Brasyer, William, 41, 78, 154; Emma, wife of, 40, 41.

Brevitor, John (monastic servant), 94.
Brewster, William, 29*, 46, 131, 138.
Brian, William, 156.
Brig, Brigg, Bryg', Brygghe, Bryghe, Richard, 35, 53; Robert (carpenter), 58, 62, 65*, 77, 114; provides timber, 72, 73, 97; repairs done by, 52, 53, 74*, 80, 86, 88, 95*, 96, 100, 107, 110.
Brigman, John, 3.
Brigmylle, Brigmylle holme, see Sutton.
Brodleg', John, 146.
Broke, John, 58.
Bronham, see Burnham.
Brow, John, 150.
Browhe, Thomas, 120*.
Brown, Browne, Davy (mercer), 111, 115; his wife, 107; H., 50; John, 53; John, junior, 167; John, senior, 167; Thomas, 167*.
Browny, John (monastic servant), 16, 22, 36, 42; Richard (monastic servant), 91*.
Bryg', Brygghe, Bryghe, see Brig.
Brygmille, Brygmylle, see Sutton.
Budde, William (chaplain), 128*.
Bunghe, John (magister), 44.
Burbroke, John, 4.
Burbryg, see Peterborough Bridge.
Burges, John, 36–38, 89, 160; John, senior, 78, 79; John, son of Richard, 78; Richard, 78, 153.
Burgus, see Peterborough.
Burle, Burley, John (fuller), 101, 104, 109, 114, 115, 127, 131, 138, 140.
Burnham, Bronham, Burnam, Burneham, John, monk, xivn, 36, 75, 132, 145, 151, 161, 164, master of the works, 22n, cellarer, 22, 40n, infirmarer, 40, refectorer, 89, 124.
Burowbryg, Burowhbrig, Burrowbrig, see Borowbrig; Peterborough Bridge.
Burrough, Burrow, Burrowh, Burrowhe, see Borough.
Burton, Peter (carpenter), 135*, 136*; Simon, 58.
Bury St. Edmunds (Suffolk), xlv.
Bury, Bery, Byri, Byrry, Byry, William, son of Joan Gattele, monk, 76*, 96, 139, 150, 165*, payments to, 83, 105, 115, 120, 134, 136, 137, 139, 145, 147, 152, fourth prior, 165n.
Bykurton, Bykyrton, John, 97*.
Byri, Byrry, Byry, see Bury.
Bysle, Bysley, Bysly, see Bisley.
Bytam, John, son of John Roper, 96, 99*, 101*, 113*, 114*, 126, 138, 146, 157, 160; his wife, 99, 124.
Bytrysche, John (carpenter), 87.

C

Caker, John (monastic servant), 94, 98, 138; W., 49.
Cambridge, 49; University, xxiii.
Canterbury, Christ Church, xlv.
Carpenter, see Bradbyry, Hubboc, John, Stephen, and Subject Index under Trades.
Castell, Castelle, William, 16*, 52*; his wife, 16.
Castor, Caster, Castur, xxxvii, 2, 18, 24, 49, 127, 128*, 139*, 140*, 156*, 166; farmer of, see Honte; Castor wood, wode, 2.
Castor, Caastur, Castur, John, 29*, 30, 52*, 57, 131, 138, 140; Robert, 27; Thomas, 155.
Cathwaite, Cathethwayte, Cathetwayte, see Paston.
Challener, Chalner, John, 79, 97, 99, 113, 127.
Chaumberleyn, Chawmeberleyne, Richard, alias Webster (weaver), 113, 126, 138, 140.
Childryns londe, 49.
Clapton, Clopton, xxxiiin, 10n, 12, 19, 56, 72, 79, 87, 106, 120; building and repairs at, 28, 29, 46*, 80, 135, 137, 146; collector of, 28, 46, and see Freyr, Henry; Old Forthe in, 28; Tychemer brook in, 28.
Clark, Clarke, clericus, Clerk, John, of Maxey, 156; his wife, 156; John, of Oxney, 54, 108; Matilda, wife of, 54*; John, of Woodcroft, alias Smyth, father of John Godeale, 29, 52, 160; accounts with almoner, 22, 23, 43, 50, 56, 79, 84, 92, 112, 129, 131, 137*, 144, 162; William, 24, 85; William, alias Netterde (neatherd), 126, 156.
Clendon, John, 138; see also Glendon.
Cley, see Deeping.
Clocsmyth, Clokmythe, Cloksmyth, Richard, 50, 65, 66, 70, 82, 133.
Clopton, see Clapton.
Clyffe, see King's Cliffe.
Clyvre, John, 155.
Cocksholme, Cokesholme, Cokkysholme, Cokkysse Holme, Coksholme, see Peterborough.
Cocus, Coke, Cooke, Coquus, John, see Bacster; Hall; Thomas, see Roceby.
Codder, John, 98.
Coker, Richard, 56.
Colchestur, John, 120.
Cold Overton (Rutland), Kold Owreton, Robert (of), 138.
Coldham, see Peterborough.
Coldwell, Coldewel, Coldewelle,

Coldwel, Coldwelle, John, alias Merstlonde (almoner's servant), xxxi*, xlii, 102, 115, 119; as financial intermediary, xxxi, 30, 31, 50, 54, 62, 63, 67, 76, 77*, 92, 93, 97–99, 103, 107, 109*, 112, 115, 120–2; as witness, 53, 60*, 65, 71, 103, 118, 138; debts and payments of, 58, 61, 67, 69, 110*, 119, 120, 125, 129, 131, 138, 140*; journeys of, xxxi, 52, 59, 81*, 85, 90, 97, 117, 122; purchases by, 56, 66*, 82, 92, 97, 109, 116, 119, 131; remuneration of, xxxi, xlii, 59*, 84, 94, 103, 106, 110, 120, 138; repairs to house of, 157, 160; sales by, xxxi, 93, 108, 135.
Colepepur, —, 26.
Colermaker, Collermaker, Kollermaker, Henry, 74, 79, 80, 95, 96, 99, 114, 138; Isabella, 145.
Collyweston, see Weston.
Columbyn, Columbyne, Robert, 32, 115.
Colyn, John, 78; Thomas, 141; William, 167.
Colyngham, John, 79, 108.
Comesse, W., 6.
Confort, Richard, 3.
Conquest, Conqueste, Anna, wife of Robert, 120; Robert, son of Thomas Priour, 19, 48, 72, 86, 90, 115, 116*, 120, 121, 131, 134, 161, 166; as farmer of Sutton, 12, 13, 62*, 63, 70, 103, 106, 130, 156, 157; sales to, 106, 136, 160; as tenant, 48*, 65, 105, 135, 136; as witness, 12, 29, 46, 70, 162.
Conway, Nicholas (knight), 4*.
Cook, see Cocus.
Coope, John, 160.
Cooper, Copar, Coper, Cowper, Benedict (cooper), 131; John, 136; Thomas, 127, 132*, 148*, 150; carriage by, 109, 124–6, 132*, 141, 142, 153, 154, 160, 162; William, 34, 106.
Coppyng, John, 105.
Coquus, see Roceby.
Corbette, John, 121, 162.
Cordel, Cordelle, John, 128*.
Coriour, Coryour, John, 136*, 137.
Corner, John, 41.
Corveser, John, alias Sowter, 136, 137.
Cosyn, see Hall.
Cotelar, Coteler, Cuttlar, Kotlar, Agnes, 95, 120*, 132; Thomas, 104.
Cotterstock, 10n.
Cowper, see Cooper.
Cowston, Richard, 121, 123, 126, 156.
Craane, Joan, wife of William, 86, 102,

154–6; John, 146; William, 66, 127, 142, 155*.
Cresby, John, 50*.
Crosse, John, 15, 36, 38, 77, 78, 86, 168; Richard, 87, 99, 126; Robert, 75, 80, 83, 95, 103, 123, 127, 139, 148, 154.
Crowland, Croyland, Croylond, 2, 3, 54, 77n, 78.
Crowland, Croyland, Croylande, Croylond, Godfrey of, abbot, xxi; John, monk (1), 83, 158, 161*, 165, refectorer, 165n; John, monk (2), 165n; Thomas, monk, 145, 152*.
Croxton, Croxston (? Lincs.), 148.
Cuttlar, see Cotelar.

D

Dalad, John (sawyer), 163.
Davy, John, 33.
Davyntre, Davyntr', Dawntr', Dawntre, Joan, 130; John, 124*; Joan or John, 126; William, 85, 98, 99, 127.
Davyson, John, 146.
Daw, Annys (Agnes), 48.
Deeping, Depyng (Lincs.), 19, 47, 79, 120, 155; fair at, 151; East Deeping, 43–45, vicar of, 44*; West Deeping, 134, 155.
Deeping, Depyng, Depynge, John, abbot, xi, xiii, xiv*, 128; Richard, monk, 28*; Thomas, monk, 123, possibly cellarer, 26, 78, warden of Oxney, 130, 139, possibly infirmarer, 139; Thomas, monk, senior, xivn; William, alias Cley, monk, 42, 168, warden of the altar of Holy Cross, 115, 124, 129, 130, warden of Oxney, 130, 139; William, senior, monk, 151, 164, 165*; William, cantor, 19, 91.
Denby, 36.
Derby, Thomas, 35, 36, 99, 162; his widow, 155.
Derneford, Derneforde, Richard, 8*.
Desborough, Deysburrow, 78.
Dey, John (monastic servant), 22, 94; his son, 133; William, monk, 88.
Deynes, Deynys, John, 4, 167.
Doddington, Great, Dodyngton, 61, 81, 93.
Dodley, Richard, 28.
Dogsthorpe, Dosthorp, Dosthorppe (hamlet of Peterborough), 3, 17*, 89, 90, 116, 135; Stibbyngs, Stybbyngs, les, apparently in, 78, 135, 162.
Donington, Donyngton (Lincs.), 155.
Donsby, John, rector of Orton or Overton, 78.
Donwyche, Reginald, 78.
Doutte, Robert, alias Grey, 37.

Dowcheman, Walter (carpenter), 2.

Downe, John, 152, 153.

Dowsdale (probably in Whaplode, Lincs.), 128, 146.

Draper, Agnes, 38, 103, 137; John, 17, 32, 35, 38*, 79, 82, 111; his wife (probably Agnes), 17; John, junior, 92.

Drews, Drewsse, Drewus, Drewysse, John, junior, son of John Drews senior, 55, 113*, 127, 138, 140; John, senior, 98, 113n, 149; sister of, 149.

Drury, John (miller), 134; Stephen, son of, 134.

Dureham, Durram, John, 24, 32, 48, 117.

Dycklon, Dyclon, Dyklon, Dyklun, Dyklyng, John, 43; Richard, rector of Northborough, 30*, 43–45, 67*, 78, 81, 168.

Dykyl, Joan, 161.

Dyllynge, John, 4.

Dyvys, Thomas, 58.

E

Eaglethorpe, Egyllethorp (in Warmington), 50.

East field, see Maxey.

Easton-on-the-Hill, Eston, 33*, 116, 120, 153; Estonfeld, Eston feelde in or near, 132, 142*.

Eastwood, see Eye.

Edgyston, Egiston, Egyston, John, 28, 46*, 72, 79, 82, 168, 169n; Richard (slater), 121, 125, 136*; his son, 121, 125.*

Edows, Thomas, 38, 105.

Edward I, King, 47, 48; Edward IV, 113n, 156*.

Edynam, Matilda, 121.

Egiston, Egyston, see Edgyston.

Egyllethorp, see Eaglethorpe.

Eldernell, Eldurnale, see Whittlesey.

Elmstow, Nicholas of, abbot, 128.

Ely (Cambs.), xxviii, xxxi, 91; fair at, 90, 110, 125, 140.

Elyotte, John, 34, 62.

Elys, Thomas, 146.

England, see Inglond.

Ermytte, see John.

Essam, John, 78.

Essex, Esex, Sarah, 55*, 69, 103, 168.

Est, Alice, xvi; John, 4; John, senior, 3; Walter, 4; William, 58*.

Estas, Estasse, Estaze, son of John Roper (almoner's servant), xxxin, xlii, 39, 146, 149; his parents, 39.

Eston, Estonfeld, Eston feelde, see Easton-on-the-Hill.

Eston, John, 72, 79, 127, 128, 139, 140; Nicholas, 128*; Richard, 11, 38, 78; Thomas, 78, 79, 93.

Eton, William (frater), 149.

Everyngham, Robert, 79; William, brother of Robert, 79.

Evysle, John, 115.

Exton, Exston, John, 22; William, monk, steward, xiv*, prior, xvii, 28*, 64, 75, 77, 78, 143*.

Eye, Ey, 3, 35*, 53, 79, 166; East meadow in, 166; Eastwood, Estwode, Estwoode in, xxxiii*, xxxvii, 1*, 33*, 86, 111, 144; Eyebury in, 91n, 108n; the Reaches, le Reyche in, 159*; Singlesole, Seyngylsold in, 146*; Tanholt, Tanholtte in, 91*, 108*, 109, 120*.

Eyl'worth, Eylesworth, see Ailsworth.

Eyr, Eyrr, Eyyr, John, 12*, 17, 24, 29, 82, 103, 105, 121*, 125, 126, 162; as bailiff, 70; as collector, 3, 10, 12, 40, 70, 86, 103, 166; John, junior, his son, 40, 57, 86.

F

Faber, see Smyth.

Fadurman, Fadyrman, Thomas, 24, 48*.

Farcet, Farsedde (Hunts.), 135.

Fayreday, Robert, 117, 126*.

Fermur, William, 50.

Flaxlonde, 126, 127.

Fleet, Fleete, Flete (Lincs.), 100, 101, 114*; Fleet Hargate in, 146, 163.

Flemyng, Richard, bishop of Lincoln, xiii.

Fletcher, see Waldyng.

Fletton, Old (Hunts.), 83, 87, 101, 109, 110, 125–7, 132*, 141, 146, 148; manor of, xx, 1; rector of, 77.

Flour, John, 4.

Foleschank, see Gunthorpe.

Foole, William, 114, 128, 129.

Forthe, Old, see Clapton.

Fotheringay, Fotheringhay, Fodryngay, Fodrynghay, 64, 78*, 145n.

Freman, Richard, 78.

Frer, Freyr, Henry, 27, 80; see also Henry.

Fretur, see Robert, William, and Subject Index under Refectory.

Fritthe, Frytthe, Richard, 61*.

Fullar, Fuller, Andrew, 162; John, 157; Robert, 50.

Fullebroke, Robert (pewterer), 53.

Fusȝarde, Fyssarde, Janyn, 135–7, and see Berkar and Janyn.

Fylyngham, John, junior, 57, 60*, 70.

Fylyp, Thomas, 167 (cf. Phylyppe).

Fyscher, Fyscherr, Richard, 83; William, 33.
Fyssarde, *see* Fusȝarde.

G

Gaale, Richard, 50.
Galantte, John, 155.
Gardiner, Gardyner, Robert, 29, 131*, 138; Stephen, 30, 140, 156; William, 87.
Garlonde, Agnes, 35.
Garrad, William, 27.
Gatelond style, *see* Peterborough.
Gattele, Gattle, Joan, mother of William Bury, 65, 76*, 96; William (butcher), 6.
Gebon, Thomas, 159.
Gedney, Robert, 155; William, 65, 78.
Geffron, Gefron, William, 24, 48*, 126, 166.
Gent, Gentle, John, monk, 161, 165*n*, sacrist, 168.
George (merchant), 7*; monk, 145 (cf. Borough).
Gervysse, William, 139.
Gilbert, *see* Holbeach, Walysse.
Glasyer, Thomas, 5.
Glatton, John, 88.
Glendon, Stephen, 163; *see also* Clendon.
Glinton, Glynton, John, monk, 68, 90, 114, 125, 146, 158, 164*, 166, possibly abbot's receiver, 158, sacrist, 165*n*; William, 95, 110, 130, 145, 154.
Godeale, John, son of John Clark of Woodcroft, 144.
Godfrey, Robert, 126, 136.
Goldsmythe, Golsmyth, Joan, 102, 115, 120; William, 8.
Gonowr, John, 18.
Gonthorp, Gonthorppe, *see* Gunthorpe.
Gosberton, Gosberkirk, Gosberkirc, Gosberkyrc, Gosmerkirc, Thomas, monk, xiii–xvi, 33, 42*, 54, 68, 70, 82.
Granger, John, 43.
Grawnte, John, 67; Richard (monastic servant), 60*, 69, 89*, 94, 116, 122, 136*; his wife, 60, 69, 89.
Gray, William, bishop of Lincoln, xiii.
Greatford, Gretteford, Gretteforde, William, monk, 22*, 40, 42*, sub-almoner, 27, 40.
Greene, Henry (magister), high steward of the liberty of Peterborough, 52, 54*; J., 50.
Greetham, Gretham (Lincs. or Rutland), 79.
Gregory, Richard (monastic servant), 89*, 107, 122.
Greneham, William, 113*n*.
Grey, *see* Doutte.

Grobbe, Stephen, 164.
Gromchestur, Emma or Emmota, 86, 115.
Gronger, John, 105, 162; Robert, 79.
Growtte, John, 141.
Grymbold, Richard, 3.
Grynston, John, 49.
Grype, Thomas, Franciscan, 148*.
Gryssle, John, 36.
Gunthorpe, Gonthorp, Gonthorpppe, xxxvii*, 9*, 10, 16, 18, 47, 78, 88, 89, 93, 142*; cottage in, xxxii, 49*, 117; manor of, xxi*; tithes in, xxxiii*, xxxviii*n*, 10*, 11; tithe barn in, xxxiii*n*, 11, 15*, 18, 36, 37, 123, 132, 140–2; Foleschank in, 49.
Gyl, William, 160.
Gyldale, Richard, 3.
Gylham, Thomas, 107.

H

Haale, — (probably William), 48; John (mason), 99; William, 32.
Haame, Havme, Hawme, Thomas, 8, 11, 17, 21, 22, 37, 38, 41; as financial intermediary, 8, 12*, 28–30, 56.
Haburgyl, Habyrgyl, Thomas (tanner), 72, 85, 98, 121, 123, 127; house of, 19, 83, 99, 118–20, 132; *see also* Peterborough, Cowgate, Haburgylle plase.
Hacbyche, John, 41.
Haddurle, Thomas, 61.
Halbotfen, 49.
Halden, John, monk, almoner, 162*.
Haldenby, Thomas (gentleman), 58*.
Hall, Halle, Isabella, wife of Nicholas, 69; John (monastic servant, cook), 25, 73, 94, 101, 125, 138, 144, 153; John o ye, alias Cosyn (probably the same: almoner's servant), 46, 47; John, monk, cellarer, 165*n*; Nicholas, 69; Thomas (monastic servant), 138.
Halyday, John (carpenter), 110, 111, 116.
Hamerton, Hamurton, John, rector of Paston, 17*, 44*n*, 76.
Hamond, Hamonde, Hamonds, Hamons meadow (probably in Peterborough), 49, 71, 73, 80, 101, 124, 132, 155.
Hanwod, Thomas, 121.
Hardy, Thomas, 11, 35, 36, 38, 47.
Hare, John, vicar of Peterborough (notary), 44*, 148*; *see also* Peterborough.
Harlton, Harleston, Harleton, Harlleton, Richard, monk, 42, 53, 61, 62, 65, 75, 149, 162, treasurer, xix*n*, 42, 53, 62, 90, 91, abbot's receiver, 91, 151*, 152, prior, 149; Richard, senior,

monk, 42, prior, xiii, xiv, xvi, xvii,
xxiv, xxxviii, 42n.
Harpmaker, Thomas, 5.
Hart, Harte, Hartte, Hertte, John, 28,
106, 119; his wife, 135; William, 146.
Haryngton, Richard (cantor), 100, 120.
Haryson, John, 116; William, 107.
Hatherley, John (ironmonger), 119.
Hatle, Richard, 36.
Hauxey, William, 34.
Havme, Hawme, see Haame.
Haw, H., 49.
Hawxby, William, 79.
Helme, John (tailor), 148.
Helpston, 80.
Henry VI, King, 2, 10n, 22, 38, 41, 58n,
61*, 93, 165n; visit to Peterborough,
77*, 140*; Henry (bailiff), 4; Henry
(collector), 46, see also Frer; Henry
(dyker), 104.
Hernes, Hernesse, Agnes, 104, 127.
Hertte, see Hart.
Hetyng, John, 98.
Heyd, Heyds, Heydys, Thomas (car-
penter), 73, 74, 80, 96, 100.
Heydon, Joan, 59.
Heygate, see Maxey.
Hither Orton, Hydur Owreton, see
Orton Longueville.
Hobard, Hobarde, Hoberd, Hoberde,
John (dyker), alias 'Long Jon', 98,
99*, 101, 104*.
Hodis, Hods, Hodys, meadow, wong
(probably in Peterborough), 57, 84,
95, 103, 123*, 127, 139, 148, 154.
Hok', Hooks, see Smyth.
Holande, Holond, Henry, 7; William,
48.
Holbeach, Gilbert, monk, 137, 165n;
William, monk, 165n.
Holland, Holond, Holondia (Lincs.)
66, 120, 122, 151, 159.
Holmys, lez, Holmz, see Paston.
Holts, le, 147.
Honnyng, Honnyg, Hunnyng, Agnes,
wife of John, 63, 72, 109; John, 63,
109; Richard, 112, 149, 156-9.
Honte, Hontte, John, 139, 140; Thomas,
farmer of Castor, 29, 47, 105.
Hontyndon, Hontyngdon, see Hunting-
don.
Hood, Hoode, John, 4; William, 90.
Hooks, see Smyth.
Hopkyn, Henry (beadle), 57; John, 7,
11, 16, 32, 51, 52, 57, 69, 78; William,
son of John, 52, 78.
Horne, John, 79.
Horton, Richard, 90; his wife, 129, 148.
Hostylar, Agnes, 127.

Hosyar, Robert, 113.
Hubboc, Hubbok, John (carpenter),
125, 135-7, 141, 153, 157*, 161, 166
(cf. John).
Hugh, 104 (cf. Walton).
Humberstone, Reginald, 57.
Humfrey, John (ironmonger), 119.
Hunnyng, see Honnyng.
Huntingdon, Hontyndon, Hontyng-
don, Huntyngdon, William, monk,
22, 54, 57, 58, 75.
Huntingdonshire, 93.
Hylle, John (slater), 141-4; John,
monk, 125, 150, third prior, 165n.
Hynton, John, 25, 70; his wife, 71*.

I

Inckle, Incle, Incley, John, 4, 16, 79, 95,
110, 111, 115, 127.
Inglond, Thomas, 141.
Ionysse, see Jonys.
Ireland, Irlonde, John of (monastic
servant), 163.
Irnarde, Irnerde, Yrnerde, John, farmer
of Maxey, 29*, 30*, 81*; John, of
Yaxley, 82.
Ives, Ivys, Ivysse, Yve, Yves, Yvis,
Yvisse, Yvysse, Athelina, 96; John,
12, 24*, 40*, 48*, 66, 80, 82, 126;
carriage by, 19, 32, 105, 121; as
financial intermediary, 29*, 126, 156*,
162; house of, 31, 34, 43, 55, 121; son
of, 40, 55, 72.

J

Jacson, Jaxson, Joan, 26, 27; William,
son of, 26, 27, 29, 70, 107.
James, 50; 105; 156; wife of, 155;
(monastic servant), 138, 146.
Janyn, 132, 140*, 156; and see Berkar
and Fuszarde.
Jaxson, see Jacson.
Jelyan, John (furber), 82.
John, Jon, 100; 105; brother of Walter
(carpenter), 2; (carpenter), 136, and
see Hubboc; (carpenter), see also
Bradbury; (cobbler, monastic ser-
vant), 121, 126; (cook), 14; hermit,
Ermytte, 38*, 92*; (sexton), 25*;
(thresher), 37, and see Beyl; see also
Hobard, Smyth.
Joly, William, 97.
Jonys, Ionysse, Jonysse, Robert
(thatcher), 96, 99*, 117.
Jordan, Roger (scribe), 44, 45*.

K

Kaker, John, 85.
Karynton, Robert, 69.

Kechelle, Geoffrey, 92.

Kelfole, Alice, 79.

Kendal, Kendale (Westmorland), 133.

Keruer', Keruere, Richard (carpenter), 5.

Keyworth, Keyworthe, Robert, 97, 123, 124.

King's Cliffe, Clyffe, 61.

King's Lynn, see Lynn.

Knott, Richard, 91, 92.

Knythe, Richard, 105.

Kold Owreton, see Cold Overton.

Kollermaker, see Colermaker.

Kotlar, see Cotelar.

Kydd, Kydde, Thomas, monk, warden of Oxney, 54, 108; William, monk, 164.

Kydman, see Schyggey.

Kydwel, Kydwelle, John (carpenter), 103, 108.

Kyllam, John, 27; Thomas, 148; his wife, 149.

Kyng, Alice, 102; Margaret, 90.

Kyrby, Kyrcby, John, 61*, 62, 73, 81, 93, 95, 105.

Kyrcby Field, 126.

Kysby, Henry, 84, 98, 104; Richard, son of, 84; William, 8, 98.

L

Lambe, Thomas (tailor), 161.

Langley, Langle, Edmund, 1st Duke of York, 152.

Laveroc, Laverok, —, 48; Walter, 24.

Lay, Laye, John, 156; William, 24, 29, 31, 32, 48.

Leasingham, Lesyngham, John, monk, 114, 150, 161, possibly refectorer, 75.

Lecetur, see Leicester.

Leche, John (goldsmith), 4*.

Legbene, Leygben, John, 80, 87.

Leggette, John, 86.

Leicester, Lecetur, Leycetur, William, monk, 41, 49, 70, 75, 144, possibly warden of the altar of Holy Cross, 40*, subsacrist, 41, treasurer, xixn, 70, 75*, cellarer, 129*, 147*, prior, 158, 164.

Lek, John, 56.

Lesse, Walter, 50; John, son of, 50.

Lesyngham, see Leasingham.

Leverysse, William, 111.

Lewyn, Thomas, 83.

Leycetur, see Leicester.

Leygben, see Legbene.

Liddington, Lydgton, Lydyngton, Lydyntone, Lythyngton, Lytington, Robert, monk, 27*, 68, 88, 158, 159, 165*.

Lincoln, Lincolnia, Lyncolnia, 43; bishop of, xii, 53, 59, 97, see also Alnwick, Flemyng, Gray; vicar general of, 44.

Lincoln, John, monk, 165n.

Lindsey, Robert of, abbot, xx.

Lolham, Loolam mill (in Maxey), 153.

Lombe, Richard, 8, 11, 41.

London, 7, 43, 45, 58, 59, 69*, 85, 119, 148; Fleet St., Flete Strete, 69n., 148; Ludgate, 148.

London, Richard of, abbot, xxi; Thomas, monk, warden of the altar of Holy Cross, 165n.

Long dalle, see Upton.

Long lane, see Warmington.

Longthorpe, Thorp, Thorppe, (hamlet of Peterborough) 2, 4.

Lorde, J. (magister), 45.

Lorre, Lorr', Lorryer, Peter, 65, 78, 82, 95, 119, 141.

Lowthe, Alice, 42.

Lucas, Lucasse, Lucaz, Richard, 3, 8, 25*; William, alias Man, 25*, 62, 123, 125, 127, 129, 154.

Lundys yard, Lunsthynk, see Sutton.

Lyderon, Robert, monk, 139.

Lydygton, Lydyngton, Lydyntone, see Liddington.

Lynn, King's, Lynne (Norfolk), 34, 68, 122.

Lynn, Lyn, Lynne, Edmund, monk, 152, 154, 165*; Geoffrey, monk, 165n; Henry, monk (previously clerk), 64, 75, 115, 120, 150, 151, 159, 161*, 164, 165*, possibly warden of the altar of Holy Cross, 115.

Lynton, Joan, 111, 126.

Lyster, Stephen, 11.

Lythyngton, Lytington, see Liddington.

Lytster, John, 69.

M

Maddy, Richard, 91.

Malden, John, monk, 54, 107, 146, 147, 150, 151*, 158, 161, 164, prior, 165n.

Malthows, John, 120*.

Malyns place, Malynsthynk, Malynyard, see Sutton.

Man, see Lucas.

Manton, John, 87.

Marholm, Marram, Merham, 27, 40, 107, 112, 120, 144, 146–8, 153, 155, 159–61; boundaries of, Marram mette, 26*; repairs in, 110, 111, 151, 157*; rector of, 120, 147, 154, 155; Mere Dyke, Mer' dyk' in, 26.

Markham, Markam, Merkam, William, monk, xiv, xv, 17, 22*, 28, 75, refectorer, xxiin, treasurer, xv, xvii, xixn, 27*, warden of Oxney, 27*, 28*, 42, infirmarer, 54, 72, 107, 130.

Martin (cobbler), 113*, 127.

Martyn, Bridget, 71; John, bailiff of Peterborough, 43, 72; William, 100, 101, 114*.

Mason, Henry, 118*, 120, 128; John and Richard, brothers, 17, 101, 114*, 121; William (carpenter), 3*, 137.

Maxey, Maxsey, 46, 52*, 57, 102, 107, 109, 138, 140, 148*, 153, 164, 168; church of, 44, 45, 97, 150*; collector of, 29; fields and meadows in, 75, 81, 117; rectory of, xxxiii*, xxxiv, 18, 81, 95, 105, 112, 147*, 149, 153*, 157, farm and value of, xxxviiin, 10n, 29, 30*, 67*, farmers of, see Irnarde, Smythe; tithes of, 26*, 27*, 81, 148, 149*, 155, 156; vicar of, see Bakon; East field in, 148; East meadow in, 27*; Heygate in, 26; Newpark probably in, 81; North field in, 148; Nunton holme in, 27; Rose Place in, 110*; Saxpole apparently in, 156; South field, Sowth feld, Sowthe felde in, 26, 81, 148; West field in, 148.

Maxey, Maxe, Thomas, monk, 8, 22*, 38, 75*, treasurer, xixn, 8n, almoner, 15*, 64*, sacrist, 10, 19, 36*.

Maydelette, William, 22, 70, 73, 83, 124*.

Mayhewhe, Richard, 78.

Medow, John (†kydder), 97, 98, 104.

Mekness, William, 17.

Melton Mowbray, Melton Mowbr' (Leics.), 9.

Melton, William, monk, xv, 22n, 68, 78, 104, 115, 122*, 155, 161, 164*, possibly sacrist, 22, infirmarer, 27, 72, 93, 94, possibly hostiller, 75; and see Stawnton.

Merbyri, Reginald (†generosus), 114.

Merche, Mersche, John (tailor), 36; William, 32.

Merchell stybbyngs, 111 (cf. Dogsthorpe).

Mere Dyke, Mer' dyk', see Marholm.

Merkam, see Markham.

Merkande, Merkawnte, William, 22, 110.

Mersche, see Merche.

Merstlonde, see Coldwell.

Meyre, John (potter), 119.

Michelle, 60.

Mil', see Myller.

Milton, 58n.

Mockehyl gap, see Muchyl.

Molton, see Moulton.

Morcott, Morcoote (Rutland), 31.

More, Mor, Moour, Mors, John, monk, xv, xvi, 54*, 164, 165.

Morton, family, xviii*; Agnes, xviii*, xxxvi, xliv, 18–20, 32, 38–40; Richard, xviii*, 155; Robert, xviii*, 25*, 40*; Robert, son of Agnes (almoner's servant), xviii*, xxxi*, 18, 94, 113, 120*, 133, 138, 146, 150, 162, 163*, 166, 168, as financial intermediary, 106, 112, 124, 133, 148*, 149*, 152, 168; Robert (miller), xviii*, 130; Thomas, monk of Ramsey, xviii*, 87, 88, 90, 135; William, monk, almoner, passim, infirmarer, xix*, 163*, warden of Oxney, xix*, 168*; William (monastic servant), xviii*, 66, 74, 98, 113, 127, 143.

Morys, John, monk, 165n.

Moulton, Molton, Multon, John, 79; Richard, monk, 165n; Thomas, 70, 73*, 74, 79, 83, 124*, 128, 153.

Mourby, Thomas, 78.

Mowncel, Mowncelle, Mowncyele, Mownecelle, Mownselle, Mownsylle, Robert (miller), 48, 66, 72, 80, 126, 156*, 157*.

Moyses, William, 27.

Muchyl, Mockehyl, Muckehil, Mukhyl, Mukhylle gap (probably in Peterborough), xxxiii, xxxvii, 71, 73, 101, 107, 132, 148, 153, 155.

Multon, see Moulton.

Murcote, Murkote, —, 27; Richard (butcher), 148.

Myl', Richard (magister), 43.

Myller, Mil', John, 105; Thomas, 157; Walter, 49; William, 126, 156.

N

N., John (carpenter), 2.

Nabbe wood, wode, see Paston.

Nafferton, John (skinner), 83.

Narhamton, Narhamtonia, see Northampton, Northamptonshire.

Nede, Neede, see St. Neots.

Neffe, Neve, William, 3, 19, 142.

Nelson, Neeleson, Paul (carpenter), 100, 105, 106, 108, 109, 138, 140*, 141, 143.

Netterde, see Clark.

Newark, Newerc, Newerk (hamlet of Peterborough), 3, 49*, 73, 74, 78, 111, 127; chapel of St. Mary Magdalene, the Park Kirk, Parke kyrc, 38n, 40*, 52, 66*, 68*, 86, 89, 92n, 111*, 122*, 147.

Newark, William, monk, 165*n*.
Newbonde tynk, *see* Sutton.
Newpark, *see* Maxey.
Newthorpe, Thomas, 44*n*.
Newton, Water (Hunts.), 10*n*.
Nicholas, 99; .abbot, *see* Elmstow; monk, 75, 150–2, 158*, 159, 161*, 165*, subsacrist, 151, 152; clerk of, 94 (cf. Overton); Pope Nicholas IV, 47; *see also* Smyth.
Noblette, Thomas, 19, 78, 82, 94, 145.
Non hylle, 124, 148.
Noox, *see* Nox.
Northampton, Narhamton, Norhamton, Northamton, 81, 112, 149.
Northamptonshire, Narhamtonia, 93.
Northborough, Norborow, Norburrow, 26*, 117; rector of, *see* Dycklon.
North field, *see* Maxey.
Northorpe, Northop, Northoppe, John, monk, 22, 42, 46, 54, 62, 68, 70, 75, 82.
North Road, Old, 59*n*, 145*n*.
Norton, William, 45, 90.
Norwich, Norwyche, xlvi, 48.
Nottingham, Notingham, Nottyngham, Notyngham, Robert, monk, 61, 65, 68, 93, 110, 150, 151, 161*, 164*, 165*, possibly master of the works, 78, treasurer, xixn, 75, 76*, 88, 93, 124, 139, 145, subprior, xixn, 165*n*.
Nox, Noox, John, 114, 127; his wife, 127.
Nunton holme, *see* Maxey.

O

Official, Ofcyel, Offecyal, Offecyel, Offycial, Margaret (monastic servant), 32*, 35*, 45, 47*.
Offord, *see* Ufford.
Olyver, Margaret, 167.
Ondell', *see* Oundle.
Orton, *see* Overton.
Orton Longueville or Hither Orton, Hydur Owreton (Hunts.), 156*.
Orwyn, Katherine, wife of Robert, 89*, 104, 122*, 131; Robert (butcher), xxxv, 37, 38*, 52, 66, 68, 69, 75, 88, 98, 132, hires winter pasture, xxxvn, 6, 7*, 22, present at dinner, 89*, 104, 122*.
Osney, Oseneia (Oxon.), abbot of, 1.
Oundle, Ondell', Owndylle, xxxvii, 4, 87, 111.
Overton or Orton, Owrton (probably Cold Overton, Rutland), 4, 78, 98; rector of, *see* Donsby.
Overton, Henry of, abbot, 128;

Nicholas, monk, master of the works and pittancer, 165*n** (cf. Nicholas).
Owen, Owyn, Morgan, 107*.
Oxford, Oxonia, 88, 135; Canterbury College, students at, xiv*, xxix, xxx*, 52, 66, 93, 97, 107, 109, 144, 146, 158, *and see Subject Index under* University.
Oxford, Oxforde, Oxforthe, Richard, monk, xiv, 26, 40, 115, 152, 161, 164, 165, third prior, 115, sub-almoner, 165*n*; Richard, junior, monk, 68, 125, 150; Richard, senior, monk, 21*, 23*n*, 27, 62*, 137, 147.
Oxney, monastic grange and rest house, xiv, xix, 22, 27, 40, 54, 108, 117, 139, 160, 166–8; prior at, 28, 34, 46, 94*, 139, 150, 151, 158, 160, 161, 164, 165; warden of, *see* Deeping, Kydd, Markham, Morton, Pytchley.

P

Paale, Palle, John, 41*, 163; Richard, 8; Robert, 149; Thomas, 55.
Palmer, Henry, 41, 46, 94, 110, 138, 146, 151, 159; house of, 18, 19, 21, 45, 109, 117, 143, 153*, 157; son of, 159; John, 132, 136; Ralph, 128; William, 157; *see also* Palms.
Palms (or Palmer), Paulms, Paums, Robert, 29, 30*, 168.
Pampe, John, 32; Thomas (monastic servant), 91*.
Panke, John, 24.
Pantre, Richard, 83, 113.
Paple, Papley, Papple, Richard, 98, 104, 107, 117, 128.
Paris, *see Subject Index under* Wax.
Parker, —, 48; Alice, wife of William, xvi.
Parteney, John, 84.
Paston, 35, 36*, 47, 49*, 82, 107, 151*, 154, 168; cottages at, 19, 94, 145; church and tithes of, xxn, xxxiii*, xxxiv, 10*n*, 76, 77, 134, 135, 168; rector of, 66, 67, 78, 134, *and see* Hamerton; Cathwaite, Cathethwayte, Cathetwayte in, 79, 93, 151*, 161; lez Holmys, Holmz in, 49*; Nabbe wood, wode in, 27.
Patynmaker, Robert, 78, 126.
Paul (carpenter), 123, 128*, 129.
Paulms, Paums, *see* Palms.
Payn, Payne, William, 3, 52, 63, 64, 68, 78, 90, 91, 126, 131, 142.
Paynsho, Paynys holme, *see* Peakirk.
Paynyll, John (magister), 45.
Peakirk, Peykyrc, 166; rector of, 26, 27,

81; Paynsho, Paynys holme in, 70*, 79.

Penel, John, 35, 36, 38, 168*.

Penyngton, James, Jamys, 106, 107.

Pepur, Thomas (butcher), 70, 71, 83*, 85, 93, 97, 103, 107, 126; his wife, 71*.

Peter (monastic servant), 40, 94.

Peterborough, Burgus, Burrow, xxxii, xxxiii*, 4*, 7, 15, 16, 104, 131, 139, 145n, 163; carriage to and from, xxxvii*, 1, 2, 9*, 16, 18, 32, 107, 125, 153; vicar of, 44, 45, 58, 59, 83*, 103, 114, 117*, 135, and see Hare; vicarage of, xxx, 33*, 105.

Peterborough Abbey, passim.

Peterborough, churches and hospitals in: Church of St. John the Baptist (old and new), xxx, 2n, 33*, 55n, 60, 85n, 101n, 117, 121, 122*, cemetery, xxxv, 7, 55, garden, xxxv, 60, 85, 97, 100, 101*, 109, 114, 125, vicarage, xxx, 33*, 105; St. Leonard's Hospital, the Spittle (in Westwood), xxviii, xxix, 22, 25, 33, 50, 55, 57, 65, 73, 127, 132, barns at, 21*, 32, 52, 71, 73, 83, 90, 100, 106, 117, 118, 127, 160*, carriage from, 21, 79, 101, 132, 153*, carriage to, 32*, 43, 46, 51*, 60*, 62, 69, 73*, 74, 80*, 81, 87, 88, 101*, 119, 124*, 125, 132*, 142*, 153*, 160, doves, dovecote at, 22, 83*, 103, croft at (cf. Westwood, Spitilcrofte), 55, 71*, hall of, 32, 50–53, 60, 63, 64, 80, 81, 87, 88, 99, hermit at, 92 (see also John), repairs and other work at, 18, 21, 24, 32, 70, 73*, 96, 98, 100, 114, 115, 121, 123, 146, 150, 159; St. Thomas's Hospital, the Sister House, ye Cyster howse, le Cystur hows, howus (also the chapel of St. Thomas or the Becket chapel), xxviii, xxix*, 54n, 64, 65, 143*, 146, 153, 156, 158, sewer at, 109, 117, 140, 144, 152, chaplain of, 72, 89, 103, 122*, clerk of, 22, prioress of, 96, servant at, 41, 54, 55, 65, and see Gromchestur, sisters at, 22, 41, 54*, 65, 69*, 76, 96, 152, and see Essex, Gattele, Ives.

Peterborough, places and streets in: Barnard's, Barnax Cross, 38*, 143n; Bolwelgate (probably in Peterborough), 50; Bondgate, Bondegate, Bongat, Bongate (now St. John's St.), 21, 33*, 35, 99*, 117*, 119*, 123, 153, and see Boongate Hook; Bondstyle, 105, 107, 135; Boongate Hook, 33n; Boroughbury, Burrowbery, 101; Brewerne, le, 161; Bull Gate, Bole ȝaate, Bolle yaate, Boylgata, Boylyaate, Bull

yate (probably identical with Bolithegate), 9*, 33, 41, 87, 95, 124*; Burbryg, Burowbryg, see Peterborough Bridge; Chapel Row, Chapelle Row, 19*, 21, 37, 66, 133, 140*, 151, 153, 156, 157*, 160; Cockesholme, Cokesholme, Cokkysholme, Cokkysse Holme, Coksholme, Coxholme, Koksholme, 50, 60, 71n, 103, 109, 110, 119, 123, 124*, 132, 148*, 155; rent of, 73, 74*, 83; Coldham, little, lytylle Coldham, 105, 139, 140; Cowgate, Cowgaate, Kowgate, 19*, 57, 74, 91, 119, 124, 132, 142, 153, 159, 160, building in, 83, repairs in, 99*, 109, 117–19, 135, 136, 160, Haburgylle plase in, 119; Cumbergate, Comersgate, 49, 79, 132, 136; Cuttlar place, 119 (cf. Cotelar); Edgerley, Egerley, Egersle, 49*; Fallam herne, see under Westwood; Gatelond style, 57; Groplane, 98; Heyate, Heygat (perhaps Hythegate), 17, 19, 74, 80, 143; Howgate, Hawyaate (now Midgate), 49, 87, 143n, 145, 146, 168; Swan's Pool on, 143n; Hythegate (now Bridge St.; cf. Heyate), 159–62; Long Causeway, 143n; Low Grange, le Low, Lowhe, 104, 129*; Market Place, Marketstede, Merket stede, 25, 33n, 168; Martin's Bridge, Martyn bryg, 143*, 160; Midgate, see Howgate; Park Gate, le Parke Gaate, 155; Peterborough Bridge, Burowbryg, Peturbryghe, 9, fair at, 34*, 67*, 165–7, and see Borowbrig; Pewterer', Pewturrer Plase, 102, 138*; Priestgate, Prestgate, 153*, 156; Raton Row, 41, 55, 70, 99, 116*, 117, 119, 132, 150; Sartry, †Sartrina (tailor's shop), 54, 98, 163; Snossels, Snorshylle, 68, 153; Sowter Row, 73, 79, 95, 99, 109, 110, 114, 136, 137, 145, 161, carriage to and from, 9, 19, 21, 74, 79, 101, 119, 124*, repairs in, 21, 65, 73, 95, 96*, 99*, 108*, 109, 111, 117*; Stoxleys place, 154, and see Stoxley; the Trenches, le Trenchys, Trenchysse, garden in, xxx, xxxv, 100, 101*, 104, 109, 113, 136, 139; Vetus Scaccarium, 18*, 19, 34; Vineyard Road, 55n; Westgate, Westegat, Westegate, Westgaate, 2, 28, 35, 49n, 83, 86, 103, 107, 127, 139, 143n, building material for, 91, 109, 118, 128, carriage to and from, 9, 74, 129, repairs in, 2, 35, 45, 129; Westwood, Westewode, Westwod, Westwode, xxxiii*, 33, 57*, 71n, 95, 145; Botolsok in, 57, 95, Fallam herne, hirne, hyrne in, xxxiii, 101, 132, 144, 145*, 155, rent for, 61, 84, 103, 108, 123, rent of, subsacrist in, 127, 133, 147, Spitil-crofte, Spytillecrofte, Spytylcroffte, Spytylcroft, 83–85, 103, 123, 124, 148; Woodehithemilne (mill), 2*; see also St. Leonard's Hospital.

For hamlets of Peterborough, see Dogs-thorpe, Longthorpe, Newark, Oxney; for places probably in Peterborough, see Bondfeld; Hamond, Hamons meadow; Hodis, Hods meadow; Muchyl Gap; Stony Pitts; Swyns meadow.

Peterborough, as surname, see Borough.

Pewys or Powys, Simon, 128*.

Phylyppe, William (carpenter), 9 (cf. Fylyp).

Pinchbeck, Pynchebec, Agnes, 139; John, junior, 74, 89, 126; John, senior, 97; Thomas, monk, 165n.

Pipewel, Pippewelle, Pyppewel, Pyppe-welle, Pyppwel, Pyppwelle, Pyp-welle, John (monastic servant), 15, 16, 24, 32, 74, 79, 85, 89, 122, 127, 138; William, 98, 108.

Pitts, Pytts, Richard, 58, 85, 118, 139; Robert, 110.

Plantagenet, Plantaginette, Richard, 3rd Duke of York, 58n, 113n*, 145n, 152.

Ploman, Plowman, William (thatcher), 17, 35, 41*, 43*, 50*, 61, 66, 70, 123.

Plomere, William, 4.

Poope, John, 21.

Porter, Portere, Joan, widow of Richard, 3; William, 4, 25.

Potter, John, 106, 110, 111, 115.

Potton, —, 48.

Powys, see Pewys.

Priour, Pryour, Dycon or Richard, 48; Thomas, father of Robert Conquest, farmer of Sutton, 12, 24*, 40, 48*, 116; his wife, 12; Thomas, junior, 24.

Prutwell, John (notary), 44n.

Pybaker, see Bacster.

Pychele, Pycheley, see Pytchley.

Pye, John, of Gunthorpe, 10, 11, 15*, 22, 35–38, 46, 66, 168*; John, of Paston, 107; William, 68; William, of Paston, 78.

Pyg, Pygge, Katherine, 95, 110.

Pyk, John, wife of, 119.

Pynchebec, see Pinchbeck.

Pyndar, Pynder, Richard, 55, 66, 73, 82, 83, 101, 123, 127, 148; carriage by, 73, 89, 91, 101, 104, 120.

Pyppewel, Pyppewelle, Pyppwel, Pypp-welle, Pypwelle, see Pipewel.

Pytchley, Pychele, rector of, 49.

Pytchley, Pychele, Pycheley, Henry of, monk, 24n, 25n, 117n; John, monk, 22n, 42n, 54, 64, 97, 104, 122*, 124, 127–9, 146, 158, at Oxney, 150*, 161*, 164*, 165*; payments to, 22, 42, 46, 53, 57, 58, 105, 152, 159, hostiller, 119, 122*, 123, infirmarer, 54, 168, warden of Oxney, 165n.; servant of, 146.

Pytts, see Pitts.

Q

Qhwyt, Qhwyte, see White.

R

Raffe, Rathe, Rave, William (magister), 43–45, 97, 146; bailiff of, 82.

Ramsey (Hunts.), 128; abbey of, 54, 72, 87, 88, abbot of, 88.

Ramsey, Rampsey, Thomas (apparently the same as Thomas of St. Neots), 133; William, monk, 115, 116, 125*, 132, 135, 150*, 151, 161, 164*, pay-ments to, 54, 83, 125, 131, 136, 137*, 143, 150*, subsacrist, 147, cellarer, 163, abbot's receiver and steward, 165n, abbot, xi, 165n.

Rathe, Rave, see Raffe.

Ravon, John (carpenter), 9, 95, 118, 120; Matilda or Maud, 104, 106, 111; William, 3, 28.

Rawlyn, John, 44n.

Rawscotte, Thomas (magister), 59.

Redyll, see Ridel.

Reede, Rede, John (chaplain and cantor), 163; William, 29, 110; William (butcher), 126, 145, 168; William (slater), 108, 118*, 126, 144.

Reffeson, Reffson, John, 167*; Robert, 141, 154.

Rest, Reeste, William, 17, 109, 127, 144*; William, senior, 105.

Reyche, le, see Eye.

Reynolde, Margaret, wife of William, 26; William, 26, 27*, 32, 48.

Reynyll, Richard (magister), 45, 58.

Richard (janitor), 52; (slater), 137; see also Smyth, York.

Ridel, Redyll, Ridell, Rydelle, Henry, 24*, 65.

Ripon, Ryppon, John, monk, 125, 137, 152, 165*, almoner, 165n.

Riseley, Ryssele (Beds.), 135.

Robert, o the fretur (refectory, monastic servant), 137, 146; parson of Wood-stone, 124; (slater), 105; farmer of Maxey, see Smyth; monk and treasurer, see Nottingham.

Roceby, Rowceby, Rowseby, — (frater), 5; Thomas, Thomas the cook (monastic servant, infirmary cook), 27, 40, 54, 94*, 97, 116*, 117, 123, 128, 138, 150, 154*; agricultural and other work, 33*, 154; food purchases, etc., 23, 43*, 54, 107*, 130, 154*.

Rockle, John (carpenter), 148.

Rodger, Rogger, William, also William sclatter (slater), 70, 91, 101*, 116, 117, 127, 141-4, 146, 149, 157, 160, 161.

Rog', G., 38.

Rolston, Alred, 168; Robert, 35, 36.

Rome, 44.

Roome, John, 50.

Roper, Ropere, J., 50; John, 5; John, father of John Bytam, 99, 101*; John, father of John Estas, 38*, 39, 89; John, of Woodstone, 79, 98.

Rose, John, 102; Rose Place, see Maxey.

Rothewel, Rothewelle, Rowthwelle, John, 12*, 22, 24, 31*, 34, 46, 48*, 55; Thomas, 24, 117, 162; see also Rowelle.

Rotlande, see Smyth.

Rowceby, Rowseby, see Roceby.

Rowelle, Rowell', Royewel, John, 24, 43, 126, 156, 157, 161, 162; son of, 72; Thomas, 121, 126, 156; see also Rothewel.

Rowsyng, John, 145.

Rowthwelle, see Rothewel.

Royewel, see Rowelle.

Royston (Herts.), 59.

Ryal, Ryalle, John, monk, 22, 75, 82, 104, 112, 122, 137, 145, 152*, 164, 165, subsacrist, 82; Thomas, 102.

Rycheman, John, 28, 33; Robert, wife of, 38.

Rydar, Ryder', Robert, 106; William (butcher), 6, 123.

Rydelle, see Ridel.

Ryette, John (weaver), 97*, 98.

Ryheston, William, 154.

Ryppon, see Ripon.

Rypse, Edmund, 4.

S

Saburton, John, 83; son of, 84.

Sadler, Thomas, 98.

St. Albans (Herts.), battle of, 145n, 146.

St. Neots, S. Neotus, Nede, Neede, Sen Neede, Seyneede, Seyn Neede, Thomas of, monk, 94*, 122, 129, 137*, 140, 150*, 158, 161*; as almoner's vicar in choir, xxx, 115, 133, 139, 158*; other payments to, 88, 102, 105, 115*, 120, 134, 137*, 139, 152, and see Ramsey.

Samon, Robert, 35*, 36, 168.

Sandur, Sawndur, John, son of William, 135; Robert, 53; William, 3, 52, 90, 111, 123*, 135, 152, 161; William, junior, 144, 145.

Sandwich, Sandewyche (Kent), 58.

Sapcot, Richard, 49.

Sawar, Thomas, 52.

Sawndur, see Sandur.

Saxpole, see Maxey.

Scarlet, Scarlette, Skarlet, John, 50, 88.

Scharppe, Richard (cantor), 134.

Schefford, see Shefford.

Schelford, Schelleford, see Shelford.

Schepey, William (mason), 50, 51, 57, 70, 99, 102; son of, 102*.

Scherwyn, Schyrwyn, John, 148*, 155.

Schort wood, see Sutton.

Schropsberi, see Shrewsbury.

Schyggey, Schyngey, Schynggey, John, alias Kydman, 140, 160; Roger, 153 (cf. Schyngle).

Schyngle, John (mason), 113; Roger, 157* (cf. Schyggey).

Sclatter (slater), see Richard.

Segraffe, Thomas, 155.

Sen Neede, Seyneede, Seyn Neede, see St. Neots.

Sewale, Sewalle, John, alias Agas, 101, 114*; Richard, 19, 20; William, 55, 83, 84*, 103, 127; his wife, 84, 127.

Seymerk', Thomas, 25*.

Seyngylsold, Singlesole, see Eye.

Shefford, Schefford (Beds.), bailiff of, 150.

Shelford, Schelford, Schelleford, Hugh, 24; William, 113; William, monk, 165n.

Shrewsbury, Schropsberi, Richard, monk, 148.

Simon, Symon, 97.

Skarlet, see Scarlet.

Skirmote, Richard (gentleman), 58n.

Skynner, John, 74.

Smyth, Smythe (Smith), John, 85; John (almoner's clerk), xxxin, 30, 35, 41; John (blacksmith), of Denby, 36; John, of Sutton, 4; John, of Woodcroft, see Clark; John, of Yaxley, 36; Nicholas (blacksmith), 34, 38*, 46, 104; Nicholas, brother of Thomas, 30, 34, 38, 81, 158, 159; hostilarius of, 81; Richard (carpenter), 103*, 108; Robert, 4; Robert, alias Hok', Hooks, farmer of Maxey Rectory, 30*, 67, 110, 112*, 150; Thomas, brother of Nicholas, 159, 167*; Thomas, alias Rotlande (blacksmith), 56, 80*, 99, 106*, 145; Thomas, of Eye, 35; Walter, 97.

Smythefelde, John, 63.

Snow, John, 114*.

Snypewel hill, see Sutton.

Socklyng, Sucklyng, John, 114, 119, 127.

Somerset, Duke of, 14, 26n.

Somur, John (thatcher), 99, 110, 117.

Somursette, John (cook), 127.

Sothworth, Roger, Franciscan, 44.

South field, Sowth feld, Sowthe felde, see Maxey.

Southorpe, Walcot, Walcotte in, xxxviin, 51, 61.

Sowter, see Corveser.

Sowthwel brook, see Upton.

Spalding, Spaldyng (Lincs.), 54.

Spalding, Spaldyng, John, monk, 28; William, monk, 22, 56, 150, 161*, 164, 165, possibly pittancer, 78*, 91, infirmarer, 165n.

Spencer, Robert, 138, 140; Thomas (saddler), 97, 126.

Stacy, William, 48.

Staffe, Robert (clerk), 146.

Stamford, Stanford, Stanfordia, Stawnforde (Lincs.), 4, 7*, 17, 91, 92, 100*, 105, 114–16, 120, 130, 131, 148; church of St. Thomas on Stamford Bridge, 4*, 5; consistory at, 43–45; fair at, 87, 97, 116, 117, 151, 167; journeys to, 39*, 43, 54, 59, 64; purchases at, 39, 64.

Stamford, Stanfor, Stanford, Stanforthe, Stawnford, Stawnforde, —, monk, 89*, 104, 151, 161; James, 69; Richard, monk, xiv, 12, 13, 42*, 53*, 130, chamberlain, 12n; William, monk, xiii, xiv, 22*, 68, 131, 158, 165*.

Stanground, Stanggrownde, Stangronde (Hunts.), 4, 33; vicar of, see Bevelle.

Starr', Thomas, wife of, 129.

Stawnford, Stawnforde, see Stamford.

Stawnton, Alice, alias Melton, 32; John (barber), 97, 114.

Stel, Stele, John (apothecary), 85, 98.

Stephen (carpenter, monastic servant), 105, 108, 109, 131, 138, 140.

Sterbrige, Ster'brige, Sterbrydge, see Stourbridge.

Sterr', Richard (monastic servant), 138.

Stevur, Styvour, Styvur, John (slater), 8, 22, 141, 142.

Steynton, Robert, 33, 34; son of, 76.

Stibbyngs, Stybbyngs, les, see Dogsthorpe.

Stilton, Styleton (Hunts.), 59, 154.

Stokton, Robert (blacksmith), 161.

Stonley, Peter, 2.

Stony Pitts (probably in Peterborough), xxxiiin, 132.

Stoon, Robert, 158.

Stourbridge Fair, Sterbrige, Ster'brige, Sterbrydge (in Cambridge), 90*, 124, 125, 167.

Stoxley, Stokysley, Stoxle, John, 143, 146, 153; William (monastic servant), 138, 146; Stoxleys place, see Peterborough.

Stranglyon, Thomas, 108, 119–21.

Stroxmans acre, 49.

Stybbyngs, les, see Dogsthorpe.

Style, Robert (clerk), 62; Thomas, 62.

Styleton, see Stilton.

Styvour, Styvur, see Stevur.

Sucklyng, see Socklyng.

Sugur, — (doctor), 58.

Surdus, Richard (apparently monastic servant), 57.

Sutor (cobbler), see Martin.

Sutton, 4*, 22, 31*, 65*, 66, 78, 79, 82, 83, 105, 109, 145n; almoner's lands and rents in, xxxii, xxxiii*, 10n, 24, 48*, accounts of, 40, 48, 62, 166, 168; carriage to and from, xxxvii*, 19, 32, 34, 40, 83*, 105, 109, 132, 133; chapel at, 13, 55; collector of, 29, 48, and see Eyr; court at, 24*; farm, farmers of, 130, and see Conquest, Priour; houses and householders, 34, 43, 48, 57, 110, 117, 136; purchases for, 43, 57, 80*; repairs at, 46, 55, 86, 110, 133, 134, 136, to manor house, 13, 40, 61, 62, 68, 74, 110, 136. Places in: Baconthink, Baconthynk, Bakonsthynk, 65, 125, 126; Benetholde, 48; Brigmylle, Brygmille, Brygmylle (Bridge Mill), 62, 63, 65, 99, 109, 130, 139, building work and materials for, 70, 72, 87, 91, 102, 103, 107, 108, 116, 131, 134, carriage to and from, xxxii, 63, 105, 115, 116, 162, revenue from, xxxiii, xxxviiin, 134; Brigmylle holme, 105; Lundys yard, Lunsthynk, 24, 48; Malyns place, Malyns, Malynsse thynk, Malynyard, 24*, 48, 65, 125, 126, 161; Newbonde tynk, 48; Schort wood, wod (apparently in Sutton), 65; Snypewel hill, 48; Sutton wood, wode, woode, 51, 57, 62, 72, 117, 119, 121*, 156*, see also Blogwyn; Warynsthynk, 162; Wolffe yerde, 48; Woodmyl dyks, 48 (for thynk, tynk, cf. glossary).

Swyns, Swynys meadow (probably in Peterborough), 60, 64, 71, 78, 83*, 84, 103, 123, 124, 127, 132, 148*.

Sybberton, see Upton.

Sydraks, 48.

Sylk, Richard, 38; William, 53.

Syyr, John, 68.

T

Tallington, Talyngton, William, monk, 28*.
Tanholt, Tanholtte, see Eye.
Tapyser, William, alias o' sandle, 158.
Tarry, Henry, 143*.
Taylour, Tallour, Richard, 138; Simon, 156*; Thomas of Castor, 24; Thomas, of Sutton, 24.
Tempyl, Tempylle, John, 94, 110, 131.
Terrington, Tyrynton (Norfolk), 37*.
Teysse, 48.
Thacker, John, 156.
Thomas (carpenter), 113; (clerk), 94; (cook), see Roceby; (monastic servant, gardener), 94; (blacksmith), see Smyth.
Thornbery, —, monk, 165*.
Thorney (Hunts.), 10n, 16, 54, 158.
Thornhaugh, Thornaw, 125, 130, 134.
Thorp, Thorppe, see Longthorpe.
Thorppe, Thomas, 87; William, 91.
Thurlby, Alice, 4.
Toche, Tooche, Laurence, 77*, 91, 142, 151, 161.
Torolde, John, 161.
Towcester, Towcetur, 66.
Townsende, Tounende, Townysende, Thomas, 83, 97, 98.
Travesse, William, 122*.
Trett', William, father and son, 38.
Trotter, John, 19.
Turvey, John, monk, 22*, 33, 42*, 46, 53, 57, 68.
Tychemer brook, see Clapton.
Tylar, Tyler, Emma, 38; William, 84.
Tylly, John, monk, 53, 59, 63, 85, 111, 133, 139, 152*, 165n.
Tyrynton, see Terrington.
Tyssington, John (magister), 44.

U

Uffington, Uffyngton (Lincs.), 45.
Ufford, Offord, Ufforde, Ufforthe, Edmund, monk, 145; William, monk, 22, 42, 46, 75, 161*, 164*, 165*.
Underwode, Richard (chaplain), 44, 45*.
Upex, Thomas (notary), 44n.
Uppyngham, Richard, 24*, 29, 48.
Upton, 24*, 25, 51, 58n; Long dalle in, 24; Sybberton in, 25; Sowthwel brook probably in, 24.
Upwell, Welle (Cambs.), 41*.

V

Venur, John, 124.
Vyncent, William, 4.

W

Waar, see Ware.
Waarde, Ward, Warde, John (tiler), 18*, 19, 40, 68.
Wakefield (Yorks.), 145n.
Wakerle, Wakerley, Wakyrle, Wakyrley, John, 61, 79, 93*, 137, 161*; son of, 137.
Walcot, Walcotte, see Southorpe.
Waldyng, John, alias Fletcher (mercer), 18, 19, 28, 38, 41, 57, 68, 82, 88, 102, 125–7.
Wales, 91.
Walker, Nicholas, 24.
Walleram, Walram, Simon, 79, 89, 111; Robert, son of, 89.
Walmisford, Walmysford, Walmysforde, Walmysforthe, see Wansford.
Walpole (Norfolk), 146.
Walsingham, Walsyngham (Norfolk), 86*, 106, 146.
Walter (carpenter), brother of John (carpenter), 2; collector, 37; (monastic servant), 94; monk, 88, 158* (cf. Warmington).
Walton, 35, 36, 78, 79, 89, 93.
Walton, Hugh of, 109; see also Hugh.
Walys, Walysse, Gilbert (almoner's servant), 151, 154; Thomas, Dominican, 148; William, 151; father of, 151.
Wansford, Walmysford, Walmysforde, xxxviin, 51, 162.
Wansford, Walmisford, Walmysford, Walmysforde, Walmysforthe, William, monk, 22, 33*, 42n, 89*, 90, 104, 144, 150, 151, 161*, 164*, 165*; payments to, 42, 68, 75, 83, 93, 131, 137.
Ward, Warde, see Waarde.
Ware, Waar (Herts.), 59*.
Warmington, Wermington, Wermyngton, xxxiiin, xxxvii, 1, 10n, 26, 39, 49, 110, 111*, 131, 143, 154; collector of, 29; Almoner's lane, alias Long lane in, 111.
Warmington, Wermington, Wermingtone, Wermyngton, Wermyngtone, Wermynton, Walter, monk, 20*, 94, 131, 137, 143, 158; payments to, 75, 82, 131, 134, 136, 137, 139, 143, 145*, 147, 152*, 159.
Wartre, John, 3.
Waryn, John, 4; Thomas, 126, 162; Warynsthynk, see Sutton.
Waxhows pond, 108.
Webster, Wevar (weaver), Laurence, 93, 97, 148; Richard, see Chaumberleyn; Robert (carpenter), 67.
Weekley, Wycle, 3.
Welle, see Upwell.

Wenham, Wennam, William, monk, 79, 104, 105, 115, 131.

Wentbrig, John (weaver), 114.

Werkry leyton (garden), le, Werkery 3ard (yard), 26, 98.

Wermele, Wormele, Wormeley, Wurmeley, Henry, 19, 24, 31*, 32*, 34, 48*.

Wermington, Wermingtone, Wermyngton, Wermyngtone, Wermynton, see Warmington.

Werrington, Werryngton, Weryngton, Wethryngton, Wyryngton, Wytheryngton, 15, 27, 49, 65, 77, 78, 86, 168; collector of, 68, 82.

West field, see Maxey.

Westminster, Westmonasterium, 58*.

Weston (probably Collyweston), 3.

Wethryngton, see Werrington.

Wevar, see Webster.

Whaplode (Lincs.), see Dowsdale.

White, Whyte, Qhwyt, Qhwyte, John (almoner's servant), xxxi*n*, 94; John (tanner), 127, 150; Walter (monastic servant), 27, 97, 107, 138; William, 69, 70.

Whittlesey, Whyttlesey, Wytlisse, Wytlissey, Wyttlyssey, Wytylsey (Cambs.), 17, 32, 73, 79, 95; Eldernell, Eldurnale in, 79, 150.

Whytside, John, 4, 5.

Wiggenhall (Norfolk), see Wygnale.

Wigtoft, Wictofte (Lincs.), 159.

William, 114, 162; (brewster), 140; (clerk), 98, 99; (plumber), 144, 150; monk, prior, 47; servant in infirmary, 94; servant in refectory (William o the Fretur), 94, 97; (thatcher), 128; see also Rodger, Tapyser, Yaxley.

Willybrook, Willybroc, Wyllybrok, hundred of, 118; bailiff of, 50.

Winchester, xlvi.

Winwick, Wynwyk' (Hunts.), 3, 4.

Winwick, Wynwic, Wynwyc, Wynwych', Wynwyk, John, monk, 3, 4, 16, 78, 119; Margaret, 167.

Wisbech, Wysbeche (Cambs.), 8*, 40, 41*, 78.

Wodcroft, Wodcrofte, Wodcroftte, Wodecroft, see Etton.

Wodnewton, see Woodnewton.

Wodston, see Woodstone.

Wolffe yerde, see Sutton.

Wollasse, Thomas, 98.

Woodcroft, Wodcroft, Wodcrofte,

Wodcroftte, Wodecroft (in Etton), 22, 26*, 29, 52, 56, 79, 84, 92, 112, 129, 131, 137, 144, 162*.

Woode, J., 49; William (clerk), 127.

Woodmyl dyks, see Sutton.

Woodnewton, Wodnewton, 50.

Woodstone, Wodston (Hunts.), 79, 98, 113, 124.

Wormele, Wormeley, see Wermele.

Wryte, Wryhete, Wryhette, Wryhte, John, 38, 41, 79; Robert, 37, 38; his wife, 47; Robert, of Fletton, 109, 116; Thomas, 135; William, father of Richard Boydyl, 100; see also Beyl.

Wurmele, see Wermele.

Wyberd, Simon, 144.

Wycle, see Weekley.

Wycle, Wyncle, Henry (butcher), 6, 25.

Wygnale, probably Wiggenhall (Norfolk), xxxvii, 87*.

Wygston, John, 162.

Wygtoft, William, 4.

Wyllyamson, John, 167.

Wyllybrok, see Willybrook.

Wymyche, Wymyheste, Wymys, Wymysche, Wymysse, Robert, 24, 48, 65, 105*; William, 156.

Wyncle, see Weekley.

Wynwic, Wynwyc, Wynwych', Wynwyk, see Winwick.

Wysbeche, see Wisbech.

Wytheryngton, see Werrington.

Wytlisse, Wytlissey, Wyttlyssey, Wytylsey, see Whittlesey.

Wyttham, Wyttheham, William (magister), 58*, 59*.

Y

Yarryngton, Yaryngton, Henry, 130, 143*, 144*.

Yaxley, Yaxle, 36, 82; deanery of, 10*n*.

Yaxley, William of, 114*.

Yonghe, Yoong, Yowng, Yownge, 3onge, Agnes, 5; John, 15, 114, 127; Roger, 163.

York, Yoork, Yorc, Dukes of, see Langley, Plantagenet; John, monk, xviii, 17*, 22*, 26*, 106, 161, 165*.

Yrnerde, see Irnarde.

Yve, Yves, Yvis, Yvisse, Yvysse, see Ives.

3onge, see Yonghe.

3

INDEX OF SUBJECTS

The nature of the text does not make it easy to provide an adequate subject index, since the bulk of its type of entry—e.g. building materials, carpentry, cloth, corn, malt, peas, slates, thatch, &c.—occur *passim*. What follows is therefore a selection of those items which can usefully be indexed, in particular an analysis of the buildings, offices, and inhabitants of Peterborough Abbey (see Abbey buildings, Abbot, Almoner, Monks, Obedientiary system, &c.).

The proper names to which cross-references are given will be found in the Index of Places and Persons.

A

Abbey buildings: Abbot's lodging, 39, 77; Abbot's gaol, 69, 117, 120, 134; Chapter House, 151, 165n; Church, altars and chapels, Holy Cross, 54, warden of, 40, 115, *and see* Borough, Deeping, Leicester, London, Lynn; Lady Chapel, 29, 68*, 91, warden of, 78*, *and see* Borough; St. Laurence, 93, 108, 142, 164; Holy Trinity, 77*; Chapel of the Novices, 29, 54, 115; Choir, xlv*, 68, vestry, 29, 113, 143; Cloister, 42, 94n, 103, 137, 145*; Guest house (*hostilaria*), 94*; Infirmary, 54, 164, 165n*, chambers in, 28*, 63, 93*, 94, 105, 106*, 108, 120, 124, 164, kitchen in, 163; Kitchen, 40, 146*; Minucio (bloodletting chambers, presumably in Infirmary), chapel of, 134, hall of, 7, 22, 26, 40*, 54, 78, kitchen of, 60, servants of, 138, 154, *and see* Peter, William; Monks' Chambers, 42, 53, 144; Monks' Parlour (*Locutorium*), xxxn, 134; Offices, almoner's, *passim*, great chamber in, 140, chamberlain's, 54, 115, treasurer's, 93; Prior's Chamber, 94*; Refectory, xxiv, 3, 94, 125, 131, pulpit (either in refectory or church), 54; Subalmonry, xxx*, 22, 39, 64, 65, 72, 90, 93, 105*, 115; *and see* Gardens.

Abbot, *abbas*, xxiv, xxv, 39, 44, 45, 53, 60, 72, 106, 111, 139, 143, 158; financial dealings of, 43, 49*, 51, 52, 86, 102; on pilgrimage to Walsingham, 86, 106; office of, xxviii, 69n, 104; *nativi* of, 42, 89; *see also* (abbots) Andrew, Ashton, Benedict, Crowland, Deeping, Elmstow, Lindsey, London, Overton, Ramsey; (abbot's confessor) More; *and* Abbey buildings.

Abbot's Receiver, *receptor*, xxin, xxiii*, xxiv, 3, 4, 77, 91*, 143*, 151*, 158, 166; *and see* Glinton, Harlton, Ramsey.

Accounts, xvi, xxiii–xxv, xxxi, xxxvii–

xxxix, xli–xlv, *and passim*; Almoner's account rolls, *see* Books and records; *see also* Bills, Tallies.

Almoner, *elemosinarius*, awmener, office of (in general), history and functions, xxv–xxviii, xxxi, xlv, xlvi; (at Peterborough), history and functions, xx, xxi*, xxiii*, xxiv, xxviii–xxx, xxxiiin; income, xxxviii*; inventory of office, 20, 34; payments of monks' stipends, for spices (on O *Sapientia*), xxiv, 22*, 42, 53, 54, (on the Feast of the Purification) 68, 82, 83, 93, 102, 115, 131, 137, 145, 152; for tunics (on St. Luke's Day), xxiv, 22*, 27, 28, 42, 53, 62, 75, 88, 105, 125, 136, 143, 152, 159; for the 'O' (festivity), 33, 46, 54, 57, 58, 70, 88, 102, 120, 133, 134, 139, 147, 158; *see also* Halden, Maxey, Morton, Ripon; *above*, Abbey buildings, *and below*, Clerks, Servants, Subalmoner.

Alms, xxv–xxx, xlii*, xlv, xlvi, ?42, 53, 125, 146, 153; distribution on All Souls' Day, 10*, 52, 89, 92, 107, 116, 131, 153*; Maundy, xxvi*, xxix, xlvi*.

Apprentices, 119, 141, 153, 157; apprenticeship, 119.

B

Bailiffs, 82, 150; royal, 50; *see also* Eyr, Henry, Martyn, Raffe.

Beadle, *see* Hopkyn.

Beer, *see* Drink.

Bells, 5, 25n, ?103*, 137.

Bills, 151, 152.

Bishops, *see* Alnwick, Flemyng, Gray, Lincoln.

Blood-letting, *see* Abbey buildings; Feasts.

Book of Roger Bird, 10n, 26n, 38n, 44n, 67n, 165n.

Book of William Morton, The, xi, xii, xxxix–xlvi *and passim*.

Books and records: books etc., xxix*,

17*, 28, 49; Bible, 132; *Doctrinale* (treatise on grammar), 145; extracts from chronicles, xl*, 47, 48, 106; chronicle roll, 115; mortuary roll, 54; *Speculum stultorum*, 106; repair of books, 5; records, monastic, xi, xii, xxxi*, xli; accounts of the church of St. Thomas on Stamford Bridge, xl, 4, 5; fabric roll of the same, 4; account of abbot's receiver, 4; almoner's account rolls, xxxvii–xxxix, xli, xlii, 9*n*, 35, 74*n*, 91, 95, 98, 99*n*, 118, 123, 128*; almoner's court rolls, xxxi, xl*, 24, 25; almoner's register, 128; almoner's white book (*albus liber*), 131*; *liber feodarius*, 117*; record of Maxey process, xxxi, 117*; schedule of repairs at Maxey, 67; rolls (unspecified), 28; *see also* Courts.

Bread, *see* Food.

Bridges, *see* Peterborough, Martin's Bridge; Peterborough Bridge; Stamford; Sutton, Brigmylle.

Building and repair work, *passim; see especially* 31 (new buildings at Sutton), 35–38 (chimneys), 51, 52 (new hall and garret at St. Leonard's Hospital), xxxiii*, 70, 103, 134, etc. (Sutton, Brigmylle, q.v.).

Bursar, *see* Treasurer.

C

Cantores, see Deeping, Haryngton, Reede, Scharppe.

Carriage and carting, xxxvi, xxxvii, *and passim*; by water, xxxvii, 83, 87, 90, 124, 125.

Cellarer, *celerarius*, *celerer'*, *selerarius*, 78*, 150, 151, 161; office of, xx, xxi*, xxiii, xxiv*, xxviii*, 26, 68, 75, 128*, 139, 147*; *see also* Borough, Burnham, Hall, Ramsey.

Chamberlain, *camerarius*, 60, 161; office of, xxiv, xxviii, 1; clerk of, 138; *see also* Baston, Stamford, *and* Abbey buildings.

Chapels, *see* Peterborough, St. Thomas's Hospital, Newark; Sutton; *and* Abbey buildings.

Chaplains, 149; of prior, *see* Moulton; of St. Thomas's Hospital, 72, 89, 103, 122*; *see also* Budde, Reede, Underwode.

Chapters, General Chapters of the English Benedictine Congregation, subsidies for, xvii*, xviii, 38, 88, 134, 140.

Churches, *see* Maxey, Paston, Peterborough, Stamford.

Clerks, 158; of prior, 94, 137; of St. Thomas's Hospital, 22; *see also* Austhorp, Ay, Bawnce, Bernylle, Bolton, Clark, Lynn, Smyth, Staffe, Style, Thomas, William, Woode.

Clock, 167.

Coins, methods of payment, xliv, *and passim*; forged coin, xliv, 77*, 93, 130, 162; gold, 46; gold farthings, xliv, 54, 81; gold halfpennies, xliv, 53, 54, 138; gold nobles, xliv, 12, 30, 31, 62, 66*, 81, 130, 136*, 137, 142, 158; gold weight, 167; silver, *passim*, *especially* 62, 155; grotes, xliv*, 28, 81, 93, 107, 112, 130, 137*, 140.

Collectors, xxxviii; *and see* Clapton, Maxey, Sutton, Warmington, and Werrington; *and* Eyr, Henry, Walter.

Convocation, 148*.

Courts, writs and legal proceedings, 7, 19, 25, 52, 58, 59, 69, 78, 82, 85, 118; consistory court, 44*, 45*; manor court, 24, 25, 29, 117, 125, 166*; *see also* Books and records.

Cows and oxen, xxxv, 18, 39, 47, 124, 158, 162; hire of, xxxv*, xxxvi, 14, 15*, 54, 104, 127, 155; pasturing, agistment of, xxxv, 7*, 16, 92; sale of, 6*, 26, 71; cowsheds (*bovaria*, *boveria*), 13, 46, 62, 74.

D

Diseases: of horses, treatment of, 46, 135; spavin, 87; vives, glanders, 34, 37, 38.

Doves, Dovecotes, 9, 12, 22*, 57*, 59*, 71, 83*, 89*, 103, 166, *and see* Food.

Drink, 21, 31, 33, 39, 77, 104, 115, 123; beer, 45, 50, 52, 59*, 64, 74, 78, 88*, 96, 104, 108–10, 118–21, 124, 127, 143, 146, 148; for the monastery, 21, 131; with meals and feasts, 20*, 25, 58*, 59, 71, 89, 103, 122, 134, 150, 151, 160; wine, 3, 41, 43–45, 49, 52, 54, 82, 120, 150, 152*, 158; for the monastery, 33, 34, 41, 53, 59, 85, 111, 112, 133*, 139, 158*.

E

Eye salve, 12.

F

Fairs, *see* Deeping, Ely, Peterborough Bridge, Stamford, Stourbridge.

Faith, pledging of, xlv, 25*, 55, 60*, 65, 92, 107, 113*, 114, 118, 162, 163.

Farmers, xxxiv, 95*; *and see* Castor (Honte), Maxey (Irnarde, Smyth), Sutton (also Conquest, Priour).

Farms, xxxiv, xxxviii*n*, 27, 49, 71, 94, 95, 102, 116, 130, 134.

Feasts and meals, *appellaciones*, 95, 147*, 154; *minuciones* (feasts at bloodletting time), 26, 28*, 39; *minucio* of the third prior (Christmastide, Sexagesima, and Quinquagesima), 13, 14, 23, 24, 43, 55, 56, 69, 84, 85, 96, 107, 130, 134, 142; on St. Mary Magdalene's day, xxx, xlii, 20*, 71, 72, 89, 103, 104, 122, 134, 150; dinners with the Prior at Oxney, 28, 34, 46, 78, 94*, 139*, 149–51, 158, 160, 161, 164, 165; other meals, 25, 35, 42, 54, 64, 65, 72*, 89, 150, 151*, 154*, 160; *see also* Drink, Food.

Food, xxiv, xxxiv, xxxv*, 5, 43, 58*, 59*, 70, 74, 109, 134, 149, 159; apples, 55, 79, 104, 127; bread, xxxiv, 25, 39, 43, 58*, 59*, 82, 109, 146, 151*, 160, on St. Mary Magdalene's Day, 20*, 71, 89, 103, 122, 134*, 150, baking of, 9, 10, 42, 52, 82; broth, 20*, 160; butter, 14, 56, 149; cheese, 9, 25, 39, 109; corn, meal, peas, etc., *passim*; doves (as food), 59*, 71, 89* (cf. Doves, Dovecotes); eggs, 13, 14, 20*, 23*, 55, 56, 85, 96, 134, 142, 149, 166*; figs and raisins, currants, 6*, 7, 34, 56, 59, 81*, 103, 111, 160; fish, 6–8, 12, 14*, 20*, 55, 85, 103*, 110, 122*, 150*, 167, shellfish, 122*; fowls, capons, 13, 14*, 16, 55, 56, 71, 72, 78, 85, 88*, 89, 96, 116, 142, 150*, 151*, 154, 160, other chicken, 12–14, 16, 18, 20, 23*, 56, 59, 71, 85*, 89, 96*, 134, 142, 150, 151*, 160*, duck, 23, geese, 13, 14, 18, 20, 23*, 55*, 56, 71*, 85*, 89, 96, 134, 142*, 151*, 160, wildfowl, 13, 23, 55*, 56*, 85*, 96*, 142*; honey, 12, 20, 160; meat, xxxv, 13*, 14, 20, 23*, 24, 26, 54, 56*, 60, 71, 72, 77, 85*, 93, 94, 96*, 107*, 149, 151*, 154*, 160*, beef, 89, 150, 151*n*, brawn, 13, 23*, 43, 56, 69, 84, 96, lamb, 56, 58, 72, mutton, 14, 20*, 43, 56, 59, 71*, 89, 103, 109, 134, 150*, 151*, 154, pork, 13*, 14*, 20, 23*, 24*, 55*, 56*, 58, 71*, 78*, 85*, 89, 93, 96*, 126, 134*, 142*, 150, 151*, 154, 160*, veal, 13, 14, 20, 23*, 24, 55*, 56*, 72, 78, 85*, 96*, 134, 142, 154; milk, 19, 25, 104, 149, 160; nuts (almonds, walnuts), 34*, 57, 68*, 103, 109, 115, 124, 140, 150, 160; onions, 103; pasties, etc., 13, 115; rabbits, 55*, 56, 96*; salt, 149; spices, 5*, 6*, 14*, 20, 34, 56, 58, 103, 115, 122, 124, 142*, 151*, 154, 155, 160, 164, 167,

cumin and pepper rents, 26, 75, 128*, 133, 147*, *see also* Almoner, payments of monks' stipends; treacle, 154; whey, 154*; *see also* Drink, Feasts and meals.

Friars, 44, 148*, possibly also 5, 149.

G

Gardens, abbey, 29; almoner's, xxx*, 21, 33, 34, 41, 60, 69, 70, 82, 85, 89, 104*, 116, 119, 122, 136, herb garden, 57, 113; other gardens, xxx*, 71, 146*; *see also* Peterborough, Church of St. John the Baptist, the Trenches.

Garnerer, office of, xxiv.

Gentlemen, *see* Haldenby, Merbyri, Skirmote.

H

Hermit, *see* John.

Horses, 43–45, 58*, 59*, 61, 74, 79, 80, 126, 135, 144–6, 154, 166, 167; gifts of, 39*, 84; purchase of, 108, 116, 135, 146; sale of, 8, 21, 72, 91, 92, 116; Sorelle, Soorelle, 34*, 37, 38*, 46, 87, 104, 116; cart horses, 149.

Hospitals, xxvi*, *and see* Peterborough, churches and hospitals in.

Hostiller, *hostilarius* (guestmaster), office of, xxiii, xxiv, xxix, 75, 122; servants of, xxiii, 94; *see also* Borough, Melton, Pytchley, *and* Abbey buildings.

I

Infirmarer, xxiii, 28*, 42, 54, 137, 139, 143, 160*; *and see* Burnham, Markham, Melton, Morton, Pytchley, Spalding, *and* Abbey buildings.

J

Janitor, *see* Richard.

K

Knight, *see* Conway.

L

Leeks, 34, 60, 89, 119, 120.

Lime-kilns, 57, 68*, 102, 114, 146.

M

Master of the Works, *magister operis, operum*, xxiii, 69, 75*, 78, 87, 106, 129, 138; *and see* Borough, Burnham, Overton.

Masters (of Arts), *magistri, see* Barkbe, Greene, Lorde, Myl', Paynyll, Raffe, Rawscotte, Reynyll, Sugur (doctor), Tyssington, Wyttham.

Meals, *see* Feasts and meals.
Meat, *see* Food.
Mills, 9*, 10*, 125; watermills, *see* Lolham Mill, Sutton, Brigmylle; windmills, 2 (Woodhithemilne in Peterborough); Millers, xxxiv, 52; *and see* Drury, Morton, Mowncel.
Money, *see* Coins.
Monks, lists of, xiii*n*, 165*n*; *and see* Aldwinkle, Ashton, Barnack, Baston, Bisley, Borough, Burnham, Bury, Crowland, Deeping, Dey, Exton, Gent, George, Glinton, Gosberton, Greatford, Halden, Hall, Harlton, Holbeach, Huntingdon, Hylle, Kydd, Leasingham, Leicester, Liddington, Lincoln, London, Lyderon, Lynn, Malden, Markham, Maxey, Melton, More, Morton, Morys, Moulton, Newark, Nicholas, Northorpe, Nottingham, Overton, Oxford, Pinchbeck, Pytchley, Ramsey, Ripon, Ryal, St. Neots, Shelford, Shrewsbury, Spalding, Stamford, Tallington, Thornbery, Turvey, Tylly, Ufford, Walter, Wansford, Warmington, Wenham, William, Winwick, York.

N

Notaries, 43; *and see* Hare, Prutwell, Upex.
Novices, 21, 29, 54, 115.

O

Obedientiary system, xviii, xix–xxv; *see also* Abbot's receiver, Almoner, Cellarer, Chamberlain, Garnerer, Hostiller, Infirmarer, Master of the Works, Pittancer, Precentor, Prior, Prior, Third and Fourth, Refectorer, Sacrist, Steward, Subalmoner, Subprior, Subsacrist, Treasurer, Wardens.

P

Parson, of Walpole and Fleet Hargate, *see* Davyson; of Woodstone, *see* Robert.
Pigs, 13, 14, 16, 20, 23, 25, 55*, 71, 85, 96, 126, 134*, 142*, 150, 151*, 156, 159, 160, 163.
Pilgrimages to Walsingham, 86, 106, 146.
Pittancer, *pitanciarius*, xxiii, xxiv*, 76*, 78, 91, 146*; *and see* Overton, Spalding.
Players or minstrels, *histriones*, 5.
Precentor, xiv, xxix*, 17, 28, 49; *and see* Borough.

Prior, 21, 28*, 40*, 42, 56, 75, 94*, 100*, 109, 120, 130, 134, 143, 158; as financial intermediary, 7, 54, 108*; payments to, 54, 102, 131, 137; at Oxney, 28, 34, 46, 78, 94*, 139*, 149–51, 158, 160, 161, 164, 165; clerks and servants of, 94, 137, 165*n*; *see also* Exton, Harlton, Leicester, Malden, William; *and* Abbey buildings.
Prior, Third, 161; *see* Feasts and meals, *minucio* of the third prior, *and also* Hylle, Oxford.
Prior, Fourth, *see* Bury.
Prioress of St. Thomas's Hospital, 96.

R

Receiver, *see* Abbot's receiver.
Records, *see* Books and records.
Rector, *see* Fletton, Northborough (Dycklon), Overton (Donsby), Paston (also Hamerton), Peakirk.
Refectorer, *refectorarius*, xxiv, 75; *and see* Burnham, Crowland, Leasingham, Markham; *and* Abbey buildings.

S

Sacrist, *sacrista*, xx, xxiii*, xxviii, 86, 93, 111, 114, 117, 124, 138; at Oxney, 150, 151, 161; payments to and for, 22, 38*, 55, 168*; purchases from and by, 82, 87, 117, 129; *and see* Borough, Gent, Glinton, Maxey, Melton.
Seneschal, *see* Steward.
Servants, monastic, xxvii, xxviii, xxxi*, 94, 137, 138, 146, 147; *and see* Brevitor, Browny, Caker, Dey, Grawnte, Gregory, Hall, Ireland, James, John, Morton, Official, Pampe, Peter, Pipewel, Robert, Roceby, Stephen, Sterr', Stoxley, Surdus, Thomas, Walter, White, William; almoner's servants, xxxi*, xlii*; *and see* Ay, Baly, Coldwell, Estas, Hall, Morton, Walys, White.
Sheep, *see* Food; Sheep-cote, 12, 90.
Shops, xxxiii, xxxiv, 17, 98, 136, 138*, 140, 143*, 158, 163.
Spices, *see* Food.
Steward, lay steward of the liberty of Peterborough, *see* Greene; monastic, *senescallus*, 166; *and see* Borough, Exton, Ramsey.
Stipends of monks, xx, xxiii, xxiv; *and see* Almoner, payments.
Subalmoner, *subelemosinarius*, xxiii*, xxx, 40; *and see* Greatford, Oxford, *and* Abbey buildings.
Subprior, xiv, 17; *and see* Nottingham.

Subsacrist, *subsacrista*, xxxiii, 59, 129*, 133*, 150; office of, 127, 128, 147*; *and see* Borough, Leicester, Nicholas, Ramsey, Ryal.

T

Tallies, xxxi, xli*, xlii, 19, 26–30, 57, 64, 103*, 107, 152, 163.

Taxation (tenths), 2, 10*n*, 22, 38, 41, 61*, 93, ? 156.

Trades, xxxiv, xxxvi; apothecaries, *see* Stel; bakers, *see* Bacster; barbers, 58, 59, 164, *and see* Stawnton; blacksmiths, *see* Smyth, Stokton; brewsters, *see* William; butchers, xxxv, xxxvi, *and see* Beyl, Bocher, Gattele, Murcote, Orwyn, Pepur, Reede, Rydar, Wycle; carpenter, 5, *and see* Asselyn, Boydyl, Bradbyry, Brig, Bytrysche, Dowcheman, Halyday, Heyd, Hubboc, John, Keruer', Kydwel, Mason, N., Nelson, Paul, Phylyppe, Ravon, Rockle, Smyth, Stephen, Thomas, Walter, Webster; cobblers, *see* Alownton, John, Martin; cooks, 150, *and see* Hall, John, Roceby, Somursette; coopers, *see* Benet, Cooper; dykers, *see* Henry, Hobard; fuller, *see* Burle; furber, *see* Jelyan; gardener, *see* Thomas; glazier, 5, 68, 122, glazing, 147; goldsmith, *see* Leche; ironmongers, *see* Hatherley, Humfrey; †kydder, *see* Medow; leach, *see* Barbur; masons, 2, 21, 38, 45, 85, *and see* Schepey, Schyngle; mercers, *see* Brown, Waldyng; merchant, xxxvi, *and see* George; millers, *see under* Mills; neatherd, *see* Clark; pewterer, *see* Fullebroke; plumber, 5, *and see* William; potter, *see* Meyre; saddler, *see* Spencer; sawyer, *see* Dalad; scribe, *see* Jordan; sexton, *see* John; shepherd, 72; skinner, *see* Nafferton; slaters, *see* Aspschaw, Batche, Edgyston, Hylle, Reede, Richard, Robert, Rodger, Stevur (cf. thackers, tilers); tailors, *see* Helme, Lambe, Merche; tanners, *see* Haburgyl, White; †thackers, thatchers, or roofers, *see* Jonys, Ploman, Somur, William (cf. slaters, tiler); threshers, *see* Beyl, John; tiler, *see* Waarde (cf. slaters, thackers); weavers, *see* Chaumberleyn, Ryette, Webster, Wentbrig.

Treasurer (or Bursar), *thesaurarius*, xix, xxi*, 134, 138, 158, 161; office of,

xxi*, xxiii*, xxiv*, 1, 42, 58, 105, 120, 125, 136; servant of, 138; *see also* Harlton, Leicester, Markham, Maxey, Nottingham, *and* Abbey buildings.

Trees and timber, xxxv; for carpentry and fuel *passim*; for woods, *see* Castor wood, Eye, Eastwood, Paston, Nabbe wood, Peterborough, Westwood, Sutton, Schort wood, Sutton wood; immersing (for seasoning) and extracting timber from water, 12, 32, 65, 91, 101, 104, 108, 132; types of wood and trees: apple, 117, ash, 3, 9, 16*, 19, 21, 33, 64, 74, 86*, 91*, 97*, 98*, 100–2, 107, 108, 113*, 114*, 120, 125, 139, 153, 169; elder, 26, 75, 97*, 147; maple, 2; oak, 9*, 16, 19, 21, 33*, 34, 46, 52*, 63–65, 72*, 79, 90–92, 107–109, 111, 118, 123, 125, 129, 140, 147, 153, 155, 166*; pear, 148*; shrub or scrub, 101, 107; thorn, 9, 61, 65, 76, 101*, 111, 136, 153*, 155, 159; walnut, 52, 91; willow, 3, 7, 16, 20, 68, 70, 86, 97*, 98, 100, 101, 113*, 114*; wych-elm, 2, 4.

U

University, monks at, xiv, xxiii, xxix, xxx*, 28, 52, 61, 66, 93, 97, 107, 109, 117, 122, 135, 144, 146, 158.

Usury, xxxvi.

V

Valuations: of 1254 (Valuation of Norwich), xxi*n*, xxxiii*n*, 47, 48; of 1291 (Taxation of Pope Nicholas IV), xxi*n*, xxxiii*n*, 1, 10*n*, 47, 48; of 1535 (Valor Ecclesiasticus), xii, xxvii–xxix, xxxiii*n*, xxxviii*.

Vicar, *see* Bakon, Bevelle, Deeping, Peterborough (also Hare).

Vicar General, *see* Lincoln.

Visitation, monastic, xi*, xii–xvii, 53.

W

Wardens, *see* Abbey buildings, Church, altar of Holy Cross, Lady Chapel, *and* Peterborough, Oxney.

Wax, candles, 5*, 6, 47, 75, 76*, 88, 91, 123, 124, 129, 151*, 158; †*hercie et reddicio*, 2, 3; candle of Paris, 34, 149; candelabra, 163.

Wine, *see* Drink.

Wood, Woods, *see* Trees and timber.

Writs, *see* Courts.

PRINTED IN
GREAT BRITAIN
AT THE
UNIVERSITY PRESS
OXFORD
BY
CHARLES BATEY
PRINTER
TO THE
UNIVERSITY